REPRESENTATION
AND THE TEXT

REPRESENTATION AND THE TEXT

❏

RE-FRAMING THE NARRATIVE VOICE

EDITED BY

WILLIAM G. TIERNEY
AND
YVONNA S. LINCOLN

STATE UNIVERSITY OF NEW YORK PRESS

Published by
State University of New York Press, Albany

For information, address State University of New York Press,
State University Plaza, Albany, N.Y. 12246

Production by M. R. Mulholland
Marketing by Theresa A. Swierzowski

Library of Congress Cataloging-in-Publication Data

Representation and the text : re-framing the narrative voice / edited
    by William G. Tierney and Yvonna S. Lincoln.
        p.   cm.
    Includes bibliographical references and index.
    ISBN 0-7914-3471-0. — ISBN 0-7914-3472-9 (pbk.)
        1. Literature, Modern—20th century—History and criticism.
    2. Point of view (Literature) 3. Narration (Rhetoric) 4. Style,
    Literary. I. Tierney, William G. II. Lincoln, Yvonna S.
    PN771.R47 1997
    809.3′04—dc21   96-44385
                                                                                CIP

10 9 8 7 6 5 4 3 2 1

CONTENTS

INTRODUCTION:
EXPLORATIONS AND DISCOVERIES

WILLIAM G. TIERNEY AND YVONNA S. LINCOLN

Social scientists who utilize qualitative research move toward the twenty-first century in many respects pondering questions that bedeviled our methodological ancestors at the turn of the twentieth century. What should our stance be vis-à-vis those whom we study? How do we know what we observe is "true?" What is the best means to present what we have discovered to our readers? Who should be our readers?

Although such questions may still be with us—like a chronic backache whose pain may subside at times but never go away—the manner in which we think about such questions has changed, and our tentative responses are also different. We once thought that the "native's" world was simple and understandable. Our role was to record what we saw and develop findings so that they would contribute to Western science. The relationship between native and researcher was unequal, in large part because we knew more than they did—we understood their world, but they did not understand ours. And we presented our work to our confreres at conferences, journals, and books in a prose laden with a technical vocabulary that demonstrated our sophistication with scientific terms and an ability to add to the scientific stock of knowledge.

Today, a culture of doubt permeates academic work in the social sciences. We are no longer sure if it is either possible or desirable (read ethical) to "leave no footprints" when we undertake a study of a group of people. Words such as "reliability," "validity," and "trustworthiness" have become contested terms in a postmodern world, and researchers have sought to reinscribe them with meanings that would have been unheard of two generations ago. Validity, for example, in part refers to how we are able to improve the lives of those we study (Lather, 1986); trustworthiness pertains to checking with our interviewees to see if they agree with what we have written and concur on our representations of them (Lincoln & Guba, 1985). How we present our work, and to whom, is also more up for grabs today than at any other time in this century.

All of these points are obviously interrelated. If those whom we study are to be co-participants in the development of our findings, then the manner in which "we" study "them" will be different from the individual who thinks of him or herself as a clinician trying to develop understandings akin to the scientist in a laboratory. The desire to create change, to lessen oppression, or to assist in the development of a more equitable world sets up a different research dynamic from that of the disengaged academic whose main purpose is to add to the stock of theoretical knowledge. And if we are to raise such issues about the research process, then the manner in which we present data, and to whom, also comes under renewed scrutiny. It is this last point that is the focus of this book. All of the authors begin with a basic premise: if we partake in the current debate that circles around postmodernists' interpretation of notions such as "reality" and "identity," then the development of qualitative texts in the social sciences demand dramatic new reconfiguration, and to a large extent, new audiences. Parenthetically, we are not saying that everything that has gone before us is false, or that the views of authors a generation ago, or of our colleagues today, are wrong. Times change, different groups have different interpretations, and even if the questions may not change, our take on how we think about those questions has afforded us a uniquely different way to situate ourselves within the research experience. We welcome constructive dialogue.

Our consistent focus here, however—such that anyone can be consistent who subscribes to postmodernism—is to discuss the implications for representational practices if we subscribe to what has come to be called "postmodernism." The book is not intended as a primer on postmodernism, and as we have discovered, as authors, we have significant disagreements with one another about the basic tenets of postmodernism. Some of us call on European strands of postmodernism and others use a feminist version; some think that postmodernism is an explicit call for political change, and others focus on the theoretical implications of postmodernism. Nevertheless, we all agree that the manner in which we present data, how we construct the "author" and the "reader," demand serious investigation in ways that would have been unheard of fifty years ago.

There are other major agreements that are shared between us, however. The agreements that we share run as explicit and implicit themes through each of chapters in this volume. We are bound first by the commitment to "break the science habit," as Lincoln's chapter calls it. We are sober resistors to what Pinar labels here the "tyranny of science," the norming and normalization of structuralism, the imprisoning strictures of science that create silences. Thus, throughout the chapters, readers will see warnings against textual adherence to conventional mandates for what science demands. Or they will see deep analyses of the "fictions" that science can create from perspectival and textual/rhetorical demands. Or they will see the effects of experiments that try to break those chains.

We are also bound by another commitment, this one ideological. While some of us are critical theorists, some of us Marxist in orientation, others feminist, our ideological commitment supersedes each of those ideological and methodological lenses. We are bound by what Tierney calls the "ideology of doubt." This ideology of doubt is explicated by Laurel Richardson, in an earlier work (1994):

> The core of postmodernism is the doubt that any method or theory, discourse or genre, tradition or novelty, has a universal and general claim as the "right" or the privileged form of authoritative knowledge. Postmodernism suspects all truth claims of masking and serving particular interests in local, cultural and political struggles. . . .
>
> The postmodernist context of doubt distrusts all methods equally. No method has a privileged status. The superiority of "science" over "literature"—or, from another vantage point, "literature" over "science"—is challenged. (pp. 517–7)

Thus, we are all suspicious. We are suspicious of those who tell us they have the only methods appropriate for conducting scientific inquiry. We are suspicious of those who tell us they have the final theories on why the world is as it is. We are especially suspicious of discourses that, without thoughtful analytic deconstructing, invisibly shape the ideas which we express, limit the views of reality with which we grapple, and silence those who are not privy to our private languages. And we are suspicious of "genre wars," the particular border skirmishes of academic provinces that declare some traditions important, powerful, legitimate, while others are ideologically impoverished.

We are also bound as authors by a commitment to intertwine the personal with the professional, because we understood "the personal was political," and "the professional was personal" long before standpoint epistemology was fully explicated. Carolyn Ellis's intensely personal writing experiment, which both comments upon and completes part I, shows us how one woman comes to grips with the intersection of the personal and the professional. Patti Lather's work on women with HIV/AIDS encounters the contradictions of the personal, the political, and the professional again in part II. Peter McLaren writes of his realization of the self as flaneur—as lounger, loafer, stroller in urban spaces sees himself becoming, as we all do to some extent, the metropolitan voyeur, the observer who has been caught up in cosmopolitan rituals of his own. His reconfiguration of space, monuments, time, and urban danger signal both the precarious, "saturated" self, and the postmodern sense of terror that invariably accompanies doubt.

We agree, too, that to claim "reality" is a "contested terrain" is to understate the case. It is a battleground where armies of the personal, the political, the cultural, the linguistic, the racial, the gendered, the classes collide in symbolic combat. It is a fractured landscape of struggle and resistance, of border crossings of all description, where margins meet the center, where no human escapes without wounds, where engagements and withdrawals mark the day from dawn to nightfall, where doubt pervades every encounter.

Finally, we are also joined by Schwandt's explication of the ethical dilemma of finding a "responsible way to compose a text that re-presents the postmodern wisdom" of how and who we are. Whether that text is a drama (as in Denzin's call for performance and storytelling), or whether it is a disavowal of the single, career-making monograph in favor of multiple texts aiming to engage multiple audiences, seeking to persuade multiple readers/players, we are all seeking forms and frames which convey our narratives with immediacy and with recognition. We are, as chapter authors, about a search for an ethical way to "be," in the personal/professional nexus that shape our lives, and in the texts we seek to present and re-present.

Our task here, and the purpose of this book is to focus specifically on authorial representations of contested reality in qualitative research. As we shall discuss, in general, the manner in which qualitative social scientists have presented the voice of the author/narrator and "subjects" has been remarkably similar. That is, even when one looks across theoretical frameworks, genres, and traditions in qualitative research, there is more similarity than diversity with regard to how data have been presented. Accordingly, our objectives in this book are twofold:

1. To provide a critique of how authors use voice in their research, and
2. To suggest ways to develop experimental voices that expand the range of narrative strategies.

We have divided the book in two. Part I maps out the conceptual terrain and outlines the issues that confront researchers as they develop their texts. Part II suggests and demonstrates possible strategies we might employ if we take seriously the points made in the first part. We conclude both parts with critiques of the points that have been made.

In chapter 1 Don Polkinghorne suggests that the traditional authorial role of the logician or debater should be dropped and the voice of the storyteller assumed. When the author takes such a role, suggests Polkinghorne, the research act takes on an entirely different light. "Subjects" become actors in a research narrative. The researcher's removed, objective stance is changed as the researcher also becomes an actor in the text. And most importantly, the understanding of the nature of knowledge is dramatically reinterpreted so that knowledge statements are no longer considered to be statements that mirror reality; instead, they become constructions or "maps" of reality. In essence, data are created, rather than discovered, and the reader becomes aware of the creation through the textual strategy employed by the author.

Tierney continues this strain of thought in chapter 2 by way of an analysis of how authors have presented qualitative research articles. He pays particular attention to two aspects of a text: (1) how the author fits within the text, and (2) the temporal structure of the text. He suggests that the authorial voice generally has been presented in one of three ways: as an omniscient narrator, as an interviewer, or as a first-person narrator within the story. Textual time has been presented in four manners: in the present tense or the past tense, and either in linear or disjunctive fashion. Tierney suggests what we might do to expand the narrative strategies of the text and raises issues of import pertaining to how we educate future scholars, what this means for scholarly journals, and how our relationships with those whom we study of necessity will change.

In chapter 3 Yvonna Lincoln dissects the textual implications for the postmodernist credo that all texts are partial, gender-specific, local, and historically and culturally situated. She suggests that the partial nature of texts, coupled with the variety of identities that any piece of fieldwork might elicit, provide opportunities for authors to explore the possibilities of multiple texts directed toward multiple readers. Texts may attract criticism, unease, and discomfort because they stand as sole testaments to a piece of ethnographic work. Multiple texts, directed toward the research, policy, social change efforts, or public intellectual needs of various audiences may better represent both the complexity of the lives we study, and the lives we lead as academics and private persons, in and out of the research contexts. Multiple texts may also better address the issues of temporality that Tierney raises, because they necessarily portray the products of an ethical reflexivity: the changing self over time, the maturing comprehension of our contexts, the deepening awareness of hidden social structures and power relations.

Joe Kincheloe suggests in chapter 4 that one problem with our texts is their inability to suggest or prompt action. They are, in the sense of realist criticism, "fictions," and they are, in the sense of action, "formulas." Our texts fail on two counts: both as true accounts in that they are partial, and as explications of how we might enact a more just world, because they imply a disinterested spectator on alien worlds. Kincheloe poses the possibility that critical theory, married to contructivism, might serve authors, texts, and readers alike in discovering the dynamics of power in shaping representations of the worlds we study and display.

He posits critical self-reflection as a form of analytic mirror wherein the text (in interaction with the self) begins to reveal macro and micro power dynamics. Uncovering the intersections of macro and micro power accomplishes a kind of "power archaeology"—a sifting of the colonies of consciousness until realization and understanding occur. Texts that act to re-present in ways that uncover, sift, and assemble evidence on power structures clearly make meaningful action more possible. Authors have choices about their texts; re-presentation can remain fictional and formulaic, or it can uncover the ancient sites of colonization and domination.

In chapter 5 Bill Pinar argues that reason is a regime imposed on the deepest symbolic structures of Western civilization. Imposition of this regime into the furthest corners of our social lives—education, relations of power, gender and sexual identities, and science—has created the divided self. The dissociated, divided, abstracted/distracted cognitive self, separated from its own body, can only cast the nonreasoning self as "other." This Cartesian creation perpetuates othering at the expense of not only one's own body, but at the expense of women, children, homosexuals, anyone at the margins. Pinar concludes that the heritage of Newtonian and Cartesian cosmologies of knowability are themselves forms of symbolic and discursive prisons, limiting our visions of the possible, colonizing not only countries but also our bodies, sustaining a white patriarchy even as the voices of the others claim recognition from outside the center.

Carolyn Ellis offers a summary of the first part in chapter 6 by arguing that the crisis of representation that the authors speak about challenges the most venerable notions of what we have come to think of as scientific truth and knowledge. By way of an experimental text, Ellis raises questions about authorial voice, academic discourse, and the relationship between fiction/formula, power/reason. In essence, Ellis critiques the chapters in part I by using the methods, techniques, and discourses that the authors themselves have developed.

Part II opens with a chapter by Peter McLaren, who argues that the ethnographer has a role in a postmodern world uniquely different from his or her brethren of the past. McLaren sees ethnographers as change agents who seek to create the conditions for the empowerment of those who are voiceless and silenced. At the same time, McLaren argues that the ethnographer is undergoing a crisis of representation within and outside of the academy and within and outside of the self. Writing in the style that we call for here, argues, McLaren, demands risks that provoke reflexivity, which in turn requires the author to become a postmodern flaneur.

In chapter 8 Norman Denzin takes up a vision of text as performance. As qualitative researchers expand the ranges of their voices an accompanying revision is likely to occur in our perspectives of what a text is. Denzin proposes that a powerful form of text builds on theater. One reader can interact with a book in a very private way. Even multiple readers can be unaware of those with whom they share a text. Theater—performed drama with live audiences—broadens the social tapestry in such a way that multiple "readers" interpret, interact with, and internalize a vivid, lived, shared text. Denzin suggest that the possibilities for reconnecting inquiry to the very human act of storytelling coalesces in performance texts.

Erica McWilliam suggest in chapter 9 that academic writers and teachers cannot get away from the issue of authority, but they can fundamentally reconfigure relationships. McWilliam delineates the academic strategies employed to utilize power, and outlines how academic rules seek to privilege some and silence others. She then moves into a discussion about how one might break the rules, and in doing so change readers' views of what constitutes an academic text. McWilliam pays particular attention to those involved in the teaching of academic texts—dissertation advisors.

In the next chapter Patti Lather delineates textual practices in an interview study of women living with HIV/AIDS. In a multilayered weaving of method, the politics of interpretation, data, analysis, and text, her chapter is a text that fosters brooding about the issues involved in telling other people's stories and living in the shadow places of history as loss. She analyzes textual decisions that create a mosaic text that is designed to interrupt the reductiveness of the restricted economies of representation that characterize mainstream social science.

In the penultimate chapter, Greg Tanaka displays one of the possible textual strategies for creating multiple voices in a variety of ranges alongside each other. A vivid and lyrical case alongside, although not totally in tandem with, an exploration of fictional poetics, provides a textual counterpoint like a painful, but very real, conversation between new lovers. The technical placement of text provides a sense of the halting, tentative quality of a dialogue moving between registers. Greg's text is a visual re-presentation of the multitonal attempt to find a common set of meanings, a language shared. It is, too, a stark demonstration of the ways in which individuals construct very different worlds from the same or related contexts. In Greg's work, the search is for a language of race and equality. In other texts, the textual poetics might represent a struggle to recover voice, a demand for identity, a body-blow delivered in a broken-field run from the margins. Explorations of many struggles—men/women, gay/straight, liberal/conservative—might be explored via graphic experiments in text that display the ragged, hoarse attempts to tell our stories, no matter how partial our personal truths.

In the concluding chapter Thomas Schwandt summarizes what the authors have attempted. He then posits challenges that await us beyond the text. He points out the nature of interpretation in a post-postmodern world and raises questions about the implications for developing "wisdom" about the myriad problems that confront.

All books are explorations of one sort or another; like ships, some have a successful voyage and others sink to the ocean's floor. Perhaps a text is fatally flawed and of little use, or perhaps it charts new waters. Given the focus of the text, we are careful about how we define our own exploration and the "new" waters. Columbus may have "discovered" the New World for Europeans, for example, but he certainly made no discovery for those first Americans who lived in the Americas. Our understandings are contingent and contextually based. Nevertheless, we intend for this book to move those of us who do qualitative research into representational areas that are often ignored or overlooked. Indeed, there are at least four issues that the book indirectly takes up that we hope gathers momentum in the next few years.

As authors, some of us have noted that there is no small amount of postmodern irony where in a text that occasionally argues for greater accessibility, a chapter may be quite laden with dense and difficult language. As we noted above, we are not arguing any doctrinaire credo that says all texts must be one way or another. We also are not suggesting that texts should be "dumbed down" for readers. To advocate for broader representational practices surely should not imply that scholarly texts in a traditional fashion should be disdained. Such a suggestion is both anti-intellectual and insulting to readers—as if they are unable to read difficult texts. At the same time, we are suggesting that not all texts need to be written for similar academic audiences, or even indeed solely for an academic audience. Thus, our first recommendation is that we hope to see more texts created for a broader range of readers.

Our second observation is directly tied to the issue of accessibility. Again, a few chapter authors have noted that some of us argue for experimentation in writing in quite standard fashion. Except for Tanaka's and Lather's chapters, in many respects this is a book about experimental writing rather than a book of experimental texts. Again, we made such a decision with the assumption that we first needed to lay out the conceptual issues and then get on with the experiments themselves. We hope, then, that the readers and ourselves are moved to experiment with new forms of data presentation. Lather offers technological ways to disrupt the text so that it becomes multivocal and Tanaka provides an example of how this might be done; Tierney suggests temporal and narrative strategies, and Denzin writes about performance. All of these are initial attempts to move one's creative energies toward experimentation. Obviously, other possibilities exist.

Our third and fourth points pertain to what this text has not discussed. On the one hand, we have discussed only representational practices that relate to writing. On the other hand, we have authors who are at the pinnacles of their careers; by and large the authors present a cohesive view of what we mean by experimentation.

It has become commonplace to point out the revolution that is occurring as the "information superhighway" is built. In small ways, we have used the highway—e-mail to one another about chapters, trading diskettes back and forth—but the book has not investigated radically different representational practices—film, video, and the like. We made a decision to focus on the written text so that the reader might get as wide a spectrum of opinions about it as possible. But by our focus, we have not meant to exclude the important advances that are taking place on the screen. If this book jars the reader into thinking about alternative venues for his or her work so that a text turns into a cinematic document, we welcome it. Indeed, a book of the kind that we have attempted here that speaks about cinematic and technological representations would be most helpful for those of us who accept that different representational practices are needed, but are unsure what that means in media other than the written text.

And finally, we are painfully aware of the need for an expansion of those of us who speak and write about representational practices. To be sure, the authors of this book are not xeroxes of one another. We have a mix of men and women, for example, and some of us are gay and some are straight. Such that it matters, some teach at public institutions and others work at private universities. Some of us are young, and some are old(er). (Tierney likes to remind us that he is forty-four, and Lincoln likes to tell us it's none of our business how young she is.) But by and large, this is a text created by white, tenured, academics.

We make no apologies for authors who are significant voices about a topic such as representation. Nevertheless, this is a topic that demands voices who will move us well beyond the realm of issues that we take up here. Off and on, in our discussions about these issues, some of us have raised the perils that we are suggesting for younger scholars. An untenured assistant professor, for example, obviously will find it easier to publish an article written in a standard format than one that is a performance text or a short story. Our hope is that our voices have at least helped cut a path that so that others are able to create their own trails and venues. If representation is the central concern in the text, then obviously we are hopeful that a much wider group of scholars—academic and nonacademic, older and younger, Anglo, Asian, African American, Native American, Hispanic, and the like—take up these concerns and translate them in their own unique ways. Who we are changes what we write about and how we write. Simply stated, if the academy is to change, if our views of reality are to be more inclusive, then we need a broader representation of authorial voices as we approach the twenty-first century. Thus, we offer here an argument or experimental representational practices that may well not enable us to discover new lands—as if they are out there, waiting to be found—but instead, help us to create new ways to see the world, and in doing so, broaden who we mean by "us."

References

Guba, Egon G., & Lincoln, Yvonna S. (1989). *Fourth generation evaluation.* Newbury Park, CA: Sage.

Lather, Patti. (1986). Research as praxis. *Harvard Educational Review, 56,* 257–77.

Lincoln, Yvonna S., & Guba, Egon G. (1985). *Naturalistic inquiry.* Newbury Park, CA: Sage.

Richardson, Laurel. (1994). Writing: A method of inquiry. In Norman K. Denzin and Yvonna S. Lincoln (Eds.), *Handbook of Qualitative Research.* Thousand Oaks, CA: Sage.

PART I

MAPPING THE CONCEPTUAL TERRAIN

❑

1

REPORTING QUALITATIVE RESEARCH AS PRACTICE

DONALD E. POLKINGHORNE

The purpose of this chapter is to encourage researchers to experiment with using a narrative format in reporting their studies. In the conventional format, which is mandatory for publication in most research journals, researchers are required to assume the voice of a logician or debater. By changing their voice to storyteller, researchers will also change the way in which the voices of their "subjects" or participants can be heard. As logicians and debaters, researchers codify, objectify, and fragment what their "subjects" have to say into factors and themes. As storytellers, "subjects" appear as actors in a research narrative. They are given their own speaking roles in the drama and interact with the researcher protagonist as contributors to the story's denouement.

Researchers are practitioners; that is, they engage in a human activity carried out over time in order to accomplish a purpose. The purpose of social science research projects is to produce knowledge and understanding of the human condition. A narrative account is the appropriate form of expression to display research as a practice. The production occurs over time and has a beginning, middle, and end (Aristotle, trans. 1954), the essential elements of a story.

The format of the research report is a fundamental artifact of the social science disciplines. Suggestions for experimentation and change in the format needs to take into account the "web of delivered discourse, social practices, professional requirements, and daily decisions" (Schrag, 1986, p. 4) in which this discussion takes place. One does not begin anew, but within his or her historical situation. The tenacity and power of the conventional approach to doing and reporting research, as well as the possibility of its evolutionary change, has been recently illustrated by its assimilation of qualitative research into its orthodoxy (LeCompte, Millroy, & Preissle, 1992, p. xvi). In this assimilation process, qualitative research accommodated the conventional approach by adapting for its own the standard format for reporting research. This format confines the presentation of research to a logically ordered justification of results and disregards the processes of discovery and decision that are essential to the actual production of research. Development of more appropriate formats for reporting qualitative research may also advance the acceptance of diverse reporting formats for research using quantitative methods. The acceptance of qualitative methods into the mainstream allows for encouragement that a change in the research report formats is possible.

Research Reports as Knowledge Claims

The conventional format of the research report is a convenient design to allow "the community of scholars" to judge the validity of the knowledge claim presented by a researcher. It provides efficient access to the determination of whether or not the claim was the product of an approved methodological algorithm. The assumed primary function of research is to create new knowledge. Social science researchers engage in research in order to have something to say about the human condition; that is, to produce a true statement about human affairs. As a result of carrying out the inquiry, the researcher claims to have found out something about human reality. The research report states the claim and presents information to justify it. Its function is not simply to inform editors about what the researcher is claiming, but to convince them of the validity of the claim. Researchers submit their reports to the scholarly community (represented by journal editors and reviewers) for its review and judgment. The editors and reviewers determine whether or not the claim will be added to the discipline's body of knowledge; that is, whether or not it will be published in a research journal.

The audience for the conventional report is the expert reviewers who decide on the validity of the knowledge claim, not the general reader or the discipline's practitioners. The conventional format is not designed to communicate the knowledge claim, but to communicate its validity. It is not surprising that practitioners, whose interests focus on the usefulness of knowledge claims, do not find the conventional format of the reports a useful means for displaying the significance of the knowledge for practice (for example, Morrow-Bradley & Elliott, 1986).

Many knowledge claims that are submitted to journals along with support for their validity (research reports) are judged to be not acceptable. Those that do not pass the muster of the review process are not added to the discipline's body of knowledge. What was claimed to be knowledge in those reports has not been accepted as, in fact, knowledge. The reports that are published have already passed the review, thus, publication of a knowledge claim signifies it has been accepted by the caretakers of the discipline's body of knowledge. The purpose of publication is not to present the claim for judgment regarding its validity by the readership of a journal; judgment has already taken place by the expert reviewers. The journals serve to distribute and communicate what their editors and reviewers have already accepted into the body of knowledge. When writers reference published articles, they generally assume the validity of the article's knowledge claim. When journals publish the articles that have passed their review, they do so in the same report format in which it was presented for review. A report format that would be most effective for communicating accepted knowledge is not the same format that was designed to facilitate reviewer's judgments. Yet this is the format our journals conventionally use to make the newly accepted knowledge public.

Within the conventional approach, successful knowledge claims, that is, those that pass the muster of the journal review process, serve other functions beside adding to a discipline's body of knowledge. They are used as an index for promotion and tenure decisions. A researcher's career advancement is often tied directly to the number of knowledge claims that have made it through the review process to publication. Thus, tampering with the conventional format and presenting one's research to reviewers in a different format is serious business.

Multiple Reports for Different Audiences

One solution to the problem of using the conventional format in publications intended to distribute and communicate the new additions to a discipline's knowledge is to experiment with alternate formats when presenting accepted claims to other audiences. Researchers could continue to use the conventional format for presenting their knowledge claims for judgment by peer reviewers and journal editors. An example of the use of alternate formats for distribution of research generated knowledge to audiences other than reviewers, is Fischer and Wertz's (1979) study of the experience of being criminally victimized. They produced five different reports of their findings. The first was a conventional research report addressed to reviewers. The purpose of this report was to convince reviewers of the validity of their findings. Even though their research was a qualitative study employing phenomenological methods, their report used the conventional format with its pattern of literature review, method section, results of analysis, and discussion. They stated that this report was too dense and technical for use at public presentations and nonprofessional discussions. Because a major purpose of their study was to affect policy changes, they produced additional reports using other formats designed to communicate their results clearly and meaningfully to community members and policymakers. Their second report consisted of a collection of individual case synopses which were intended to provide the audience "with concrete examples that reverberate with their own lives" (p. 143). The third report was in the format of an "illustrated narrative." In this report they placed the experiences of the victims into five sections ordered in a temporal sequence. The first section was about "living routinely," the middle three sections described the life changes participants went through as a result of being assaulted, and the final section was the denouement which described how victims "got on" with their lives after the trauma of the assault. Their fourth format was a collection of individual case materials in a shortened form. The fifth format was prepared for an audience of psychotherapists and was a more technical discussion of their findings as they related to the psychological dynamics of trauma experiences and a presentation of the implications of their results for counseling the criminally victimized.

The use of a variety of formats by Fischer and Wertz issued from their desire to communicate their findings to audiences that could make most effective use of them. They presented to neighborhood groups, police departments, and therapists, as well as to journal reviewers. The usefulness of multiple formats for the communication and distribution of results seems an obvious and necessary addition to the conventional format used to present knowledge claims to reviewers. In this chapter I want to make a stronger proposal than merely the use of multiple formats for reporting research. The understanding of the nature of knowledge and its validation have undergone change as we have passed from a positivistic philosophy of science to a period of "posts"—postpositive, poststructural, and postmodern. The formats in which research is reported are not neutral and transparent, but reflect particular epistemological commitments. The conventional social science research report format was designed to allow an efficient judgment about the validity of knowledge claims as they were understood within a positivist framework (Bazerman, 1987; Madigan, Johnson, & Linton, 1995). In the positivist framework the determination of validity of research results was based on the judgment that prescribed methods had been correctly followed. My stronger proposal is that the use of a narrative format for reporting research should be privileged over the conventional format, even in presenting knowledge claims for reviewer judgment. The narrative provides a more epistemologically adequate discourse form for reporting and assessing research within the context of a postpositivistic understanding of knowledge generation.

Report Format and Types of Proof

The conventional format mandated for social science research reports has been conditioned by how the disciplines came to understand the properties of their knowledge and how this type of knowledge was to be ratified. The stance regarding the properties of knowledge mandated the "voice" and grammar employed by the report writer. In the heyday of positivism, knowledge was held to have the property of a logical conclusion, akin to a mathematical derivation. Knowledge statements were products of a hypothetical-deductive process. In this process the consequences of a knowledge claim (a hypothesis) were logically deduced, and then observations were made to determine if, in fact, the consequences followed the hypothesized conditions. If they logically followed, the claim was held to be demonstrated (or inductively verified, see Gordon, 1991). A true knowledge statement has logical certitude because it was the product of a formal process. As was the case with mathematical solutions, the validity of research conclusions were understood to be independent of both the person making the claim and the audience to whom the claim was presented.

More recently, the property of knowledge has been reconsidered. Instead of a logical certainty, knowledge is understood as an agreement reached by community of scholars. Knowledge is the best map or description of reality about which the community has reached consensus (Habermas, 1979). This shift in the understanding of the property of knowledge reflects the change in the philosophy of science from a "hard" or naive realism to a "soft" or subtle realism (Hammersley, 1990). No longer are knowledge statements considered to be mirrored reflections of reality as it is in itself; rather, they are human constructions of models or maps of reality. Through exchanges with the world, these constructions evolve (Campbell, 1974) toward more useful depiction. The more evolved models are not necessarily more accurate descriptions of reality, but their use provides a more successful interaction with the world than previous models. Research reports informed by this understanding of knowledge may be presented as arguments (Nelson, Megill, & McCloskey, 1987; Perelman, 1982) or as narrative accounts. Their purpose is to convince reviewers of the pragmatic reasonableness of their knowledge claims. In this mode, the members of the audience are crucial, because they are the ones who need to be convinced by the report.

The philosophies of knowledge are quite different for those who understand knowledge as a certain product of logical operations and those who understand it as a map or model of aspects of self, others, society, or the material realm. Nevertheless, researchers committed to the recent shift in the philosophy of science have retained the general format for reporting research; even though this format reflects the principles of a positivistic understanding of science. Both groups of researchers continue to employ the standard format which is designed to display a formal demonstration of the research conclusions and to recount the correct use of acceptable methods of data collection and data analysis.

One consequence of retaining the conventional format by those holding the new understanding of knowledge is that their research reports continue to display the knowledge process from a synchronic perspective. Saussure (1907–11/1966) contrasted two approaches to the study of language—the synchronic and the diachronic. The diachronic (through-time) study of language, which had been the way language was studied before Saussure, investigated the development of language through time. Its focus was on the changes that occurred in words, grammar, and vocabulary through history. The synchronic (same-time) study called for a slice through a living language as it existed at a particular time. By approaching language synchronically, Saussure exhibited the structural relations that existed among the signs of a language system. He found that the meaning of a sign was dependent on its differences from other signs, not on an evident connection to a reference. Saussure's discoveries were recovered by Lévi-Strauss (1958/1963) and were foundational for the structuralist movement in France.

A synchronic research report presents its support for its knowledge claim in stop-time. The data and analysis are presented without temporal depth. The report submits its information as if it were all present at the same time. The order of the presentation is determined by the structure of a validity demonstration, not the actual sequence of progressions and regressions in which the research project unfolded. The blocks of a synchronic report are expected to fit into the structured cut outs of the format board. The order in which the blocks were collected is not considered as significant as the fact that each block can fill its place in the demonstration. For the positivist reviewer the concern is whether or not a part fulfills the requirements of its particular place in a formal argument; for the postpositivist reviewer the question is whether the journey by which the knowledge was accumulated was productive.

In the next section I address the use of a diachronic or narrative form of report. I hold that the synchronic presentation of research misses the crucial temporal dimension through which research projects develop. The meaning of research results is not independent of the process that produced them; research findings retain the traces of the productive activities that generated them. In the spirit of experimentation, I propose that qualitative researchers use a diachronic type report to present their research. The format of such a report is a diachronic account of the events, happenings, actions, and choices through which a research project moved.

Diachronic Research Reports

The diachronic research report is based on the understanding that research is a practice, a product of human action. Research practice shares with other human practices movement through time. Researchers are the protagonists in the drama of their quests for understanding. The drama consists of a sequential composition of decisions, actions, chance occurrences, and interactions with subjects and colleagues. Values, desires, inadequacies, skills, and personal characteristics make their appearance at various points in the researcher's performance.

Action is the basis for creating meaning (Valdé, 1991) and a knowledge claim is an accomplishment that comes through a researcher's actions or performance. To cut the claim off from the actions and happenings that led up to it is to strip it of its full meaning. The research process needs to be reported as a temporal whole in which the knowledge claim is a conclusion whose meaning is dependent on the developing actions and events of the whole research process. As temporally sequenced actions, research follows the logic of practice; not the formal logic of a positivistic approach to research, nor the argumentative reasoning of the constructivist approach.

Narrative is the discourse form which can express the diachronic perspective of human actions. It retains their temporal dimension by exhibiting them as occurring before, at the same time, or after other actions or events. "Perhaps the most essential ingredient of narrative accounting (or storytelling) is its capability to structure events in such a way that they demonstrate . . . a sense of movement of direction through time" (Gergen & Gergen, 1986). Narrative, however, not only retains the temporal sequence of actions, but links them together as contributors to the accomplishment of a common purpose.

Approaching research diachronically emphasizes that research is composed of a connected set of human activities and that the discourse form which is best suited for reporting human actions is the narrative. The next two sections concentrate on these aspects of diachronically conceived research, that is, action theory and narrative discourse.

Action Theory

Research is a performance carried out by investigators. As a performance it takes place within the context of social norms and scripts; that is, it is social practice. Bourdieu (1990b), a noted French anthropologist, has presented a theory of social practice that I have found helpful in situating the practice of research. Jenkins's (1992) excellent review has provided a guide for my reading of Bourdieu.

Bourdieu holds that through the business of everyday life people learn and construct models of how the world is, of how the world ought to be, of human nature, of cosmology. These models do not simply fulfill purely theoretical or cognitive functions; they are about doing, as much as they are about knowing. Only as one does things is it possible to know about things (Bourdieu, 1977).

Bourdieu describes three features of practice: (1) it is located in time and space, (2) it is most often guided by tacit understanding instead of rational decisions, and (3) it has purpose and strategies for accomplishing its goal.

First, practice is located in space, and, more significantly, in time. It is something that can be observed not only in three dimensions, but also from moment to moment. Temporality is an basic feature of practice.

> Time is both a constraint and a resource for social interaction. More than that, practice is "intrinsically defined by its *tempo*." Time, and the sense of it, is, of course, socially constructed; it is, however, socially constructed out of natural cycles—days and nights, seasons, the human pattern of reproduction, growth and ageing. Similarly, and more immediately, interaction *takes* time— and it occurs in space. Time and space are both capable of being modeled in different ways, and are thus equally social constructs, but movement in space always involves movement in time. Practice as a visible, "objective," social phenomenon cannot be understood outside of time/space. Any adequate analysis of practice must, therefore, treat temporality as a central feature of its very nature. (Jenkins, 1992, p. 69)

Second, practice is not wholly consciously organized. "Nothing is random or purely accidental but, as one thing follows on from another, practice happens" (Jenkins, 1992, p. 70). Bourdieu holds that practice follows the practical sense or "a feel for the game."

The practical mastery of the logic or of the imminent necessity of a game—a mastery acquired by experience of the game, and one which works outside conscious control and discourse (in the way that, for instance, techniques of the body do). (Bourdieu, 1990a, p. 61)

Bourdieu's notion that practice is not primarily guided by logically derived decisions places it in what Epstein (1993) refers to as the *experiential* system. Epstein contrasts the experiential system with the rational system and proposes that the experiential system is holistic, makes associationistic connection, and its processes occur "instantaneously and normally outside of conscious awareness . . . [with the result] that people are generally unaware of intervening interpretative and affective reactions and assume that they react directly to external events" (p. 403). Thus, actions in the social world are experientially guided and responsive to changing contexts without the necessity to "stop and think" before the act. Research practice can be characterized as a dance in which investigators' respond to the opportunities and challenges of their projects through "felt meanings" (Gendlin, 1991).

The coincidence of the objective structures and the internalized structures which provides the illusion of immediate understanding, characteristic of practical experience of the familiar universe, and which at the same time excludes from that experience any inquiry as to its own conditions of possibility. (Bourdieu, 1990b, p. 20)

Actions, of which practice is composed, would not be possible unless it were taken for granted most of the time. "We don't spend our time questioning the meaning of life because we cannot afford to and social imperatives do not allow—in both senses of the word—us to do it" (Jenkins, 1992, p. 71).

Practice is characteristically fluid and indeterminate. It is "the 'art' of the *necessary improvisation* which defines excellence" (Bourdieu, 1977, p. 8). Social life, in all of its complexity and variety, is not accomplished on the basis of rules, recipes and normative models. "We cannot have 'on file' a rule or prescription for every conceivable situation which one might encounter in routine social life. The depiction of practice as an improvisatory performance reemphasizes the importance of recognizing the temporal dimension of practice. Improvisation is the exploitation of pause, interval and indecision. The delay or, its opposite, the swift execution of the surprise move—is manipulable as a strategic resource" (Jenkins, 1992, p. 71). Bourdieu is critical of decision and game theory that picture human action as intrinsically rational and calculating.

Third, practice, even though accomplished without conscious deliberation for the most part, has purpose. Practice is not the product of structural rules, but of actor's strategies. Actors have goals and interests and use strategies to accomplish them. In his ethnographic analyses, Bourdieu describes "the inter play of culturally given dispositions, interests and ways of proceeding" and "individual skills and social competences, the constraints of resource limitations, the unintended consequences which intrude into any ongoing chain of transactions, personal idiosyncrasies and failings, and the weight of the history of relationships between the individuals concerned and the groups in which they claim membership" (Jenkins, 1992, p. 72).

For Bourdieu, the logic of practice consists of these three features—it occurs in space and time, it is guided by tacit understanding which neither wholly conscious nor wholly unconscious, and it is purposeful and strategic. Thus, practice is a mixture of constraint and freedom.

Using Bourdieu's theory as a guide, the practice of research has: (1) temporality as its central feature; (2) proceeds by way of "necessary improvisation" and tacit knowing, rather than by its own rationality and powers of decision-making; and (3) is strategic and goal-oriented. The description of research as practice differs significantly from the descriptions given in research textbooks or presented in conventional research reports. Instead of a performance choreographed according to logically ordered algorithmic methodical steps, the research process consists of often tacit strategic improvisations in the service of a guiding purpose. From my own and my colleagues' research experiences, I hold that the flowing logic of practice more accurately describes the texture of actual research practice than does the logic of formal demonstration.

In the new philosophy of science, knowing the actual unfolding process of the research is important to the understanding the meaning of the results. Thus, it is important that the research be reported in a form that can communicate the complex and fluid unfolding of the performance. The conventional reporting format reconstructs the actual research performance into a series of rationally calculated actions that moved the process straight forward toward a knowledge claim. More closely aligned with the diachronic and improvisational characteristics of the logic of practice is the narrative form. When constructing their reports of the temporal, tacit, and purposeful dimensions of their research endeavors, researchers need to use a format that can communicate the depth, complexity, and contextuality of their knowledge generation.

The Discourse Form of Narrative

The discourse form that is most appropriate for describing human action is narrative (Ricoeur, 1984). Bruner (1990) has argued that narrative is the natural mode through which human beings make sense of lives in time. Narrative discourse produces stories whose subject matter is human action. Stories are concerned with human attempts to progress to a solution, clarification, or unraveling of an incomplete situation. Narrative transforms a mere succession of actions and events into a coherent whole in which these happenings gain meaning as contributors to a common purpose. The research narrative draws together into a story the diverse actions and events that contributed to the research outcome—the findings.

"Other things exist in time, but only humans possess the capacity to perceive the connectedness of life and to seeks its coherence" (Vanhoozer, 1991, p. 43). Stories are linguistic expressions of this uniquely human experience of the connectedness of life (Ricoeur, 1992). The ground of storied expressions is the phenomenon of individual protagonists engaged in an ordered transformation from an initial situation to a terminal situation. The capacity to understand stories derives from the correlation between the unfolding of a story and the temporal character of human experience and the human pre-understanding of human action (Ricoeur, 1984). Although the protagonists of stories can be expanded by analogizing to institutions, organizations, or groups of people and by anthropomorphizing to animals (as in fairy tales), the story form retains its primary character of an imitation of personal action (Aristotle, 1954).

"People do not deal with the world event by event or with text sentence by sentence. They frame events and sentences in larger structures" (Bruner, 1990, p. 64). Plot is the narrative structure through which people understand and describe the relationship among the events and choices of their lives. Plots function to compose or configure events into a story by:

1. Delimiting a temporal range which marks the beginning and end of the story,
2. Providing criteria for the selection of events to be included in the story,

3. Temporally ordering events into an unfolding movement culminating in a conclusion, and
4. Clarifying or making explicit the meaning events have as contributors to the story as a unified whole.

Plots mark off a segment of time in which events are linked together as contributors to a particular outcome. The segment of time can range from the boundless (the story of God's creation of the universe), to centuries (the story of the settlement of the United states), to lifetimes (biographies), to daily or hourly episodes (the story of going shopping). In each case the plot establishes the beginning and end of the storied segment, thereby creating the temporal boundaries for the narrative gestalt.

Plots also function to select from the myriad of happenings those that are direct contributors to the terminal situation of the story (Carr, 1986). When the plot of the story concerns a researcher's production of a knowledge claim, those events and actions pertinent to the production of the claim are selected for inclusion in the highlighted figure of the story. Other events, such as the clothes worn, the room in which the analysis was undertaken, the eating of breakfast, and so on, because they are not central to the plot, may be included as background.

Narrative thinking is the most effective method of organizing action (Robinson & Hawpe, 1986). In a narrative approach, action is viewed as an expression of existence, and "its organization manifests the narrative organization of human experience" (Polkinghorne, 1988, p. 142). As the syllogism is the appropriate form for expressing a formal logic demonstration, and argument is appropriate for using evidence to convince an audience, narrative is the appropriate form for displaying the logic of practice.

Narrative discourse functions to transform a list or sequence of disconnected research events into a unified story with a thematic point (Polkinghorne, 1988). Narrative grammar performs this transformation through the operation of "emplotment" (Ricoeur, 1984). In emplotment actions and happenings are "grasped" together into a temporal whole and displayed as contributors to a particular outcome or achievement. Emplotment has a gestaltlike organizing quality that draws attention away from individual research events and draws attention to the unfolding of the whole project. The interest of Gestalt psychology is in the formation of spatial elements into whole figures (for example, the mental operation whereby by three non aligned dots take on the appearance of a triangle). Narrative grammar operates to configure research events into elements of a temporal whole that is located between the beginnings of a research project and its final denouement. Although emplotment can operate as a single thread that serves to draw all the elements together, it often employs multiple threads or subplots which are woven together into the complex and layered whole. Because of the synthesizing operations of emplotment, a narrative research report is able to accommodate and integrate the multiple elements that affect the progress of the project. Dispositions, values, emotions, purposes, deliberations, choices, chance events, and bodily and physical processes are synthesized into a single research story.

The narrative research report is a history of the research project. It is not, however, an unedited motion picture depicting the process as it happened. Stories are recollections and recreations of past episodes. The meanings of events flows from their appearance in the researcher's reflections on them from the perspective of what has happened (Schön, 1983). Stories select from the myriad instances of the research process as it occurred. Not all the elements will be used for the telling of the story. As mentioned above, elements which do not contradict the plot, but which are not pertinent to its development, do not become part of the narrative research report. This process has been called narrative smoothing (Spence, 1986). An actual research project does not match a carefully crafted, congruent story. It consists of extraneous happenings and everyday distractions (Carr, 1986). The very act of bringing these happening into language imposes a higher level of order on them than they have in the flux of the everyday experience. The move to narrative configuration extracts a still higher order from the fullness of lived experiences (Kerby, 1991). Narrative configuration, however, cannot impose just any emplotted order on the selected events. The final story must fit the events while at the same time bringing an order and meaningfulness that was not necessarily apparent in the event as it happened.

Through the use of narrative, researchers can integrate the three themes of the logic of practice described by Bourdieu. The temporal unfolding of the project in which prior actions and events affect, limit, and contribute to subsequent actions can be expressed by using a narrative format. The meaning and significance of actions that were improvised or guided by tacit understanding at the time of their occurrence can be retrospectively clarified in light of subsequent developments in the project. Narrative can select and organize the various acts and events of a research endeavor from the perspective of their positive or negative contribution to the accomplishment of the purpose for which the project was undertaken.

In the narrative research report, researchers speak with the voice of the storyteller rather than the impersonal voice of the logician or the arguer. They speak in the first person as the teller of their own tale. Stories are told to (written for) audiences and can be adapted to the interests and needs of the hearers (readers). When addressed to reviewers of its knowledge claim, stories can be framed to speak to their interests. A narrative report, however, displays the acceptability of a claim rather than argues for it. The display operates by eliciting the kind of trust that accompanies observing a person's performance. The voices of the subjects who participated in the research are allowed to speak in the narrative report. What they had to say need not be fragmented into brief supporting examples for themes; but as characters in the story, they appear as co-actors affecting and contributing to the unfolding research process.

Examples of Narrative Research Reports

Over twenty years ago Golden (1976) published a collection of twenty-one narrative research reports titled *The Research Experience*. Each narrative report was preceded by the original article, which was published in the conventional synchronic format. Golden, in describing the narrative reports wrote:

> [The narrative reports] take into account the unplanned as well as the planned aspects of discovery. These first-person accounts are intended to provide a broader perspective of the research experience than is usually found in the professional literature of the field. The contributors review some of the considerations and constraints—theoretical, practical, and personal—which influenced their decisions at crucial choice points in the research experience.

She noted that the personal journals (narrative reports) took into account "the unplanned as well as the planned aspects of discovery." They showed the "feeling, thinking component—the human side—of research." The narratives "confront the disorderly, the overlooked, the unpredictable, and even the boring and routine aspects of research" (p. 30). In one of the narratives Doob and Gross (1976) include in their story incidents that changed their design. Their research called for a car remaining still when a traffic light turned green. Their frustration measure was to be the time it took before the driver in the car behind the stopped car began honking. Because the researchers couldn't get their car washed before beginning the experiment, several of the drivers thought the car was broken down and never honked; on the other hand several others chose to crash against their bumper instead of honking. The narrative format promotes the inclusion of this kind of detail and rich description; elements neglected in the contemporary demonstration format.

Golden, who wrote before the new philosophy of science had made inroads into American social sciences, depicted the narratives as describing the process of discovery, and saw the conventionally formatted reports as serving the process of justification. She writes, "science tells us what ought to be done" (Golden, 1976, p. 30). The new philosophy of science proposes that the bifurcation of research into a context of discovery and context of justification is a misunderstanding of the reciprocal influence these two contexts have on one another. The storied presentation of the research process allows for the integration of both notions within the diachronic perspective of research as practice.

The narrative research reports collected by Golden remain as exemplars for contemporary qualitative researchers. The reports are in the form of a story in which the researcher is the protagonist whose purpose is to generate knowledge. The story includes a presentation of a setting in which the action takes place, marks the beginning of the drama (the reason for the researcher's interest in generating knowledge about a particular question) and the denouement or ending of the drama (the accomplishment of the project). Between these beginning and ending points, the stories weave together: (1) the accidental and planned happenings; (2) the motives, strategies, and actions undertaken by protagonist and other characters (research participants, assistants, administrators, and others) who affected the outcome; and (3) the weight these factors had in moving the research process toward the goal or away from the goal.

There is increasing interest in the use of narrative data in qualitative research. Cortazzi (1993) and Mishler (1995) give overviews of the many uses of narratives in current research. Nevertheless, most of these narrative inquiries continue to report their results in the conventional form. Van Maanen (1988) and E. M. Bruner (1986) propose that organizational and anthropological research results be presented in narrative form. Although I support the increased use of narrative data and analysis and presentation of results in narrative form, the focus of this chapter is on a different issue—the format of the research report. Reporting research in narrative form is appropriate for the many types of qualitative investigations (as well as, quantitative investigations). Examples of research reports in narrative form more current that Golden's 1976 collection are relatively rare. An early example of a narrative report of a qualitative study is Moustakas's (1961) investigation of loneliness. Moustakas relates the story of his inquiry beginning with the illness of his daughter and moving through to the conclusion of his increased understanding of the experience of loneliness. More current examples of narrative reports of research are included in McLaughlin and Tierney's (1993) collection of studies of the experiences of people who have traditionally been left out of the educational mainstream. The contributors to this volume tell the story of how their research was conducted, including their connections with the participants that are the focus of their studies and the process by which their engagements with the participants produced the results. Wells, Hirshberg, Lipton, and Oakes (1995) provide another exemplar of narrative reporting of research. In describing their report they write: "This article presents the story of our research team's efforts to conduct a multisite case study of 10 mixed schools engaged in efforts to reduce ability grouping or tracking" (p. 18). The report is a narrative of the deliberations and choice-points made throughout their evolving project.

Conclusion

The next step in the development of a qualitative research informed by the new philosophy of science is to move out from under the conventional format for reporting research. Although there is continuing experimentation in data collection and analysis by qualitative researchers; in the main, less experimentation has been undertaken in the format for reporting results. However, in a recent symposium (Tierney, Lincoln, Denzin, Kincheloe, Lather, Pinar, & Polkinghorne, 1994), new experimental forms for reporting research were presented. Lather described a report format in which different columns are used to display interview protocols and researcher interpretations. Denzin presented the possibility of reporting research through performances in which research reports are transformed into scripts that are enacted by the authors who play themselves.

In this chapter I have argued for experimentation with a narrative format for reporting research. I have contrasted the conventional synchronic approach to report formats with a diachronic format and suggested that research should be understood as a human practice, and, thus, is best presented in a diachronic format. The synchronic approach displays the structure of a research project; the diachronic captures the human actions and temporal character of the research process. Yet I do not believe that the disciplines must choose between these two approaches. Both are useful and the strengths of one are often the weaknesses of the other. However, I believe the diachronic perspective expressed through the narrative discourse is the more privileged form for reporting research in the context of the new science. I encourage social science researchers to conceive of their research endeavors as journeys whose destination is increased understanding of human beings and to use the narrative format to report their investigative travels.

References

Aristotle, *The poetics of Aristotle* (I. Bywater, Trans.). In *The rhetoric and the poetics of Aristotle* (New York: Modern Library, 1954), 223–66.

Bazerman, C. (1987). Codifying the social scientific style: The APA Publication Manual as a behaviorist rhetoric. In J. S. Nelson, A. Megill, & D. N. McCloskey (Eds.), *The rhetoric of the human sciences: Language and argument in scholarship and public affairs* (pp. 125–144). Madison: University of Wisconsin Press.

Bourdieu, P. (1977). *Outline of a theory of practice* (R. Nice, Trans.). Cambridge: Cambridge University Press.

———. (1990a). *In other words: Essays towards a reflexive sociology* (M. Adamson, Trans.). Cambridge, England: Polity.

———. (1990b). *The logic of practice* (R. Nice, Trans.). Cambridge, England: Polity.

Bruner, E. M. (1986). Ethnography as narrative. In V. W. Turner & E. M. Bruner (Eds.), *The anthropology of experience* (pp. 139–155). Urbana: University of Illinois Press.

Bruner, J. (1990). *Acts of meaning*. Cambridge, MA: Harvard University Press.

Campbell, D. T. (1974). Evolutionary Epistemology. In P. A. Schilpp (Ed.), *The philosophy of Karl Popper* (pp. 21–37). La Salle, IL: Open Court.

Carr, D. (1986). *Time, narrative, and history*. Bloomington: University of Indiana Press.

Cortazzi, M. (1993). *Narrative analysis*. London: Falmer.

Doob, A. N., & Gross, A. E. (1976). Status of frustrator as an inhibitor of horn-honking responses: How we did it. In P. M. Golden, *The research experience* (pp. 487–494). Itasca, IL: F. E. Peacock.

Epstein, S. (1993). Implications of cognitive-experiential self-theory for personality and development. In D. C. Funder, R. D. Parke, C. Tomlinson-Keasey, & K. Widaman (Eds.), *Studying lives through time: Personality and development* (pp. 399–434). Washington, DC: American Psychological Association.

Fischer, C. T., & Wertz, F. J. (1979). Empirical phenomenological analyses of being criminally victimized. In A. Giorgi, R. Knowles, & D. L. Smith (Eds.),

Duquesne studies in phenomenological psychology (Vol. 3). Pittsburgh: Duquesne University Press.

Gendlin, E. T. (1991). Thinking beyond patterns: Body, language, and situations. In B. den Ouden & M. Moen (Eds.), *The presence of feeling in thought* (pp. 22–151). New York: Peter Lang.

Gergen, K., & Gergen, M. (1986). Narrative form and the construction of psychological science. In T. R. Sarbin (Ed.), *Narrative psychology: The storied nature of human conduct* (pp. 22–44). New York: Praeger.

Golden, P. M. (1976). *The research experience*. Itasca, IL: F. E. Peacock.

Gordon, S. (1991). *The history and philosophy of social science: An introduction*. New York: Routledge.

Habermas, J. (1979). *Communication and the evolution of society* (T. McCarthy, Trans.). Boston: Beacon Press. (First published 1976)

Hammersley, M. (1990). *Reading ethnographic research: A critical guide*. London: Longman.

Jenkins, R. (1992). *Pierre Bourdieu*. New York: Routledge.

Kerby, A. T. (1991). *Narrative and the self*. Bloomington: Indiana University Press.

LeCompte, M. D., Millroy, W. L., & Preissle, J. (Eds.). (1992). *The handbook of qualitative research in education*. San Diego: Academic.

Lévi-Strauss, C. (1963). *Structural anthropology* (C. Jacobson & B. G. Schoepf, Trans.). New York: Basic Books. (Oringinal work published 1958)

Madigan, R., Johnson, S., & Linton, P. (1995). The language of psychology: APA style as epistemology. *American Psychologist, 50*(6), 428–436.

McLaughlin, D., & Tierney, W. G. (Eds.). (1993). *Naming silenced lives: Personal narratives and the process of educational change*. New York: Routledge.

Merleau-Ponty, M. (1968). *The visible and the invisible* (A. Lingis, Trans.). Evanston, IL: Northwestern University Press. (Original work published 1964)

Mishler, E. G. (1995). Models of narrative analysis. *Journal of Narrative and Life History, 5*(2), 87–123.

Morrow-Bradley, C., & Elliott, R. (1986). Utilization of psychotherapy research by practicing psychotherapists. *American Psychologist, 41*, 188–206.

Moustakas, C. (1961). *Loneliness*. Englewood Cliffs, NJ: Prentice Hall.

Nelson, J. S., Megill, A., & McCloskey, D. N. (Eds.). (1987). *The rhetoric of the human sciences: Language and argument in scholarship and public affairs*. Madison: University of Wisconsin Press.

Perelman, C. (1982). *The realm of rhetoric* (William Kluback, Trans.). Notre Dame, IN: University of Notre Dame Press.

Polkinghorne, D. E. (1988). *Narrative knowing and the human sciences*. Albany: State University of New York Press.

Ricoeur, P. (1984). *Time and narrative* (Vol. 1). (K. McLaughlin & D. Pellauer, Trans.). Chicago: University of Chicago Press.

————. (1992). *Oneself as another* (K. Blamey, Trans.). Chicago: Chicago University Press.

Robinson, J. A. & Hawpe, L. (1986). Narrative thinking as a heuristic process. In T. R. Sarbin (Ed.), *Narrative psychology: The storied nature of human conduct* (pp. 111–125). New York: Praeger.

Saussure, F. de. (1966). *Course in general linguistics* (W. Baskin, Trans.). New York: McGraw-Hill. (Original work published 1907–11)

Schön, D. A. (1983). *The reflective practitioner*. New York: Basic Books.

Schrag, C. O. (1986). *Communicative praxis and the space of subjectivity*. Bloomington: Indiana University Press.

Spence, D. P. (1986). Narrative smoothing and clinical wisdom. In T. R. Sarbin (Ed.), *Narrative psychology: The storied nature of human conduct* (pp. 211–32). New York: Praeger.

Tierney, W. G., Lincoln, Y. S., Denzin, N. K., Kincheloe, J., Lather, P., Pinar, W., & Polkinghorne, D. E. (1994). *Representation and the text: Reframing the narrative voice*. Symposium presented at the Annual Meeting of the American Educational Research Association, San Francisco, CA.

Valdé, M. J. (1991). Introduction. In M. J. Valdé (Ed.), *A Ricoeur reader: Reflection and imagination* (pp. 3–40). Toronto: University of Toronto Press.

Vanhoozer, K. J. (1991). Philosophical antecedents to Ricoeur's *Time and Narrative*. In D. Wood (Ed.), *On Paul Ricoeur: Narrative and interpretation* (pp. 34–54). London: Routledge.

Van Maanen, J. (1988). *Tales of the field: On writing ethnography*. Chicago: University of Chicago Press.

Wells, A. S., Hirshberg, D., Lipton, M., & Oakes, J. (1995). Bounding the case within its context: A constructivist approach to studying detracking reform. *Educational Researcher, 24*(5), 18–24.

2

LOST IN TRANSLATION: TIME AND VOICE IN QUALITATIVE RESEARCH

WILLIAM G. TIERNEY

Some years ago, for a case study on curricular change, I interviewed an individual who described life at the college in the following manner: "Life here is like a movie. You wouldn't believe it, and you won't be able to portray it either. Actually it's more like a soap opera than a movie." The individual went on to relate how the business of the institution revolved around petty jealousies, sexual encounters, and madcap grabs for power that actually did have more to do with what one might encounter on television's *Dallas* than in our staid academic journals.

As researchers, we dutifully record the stories of our informants; as writers we translate their stories into acceptable academic prose. "Faculty bring to their work experiences different cultural baggage," I wrote about this individual's institution, "and as they sit on committees and deliberate over curricular change, the serious differences of opinion that stem from their own cultural backgrounds stymie change" (Tierney, 1989, p. 97).

In what follows I argue that our representations of reality in qualitative research have been remarkably similar to one another. I employ examples from two journals over the last decade to highlight how authors use voice and time in their articles. I then suggest that in an age many describe as postmodern we develop experimental voices that expand the range of narrative strategies. In doing so, we underscore how authorial voice translates research narratives, and we move away from a linear view of time. I conclude with implications for teachers, researchers and authors who subscribe to the ideas developed here.

Translating Reality

The last two decades have witnessed a wealth of discussion about different aspects of the research endeavor. Researchers have argued about how to collect and analyze data (Lincoln & Guba, 1976), how to approach those whom we research (Lather, 1986), and how to choose sites and informants (McLaughlin, 1992). Most of these analyses have critiqued modernist assumptions of what we mean by reality; to varying degrees, the critics have taken theoretical stances—constructivism, critical theory and feminist theory, for example—that have rejected modernism's reliance on science as the arbiter of truth. From these perspectives, reality is created rather than discovered.

Although narrative forms have been widely discussed in the anthropological literature (Clifford & Marcus, 1986; Marcus & Fisher, 1986) qualitative researchers in education in general have not undertaken a wide-ranging analysis of how we present data; as I shall elaborate, for the most part we have not seen a deviation from standard, accepted practices of social science writing for scholarly publications. Consequently, comments such as the following represent the norm for the development of qualitative texts:

> One practical problem that faces the author of an ethnographic report is determining how much field data to include. This is particularly true if the report is shorter than monograph length. The solution is to incorporate examples from field data to illustrate the interpretation. . . . Does the ethnography provide statements at a high level of inference about overall trends and patterns and about causal relationships that may be interesting but inadequately supported by data? (Chilcott, 1987, p. 211)

Although all authors must deal with issues such as the length of a text or the choice of data to include or exclude, what goes unquestioned is the manner in which the author presents him or her self in the text, the relationship one develops—*in the text*—with those involved in the study, and the temporal sequence in which data gets presented. In effect, an author has data that needs to be shaped to prove specific points. The unstated assumption is the existence of underlying truths that govern social relations, and the struggle for the author is to ensure that the data accurately reflects social reality.

Kenneth Gergen points out that with modernity, "one could make comfortable distinctions between *fiction* as opposed to *factual* or scientific writing. . . . With the breakdown of things-in-themselves, and the sensitivity to multiple realities, such borders begin to dissolve" (1991, p. 116). With postmodernity, then, we make decisions not simply about the length of a text or about whether our data accurately represent reality, but rather how we as authors create and present reality. We struggle to understand ourselves as researchers and authors who are historically positioned. The text, for its part, becomes a construction rather than a realist interpretation (Richardson, 1993), one version of reality rather than the only version.

Accordingly, the manner in which data gets presented undergoes dramatic reconfiguration. One needs to consider the temporal aspects and structure of the text, for example, in a manner more akin to what we are accustomed to find in fictional texts than in the realism of the social sciences. Van Maanen has offered a helpful critique of the "realist" styles used in qualitative research (1988). *Realist tales* refer to texts where the author is presented unproblematically. The reader learns about a particular people or topic and the author's voice is omniscient. The styles of realist tales may differ, but the assumptions do not. "Experiential tales," for example, highlight an absent narrator who takes the reader through an experience that he or she has had; in an alternative form, the "native's tale," the reader learns about a culture or topic from the native point of view as if the researcher did little more than transcribe fieldnotes.

From a postmodernist perspective the author's role is to deal with one's self—or multiple selves—and to enable reflexivity in the reader so that we come to terms with the "ideology of representation" (Morrow, 1991, p. 161). In doing so, data presentation may be dramatically different from the past. As we now have different ways to collect and analyze data, I am suggesting that different ways to present data also need to be encouraged. In what follows, I offer an analysis of how authors in two journals have dealt with two aspects—narrative and time—of qualitative data over the last decade. I have chosen the *Anthropology and Education Quarterly* (AEQ) and *The Review of Higher Education* (RHE) primarily because they (a) are educational journals, (b) have different audiences and authors, and (c) have made qualitative research a centerpiece of their issues. My point in discussing specific pieces of data is not to suggest that one author's article is good or another's bad. Indeed, a central goal of this text is to encourage diversity in the presentation of data; what I shall show is the orthodoxy with which qualitative researchers present their research findings. One caveat also needs to be underscored: I have drawn from ethnographies, case studies, or qualitative projects that are not linguistically oriented, for the analysis of specific pieces of language differ in purpose from what I have discussed here.

Problems of Style

Authorial Voice

The "I." In a 1986 article in *AEQ* Dehyle wrote, "The students asked if I was a new teacher or just a visitor. I asked the boy in front of the trophy case where he had learned to do that dance. With a grin he said, 'I read a book at K-Mart'" (1986, p. 111). Dehyle's article highlights one style authors have employed in *AEQ* and *RHE* to place the author. The author is a stable figure who exists within the story. Similarly, in *RHE* Tierney wrote, "It is early in the fall semester, and I am interviewing faculty, students and parents" (1991, p. 199). The authors employ a first-person narrator to move the events of the text along to a conclusion and to highlight that the author is involved in the construction of the text. The author is seen as a single narrator and as a consistent figure within the action. That is, the "I" of the text is not someone who creates the text, but rather is the data-gatherer.

The Interviewer. Another form for the author is to enter the text as a researcher who provides the reader with partial transcripts from the interview protocol. In 1992 Asal and Farrell presented the following:

AA: Do you carry guns? Why yes or no?
Amer: Yes, I like to have guns because we have to defend ourselves. I
        am not scared of machine guns. (1992, p. 284)

What one finds in this text is again the stable presence of a researcher; readers are ostensibly able to be as close to the data as is possible: we read the transcripts. This style has been consistently used over the last decade. In 1984, for example, we saw in AEQ:
As we talked further, a new twist to my teacher role came about:

Student: I know for myself, living here as the only black RA
              [Resident Assistant]in this building, the things that hap-
              pen to me that I can say have to do with my race or my
              sex, it's the racism that comes out first.
Interviewer: Yes, I know exactly what you mean. Throughout my life
              I've always felt that when I walk into a room where there
              are mostly white people, I'm first seen as a black, then as
              a woman. (Wade, 1984, p. 221)

Although the narrative style is similar, there are also significant differences. In effect, the author has three voices. One voice is the "I"—"as we talked further." The second voice is "the interviewer." Indeed, unlike the first example where the author's initials are presented, we read the role rather than the individual—"the interviewer." And yet the author also enters the text not simply to move the action along as a narrator, but also to present a human side to the discourse—"I know exactly what you mean." Thus, in this text, the author offers three different identities—narrator, interviewer, participant.

The Omniscient Narrator. This style is by the far the most pervasive form in which authors have written qualitative articles in both journals over the last decade. "Starting with the collegial frame," wrote Bensimon in 1989, "this president explained that good presidential leadership means 'accomplishing commonly determined goals in such a way that all involved are satisfied with the path taken to get there'" (1989, p. 114). "Like Joan," wrote Lesko, "Tim discussed the special relation between teachers and students: 'Teachers seem to care. Even if you don't have them for a class, you can go to them—talk, ask for help'" (1986, p. 26). Kempner wrote, "Not all the faculty shared a sense of common purpose. 'In the beginning days,' observed one faculty member, 'there was a terrific sense of purpose'" (1990, p. 220).

What occurs in these texts is that we again see a stable narrator—or rather do not see, but hear the action move along in a singular narrative fashion. The researcher entered a site and recorded data; the writer presented the data in the form of a story that set out to prove a point. The textual strategies may differ—Bensimon and Lesko were more concerned with the analysis of individuals ("Starting with the collegial frame")—and Kempner offered a case study of an institution, but the uses of the narrator are similar.

Although there are slight variations on the use of these three narrative voices, no other dramatically different strategies are employed by authors of qualitative research in either journal over the last ten years. I offer three points about this observation. First, each strategy posits the author as a researcher who unproblematically collected data and then presented it. Any sense of the author's role in the construction of reality is absent. Second, in a decade where we have seen an explosion of writing about the research method, one wonders why social scientists engaged in analyzing educational processes continue to employ only three strategies with regard to the author. If we analyzed fictional stories of even fifty years ago, we would find more narrative strategies than have been called upon here. To be sure, some texts at some times may wish to employ the three strategies used in *AEQ* and *RHE* over the last decade. And yet, is it not possible to expand the range of narrative possibilities, and in doing so to present data in dramatically different ways? Third, if we wish to employ alternative forms of representation, we may desire to turn to literary criticism as a vehicle more suited to understanding how an author develops a relationship to a text than to rely on the traditional criteria we have used to judge its worthiness.

Textual Time

Linear Time. One way to express the events in a text is chronologically, so that the reader discovers a beginning, a middle and an end. The manner in which an author presents him or her self in the text often coincides with the temporal nature of the text. In Dehyle's interaction with the students, the text revolves around the author's entrance at a school where Native American students had recess. She continued, "The assistant principal appeared and asked, 'Where are you boys supposed to be? I know it's not here!' They gave excuses (among them, that they were talking to 'that lady') and as they moved back to their gym class, the bell rang" (1986, p. 211). This recounting of an event enables the reader to engage a text where action unfolds in a familiar manner. The story makes sense because, seemingly, we capture the action as it unfolded. The same can be said of the quote by Tierney where we heard "it is early in the fall semester" (1991, p. 199). Presumably, the action moves along in the text so that we hear what occurs in the winter and spring as well.

Disjunctive Time. A more commonplace way for the author to deal with time is to disregard it. "The child's father expressed his feelings about communication with his daughter and about his role as a parent," stated Erting, "Kids are supposed to learn so much from parents through their conversation, what it's like to be an adult" (1985, p. 231). Similarly, Creswell and Brown commented, "department heads visited informally and formally with senior administrators and promotion and tenure committees about faculty accomplishments because they felt a responsibility to support their staff. 'Somehow I think the measure of the chairman is partially on how good they are in getting their people tenured'" (1992, p. 47).

These kinds of comments assume that the temporal nature of the data is unimportant. On the one hand, the reader hears an individual's beliefs about how children learn to be an adult; on the other hand, we hear how one defines the role of a good chair. Presumably, the time in which the comment was taken and the author's relation to the comment is relatively trivial. This form of comment is the temporal equivalent of the omniscient narrator.

Present Tense. "A college trustee," wrote Neumann, "sums up the tone and meter of the college life by saying that the campus runs 'like a fine-tuned Swiss watch'" (1992, p. 425). Eisenhart wrote of a student's discussion of career interests in the following manner, "Marie says, 'Everything [I tried] where I went to school, I always came back to gymnastics'" (1985, p. 255). The decision by the authors is to present the data in a narrative style that unwinds. The reader is with the author as the story unravels.

As with the narrative strategies, the use of the present tense is open to different interpretations. Neumann, for example, wrote so that the story unfolded chronologically. Eisenhart used the present tense as a way to switch from an authorial voice to a narrative one. That is, the story of Marie (mentioned above) is told in the present, ("Marie says . . .") but the narrative is contextualized in the past. Eisenhart wrote, "Subsequently, she became a member of her high school's gymnastics team and entered AAU competitions" (1985, p. 255). Thus, both linear and disjunctive time have been utilized.

Although it is possible for an author to use the present tense with either linear or disjunctive time, the norm has been to use linear time and the present tense together. We hear a story in much the same way a storyteller might begin, "We're going on a trip . . ." Such a stance calls for a willing suspension of disbelief; like all listeners, we know that the storyteller knows the end of the story. The story already has happened. But we join in a sense of disbelief because we want to be told how the story ends. When disjunctive time is used in the present tense, as with the case of Eisenhart's article, the reader is aware that the story has concluded; we do not need a sense of disbelief.

Past Tense. By far the most common narrative style over the last decade has been the use of the past tense. "In an individual interview," wrote Tutt, "Beverley explained her recent, poor attendance by explaining that getting to poker can be a hassling experience; in her words, 'I pay the price the next day'" (1989, p. 31). Smith-Hefner wrote, "His wife, who was obviously distraught and on the verge of tears, interrupted him: 'I am afraid about my children because American culture is very different from Khmer culture'" (1993, p. 149).

Here we learn that the action has happened and the author is retelling the story. We again do not need to suspend disbelief because we are not expected to be involved in the text. The past tense can be used with either linear or disjunctive time. We may hear a story that occurred, or the temporal nature of the text may be unimportant. The author who provides interview data, for example, will use disjunctive time and the past tense. The interviewer asked the informant a question and he/she responded. Conversely, one may insert one's self in the text, tell a chronological tale, and let the reader hear all of the events in the past.

What we learn, then, is that the proposition of time in our qualitative texts seems to be either-or. We use either the present or the past. Time either unfolds chronologically or is irrelevant. As with my comments about the author's narrative voice, I am not suggesting that any one strategy is mistaken. And yet, we know that different cultures have different ways to express time. Leslie Marmon Silko, for example, writes about how Pueblo people think differently about history and time so that texts do not naturally flow in linear fashion from point A to point B to point C; instead, "the structure emerges as it is made. . . . Pueblo expression resembles something like a spider's web—with many little threads radiating from the center crisscrossing one another" (1991, p. 83).

We know from Western notions of time that events and stories do not always unfold sequentially. Similarly, Michelle Wallace writes about how we must reinscribe notions of temporality and myth if we are to come to terms African American history (1991, p. 139). We know from our own experience that life's actions are often not chronological. In what ways might an author deal with time other than the fourfold responses that have been used over the last decade?

Discussion

If postmodernism has created an ideology of doubt, it stands to reason that our research endeavors also need to reflect that doubt. As previous authors have critiqued the stance a researcher assumes with those whom he/she researches and offered alternative venues, we now need to critique narrative styles and to offer alternative modes of representation. As objectivity/subjectivity are issues of concern in the collection of data, they are also issues in the presentation of data. And as we have reinterpreted the meaning of objectivity in the collection and analysis of data, we also must reinterpret such meanings for our texts.

As Stephen Webster highlights, a postmodern effort "can not take itself undialectically for granted as given (as Descartes did). . . . [Qualitative research] must hang on in good faith to the myriad contingencies and opaque personalities of reality, and deny itself the illusion of a transparent description, a luxury reserved for less reflexive sciences" (1982, p. 111). What I am arguing here is that if we accept Webster's idea, then we must accuse our research efforts of having operated within an "illusion of transparent description." The author positions him or her self unproblematically and presents a serial or disjunctive narrative.

In contrast, what I am suggesting is that we develop an openness in qualitative writing. What we need, then, is to create a textual dialectic whereby we problematize "the privileged authorial perspective, monologue, assumption of descriptive adequacy, political neutrality, and other epistemological preconceptions intrinsic to the structure of ethnographic texts" (Webster, 1983, p. 195). To do so suggests that authors move away from standard representations of reality and toward more experimental forms. Accordingly, rather than try to replicate the positivist aspects of the natural sciences, we might call upon literary genres as exemplars for the development of our writing schemes. The multiple forms of fiction, for example, offer insight about how we might present a narrator in ways other than those used by social scientists. Fiction also offers multiple accounts that utilize time in ways different from the four schemes presented above. To be sure, not every narrative and temporal choice will work, but it seems foolhardy to ignore how authors in other fields have developed their texts as we struggle to create our own. One implication of experimentation, of course, is that some efforts will fail and others will succeed. As we explore the epistemological no-man's-land between factual realism and fiction we will enrich our ways to explain the worlds we study, interpret, and create. In many respects, such an undertaking is the essence of a reflexive postmodernism. Because the landscape is uncharted I offer three possible avenues for those of us who are teachers, researchers, and ultimately, writers, as we explore this no-man's-land.

The Art of Teaching. If students are to acknowledge alternative forms of representational styles, they must be made aware of these alternative styles. In those classes where we teach qualitative research, we need at a minimum to enable individuals to see a range of narrative and temporal styles. As authors, we make choices, often unaware why we have made them. Putting a text in the present tense as opposed to the past, for example, ought to be an active authorial decision, rather than a default choice made because the author was not aware when he/she developed the text. Thus, in a class we might develop writing exercises where students transform the same text into different tenses and different authorial voices. In order for students to see the range of possibilities, we will need to bring into the classroom examples of writing that may fall outside the domains of social science and within the field of literature. Simply stated, to enable an individual to envision alternative forms of representation, we must create the conditions for such acts to take place. A classroom where we maintain conventional standards of writing and provide "classics" will not afford the student the opportunity to consider the available options that might exist as he/she develops a text.

A criticism of opening our classrooms in this manner might be twofold. On the one hand, many instructors already feel overwhelmed with what needs to be presented; if additional texts are added, one needs to consider what texts will be deleted. On the other hand, if our dissertation committees and journals define their standards according to traditional social science standards, are we not doing a disservice to students in helping them develop writing that will be viewed as unacceptable?

My response to the first issue is akin to my ideas about the nefarious debates that have circulated about the "canon." No one is suggesting that a traditional course syllabus be scrapped in favor of another syllabus. At the same time, at this point in the history of qualitative research, to avoid any discussion about issues of postmodernism and textual authority in our research classes seems to be as major a flaw as to overlook discussions about interviewing techniques. Again, I am not suggesting that all course readings be changed, but instead that we reconfigure how we teach and what we teach. In doing so, we enable students to participate in key debates of the moment.

The second concern is more central. Few dissertation committees will allow experimental fiction, for example, as a means to present one's findings. Standard social science journals will reject out of hand alternative forms of writing. And yet, standards do change. We once believed that the passive voice was the only way to write a dissertation, but such a belief is now rejected in virtually all areas except the far reaches of educational psychology departments. Journals and monographs also have changed. Recently we have seen poetic representation as one textual offering (Richardson, 1992) and a short story as another (Tierney, 1993). At a minimum, we ought to make students aware of the debates that rage in the academic community and let them make informed decisions about where they wish to position themselves in the discussion.

The Crisis of Purpose: Defining the Audience. One possible critique of the advocacy of experimental writing is that the purpose of educational research is to enable policymakers to arrive at informed decisions at a variety of levels. Information about school principals, for example, conceivably might enable a school principal to improve his or her work. Data about minority student retention could stem the tide of attrition. Ethnographies about gay and lesbian college students may lead to policies that lessen homophobia and heterosexism.

Three responses exist. First, as with one's course syllabus, I am not suggesting that all qualitative research be somehow transformed into a standard format. If anything, I am suggesting the opposite—that we need to develop multiple formats of narrative styles. Consequently, some research for some audiences presumably does need to be presented in manners that have become standard.

Second, one might also question how much standard educational research actually has impacted policies at any level. One of the central concerns of policy analysts over the last two decades is the utility of educational research. As we have developed measures of reliability and standardization we have developed a private academic language that is accessible to few individuals other than our scholarly peers. One might plausibly argue that the opening up of textual authority will enable greater utility rather than less.

Finally, the kind of experiment that I am suggesting here has been attempted before, and such works often have had considerable impact on discussions, for example, about education (Kozol, 1991), and poverty (Harrington, 1962). Again, I am not suggesting that we simplemindedly mimic one style over another or that we disregard one's audience. However, to say simply that one should not experiment with textual authority because it does not suit our purpose seems to assume unproblematically that all research has the same purpose, and that the manner in which we have presented our findings over the last two decades has been flawless.

Judging the Postmodern Text. If one accepts the goal suggested here then the greatest challenge and logical next step is to come to terms with how one evaluates whether the text is good or bad. We have developed standard criteria for judging the worthiness of traditional social science articles. Chilcott's statement in the first part of this text, for example, offers insight about how to judge a modernist article. But analyses based on realist tales of life will fail when applied to experimental texts.

Because we are embarking on a new journey, I have no clear-cut method for judging these texts, but two ideas offer a point of departure for discussion. On the one hand, we need to turn to literary criticism, considering recent attempts to analyze texts, and how such attempts might aid us in the analysis of our own work. And on the other hand, in a postmodern world where we develop reflexive texts, it seems incumbent that we logically continue with calls for self-reflexive analysis. Are the characters believable? What is the quality of the narrative voice? Does the text capture a moment or a situation or idea? At a minimum, it seems incumbent on us not to resist engaging in such experiments because we do not know how to analyze them, but rather to undertake such ventures so that we might develop ways to understand them.

Conclusion

Not everyone will concur with the suggestion that narrative experimentation needs to take place. However, if one agrees with the assumptions presented here what actions await us? Depending on how one interprets the text at least two possible challenges exist.

At a minimum, as teachers, researchers and authors we might expand our repertoire beyond what we have done for the last decade. Surely, we can develop the range of our voices and temporal conditions so that in the next ten years we offer new ways of presenting data. On a more ambitious level, we might confront the authorial role in educational research as is being done in the social sciences. Experimental anthropological texts such as *Translated Woman* (Behar, 1993) and *Mama Lola* (Brown, 1991) are examples of the kinds of work that might be attempted for educational settings. Both authors bring themselves forcefully into the text, question the conditions of reality in which they are involved, and constantly move the reader in and out of an interweaving tale.

I have offered a critique of where we have been and hinted at where we might go. In a postmodern world, where interpretation and translation are paramount, we—as subjects, objects, authors, and narrators—will often feel lost and ill at ease. The point, of course, is not to ignore the discomfort or to wish it away, but to confront the issues of identity and representation and consider how we might develop texts that highlight the problematic worlds we study, our relationship to such worlds, and how we translate them.

Note

The author wishes to acknowledge the helpful comments of Rebecca Kline, Robert Rhoads, Julie Neurerer, and Philo Hutchinson.

References

Assal, A., & Farrell, E. (1992). Attempts to make meaning of terror: Family, play, and school in time of Civil War. *Anthropology and Education Quarterly, 23*(4), 275–290.

Behar, R. (1993). *Translated woman: Crossing the border with Esperanza's story.* Boston, MA: Beacon Press.

Bensimon, E. M. (1989). The meaning of "good presidential leadership": A frame analysis. *The Review of Higher Education, 12*(2), 107–123.

Brown, K. M. (1991). *Mama Lola: A voodou priestess in Brooklyn.* Berkeley and Los Angeles, CA: University of California Press.

Chilcott, J. H. (1987). Where are you coming from and where are you going?: The reporting of ethnographic research. *American Educational Research Journal, 24*(2), 199–218.

Clifford, J., & Marcus, G. E. (Eds.). (1986). *Writing culture: The poetics and politics of ethnography.* Berkeley: University of California Press.

Creswell, J. W., & Brown, M. L. (1992). How chairpersons enhance faculty research: A grounded theory study. *The Review of Higher Education, 16*(1), 41–62.

Dehyle, D. (1986). Break dancing and breaking out: Anglos, Utes and Navajos in a border reservation high school. *Anthropology and Education Quarterly, 17*(2), 111–127.

Erting, C. J. (1985). Cultural conflict in a school for deaf children. *Anthropology and Education Quarterly, 16*(3), 225–243.

Gergen, K. (1991). *The saturated self.* New York: Basic Books.

Harrington, M. (1962). *The other America: Poverty in the United States.* Baltimore: Penguin.

Kempner, K. (1990). Faculty culture in the community college: Facilitating of hindering learning? *The Review of Higher Education, 13*(2), 215–235.

Kozol, J. (1991). *Savage inequalities: Children in America's schools.* New York: Crown.

Lesko, N. (1986). Individualism and community: Ritual discourse in a parochial high school. *Anthropology and Education Quarterly, 17*(1), 25–39.

Lincoln, Y. S., & Guba, E. G. (1985). *Naturalistic Inquiry.* Beverly Hills, CA: Sage.

Marcus, G. E., & Fisher, M. J. (1986). *Anthropology as cultural critique: An experimental moment in the human sciences.* Chicago: University Of Chicago Press.

McLaughlin, D. (1992). *When literacy empowers: Navajo language in print.* Albuquerque: University of New Mexico Press.

Morrow, R. (1991). The challenge of cultural studies to Canadian sociology and anthropology. *Canadian Review of Sociology and Anthropology, 28*(2), 153–172.

Neumann, A. (1992). Double vision: The experience of institutional stability. *The Review of Higher Education, 15*(4), 417–497.

Richardson, L. (1992). The consequences of poetic representation: Writing the other, rewriting the self. In C. Ellis & M. G.Flaherty (Eds.), *Investigating Subjectivity.* Newbury Park, CA: Sage.

———. (1994). Writing: A method of inquiry. In N. Denzin & Y. Lincoln (Eds.), *Handbook of qualitative research.* Beverly Hills, CA: Sage.

Silko, L. M. (1991). Language and literature from a Pueblo Indian perspective. In P. Mariani (Ed.), *Critical fictions: The politics of imaginative writing.* Seattle: Dia Center for the Arts.

Smith-Hefner, N. J. (1993). Education, gender, and generational conflict among Khmer refugees. *Anthropology and Education Quarterly, 24*(2), 135–158.

Tierney, W. G. (1989). *Curricular landscapes, democratic vistas: Transformative leadership in higher education* New York: Praeger.

———. (1991). Academic work and institutional culture: Constructing knowledge. *The Review of Higher Education, 14*(2), 199–216.

———. (1993). The cedar closet. *Qualitative Studies in Education, 6*(4), 303–314.

Tutt, B. R. (1989). Report of a pilot study in girlfriending: An ethnographic investigation of a women's poker group. *Anthropology and Education Quarterly, 20*(1), 23–35.

Van Maanen, J. (1988). *Tales of the field: On writing ethnography.* Chicago: University of Chicago Press.

Wade, J. E. (1984). Role boundaries and paying back: "Switching hats" in participant observation. *Anthropology and Education Quarterly, 15*(3), 211–224.

Wallace, M. (1991). Conference presentation. In P. Mariani (Ed.), *Critical fictions: The politics of imaginative writing.* Seattle: Dia Center for the Arts.

Webster, S. (1982). Dialogue and fiction in ethnography. *Dialectical Anthropology, 7*(2), 91–114.

———. (1983). Ethnography as storytelling. *Dialectical Anthropology, 8*(3), 185–205.

3

SELF, SUBJECT, AUDIENCE, TEXT: LIVING AT THE EDGE, WRITING IN THE MARGINS

YVONNA S. LINCOLN

The writer writes and the reader reads—or so it appears. And there the matter rests, for most. But in truth, this simple proposition is a mask for a vast system of ambiguities and entanglements.

—Sven Birkerts, *The Gutenberg Elegies*

Postmodernism and the Text

As the world and our views of it have changed, so, too, have changed the kinds of texts we hope to have represent us to ourselves. As we absolve ourselves of the modernist fancy that texts can stand as memorials to the truth about the world, we let go of the last measure of certainty to which we might have clung. Postmodernism's accusation against modernism is that it is a liar; it promised us truth, but delivered thickly veiled polemic tracts in the name of science. "Central to the modernist view," notes Gergen, "was a robust commitment to an objective and knowable world, and to the promise of truth about this world" (1991, p. 83). But postmodernist textual analysis suggests that all texts are created from partial perspectives, and that furthermore, that is the best we can hope for. Laurel Richardson summarizes the postmodernist critique:

> The core of postmodernism is the *doubt* that any method or theory, discourse or genre, tradition or novelty, has a universal and general claim as the "right" or the privileged form of authoritative knowledge. Postmodernism suspects all truth claims of masking and serving particular interests in local, cultural, and political

struggles. . . . *The postmodernist context of doubt distrusts all methods equally. No method has a privileged status.* The superiority of "science" over "literature" . . . is challenged. But a postmodernist position does allow us to know "something" without claiming to know everything. Having a partial, local, historical [situated] knowledge is still knowing. (Richardson, 1994, pp. 517–18, emphases in the original)

If all texts are only partial, historically and culturally situated and highly gendered, then it is but a small leap to conclude that the multiple understandings which come from any ethnographic project have only a limited chance of being presented in a single text. If texts are necessarily partial and situated, then it is a type of realist pretense to hope that any given text can tell the "whole story." Multiple stories feed into any text; but, equally important, multiple selves feed into the writing or performance of a text, and multiple audiences find themselves connecting with the stories which are told. What are the implications for this polyphonic chorus of author/selves, subjects and participants, audiences, and texts?

The idea that we can think consciously about presenting and re-presenting the stories we tell proffers an enticing invitation to think reflexively and self-consciously—not just about the fieldwork we do, but also about the means we choose and use to relay our fieldwork tales to audiences. The choice implied in reflexivity leaves open the possibility that we can consciously take out our narrative voice and reframe it. We can speak in narrative voices which represent our different selves, or which may have special meaning for particular audiences.

Our academic discussions of "the text" suggests, via its choice of articles, that we typically have under consideration a text, some text, the final end-product or by-product of our fieldwork. Indeed, even before we have completed a significant period of time in the field, we have already begun contemplating the written work it will produce—a book, several articles, one or more conference presentations. The rational planning of scholarly products is a heritage from early fieldworkers, who often immersed themselves deeply in the site, then starkly and anxiously disengaged in order to reflect and summarize their findings, often by "cataloguing" their "subjects" (Vidich & Lyman, 1994). Our ideas about reframing narratives fails to challenge this heritage of summarization and cataloguing, especially in the sense that we still assume that a major piece of research produces—or ought to produce—a magnum opus.

The concept of choice, however, is a powerful one. Choice implies intention. Intention implies a kind of deliberation, and deliberation is at the center of our "story" here: we have choices, and those choices can and will reveal different intentions. Our choices are compounded by their sheer range—the self we choose to be, our participants and the way we/they present themselves, the forms the texts take, and the audiences with whom we and our research participants wish to interact via the text.

Authors as Selves

Alma Gottleib observes there is a "widespread Western tendency to see the author, in particular, as a singular creation, standing alone in her or his artistic achievement" (1995, p. 21). The implication is that there is an author, a unitary personality, from whom is evoked a singular text, the artistic creation that is the singular product of the ethnographic experience. We know otherwise now. Geertz's (1988) *Works and Lives* dismantles the fiction of an absent author. Van Maanen's (1988) *Tales of the Field* explicitly dismantles the fiction of a unitary author with his discussion of the confessional tale. We now see the author's hand there, albeit in carefully disguised form, part and parcel of a "text-building form" that renders the author invisible. The confessional tale, often following by some years the realist tale, specifically takes up the personal experiences of the ethnographer in the field, intimating the hidden truth of the realist's tale—the presumed absence of the ethnographer's voice from the "truth" of the context (Geertz, 1988). A second self emerges in the confessional tale, a self specifically excluded from the original fieldwork narrative, a self in touch with loneliness, frustration, and the inevitable ambiguities of ethnography. Gergen (1991) suggests that in social science as in social life the "romantic self" and the "modernist self" have existed side by side for some time (the modernist self producing the realist tale, the romantic self producing the confessional tale), but that both are giving way to a postmodern, "saturated" self. This saturated self, living a "protean life-style" (Gergen, 1991, pp. 248–49) , engages in multiple relationships capable of producing multiple expressions of the self. As Gergen describes this postmodern, protean life, it is characterized by "a continuous flow of being, without obvious coherence through time . . . [an ability which means that one] holds in one's head, and does frequently and in a great variety of ways, images that are contradictory and seem to take one in opposite directions simultaneously" (p. 249). David Miller (1974, cited in Gergen, 1991, p. 249) describes this postmodern, protean experience of reality as "a matter of the radical experience of equally real, but mutually exclusive aspects of the self.

Personal identity cannot seem to be fixed. . . . The person experiences himself as many selves, each of which is felt to have . . . a life of its own."

> "Most of us fail to appreciate how profoundly we influence each other and how larger systems influence us," Harriet Lerner has observed. Instead, we learn to think in terms of individual characteristics, as if individuals are separable from the relationship systems in which they operate. . . . *We do not, however, have one "true self" that we can choose to either hide or authentically share with others. Rather, we have multiple potentials and possibilities* that different situations willl evoke or suppress, make more or less likely, and assign more or less positive values to. (1993, p. 206)

Lerner's intention is to say that we are not just one single person, a unitary author, but rather a multitude of possibilities any of which might reveal itself in a specific field situation.

This concept of multiple selves enters the conversation about textual representation because it suggests that we might choose a "self," one particular identity which was evoked by some aspect of the fieldwork, by some set of interactions with our research participants, by some confluence of circumstance, that we might evoke for a given text. Just as earlier anthropologists choose the "absent authorial voice" for their realist tales, and the personal, present, immediate (and sometimes grumpy [see, for instance, Geertz's descriptions of the Malinowski diaries, 1988]) self for their confessional tales, we might choose our voice, range and register for a given text.

Geertz explains that the realist tale is contrived by means of an "elaborate text-building strategy . . . [which] rests most fundamentally on the existence of a very strictly drawn and very carefully observed narrative contract between writer and reader" (1988, p. 58). This "theatre of language" (p. 59) relies on the adoption of a self that exists in formal discursive conventions. It is the adoption, in this "theatre of language," of a specific character, a "dramatis persona," the onstage role we are to play in the text. To the extent we can uncover and dissect the discursive conventions, we are able to redeploy the self in another direction, to another purpose, or in another role. It is here that the multiple selves come into play.

I would not wish to indicate that the selves of which we are composed can be taken off the shelf, much as we might Shakespeare's plays. Rather, they are uncovered and identified as a part of the intense reflexivity which now marks postmodern ethnography and text-building.

Who we are, how we portray ourselves in a text, are very largely a function of intense analysis of the self-in-context. Matching self with text (and matching self in text vis-a-vis research participants and with audiences) is never easy. Further, the discursive conventions which marked the authors whom Geertz disassembled fail on every count to work in today's fieldwork genres. The cultural, social, and gendered nature of those narrative genres mark them as unsuitable for nonmodernist narratives, and unable to meet the demands of social praxis.

As a result of deliberating about the self-in-action, or the self-in-text, we realize we have a range of choices and voices. The only voice not available to us is that of the "detached observer" (Lincoln, 1991). But how do we choose? In the next section, I discuss issues that will guide our choices, at least in part.

Choosing Identity

But finding the self—locating which self, capturing which historical moment, delineating which identity—who needs to write is more than the choice of a particular perspective. The search is not that of Sweeney of Irish legend, seeking to find his lost sanity, alone among the birds and wild things in the wild places (Heaney, 1983). We are not alone. Rather, we speak among many voices—those whom we write, and those who listen to us read. How to choose which self we want to expose, which persona we will risk to audience gaze?

No one has suggested criteria yet, but it might be possible to do so, however inadequately or even wrongheadedly. For example, we might consider which audience we want to address: our professional colleagues (e.g., scholarly conferences, disciplinary readers); our research respondents and participants, or others like them (e.g., community forums, plays, oral presentations, or more informal writing styles that rely on discursive conventions more like ordinary and natural language); or those readers/audiences who might wish to become involved in debating the social issues our work embraces (e.g., publicly accessible books such as Kozol's *Rachel and Her Children* [1988], or widely available newsmagazines such as *Atlantic Monthly* or *The New York Review of Books*). The choice of audience, the conscious imagining of those who might read our work, will have some influence on who we are in a text.

We might want to think about the purpose of a text when considering the authorial voice. Is the text a prompt to public debate or intended to influence policy choices? If so, we might consider the affecting, tender, observer-self of Kidder's *Among Schoolchildren* (1989). Is the intent to prompt action? We might want to see the self in praxis: a self which identifies with social action, which is in sympathy with change, which can paint stories in sharp relief and the participants' own language, and who is comfortable with the label "activist." Is the purpose to create extended understanding and a sense of shared destiny? The self who sees herself as one with others, whose realization is of one interconnectedness and community, is the self to be found.

If we are not just a single person, but rather a multitude of possibilities, I might assert that as ethnographers we could be about utilizing those multiple selves to create multiple texts, each of which speaks to a different audience. The recognition of these multiple selves could serve not to undermine our own authenticity, but rather, create larger repertoires from which we might respond with serious, audience-focused action. Clifford and Marcus (1986) call such writing the "writing of cultural accounts," a "crucial form of knowledge—the troubled, experimental knowledge of a self in jeopardy among others."

Some reader might argue that all of these identities could and should be found in a given text. And perhaps they could. More likely, multiple selves demand multiple texts. It might be the case that for many social scientists, moving away from the discursive conventions of our own histories will be experiments, only partially realized, as we make text a form of play. We will have to find ourselves and our voices, since breaking out of our scholarly "native languages" and learning new ones to match our new commitments will not be easy.

Once we have located our voices in the text, however, we confront the problem anew. This is because our respondents—the subjects of the text, its raison d'etre—have a multiple range of voices likewise. How we help them "find" their voices, and place them whole in our texts, is the next issue.

Subject Voices: The Storied Participant

Elsewhere (Lincoln, 1993), I have written on breaking the silence of the silenced, and ways of achieving "voice" for those who have been voiceless. By convention, those who have access to the conduits of power—journals, policy circles, education more broadly—have arrogated the power to "name." But in the re-presentation of storied lives, others may choose for themselves the power to name, to describe, to evoke the emotion and humanity denied by the language of social science (P. Smith, 1990).

Formerly, when subject-respondent voices entered into social science research, the researcher him/herself still made the decision about when, how, and under what circumstances. Typically, too, the research participant's (subject's) words were used to provide evidence of some point which researchers wished to make (indeed, I have chosen particular quotations from my research respondents for exactly and precisely the same reason—to buttress some point of my own interpretation, not necessarily a point of theirs [see Lecompte,1993]). This creates the appearance of a multivocal text, but such a text is still transparently under the control of the ethnographer. Recent experiments with research texts which represent more shared decision-making have created a more balanced textual form (see, for instance, Karen McCarthy Brown's *Mama Lola* [1991]). But even more egalitarian textual forms, while they suggest ways in which we might "be" in our texts, and ways in which our "subjects"—both the topics of our inquiries and the research participants— might choose to "be" in our texts (or in our lives), tell us little about how to create such an egalitarian relationship, or how to construct such a text. And even while talking only indirectly about voice, they do suggest that presentation can and does move beyond the "soulless language" (P. Smith, 1990) of social science. How is another question.

Greg Tanaka's chapter in this book points to one form of experiment in textual re-presentation, an experiment that I would call (although he does not) a *pas de deux*—storied topics, not necessarily voices, in counterpoint. The tension generated between the ruminative, analytic voice of the intellectual dissecting Dostoyevsky and the practical, pained circumstance of a context in flux, not necessarily for the better, created spaces for interior and public selves to be shared. Here, at least, the contradictions between the inner contemplations of the researcher, and the private and public torments of a university administrator, come face-to-face in a story whose textual design sharpens our sense of the disconnect. This dangerous and paradoxical threat to such a story is that we will understand—from watching this alien and disorienting *pas de deux*—that they are both the other.

But design/graphic experiments are but one way of including or inviting other voices. I and others have explored various means of coaxing other voices into texts. Since social scientists are most often charged with, or funded for, social science research, I once advised them to check at every step of the way with research participants to ensure that participants assent to what is presented in text about themselves (Lincoln & Guba, 1985; Guba & Lincoln, 1989). While it is still a useful technique, it still is predicated on the researcher in charge of the creation of a text. Peter Reason and his colleagues (1994) go much farther and argue that the only way in which to accomplish the representation of what was learned is through joint negotiation about what will be said ("coopera-

tive inquiry") and joint creation of the text(s) that transmit those understandings to wider audiences.

Somewhere between the fine advice and the growing number of
experimental examples lie possibilities for our participants—the subjects
of our works and their lives—to be fully present, unmarginalized, in
works. Choosing how is not necessarily our decision to make.
Herrington and Curtis (1990, p. 490) speak of creating a writing course
that acts to move "voices on the margin to the center" by creating the
conditions in which their students might "move confidently and
thoughtfully through private meaning-making to significant communication with others." Although bell hooks (1984; 1994) and other writ-
ers/authors might resist moving to the center in favor of the freedom of
the margins, it seems to me that creating new textual forms explicitly
calls for the kind of work that Herrington and Curtis attempted.
Somehow, without violating privacy, we have to find a way to help
those we study and study with to move from private meaning-making
to public communication. In so doing, we also have to search for ways,
with them, for them to co-create our joint texts and in so doing, find
ways to "be" with us, whether in communion, consensus, or conflict.

To follow this line of reasoning, "voice" is not something we "discover" for "subject voices"; it is a process of discovery we may start, but
which they complete. Clifford and Marcus make the point that "it has
become clear that every version of an 'other,' wherever found, is also the
construction of a 'self'" (1986, p. 23), but this is equally true in the
reverse; as 'others' create themselves, our singular selves are likewise
reconstructed. Just as "ethnography irrevocably influences the interests and lives of the people represented in them" (Van Maanen, 1988, p.
5), the life/lives and interests of the researcher are equally influenced
and often transformed. As our "subjects" become respondents and co-
participants in our research, so too do we become more engaged and
thereby transformed.

The interaction between participants, author/selves, and their
antiphonic voices act both to complicate choices about voices in the
text, and at the same time, to create new possibilities, textual and relational. The choice of author-self to present textually is moderated by
participants' choices about who they will be in the text. The "authority
to produce knowledge" (Gitlin, 1990) implicit in a commitment to hearing silenced voices creates a new form of dominion: the authority to
decide how one wishes to be presented publicly. If I possess some form
of knowledge which you do not have, then I have the power to decide
both how I will share this knowledge with you, and how I will permit
you to share it with others, because in the sharing of it with others,

there will be an "I" behind this knowledge which has the power to advantage or to disadvantage me. My sharing with you thus portends the capacity to empower or disempower me; my sharing with you becomes an ethical question for both of us.

Because the issue of voice is therefore is neither solely a problem of authorial choice, nor is it politically neutral, it can subvert the entire research and writing effort. But beyond our voices and theirs lies another issue: To whom do we speak? It is becoming clear that to whom we speak influences the voice we choose for ourselves, and the voices we might recommend for our research participants. "Audiencing" will provoke a whole new set of considerations for authors.

The Invisible Voyeurs: Audience(s) at the Edge

We have all been both on the stage, and in the audience. We are "audiencing" even when not consciously aware of the stages on which others are face-making. We review papers for journals; we act as critics for scholarly sessions at conferences; we engage in academic "shop-talk" when around both friends and mere acquaintances; we read the books of others (sometimes eagerly finishing them, other times, setting them down, half-finished, in a kind of weary disappointment at their tiresomeness). We watch our colleagues chatting or politicking, we watch our students get their sea-legs in national groups, we watch as small personal dramas unfold and die. And we listen. And even while we're attuned to the unfolding of our own multiple selves, lives, and careers, we give little specific attention to either our own audiencing or to our own audiences beyond a short span that typically includes our disciplinary colleagues, or a few scholars beyond our own disciplines. We have given little attention to how our work feeds into the public discourse (if it does at all) surrounding public policy issues, save for some few scholars who study the dispersion, dissemination, and integration of new knowledge and understanding. As a result, it should not surprise us to find that conscious choice of audience by writers for our work receives scant attention. We have, for the most part, written for ourselves, and have, consciously or unconsciously, considered the research community to be our primary "consumer" of new knowledge.

In part, this inattention to our audiences has left us with the realm of public discourse safely corraled by the political right, who appear to be astonishingly conscious of and deliberate about audience. If we know how as ethnographers to do this, why are we not doing it? I would argue that we do not know how to imagine audiences beyond our own disciplinary purviews well. We do not know how to carry on a textual conversation with people unlike ourselves. We do not know very much about consciously projecting a particular self or identity while writing, and carrying that single persona clearly and authentically throughout a piece of writing when it is to individuals or groups beyond those with whom we normally engage in professional concourse.

Identifying our Audiences

Simple as it may sound, we have not spent a large amount of time identifying our possible audiences. But the evaluation literature is useful here. If we stopped, for a moment, calling these groups of people audiences, and called them instead "stakeholders," we might find them somewhat easier to identify (see, for instance, Guba & Lincoln, 1981). One way to ask who these groups are would be to ask who could benefit from our research. Clearly, those with whom we do research would be audiences under this guideline. We might ask also about those who will clearly not benefit from our doing this research; they will be those who stand, for instance, to lose some power or privilege if we are investigating oppression. We might ask who would be affected if social arrangements were reorganized, or who would be affected if social goods were redistributed. We might ask what groups or individuals could make common cause with the particular community in which we engage in research; are there possibilities for mutual action, or at least support? And of course, we, too, are stakeholders: we have much to gain or lose in terms of status, prestige, and other benefits which accrue to the knowledge-producing elites; and we have gains or losses in terms of our own personal political commitments, and even greater stakes in our long-term transformations as human beings, if we permit the research we do to change us. Since much of our ethnographic or interpretive work is funded, we might ask who funds this work, and what is their stake in this knowledge? That question could well lead to designations of interests and stakeholders far afield of our disciplines, but deeply concerned with the outcomes of our work. All of the possible stakeholders lead us to specific audiences, each of which might use, or at least evince interest in, our work, if they but had access to it, in a form which they considered usable.

Kuhn (1976) proposed that meaning is only achieved within a "disciplinary matrix," while Van Maanen, in broadening the range of audiences we might have, proposed that meaning is communicated among and between individuals who occupy an "interpretive community" (1988, p. 41). An alteration in the interpretive community (by, for instance, reaching out to unfamiliar audiences beyond our academic world) has the potential effect of changing meanings, creating new meanings, obviating them, reversing them, or even creating a kind of untranslatable foreign language. Text producer and text reader have to share some common meaning framework for a text to be at all meaningful to readers. This sense of an interpretive community directs researchers' attention to the kinds of values that readers might hold, and therefore, to what kinds of realities might provide connective and sense-making opportunities for those readers.

The idea of an "interpretive community" also implies that different audiences might require different cultural "texts." Different audiences, who will arrive at small or substantial differences in interpretation, will form these distinct interpretive communities. ("Text" itself is a word loaded with culturally imperial meanings, suggesting literature and a willingness to read, denying functional illiteracy and a-literacy.) Stake imagined (1975) that different audiences might require vastly different "presentations": portrayals, plays, theater, forums, community meetings, even mime and dance. Contemporary action researchers, more mindful than conventional researchers of the need for research to be grounded in praxis and the various utilities and purposes of different interpretive communities, recognize the same dilemma. As a result, they have called for variegated cultural "texts" (including "group discussions, public meetings, community seminars, open-ended community surveys . . . fact-finding tours, collective production of audiovisual materials, popular theatre, group mapping and drawing exercises, group writing"; see Woodill, 1992). Variegated rather than monolingual texts are responsive to the cultural, linguistic, or presentational formats of a wide range of audiences. Despite such possibilities, and in spite of their potential accessiblity, most of us are unaccustomed to writing in literary, nonscholarly genres unlike what we have always done (fictional formats, plays, community presentations, and the like). This is the case even though such efforts might reach audiences outside our own disciplines, or within the contexts where we do our research.

Texts: Writing in the Margins

Texts stand as testaments to the facts of our existence, to our having "been there," and to the many voices of the individuals with whom we have interacted. But much is being demanded of postmodern texts. Beyond being testamentary, they are expected to fulfil purposes never premised until the latter half of this century. Readers and theoreticians alike ask that texts "come clean" with the author's partial, situated, but authentic self, preferably the "self" that showed up to begin the field-work, the self that accomplished the fieldwork, and the self who left changed (since authentic fieldwork inevitably changes a person; see, for instance, Mary Savage, 1988).

Second, our friends and critics alike demand that they see evidence that our representational and "othering" practices have not done violence to our respondents and their lives. They look for proof against our having acted colonially or in ways which further marginalize or disadvantage. Our critics are quick to locate ways in which we have fenced round the center to keep strangers out. Often this means that voices other than the author's need to be heard. But this problematic on two counts: (1) how to seek out and find those voices, and (2) how to midwife their "being" in our text in ways which they find both mean-ingful and honest (Lincoln, 1993). Thus, while our "range of textual strategies is quite narrow" now (Tierney, 1995), that will have to change.

Third, texts seem to have built-in "homing" devices, finding the audiences for which they are intended. Those audiences for whom we have written, however conventionally or experimentally, have been pri-marily ourselves. Marianna Torgovnik reflected:

> No one who gets around to writing a book, or even an essay, ever reads everything that has been written about a subject. Yet we cling to the fiction of completeness and coverage that the academic style preserves. This style protects us, we fondly believe, from being careless or subjective or unfair. It prescribes certain moves to ensure that the writer will stay within the bounds that the acad-emy has drawn. . . .
>
> If all we want to do is to write for professional advancement, to write for a fairly narrow circle of critics who exist within the same disciplinary boundaries as we do, there is nothing . . . wrong with the traditional academic style. . . .
>
> But when [researchers want] to be read, and especially when they want to be read by a large audience . . . [this] . . . means writ-ing as persons with feelings, histories and desires—as well as information and knowledge. (Torgovnik, 1991, p. 33)

We have often ignored the community of public discourse, and we have equally ignored the policy community. The damage of the latter void has created the contemporary situation wherein those who would reverse the social gains of the marginalized of the last half century are virtually the only voices that are heard. Perhaps we are afraid, in the current climate, to be known as persons of histories, feelings, and desires; perhaps we fear that when policy designers see and feel our passion (Lincoln, 1991), they will be repulsed and fearful, and accuse us of lack of objectivity. And indeed, the "warnings and advice" we give ourselves as a disciplinary community might well be reversed, were we to recognize that we speak to a policy community that is firmly grounded in modernist thinking on research "objectivity." It might pay us well (as the funding agency referred to earlier was unwilling to do) to study what forms of texts are thought to be most persuasive to the policy community(ies) with whom we should be engaged.

A critical reason for texts to reach the policy community is provided by McCarthy (1992), who worries that "cultural representations help form the images we have of others; if assimilated by those others, they help form the images they have of themselves as well; they get embodied in institutions and inform policies and practices" (1992, p. 641). If our intent as praxis-oriented postmodernists is to alter images, and to "inform policies and practices" in a public sense, then intersecting texts will have to be written which crosscut the interests of both our research participants and the policy communities who shape policy on them. We are Valerie Walkerdine's "surveillant others" (1990), in a sense, "who not only watch but also produce written records meant to inform the policies and practices regulating those whom we observe" (Alvermann, 1992). The politics of that particular representational paradox constitutes a mandate not only to create texts which are just and authentic, but also to do so in ways which reach the regulatory realm "whole, bright and deep with understanding" (Pinar, 1988) as well.

Fourth, it seems evident in both the ongoing experiments as well as the theoretical literature that representational practices have to move beyond Torgovnik's "narrow circle of critics." Some examples of this kind of work appear in this volume. Others are alluded to, as for example when Patti Lather comments that she is working with a graphics/text designer to find print strategies that will convey the multivocality of the voices in the text on which she is collaborating. Besides textual representations, however, we may need to rethink the telling of stories. It is not simply because increasingly the audiences we want to reach have ripened under the sun of the technological age and television; they are attuned more to visual images and less to the written word. We may be seeing another powerful paradigm shift underway—not a paradigm shift in the sense of models of inquiry, but a rather larger shift in the kinds of consciousness some of our audiences bring to our science, and therefore, to the kinds of "texts" that may interest, appeal to, or affect them.

As Postman has suggested (1985), and Birkerts laments (1994), we may be leaving the "two dimensional process of book-based learning," and moving toward some three-dimensional space for learning, the outlines of which are but dimly understood (1994, p. 139). Comfortable or not with the new technologies, our choices are but two: to engage with technology and attempt visual/press images that somehow convey immediacy, engagement, and multivocality, and/or to "lower" our technology and somehow re-create/re-present in that most human of forms, storytelling. I use the "and/or" locution simply because we must do both, in my opinion. Just as we needed the grounding in the human as instrument to understand qualitative methodologies deeply (Guba & Lincoln, 1981), so too do we need a deeper understanding of how we have always told each other stories, such that our personal meaning-making became communal knowledge, communal images, communal direction. This is not an either-or proposition. We need high technology—the firm understanding of not only how we tell stories in text, but also how text can be made to tell our halting and incomplete inquiries more powerfully. But we also need low technology—rebuilding our skills in storytelling, in meaning-sharing, for groups and persons who are not now a part of our narrow circle of critics.

I recall growing up in a family where my parents intuitively knew that reading was important, probably because they had little formal education themselves, and understood well, if unconsciously, the limits on their socioeconomic status placed by narrow educational opportunity. As a result, my sister and I were encouraged to read with a variety of what would be called today in reading research "literacy practices": we were regularly bought books, tutored in reading by both our parents long before we went to school, read to as small children, and the like. But one "literacy practice" that has made an enduring, if late-appearing, impact on me was "The Children's Story Hour." The Children's Story Hour was a project that encouraged children to read (in this instance, fairy tales from many countries), and repeat the stories to each other. The "organization" of the group has been long lost to my memory, but I do recall that we had some time to read and prepare our own stories, and each Saturday morning we would meet in a nearby community center, and "tell" our fairy tales to groups of our peers, parents, and interested adults (who often brought small, nonreading children to listen). I recollect most vividly my own story from one year, "Wassilika the Golden-Haired," a Russian fairy tale, and have, as a "grown-up," told the story from time to time to the small children of my closest friends.

This experience from my early elementary education years, coupled with having a father who was himself an amazing raconteur of "true stories" of astonishing wit, sophistication and split-second timing, has led me to a somewhat belated understanding of the roles that "stories" play in our lives. This is true whether we are talking of the selves we invent for public consumption, the private self, or how we "are known, or not known to others" (Krieger, 1985). I have come to see storytelling as an imperative human practice, but also, at another level of abstraction, as a metaphor for the texts we present to each other and the world. In the metaphoric sense, storytelling enables us to reconnect with the ceremonial, sacerdotal, and quotidian dramas that mark our own worlds and work.

Self, Subject, Audience, Text: Writing in the Margins

Yes, but how is this accomplished?, the reader asks. One by one, and with some problems, is my answer. Like the ancient maps which labeled unexplored territories with the warning, "Here ther be beastes and monsters," we have many beasts and monsters. We are, as I am fond of telling my graduate students when they are breaking ground, making it up as we go along. The problems that I see in creating newer textual representations are fourfold. First, we probably need to find the voice in which we will speak. Some of us are still struggling with shifting registers, with trying to write narratives which are at once authentic and which signal science. We may need to break the science habit, and go cold turkey into a new life. Breaking the science habit can only come when we have sufficient self-knowledge (read: reflexivity) to understand ourselves deeply, and to accept our selves with all our fieldwork, collegial, and human frailties. When we can exorcise the academic writing, or at least view it as only one of many languages of the self, we will see the self emerging textually.

The second problem will require a restructuring of our field relationships. Working with our respondents to help them find their own voices implies a connectedness with them that we only rarely see now in text form. Such closeness implicates a fraternal or sororial relationship that may be uncomfortable, unfamiliar, awkward, or graceless. But paternalistic colonialism can no longer suffice. The sharing of work implies egalitarian ends. Such ends necessarily define who we are and how we approach those whose voices become the subjects of our stories.

The third problem will be imagining, and finding, our audiences. It is difficult to sit before a keyboard and "talk" to a group of individuals I may never have met, interacted with, or from whom I can only imagine a set of responses. And yet, after finding ourselves, we have to find our audiences. In some instances, they will have found us, simply because we have been working with them all along; in other instances, we will create them just as we create our texts.

The fourth problem is that we will have to find or invent a form. The "form" may be a literary genre with which we are familiar and comfortable (plays, short stories, novels, poems), or it may be a textual/print format that we "design" whole cloth, with technical experts who can initiate us into the mysteries of graphic design principles. Or it may be subjectivizing and making reflexive and systematic the informal tales we tell of the field, long after the seminar rooms are closed and the restaurants and bars attract us for one last conversation. It may mean spending evenings and weekends, not hiking or sailing or catching new plays, but working with our research participants, looking for form, structure, meaning, and coming to terms with what elements of that will become public knowledge.

If this signals a merger of public and private selves, that is my intent. By this, I do not mean to imply that researchers should have no private lives. Rather, I am suggesting that much of what has happened to us in the field has gone unnoticed, unmarked, in any public sense. But in the interests of locating voices, both our own and those of others, in the text, the private side of research—the unrecorded conversations, the shifts, changes, transformations—will move into our texts. The "othering" of our own selves will cease to become a useful tool for achieving an obsolescent objectivity. It is the only way I see to manage the vicarious experience which precedes believability and "a feeling for the organism" (Keller, 1983).

Conclusion

We will never totally "get it right." Perfection is not a requisite for social science research, and the postmodernist doubt which we share leads us to believe that "getting it right" is a project best abandoned. But within our partial and situated knowledges, we can nevertheless still move outward, inclusive in our orientation, thinking not first and last about our own research productivity, but rather about the selves we bring to our storytelling lives. In moving outward, we can engage both our own multiple and complex selves, and also those with whom we would speak: our subject-topics and respondents, our audiences, and our and others' texts. We can share the possibilities of an intertextual and dialogically dramatic life; and we can share Stephen Tyler's vision:

The ethnographic text will thus achieve its purposes not by revealing them, but by making purposes possible. It will be a text of the physical, the spoken, and the performed, an evocation of the quotidian experience, a palpable reality that uses everyday speech to suggest what is ineffable, not through abstraction, but by means of the concrete. It will be a text to read not with the eyes alone, but with the ears. (1986, p.136)

References

Allen, C. J., & Garner, N. (1995). Condor qatay: Anthropology in performance. *American Anthropologist, 97*(1), 69–82.

Alvermann, D. E. (1992 December 2). *Researching the literal: Of muted voices, second texts, and cultural representations.* Presidential address, National Reading Conference, San Antonio, Texas.

Birkerts, S. (1994). *The Gutenberg elegies: The fate of reading in an electronic age.* Boston: Faber and Faber.

Brown, K. M. (1991). *Mama Lola: A Vodou priestess in Brooklyn.* Berkeley: University of California Press.

Clandinin, D. J., & Connelly, F. M. (1994). Personal experience methods. In N. K. Denzin & Y. S. Lincoln (Eds.), *Handbook of qualitative research* (pp. 413–427). Thousand Oaks, CA: Sage.

Clifford, J., & Marcus, G. E. (Eds.). (1986). *Writing culture: The poetics and politics of ethnography.* Berkeley: University of California Press.

Geertz, C. (1991). *Works and lives: The anthropologist as author.* Stanford, CA: Stanford University Press.

Gergen, K. J. (1988). *The saturated self: Dilemmas of identity in contemporary life.* New York: Basic Books.

Gitlin, A. D. (1990). Educative research, voice, and school change. *Harvard Educational Review, 60*(4), 443–466.

Gottleib, A. (1995). Beyond the lonely anthropologist: Collaboration in research and writing. *American Anthropologist, 97*(1), 21–25.

Guba, E. G., & Lincoln, Y. S. (1981). *Effective evaluation.* San Francisco: Jossey-Bass.

Heaney, S. (1983). *Sweeney astray: A version from the Irish.* New York: Farrar Straus Giroux.

Herrington, A. J., & Curtis, M. (1990). Basic writing: Moving the voices on the margin to the center. *Harvard Educational Review, 60*(4), 489–496.

Keller, E. F. (1983). *A feeling for the organism: The life and work of Barbara McClintock.* San Francisco: W. H. Freeman.

Kennedy, E. L. (1995). In pursuit of connection: Reflections on collaborative work. *American Anthropologist, 97*(1), 25–32.

Kidder, T. (1989). *Among school children.* Boston: Houghton Mifflin.

Kozol, J. (1988). *Rachel and her children: Homeless families in America.* New York: Crown.

Krieger, S. (1985). Beyond "subjectivity": The use of the self in social science. *Qualitative Sociology, 8*(4), 309–324.

Kuhn, T. S. (1970). *The structure of scientific revolutions.* Chicago: University of Chicago Press.

Lather, P. (1986). Research as praxis. *Harvard Educational Review, 56,* 257–277.

LeCompte, M. D. (1993). A framework for hearing silence: What does telling stories mean when we are supposed to be doing science? In D. McLaughlin and W. G. Tierney (Eds.), *Naming silenced lives* (pp. 9–28). New York: Routledge.

Lerner, H. G. (1993). *Dance of deception: Pretending, and truth-telling in women's lives.* New York: HarperCollins.

Lincoln, Y. S. (1993). I and thou: Method, voice and roles in research with the silenced. In D. McLaughlin and W. G. Tierney (Eds.), *Naming silenced lives* (pp. 29–50). New York: Routledge.

———. (1991, April). *The detached observer versus the passionate participant: Discourses in inquiry and science.* Paper presented at the annual meeting, American Education Research Association, Chicago.

Lincoln, Y. S., & Guba, G. (1985). *Naturalistic inquiry.* Thousand Oaks, CA: Sage.

McCarthy, T. (1992). Doing the right thing in cross-cultural representation. *Ethics, 102,* 635–649.

McLaughlin, D., & Tierney, W. G. (Eds.). (1993). *Naming silenced lives: Personal narratives and processes of educational change.* New York: Routledge.

Miller, D. (1974). *The new polytheism.* New York: Harper & Row.

Pinar, W. F. (1988). "Whole, bright, deep with understanding": Issues in Qualitative research and autobiographical method. In W. F. Pinar (Ed.), *Contemporary curriculum discourses* (pp. 134–154). Scottsdale, AZ.: Gorsuch Scarisbrick.

Postman, N. (1985). *Amusing ourselves to death: Public discourse in the age of show business.* New York: Penguin.

Reason, P. (Ed.). (1994). *Participation in human inquiry*. London: Sage.

Richardson, L. (1994). Writing: A method of inquiry. In N. K. Denzin & Y. S. Lincoln (Eds.), *Handbook of qualitative research*. Thousand Oaks, CA: Sage.

Sanjek, R. (Ed.). (1990). *Fieldnotes*. Albany: State University of New York Press.

Savage, M. (1988). Can ethnography be a neighborly act? *Anthropology and Education Quarterly, 19*(1), 3–19.

Smith, L. M. (1990). Ethics in qualitative research: An individual perspective. In E. W. Eisner & A. Peshkin (Eds.), *Qualitative inquiry in education: The continuing debate* (pp. 258–276). New York: Teachers College Press.

Smith, P. (1990). *Killing of the spirit*. New York: Viking.

Stake, R. (1975). *Evaluating the arts in education: A responsive approach*. Columbus, OH: Charles E. Merrill.

Tierney, W. G. (1995). (Re)presentation and voice. *Qualitative Inquiry, 1*(4), 379–390.

Torgovnik, M. (1991). Three women, three voices: Excerpt from "Experimental critical writing." *Lingua Franca: The Review of Academic Life, 1*(3), 19, 33.

Tyler, S. A. (1986). Post-modern ethnography: From document of the occult to occult document. In J. Clifford & G. E. Marcus (Eds.), *Writing culture: The poetics and politics of ethnography* (pp. 122–140). Berkeley: University of California Press.

Van Maanen, J. (1988). *Tales of the field: On writing ethnography*. Chicago: University of Chicago Press.

Vidich, A. J., & Lyman, S. M. (1994). Qualitative methods: Their history in sociology and anthropology. In N. K. Denzin & Y. S. Lincoln (Eds.), *Handbook of qualitative research* (pp. 23–59). Thousand Oaks, CA: Sage.

Walkerdine, V. (1990). *Schoolgirl fictions*. London: Verso.

Wolf, M. (1992). *A thrice told tale: Feminism, post-modernism, and ethnographic responsibility*. Stanford, CA: Stanford University Press.

Woodill, G. (1992). Empowering adolescents through participatory research: Final summary report of the project "Community Needs Assessment for Base Empowerment for Health Promotion." Toronto, Ontario, Canada: Ontario Ministry of Health. (Internet Summary)

4

FICTION FORMULAS: CRITICAL CONSTRUCTIVISM AND THE REPRESENTATION OF REALITY

JOE KINCHELOE

Constructivism has implied that nothing represents a "neutral" perspective, in the process shaking the epistemological foundations of modernist grand narratives. Indeed, no truly objective way of seeing exists. Nothing exists before consciousness shapes it into something we can perceive. What appears to us as objective reality is merely what our minds construct, what we are accustomed to see (Leshan & Margenau, 1982; Bohm & Peat, 1987). The knowledge that the world yields has to be interpreted by men and women who are part of that world (Besag, 1986). Whether we are attempting to understand football, education, or art, the constructivist principle tacitly remains. For example, most observers don't realize that the theory of perspective developed by fifteenth-century artists constituted a scientific convention. It was simply one way of portraying space and held no *absolute* validity. Thus, the structures and phenomena we observe in the physical world are nothing more than creations of our measuring and categorizing mind (Frye, 1987). As such, these creations always take on a fictional dimension, a dimension dependent upon a variety of social, psychological, and discursive dynamics. One important thread running through these dynamics involves the role of power and its ability to shape our representations of the world along the lines of particular patterns. In this context our fictions, though complex and idiosyncratic, become literary constructs (fiction formulas) reflective of dominant ideologies and ways of seeing at work in the larger society.

Because researchers are often unable to discern the way in which power and its dominant ideologies position them in relation to the texts they produce, the development of analytical methods for exposing this dynamic becomes a central feature of critical and constructivist research. This is where critical postmodern theory collides with constructivism, thus, the etymology of the term "critical constructivism." Critical theory, of course, is concerned with extending a human's consciousness of himself or herself as a social being. An individual who gains such a consciousness would understand how his or her political opinions, religious beliefs, gender role, racial self-concept, or educational perspectives had been influenced by the dominant culture. Critical theory thus promotes self-reflection. This self-reflection is grounded upon an ever-evolving conception of power. One of the most important elements of critical constructivism involves the development of a dynamic and textured understanding of the way power works at both macro (deep structural) and micro (particularistic) levels to shape our understandings of the world and our role in it. Such theoretical work might begin its analysis of macro-power with Gramscian notions of hegemony and its analysis of micro-power with Foucauldian notions of discursive construction with its intrapersonal and interpersonal dimensions. The theoretical innovation critical constructivism seeks involves the identification of "contact points" where these macro and micro manifestations of power connect. The search for these contact points takes place on the individual terrain of consciousness, necessitating in a sense a phenomenology of power—in a Foucauldian sense, an archeology of consciousness.

Researcher Positionality: Power Eclipses

These contact points can always be found in archaeological excavations of artifacts of researcher positionality. Such explorations of researcher consciousness are central to critical constructivism's effort to expose the worldview she or he takes for granted. It was this notion that Antonio Gramsci had in mind when he argued that philosophy should be viewed as a form of self-criticism. Gramsci asserted that the starting point for any deeper understanding of the self involves consciousness of oneself as a product of sociohistorical forces. A critical philosophy, he wrote, involves the ability of its adherents to critique the ideological frames they use to make sense of the world (Reynolds, 1987; Mardle, 1984). The success of such an effort hinges on the ability of the self, the researcher in this case, to make sense of power and to flush it out of the places in which it hides. At this point critical constructivist researchers begin to appreciate the subtle ways power shapes their research, their methods of representation and their narrative voice. Knowledge of self, of positionality (one's location in the web of reality), creates a consciousness that empowers researchers to choose between models of inquiry that avoid power relations and depersonalize knowledge and models that use intuition and emotional empathy to uncover fibers of power in modes of representation and narrative formats (Yeakey, 1987). As they develop a sense of reflexive awareness, they focus on the ways their narrative voices are shaped by linguistic codes, cultural signs, and embedded ideology. At this point they begin to reconstruct their perception of the world in a manner that prepares them not only to deconstruct what has always appeared natural but to rethink the manner in which they might present their social and cultural reformulations to their audience (Lincoln & Guba, 1985; Lincoln & Denzin, 1994; Noblit, 1985; Slaughter, 1989; Fine, 1994).

The discourse of cultural studies aids the critical constructivist effort to address researcher positionality and the historically and socially produced features of the research traditions they embrace. Such traditions often assert that there is a correct way to represent reality. Cultural studies with its poststructuralist critique of modernist inquiries contends that such traditions are *fraudulent* in their representational certainty, in their denial of ideological complicity in the dynamics of their construction (Fontana, 1994; Rosenau, 1992; Probyn, 1993). The unitary modernist self, the narrative reflection of liberalism's abstract individual (the subject who transcends the weight of historical and cultural engagement) is removed from power's construction of consciousness. As a *covert* form of autobiography, the narrative formula of traditional data presentation positions the reporter as a privileged producer of texts; the researcher cum disavowed autobiographer in this context fails to interrogate the shadowy role of power. At this juncture the critical constructivist meta-analyst specifies the discursive forms of the modernist narrative (the fiction formulas) and their power-connected seductions. Understanding power's pervasiveness as well as its construction of a researcher's ideological horizon, the critical constructivist analyst itemizes the male-specific, class-dominated, white-oriented, unified-subject-assumed fiction formulas that produce the naive narratives at the hub of academic research. These same type of secretive formulas can be uncovered in the attempt to mobilize public memory, justify a succession of institutional failures, or create a corporate tradition that never existed. Such historical fiction formulas operate on both academic and public terrains creating narratives that are conflict-free, seamless, objective, and official. Such fiction formulas arise not from the need to remember but from the need to forget. The formula calls for a bleaching of bloodstains that helps prop up established power.

Subverting the Stable Positionality of the Researcher
Who Produces the Seamless Narratives

Critical constructivism makes no attempt to conceal its subversion of the researcher's perception of her or his stable positionality in the web of reality. Researchers with unitary and stable self-perceptions often control their interpretations of the world so as to protect their coherence and consistency. The narratives that ensue aspire to a mimetic (imitational) representation of the already existing world. Whatever the intention, the cosmos represented is one of the researchers' own making, typically a bounded reality that derives its closure from the solution to the puzzle. The questioning of researcher positionality undermines such facile resolutions, such glib narrative representations. Such questions do not encourage a view that denies researcher agency or self-direction. Indeed, researchers act intentionally, but, the perceptions and appreciations that inform their actions are inscribed by the social and the political. From the critical constructivist's perspective the challenge involves understanding the ways researchers' potential field of actions is structured and how such structures are addressed in the formulation of the research act (Smith, 1988; Donald, 1993).

The power gestalt that helps construct the researcher does not contribute to the construction of a unified and stable positionality. No hermeneutic (interpretive) closure awaits the last word of the researcher's narrative; no final reading/representation of the *Lebenswelt* (lifeworld) brings the story to a tidy ending. Like a 1950s sci-fi movie about ants transformed into gargantuan killers by atomic radiation, "the end" becomes "the end?"—what will be the next species to mutate as a response to the by-products of modernist science? The feminist notion of voice when transmogrified by poststructuralist insight helps us negotiate the discomfort produced by critical constructivism's encounter with open-ended and migratory postionality. Such a conception of voice depicts it as not independent and preexistent but forged out of the individual's discursive and semiotic interplay with the power of patriarchy, racism, class-bias, and other social forces. Thus, an individual does not *discover* a voice that was there all the time but *fashions* one in negotiation with his or her environment. In the context of inquiry, critical constructivism intervenes in the fashioning process by pointing out the omnipresence of power (Finke, 1993). Thus, an informed voice is fashioned that is empowered to speak/write in the cause of social justice and egalitarian social change.

Discourse, Language, and Power

Too rarely do we analyze the deep social assumptions and power relations embedded in everyday language. School in general and the study of research in particular fail to question the ways unexamined language shapes education, the research about it, and the narrative format that transmits it to the reader. Critical constructivists aware of these dynamics advocate not only linguistic analysis of research traditions but autobiographical studies of the student researcher. The emphasis of such studies center around self-reflection and the production of (un)consciousness. The narratives emerging from such a self-conscious researcher would be far more attuned to the nuance of representation and the ideological and epistemological dimensions of narrative format. Both language and literary form are inscribed by the language of the power bloc. Creations of particular narrative forms, certain fiction formulas, mobilize meanings that often sustain domination. Any critical constructivist reading of a text, fiction or nonfiction, examines language, narrative, and representation in light of these power plays (Probyn, 1993; Fiske, 1993; Thompson, 1987; Suvin, 1988).

Traditional ethnographies have been comfortable with the supposition that language neutrally conveys a description of reality. Critical constructivist researchers understand that linguistic descriptions are not as much *about* society as they are *constitutive* of the social cosmos— that is, they create reality. Borrowing from discourse analysis, critical postmodernist scholars understand language as the substance of social action, not simply the reflection of it. Modernist ethnography assumed that as a neutral medium language could be refined to the point that a "proper" ethnographic vocabulary could be developed. From this professional lexicon objective representations of the social world could be generated that would legitimate ethnography as a "hard" scientific enterprise. Once such a project is abandoned and the constituent aspects of language are understood, critical qualitative researchers can embark on a quest for new literary strategies that break down the addiction to authorial certainty. In such a context readers are invited into a dialogue between researcher and researched where former hierarchies and formal methodological artifices of positivist science are relegated to the junk pile of epistemological history (Holstein & Gubrium, 1994; Sherrard, 1991; Fontana, 1994; Agger, 1991; Derrida, 1976; Foucault, 1980).

Any analysis of research narratology and representation and their relation to power must make use of poststructuralist discursive analysis. Michel Foucault describes discourse as a constellation of hidden historical rules that govern what can be and cannot be said and who can speak and who must listen. Discursive practices are present in technical processes, institutions, and modes of behavior and in their forms of transmission and representation. Discourses shape how we operate in the world as human agents, construct our (un)consciousness, and what we consider true (McLaren, 1994). Indeed, knowledge is interdependent with discourse in that it acquires its meaning through the context provided by the rules of discursive practice. As with particular forms of knowledge itself, discourses validate particular narrative formats and modes of representation (Fiske, 1993, p. 14). The discourse of traditional ethnography, for example, was quick to exclude nonlinear narratives and surrealistic forms of representation. Like the nineteenth-century gatekeepers of the Parisian art world who rejected impressionistic representations of reality, ethnographic guardians dismissed literary forms that fell outside the boundaries of the dominant discourse. Often their judgments were based on literary grounds as much as on ideological justifications.

Constructing Research Narratives Is a Discursive Process

All language is multiaccentual, meaning that it can be both spoken and heard, written and read in ways that reflect different meanings and different relationships to social groups and power formations. When language is used in an imperializing manner, meaning as a form of social regulation, this multiaccentual is repressed. Power wielders attempt to establish one correct meaning among listeners or readers in an effort to implant a particular ideological message into their consciousness. Such a linguistic act is an example of what is labeled discursive closure—a language game that represses alternate ways of seeing, as it establishes a textual orthodoxy. In this context discursive practices define what is normal and deviant, what is a *proper* way of representing reality and what is not. Indeed, this process of definition, inclusion, and exclusion connects discourse to modes of social ordering and of regulation of knowledge production. For example, mainstream research discourses avoid representations of the concept of oppression when examining questions of justice or injustice. Often terms such as discrimination or prejudice are used to represent race, class, and gender injustice—the concept of oppression, being a much more inclusive and damning concept, is inappropriate in a discourse complicit with the dominant power bloc (Fiske, 1993; Brown, 1994; Young, 1992). Thus, discursive closure is effected; the status quo is protected.

When researchers are acquainted with discursive analysis, a new realm of understanding about knowledge production is opened. They begin to realize, for example, that methods of *reporting* one's research is separate from the *doing* of the research. Obviously the same ideological factors can shape both tasks, but simply attending to the ways discourse and power shape the "doing aspect" (research methodology) does not guarantee continued freedom from power colonization at the reporting phase. Critical constructivism drawing upon poststructuralist theory understands that there is no such thing as neutral format of representation. Thus, the theoretical position demands an informed discursive understanding of modes of representation and narrative. The insight derived in the acquisition of such understanding has led critical constructivists to question the status of qualitative research as a *factual representation of reality*. Such an inquiry induces researchers to rethink their own positionalities as "authoritative truth tellers." Considered in this way the researcher becomes a part of the study to the degree that autobiographical analysis is necessitated. Researcher autobiography and researcher dialogue with both self and individuals researched undermine traditional narrative formulas, replacing them with more dialogical, less certain representations of cultural phenomena (Fontana, 1994).

Humility, Positionality, and Feminist Narrative Experimentation

In this *humble*, less dominant position researchers gain insight into their own location in the web of reality. Locating their own voice as one among many, researchers search for innovative ways to represent the new perspectives gained. Auto-phenomenological descriptions of researcher consciousness are interwoven with open-ended requests of the reader to help in the interpretation process, for example, "What did the white student's anger toward the course represent?" The implication here, of course, involves the hetereoglossia of textual reading, that is, the multiple interpretations possible in regard to any social expression. In this same context critical constructivist ethnographers search for excluded voices whose world views and modes of expression provide new insights into narratology (Kincheloe, 1991). Women's voices in qualitative research are valuable not only for purposes of inclusivity and gender justice but also for new modes of representation and narrative construction. A brief analysis of feminist foremothers indicates how they employed fictional narratives to make sociological points: Harriet Martinean in *Deerbrook*; Charlotte Perkins Gilman in *The Yellow Wallpaper* and *Herland*; Mari Sandoz in *Capital City*; and Zora Neale Hurston in *Their Eyes Were Watching God, Dust Tracks on a Road*, and *I Love Myself When I Am Laughing*.

Emerging from this tradition of creative narratology contemporary feminists point the way to a wide variety of formats for the presentation of their research. Feminist conversational narrative is an innovation that experiments with researcher voice by using multiple speakers. Jane Roland Martin (1985), for example, invented a conversation between Plato, Jean-Jacques Rousseau, Mary Wollstonecraft, Catharine Beecher, Charlotte Perkins Gilman, and herself. Martin's narrative format is similar to Judy Chicago's "dinner party" with its fictional conversation between historical figures. In their edited book, *Sex and Other Sacred Games*, about friendships between women, Kim Chernin and Renate Stendhal (1990) and their authors use letter writing, storytelling, surprise visits, journal entries, and descriptions of everyday activities to create a provocative and at times puzzling narratology.

In Susan Griffin's *Woman and Nature: The Roaring Inside Her* (1978) the author contends that in order to present her interpretations of the logocentrism of "civilized man," she had to burrow underneath the rationality of the discourse of mainstream research in order to find her intuition and "uncivilized self." Tapping into these sources she was able to write associatively, producing in the process a narrative format more a form of poetry than prose (Reinharz, 1992). Examples of such feminist experimentation are quite numerous. In almost all of these examples a particular power dynamic is present: the attempt of feminist researchers to resist androcentric forms of authoritative positionality and the modes of representation and narratology that result from such a standpoint.

The Literary Nature of Science

Understanding that science is a sociohistorical construction that took shape in a particular place (Western Europe) at a particular time (1650–1800), critical constructivists focus on the literary dynamics of that construction. Poststructuralism reads science not as a giant mirror of the world as much as a dynamic, imaginative, and often duplicitous literary dynamic with serious political, economic, and cultural implications. On this level the poststructuralist literary critique extends the Frankfurt School's critical theoretical analysis of science, exposing even more aspects of its subjectivity, its historical complicity. Such a charge is no less true in the social sciences, as ethnographic, semiotic, psychological, economic, and historical knowledges give up their rhetorical formation under critical cross-examination. Covering these rhetorical formations are the fingerprints of power left by many hands for many different reasons with a variety of effects. One of these influences involves the establishment of an elitist, cult-of-the-scientific-expert effect that serves to elevate the practice of science to a high priestly plain. As high priests, scientists close off physical and social analysis to "members only." Analysis of scientific discourse from a rhetorical perspective exposes the metaphorical, narratological, and tropological (pertaining to literary devices and figures of speech) dynamics that support the illusion of omniscience (Weisband, 1992; Agger, 1991; Brown, 1994; Shotter, 1993). As the result of such deconstruction, critical constructivists can promote a less technical form of scientific writing, new creative forms of representation, and experimental forms of narrative.

Perception, Language, and Fiction

If one had to characterize the complex work of Michel Foucault in one sentence, she might say: he recovered the lost importance of language—involving in particular its generational (productive/constructive) effect—that was hidden by the scientific revolution. Indeed, Foucault's basic observation involved the ways that language shapes the act of perception itself. Given such a reality, the basis of modernist epistemology is undermined—truth is always compromised by the instability and uncertainty of language. Such insight cannot be separated from any effort to rethink narrative and representation. The confident unity, for example, of qualitative narratives can no longer be naively accepted after Foucault. The reconceptualization of narratology becomes one more aspect of the larger reformulation of science itself (Foucault, 1970; Iser, 1993); the innate uncertainty of any particular mode of representation is another. The story of late-twentieth-century epistemology is a tale of lost foundations, vanished rules of representation. Social scientists used to know that "the order of things" could be represented if only the *correct* order of words could be discovered. After poststructuralism, qualitative research can accept no fact as self-evident, no representation as pure. Any research that assumes subject accounts are simple truths can no longer be trusted (Smith, 1988).

Thus, such poststructuralist insight leads critical constructivists to conclude that there are fictive elements in all representations and narratives. The central question of this essay involves the patterns of these fictions and their relationship to power. One way to view these patterns (formulas) may involve emplotment strategies such as:

1. *Romance*—fables and epics, the animation of insensate things with sense and passion. Here knowledge is identified with the appreciation and celebration of the uniqueness and particularity of all things. A romantic analyst's work is completed when she or he finishes describing the phenomena in question.

2. *Tragedy*—classical Marxism, positivism, behavioral psychology, and reductionistic cause-effect explanations. Here there is little real resemblance between the objects of the world. The process of change is best explained by the development of laws and/or mechanistic explanations of causality.

3. *Satire*—critical theory, psychoanalysis, existentialism, phenomenology, and other analytical forms that question previously established tropological/rhetorical explanations of the social world. Here existing structures are explained contextually and often ironically. Satirical analysis is innately critical of all forms of metaphorical identification or reductionism.

4. *Comedy*—Parsonian functionalism and the development of equilibrated cultural systems. Here attributes of ordered essences are established and particulars are generalized into stabilized universal truths (White, 1978).

5. *Absurdism*—nihilistic postmodernism, the post-ironic Baudrillardian breakdown of the relationship between signified and signifier. Here the possibility of meaning itself is brought into question. A return to prelinguistic perception and the loss of Enlightenment rationality in the return to myth is sought.

Obviously, these points are ideals and presented for heuristic purposes. In reality different formulas may bleed over their boundaries in particular narrative forms. For example, the analytical/narratological form on which this essay is constructed, critical constructivism may embody features of satire, absurdism, and a whisper of romance—it certainly cannot be confined to one fictive format.

The attribution of fictive elements to qualitative inquiry will not sit well with some researchers. Research narratives and fiction, they will argue, are oil and water; they represent distinct aspects of experience and, therefore, different forms of discourse. Within the modernist traditions of social research narratives of inquiry would consist of factually accurate information arranged in the order of their actual occurrence or their thematic pattern. Such organization would allow for the *true meaning* of the experience to reveal itself. All insinuations of the fictive would be deleted from the record (the objective narrative) including the taint of the intuitive in the researcher's delineation of reality. Informed by the irony of poststructuralism, critical constructivism no longer views fiction as merely a form of deception; instead, it is viewed as a fundamental dynamic in the human attempt to make meaning. Any narrative text is a compound of reality and fiction, as it brings together the given and the imagined. The recognition of the synergy produced in this relationship is a key to the reconceptualization of qualitative research narratives.

The fictive act, however, is not necessarily the most creative aspect of narrative production, as it is directed often times by tropological formulas—for example, romance, tragedy, irony, comedy, and absurdism. In this context the reality-fiction dyad is expanded to the synergetic triad of reality-fiction-imaginary. Just as the production of the narrative cannot be narrowed to features captured from referential reality, so it cannot be confined to its fictive mechanics. Such mechanics furnish the medium for the third feature of the harmonious triad—the imaginary. As a guiding act, the process of fictionalizing endows the creative imaginary with an enunciated grounding. In this articulated context the imaginary creates relationships between the given and the non-given, concocts methods of traversing the netherworld that separates them (Iser, 1993). A critical constructivist researcher examining power relations, for example, in the cultural pedagogy of Disney and Mattel would draw upon her or his awareness of the relationship between narratology and fiction formulas and turn loose the imaginary in the attempt to understand and depict the cultural/educational dynamic in question.

Representation and Power: Catatonic Seizure or Divine Trance?

Any representation of the world manifests its power through its foreclosure of worlds not represented—that is, the world is always larger than its maps. When cartographers employ the official mode of geographical representation, they reduce reader cognizance of alternative ways of "knowing" the topography. Which map is real: the Mercator projection or Peter's projection? A Western schizophrenic's catatonic seizure or an aboriginal shaman's divine trance? A critical constructivist pedagogy of representation grapples with the relationship between the production of an image and the mode of its presentation to an audience. As critical researchers come to understand the historical/social nature of representational form and content, they are better prepared to represent their own subjectivities and personal contexts outside the orbit of hegemonic representational formats. Here they are able to rescue both their scholarship and their "selves" from the structuring of dominant modes of representation. In the process such researchers are sensitized to the erasure of particular groups and individuals by power wielders and to the ways particular hegemonic representational forms mobilize their desire and thus their complicity in such deletions (Brown, 1994; Giroux, 1993, 1994).

Such representational themes are relevant in a variety of intersections between the textual and material reality. In the context of the political economy of the late twentieth century, for example, these representational themes can be uncovered in the post-Fordist corporation's power to represent the ways of the economic world to its workers. Indeed, corporate power to control the depiction of reality to both workers and consumers of the firm's products and services is a precondition of ideological domination. The most dramatic manifestation of postmodern power involves its capacity to define individuals' priorities, curiosities, incentives, and desires (Miller, 1990; Cooper, 1994; Patton, 1989; Rorty, 1992; McLaren, 1995). One of the most important goals of critical constructivist research involves the unveiling of these conditions and methods of textual production and the relationship between cultural representation and ideological domination. While power interests have always concealed the process by which they attempt to depict reality, the strategies by which dominant interests represent the world at the end of the twentieth century are far more sophisticated than ever before (Brown, 1993). The need for researchers capable of decoding the power relations embedded in cultural texts, therefore, has never been more urgent.

Modes of, for example, ethnographic representation cannot be separated from Western "discovery," exploration, exploitation, and colonization of "foreign lands," nor from the postcolonial unfolding of new models of social and economic hegemonies and oblique military imperialism. Modes of representation of educational research cannot be separated from classification systems in special education with their power to regulate the children of the poor and nonwhite. When such students are represented as abnormal a variety of ethically questionable strategies of control are justified. The significance of the critique of such oppressive representational practices typically perceived as natural cannot be ignored. Studies of ethnographic representational practices and literary theory's narratology have been slow to recognize the power relations implicit in the contact points between literary and social formations (Smith, 1988).

Critical literary studies can expose the ways power wielders employ orthodox rhetorical forms to justify hegemonic representations. Often when a particular representation is viewed as objectively true, it is seen as such because its mechanics of construction have become familiar to a point that they are rendered invisible. A chart designed to represent educational progress within the high schools in a particular school district is not typically viewed as a particular manifestation of statistical interpretation, demographic research, or social theory—obviously, all representations emanate from a variety of tacit assumptions and a particular frame of vision. Deconstructing the relationship between rhetorical and political practices, critical constructivist researchers begin to understand the ways the "truth" is produced. They appreciate the ways any discipline commits itself to particular approved styles of representation. Reacting to such recognitions, Jean-François Lyotard calls for a politics of the irrepresentable that struggles to subvert the power of realist representations to reduce the heteroglossia of all readings of the world to a unified perception. It is in his call for a transgression of the realist concept of representation that Lyotard grounds his conception of human agency, of resistance to embedded power (Brown, 1994; White, 1978; McLaren, 1995).

Extracting Representation from the Embrace of Classic Realism

Critical constructivist research attempts to remove representation from the restrictions of classic realism. Human scientific attempts to be *realistic* in the depiction of reality suggest a basic misreading of language, a failure to perceive its opaqueness, instability, and inherent inability to denote a reality existing outside the sphere of its usage. Where do we begin the journey beyond realism? As is often the case in efforts to transcend modernist formations, the work of Theodor Adorno provides a sophisticated starting place. As a reflection of his literary and aesthetic interests, Adorno grappled with questions of representation, narrative, and *form* (the domain that concerns the arrangement or expression of ideas). Combining the representational with the concerns of his radical aesthetic, Adorno contended that concepts should not be defined and classified but merely brought into relationship with one another in terms of a mosaic or the weave of a cloth. In these terms Adorno was anticipating the critical constructivist call for the exposure and abandonment of formulaic and privileged rhetorical forms (Ulmer, 1989).

Form, he continued, should involve the nonoppressive synthesis of diverse concepts or particulars. Representational form mitigates "its strangeness while at the same time keeping it intact"—that is, at the same time it conspires with civilization, form is perceived by civilization as an affront. In quintessential Frankfurt School terms, Adorno theorized that while the empirical represents repression, a critical conception of form represents freedom. Empirical representation is a secularized version of the attempt to create, like God, the world in His/ Empiricism's own image. Thus, Adorno's representation is unholy: it proudly displays the imprint of the human hand and the ways it touches the world. Critical form is not an unfiltered representation and is definitely not taken, as he says, "straight from the rule book." Critical form merges with critique and human agency, as it confronts naive representations of the past. Anticipating Foucault and Derrida's refusal of representational closure, Adorno concludes that critical form rejects the "facade of consistency and unbroken harmony" that owes its existence to the chimera of translucent language (Adorno, 1984).

Power, Narrative Construction, and Reality

All wordings are connected to the social networks of which they are a part; as a result, narrative format helps construct the meaning of human living, knowing, and feeling. As narrative fictionalizing straddles the boundaries that separate external reality and the gestalt of the imaginary, it toys with both the conception of a nongiven world and an interpretation of a social phenomenon. The discursive strategies of the researcher and the imaginative writer overlap in the fictions of fact or the fact of fictions. One can hear Foucault's laughter and imagine his subversive mind at work, as he read Borges taxonomy of categories into which animals are divided: "(a) belonging to the Emperor, (b) embalmed, (c) tame, (d) sucking pigs, (e) sirens, (f) fabulous, (g) stray dogs, (h) included in the present classification, (i) frenzied, (j) innumerable, (k) drawn with a very fine camel hair brush, (l) *et cetera*, (m) having just broken the water pitcher, (n) that from a long way off look like flies" (Foucault, 1970, p. xv). Such a list makes us immediately aware of the omnipresence of narrative construction. Foucault's reading of the taxonomy signifies a philosophy of research that cultivates the ability of its adherents to criticize the ideological frames they employ to make sense of the world (Gergen, 1994; Iser, 1993; Keat, 1994; Reynolds, 1987; Mardle, 1984). The question becomes not "What are the facts?" but "How can the facts be described in order to validate one way of explaining them over another?" In other words, "How are authoritative narratives devised?" By asking such questions, critical constructivists hope to avoid the paranoia inherent in many modernist narratives—a paranoia that disallows the researcher from recognizing the fictive nature of his or her "realistic" narratives (Valverde, 1991; Smith, 1988).

Concealing the World as We Know It

As postmodernist theory has rejected modernist grand narratives along with their totalizing claims—that is, the rejection of omnifictionalization as a narrative act—a space for a new look at narratology has opened. Moving beyond the empirical belief that social reality is both perceivable and coherent in its structure, qualitative researchers have struggled to fill the liberatory space. While the replacement of mono-logical holism with heteroglossic textual interpretations and polyphonic voices has been helpful on a number of levels, such innovations have not necessarily revolutionized qualitative research narratives. Until such narratives and their formulations are reconceptualized, realist nar-ratives will continue to imperialize consciousness by constructing a particular subject position for the reader. As realist narratives resolve contradictions, an unproblematized hallucinatory social whole is cre-ated. Such totalisms are undermined by the satirical mini-dramas of the poststructuralists who argue that modernist structures of con-sciousness actually work *to conceal the world*. Such masking is accom-plished via narrative harmonization of disparate elements in a social field—aspects of the world power wielders often want covered up. In this context critical constructivism's destabilized narrative voice upsets stable notions of the subject, as it unsettles narrative flow (Agger, 1991; Westwood, 1992; Pagano, 1991).

As power rewards particular ways of seeing the world, some nar-rative forms are compensated and others are not. Qualitative researchers who experiment with narrative form are often made to feel as outsiders in their respective fields. As such researchers challenge the accepted ways validated narratives are put together, they question hegemonic reality itself. They are the bearers of what the orthodox see as bad news, the revealers of the patterns of the fraud—the fiction formulas. Structuralist analysis delineated types of narratives around formal ele-ments including distinction between author and narrator and between story (hypothetical events) and discourse (the ordering of *reported* events). A more poststructuralist analysis moves beyond such formalist criticism to more buried fiction formulas. The postmodern assault on the unified subject exposes the way such an understanding of subjec-tivity establishes certain narrative formulas. A unified "I" appropriates cultural stories of, for example, acceptable masculinity or femininity, in the process providing unquestionable beginnings, middles, and ends to problematic life situations (Probyn, 1993). Such fiction formulas reflect the nature of reality less than they express deep-seated cultural and psychological needs. Not surprisingly these well-oiled fiction for-mulas provide closure to open-ended questions and premature resolu-tion to disconcerting contradictions.

Formulaic Confusion: Narrative as Defamiliarization

The critical constructivist questioning of qualitative fictions helps preclude the possibility of paradigmatic stagnation—it opens a conversation the field needs. Such a conversation spotlights the invented nature of knowledge and knowledge production, while at the same time revealing the chaos lurking in what is labeled "order." Critical analysis of this type refuses to allow a fiction formula to be viewed as the "real story." Indeed, the attempt to transcend standard fiction formulas may sometimes lead to an abandonment of storytelling and plot—à la Foucault in *The Order of Things*, a book without heroes, villains, or chorus that explores representation in the human sciences. In such transgressive works radical approaches to narrative open spaces for previously unheard voices. For example, particular fiction formulas in psychology place victims in specific silenced locations, refusing to analyze individual lives outside of a "narrative of pathology/abnormality." The professional in this context is induced to ask questions about the patient only as a "case" or an "example" within the narrative of mental illness. A transgressive narrative such as Norm Denzin's (in this volume) concept of narrative as performance art might empower mental patients to free themselves from the narrative of pathology/abnormality and confront their silencing (Sultana, 1995; McLaren & Giarelli, 1995; Westwood, 1992). The silenced are remade in the narratological challenge; in their transgression they resituate themselves through their reconstruction of experience.

Transgressive narratology thus views its purpose as an act of defamiliarization not refamiliarization. The critical postmodernist researcher as agent of defamiliarization plays a poetic role not all that different from Yeats, Kafka, or Joyce—a return to an awareness of the bizarre nature of the mundane. In a poststructuralist context transgressive research is a decentering of the text, restoring to audibility voices that were unheard. For the traditional narrative to retain its *coherence*, the silencing had to be done. As an act of power, this silencing excluded dangerous meanings, echoes of resistance, and clips of alternative realities that at some level of dominant perception posed a threat. Narrative order is not treated deferentially, standard meanings are not respected, and (in the spirit of Lévi-Strauss) the savage is viewed as more humane than the civilized. Transgressive narratology as mode of defamiliarization leaves us estranged from rhetorical forms that have been viewed as proof of human civility (Fiske, 1993; White, 1978).

Language as a Problem of Consciousness: The Transgressive Fiction Formulas of White and Foucault

As the consummate unmasker, Foucault celebrates the act of disordering and unnaming. Refusing to respect the relationship between words and things, Foucault's work becomes a post-Nietzschean "phe-nomenology of ghosts"—that is, a study of human consciousness removed from the tyranny of temporal or spatial ordering. Thus, language is viewed by Foucault and historian of consciousness Hayden White as a *problem* of consciousness, not as a vehicle to it. From Foucault's perspective language has been treated by social researchers in the same way madness was treated by Enlightenment philosophers: the human passageway to understanding the operation of the mind. On the basis of these understandings of modernist *misunderstandings*, transgressive fiction formulas are constructed, for example, Foucault's absurdist plays built around his descriptions of the epochs of epistemic coherency in *The Order of Things* (1970) and *The History of Sexuality* (1978). There are few romantic, comedic, or tragic formulas here; the human sciences are little more in Foucault's absurdist "plays" than Sisyphean efforts to categorize the social/psychological world.

Based on this understanding of linguistic misunderstanding, tropo-logical exposè reveals fiction formulas of different types and effects. Metaphorical tropes comparing machines to human minds as a foun-dation on which modernist forms of cognitive psychology are built have backed the discipline into an analytical corner where participants must agree to ignore every aspect of the mind-machine relationship that falls outside the parameters of the metaphor. The Right to Life movement's use of the trope of apostrophe often found in English lyric poetry that involves representing inanimate objects or natural forces as if they were human beings. The trope is easily identified by the use of "O," as in "O tree of life, direct me with your branches to my lover's arms." In this con-text the success of the anti-abortion movement has involved the tropo-logical deployment of the apostrophe to institute a relationship between speaker and hypothetical fetus—erasing, in the process, the pregnant woman. The speaker (often a man) rhetorically converts fetus to person through the magic of the fiction formula—"O little fetus so delicate and dependent, tell us of your hurt and betrayal." The expectant mother in this situation is relegated to the role of audience, not by a logical argu-ment but by a tropological technique that endows the object being addressed with subjectivity. The apostrophe accomplishes rhetorically what the photography of the fetus cropped to hid the mother's body executes pictorially (Shotter, 1993; Valverde, 1991).

Nothing from Nothing Leaves . . . ?

Transgressive ethnographer Allen Shelton (1995) is dedicated to the effort to expose fiction formulas. Shelton's technique involves, in his words, "writing about nothing." Nothingness as a subject uses its lack of currency, action, and drama to pry open the personal and challenge the order of things—that is, how the social world is put together. Freud did it in his transgressive narratives, improvising in response to trivial occurrences. In his study of Dora Freud alludes to two dreams, memories, and a woman's small netted handbag. Using only these mundanities Freud makes strange the proper bourgeois home positioning the family and their neighbors in a web of desire. Richard Brautigan exposed the bizarre humor of nothingness in his description of an adolescent making of Kool-Aide in *Trout Fishing in America*. Nicholson Baker has scanned nothingness in *The Mezzanine* (a thirty-second ride on an escalator), *Room Temperature* (a father sitting in a chair giving a bottle to his child), and *Vox* (a conversation between two strangers over a 900 number). The point is that the ability of traditional fiction formulas to impose meaning is subverted. Baker, Brautigan, Freud, and Shelton annihilate standardized meanings and replace them with previously uncontemplated insights into the social/psychological world.

Conclusion: Questions of Word Made Flesh,
Flesh Made Word, and Word Made Flesh Again

The transgressive challenge to traditional textual representation does not reassure the rhetorically and epistemologically timid, it pays no homage to the traditionalist's historical, social, and narratological certainties. Such transgression not only calls sacred memories into question but diverts and dams up their comfortable narrative flow. An ever shifting, protean subject cannot speak with the same comfort of the male voice-over of a National Geographic Special TV presentation on "the Bantu natives of the copper-rich Belgian Congo." The understanding derived from the existence of narrative fiction formulas turns the traditional Christian epiphany of the Word made Flesh on its head (White, 1978). As conceptualized by the transgressors, the Flesh is made Word—that is, a reference to the textualization of social experience. Flesh made Word induces us to bracket the male voice-over of National Geographic Specials, the Tidy-Bowl commercials, and a standard textbook on qualitative report writing:

> An Appropriately Elaborated Analysis. The efforts to "balance" and "interpenetrate" data and analysis tend, by their own logic, to result in a third feature, an appropriately *elaborated* analysis. "Appropriate elaboration" refers to the number of major divisions and subdivisions of the general design that form the main body of

the report. The rule ofthumb commonly encountered is that analyses in article-length reports ought to have on the order of three to five major divisions and perhaps a similar number of subdivisions within each division.

We would also like to note that despite some distinctive features, qualitative research and analysis is, basically, the same as all other research and analysis. The particulars of the source materials may vary, as may the difficulties in gathering material and the content of the analysis itself, but the essential process is identical to other kinds of intellectual endeavor. The elements of this essential similarity include tenacity, commitment, thought, reflection, organization, and flexibility. Happily, all these qualities can be learned. Like all learning, they are acquired through practice and repetition. (Lofland & Lofland, 1984, pp. 146–47, 151)

Flesh made Word, of course, informs us that the cognitive processes particular narratives induce are acts shaped by tropology. Flesh made Word transposes narrative prose into poetry, sometimes even into music. As an absurdist, Foucault found closure at this point. What separates the critical constructivists from Foucauldian absurdism—despite critical constructivism's intense appreciation of Foucault's project—is that they don't rest with Flesh *hypostasized* as Word. The trouble with absurdism is that it dances with fate around the quicksand of nihilism—"In the beginning was the Text." Because it takes the poststructuralist critique so seriously, critical constructivism understands its kinetic possibilities. In this context critical constructivism, clutching its *critical* roots, insists on turning the Word back to Flesh. Here it transforms the Flesh as a result of its improved understanding of the power of the Word. Critical constructivism understands that the power to narrate, to represent, and to silence is the power to oppress, to perpetuate suffering in the world. Absurdism rests too soon; oppression is left undisturbed.

References

Adorno, T. (1984). *Aesthetic theory*. Trans. C. Lenhard. New York: Routledge and Kegan Paul.

Agger, B. (1991). Critical theory, poststructuralism, and postmodernism. Their sociological relevance. *Annual Review of Sociology, 17*, 105–31.

Besag, F. (1986). Reality and research. *American Behavioral Scientist, 30*(1), 6–14.

Bohm, D., & Peat, F. (1987). *Science, order, and creativity.* New York: Bantam.

Brown, R. (1994). Rhetoric, textuality, and the postmodern turn in sociological theory. In S. Seidman (Ed.), *The postmodern turn: New perspectives in social theory.* New York: Cambridge University Press.

Chernin, K., & Stendhal, R. (1990). *Sex and other sacred games.* New York: Fawcet Columbine.

Denzin, N., & Lincoln, Y. (1994). Introduction: Entering the field of qualitative research. In N. Denzin & Y. Lincoln (Eds.), *Handbook of qualitative research.* Thousand Oaks, CA: Sage.

Derrida, J. (1976). *Of grammatology* (G. Spivak, Trans.). Baltimore: Johns Hopkins University Press.

Donald, J. (1993). The natural man and the virtuous woman: Reproducing citizens. In C. Jenks (Ed.), *Cultural reproduction.* New York: Routledge.

Fine, M. (1994). Working the hyphens: Reinventing self and others in qualitative research. In N. Denzin & Y. Lincoln (Eds.), *Handbook of qualitative research.* Thousand Oaks, CA: Sage.

Finke, L. (1993). Knowledge as bait: Feminism, voice, and the pedagogical unconsciousness. *College English, 55*(1), 7–27.

Fiske, J. (1993). *Power plays, power works.* New York: Verso.

Fontana, A. (1994). Ethnographic trends in the postmodern era. In D. Dickens & A. Fontana (Eds.), *Postmodernism and social inquiry.* New York: Guilford.

Foucault, M. (1978). *History of sexuality* (R. Hurley, Trans.). New York: Vintage.

———. (1970). *The order of things: An archaeology of the human sciences.* New York: Vintage Books.

———. (1980). *Power/knowledge: Selected interviews and other writings* (C. Gordon, Ed.). New York: Pantheon.

Frye, C. (1987). Einstein and African religion and philosophy: The hermetic parallel. In D. Ryan, (Ed.), *Einstein and the humanities.* New York: Greenwood Press.

Gergen, M. (1994). The social construction of personal histories: Gendered lives in popular autobiographies. In T. Sarbin and J. Kitsuse (Eds.), *Constructing the social.* Thousand Oaks, CA: Sage.

Giroux, H. (1994). *Disturbing pleasures: Learning popular culture.* New York: Routledge.

———. (1993). *Living dangerously: Multiculturalism and the politics of difference.* New York: Peter Lang.

Griffin, S. (1978). *Women and nature: The roaring inside her*. New York: Harper & Row.

Holstein, J., & Gubrium, J. (1994). Phenomenology, ethnomethodology, and interpretive practice. In N. Denzin & Y. Lincoln (Eds.), *Handbook of 1ualitative research*. Thousand Oaks, CA: Sage.

Iser, W. (1993). *The fictive and the imaginary: Charting literary anthropology*. Baltimore: Johns Hopkins University Press.

Keat, R. (1994). Skepticism, authority, and the market. In R. Keat, N. Whiteley, & N. Abercrombie (Eds.), *The authority of the consumer*. New York: Routledge.

Kincheloe, J. (1991). *Teachers as researchers: Qualitative paths to empowerment*. New York: Falmer.

Leshan, L., & Margeneu, H. (1982). *Einstein's space and Van Gogh's sky: Physical reality and beyond*. New York: Macmillan.

Lincoln, Y., & Guba, E. (1985). *Naturalistic inquiry*. Beverly Hills, CA: Sage.

Lofland, J., & Lofland, L. (1984). *Analyzing social settings: A guide to qualitative observation and analysis*. Belmont, CA: Wadsworth.

McLaren, P. (1995). *Critical pedagogy and predatory culture: Oppositional politics in a postmodern era*. New York: Routledge.

————. (1994). *Life in schools: An introduction to critical pedagogy in the foundations of education*. White Plains, NY: Longman.

McLaren, P., & Giarelli, J. (1995). Introduction: Critical theory and educational research. In P. McLaren and J. Giarelli (Eds.), *Critical theory and educational research*. Albany: State University of New York Press.

Mardle, G. (1984). Power, tradition, and change: Educational implications of the thought of Antonio Gramsci. In J. Codd (Ed.), *Philosophy, common sense, and action in educational administration*. Victoria, Australia: Deakin University Press.

Martin, J. (1985). *Reclaiming a conversation: The ideal of the educated woman*. New Haven, CT: Yale University Press.

Miller, J. (1990). Carnivals of atrocity: Foucault, Nietzsche, cruelty. *Political Theory, 15*(3), 470–491.

Noblit, G. (1984). The prospects of an applied ethnography for education: A sociology of knowledge interpretation. *Educational Evaluation and Policy Analysis, 6*(1), 95-101.

Pagano, J. (1991). Moral fictions: The dilemma of theory and practice. In C. Witherell & N. Noddings (Eds.), *Stories lives tell: Narrative and dialogue in education*. New York: Teachers College Press.

Patton, P. (1989). Taylor and Foucault on power and freedom. *Political Studies, 37,* 260–76.

Probyn, E. (1993). True voices and real people: The "problem" of the autobiographical in cultural studies. In V. Blundell, J. Shepherd, & I. Taylor (Eds.), *Relocating cultural studies: Developments in theory and research.* New York: Routledge.

Reinharz, S. (1992). *Feminist methods in social research.* New York: Oxford University Press.

Reynolds, R. (1987). Einstein and psychology: The genetic epistemology of relativistic physics. In D. Ryan (Ed.), *Einstein and the humanities.* New York: Greenwood Press.

Rorty, A. (1992). Power and powers: A dialogue between Buff and Rebuff. In T. Wartenberg (Ed.), *Rethinking power.* Albany: State University of New York Press.

Rosenau, P. (1992). *Postmodernism and the social sciences: Insights, inroads, and intrusion.* Princeton, NJ: Princeton University Press.

Shelton, A. (1995). Where the Big Mac is king: McDonalds U.S.A. *Taboo: The Journal of Culture and Education, 1*(2), 1–15.

Sherrard, C. (1991). Developing discourse analysis. *The Journal of General Psychology, 118*(2), 171–79.

Shotter, J. (1993). *Cultural politics of everyday life.* Toronto: University of Toronto Press.

Slaughter, R. (1989). Cultural reconstruction in the postmodern world. *Journal of Curriculum Studies, 3,* 255–270.

Smith, P. (1988). *Discerning the subject.* Minneapolis: University of Minnesota Press.

Sultana, R. (1995). Ethnography and the politics of absence. In P. McLaren & J. Giarelli (Eds.), *Critical Theory and Educational Research.* Albany: State University of New York Press.

Suvin, D. (1988). Can people be (re)presented in fiction?: Toward a theory of narrative agents and a materialist critique beyond technocracy or reductionism. In C. Nelson & L. Grossberg (Eds.), *Marxism and the interpretation of culture.* Urbana: University of Illinois Press.

Thompson, J. (1987). Language and ideology: A framework for analysis. *The Sociological Review, 35,* 516–536.

Ulmer, G. (1989). My story: The law of idiom in applied grammatology. In R. Cohen (Ed.), *Future literary theory.* New York: Routledge.

Valverde, M. (1991). As if subjects existed: Analyzing social discourses. *Canadian Review of Sociology and Anthropology, 28*(2), 173–187.

Weisband, E. (1992). Justice and the challenges of constructivist pedagogy: Normative perspectives in teaching political economy. In L. Gonick & E. Weisband (Eds.), *Teaching world politics: Contending pedagogies for a new world order*. Boulder, CO: Westview Press.

Westwood, S. (1992). Power/knowledge. *The Politics of Transformative Research, 24*(2), 191–198.

White, H. (1978). *Tropics of discourse: Essays in cultural criticism*. Baltimore: Johns Hopkins University Press.

Yeakey, C. (1987). Critical thought and administrative theory: Conceptual approaches to the study of decision-making. *Planning and Changing, 18*(1), 23–32.

Young, I. (1992). Five faces of oppression. In T. Wartenberg (Ed.), *Rethinking power*. Albany: State University of New York Press.

5

REGIMES OF REASON AND THE MALE NARRATIVE VOICE

WILLIAM F. PINAR

In the writing of narrative, it becomes important to sort out whose voice is the dominant one when we write "I."

—F. Michael Connelly and D. Jean Clandinin,
"Stories of Experience and Narrative Inquiry"

Reason is only a concept, and a very impoverished concept for defining the plane and the movements that pass through it.

—Gilles Deleuze and Felix Guattari, *What Is Philosophy?*

[A]n understanding of virtually any aspect of modern Western culture must be, not merely incomplete, but damaged in its central substance to the degree that it does not incorporate a critical analysis of modern homo/heterosexual definition

—Eve Kosofsky Sedgwick, *Epistemology of the Closet*

Introduction: Speak Your Mind

The concept of voice has been an evocative one in several contemporary curriculum discourses. In a 1993 paper that reviewed the concerns of his scholarly career, Dwayne E. Huebner spoke of being called to teaching. Huebner (1993) reminded that: "teaching is a vocation. . . . A vocation is a call" (p. 8). The vocation of teaching, he explained, involves three aspects: "Three voices call, or three demands are made on the teacher. Hence the life that is teaching is inherently a conflicted way of living. The teacher is called by the students, by the content, and by the institution within which the teacher lives. . . .

Spiritual warfare is inherent in all vocations" (Huebner, 1993, p. 9). In the contemporary field—which Huebner's own work helped bring into being—voice has become crucial in portraying these calls to speak and teach. In the efforts to understand curriculum as political, racial, gender, phenomenological, and autobiographical text, voice has been elaborated and employed extensively. Voice is also central to teacher education and supervision/evaluation. (For a review of the former see Elbaz, 1991; also Giroux & McLaren, 1986; for the latter, see Gitlin, 1990; Gitlin & Price, 1992, Gitlin, Siegel, & Boru, 1988.)

During the 1980s Janet L. Miller employed voice in her groundbreaking exploration of the relationships among identity, the self, and others. In "The Sound of Silence Breaking" (1982), she wrote: "The dream is recurring: the quiet is everywhere. It surrounds my classroom, penetrates the halls of the building in which I teach. I wait with my students for the voices, horrified that they might scream in rage, trembling that they may never whisper" (p. 5). This silence is the silence of women's experience and voices, the splitting off of women's lived worlds from the public discourse of education. In this situation, Miller asked: "How much [does] it take to break silence?" (p. 5). Miller suggested that "breaking silence with my students creates a way for me to ground my fears of the unnatural silences and to focus my voice, my energies upon the articulation of our work together" (p. 10). In *Creating Space and Finding Voices*, Miller documented in a lyrical, autobiographical voice her collaboration with several teachers:

> This narrative, then attempts to brings teachers' voices to the center of the dialogue and debate surrounding current educational reform, teacher education restructuring efforts, and research on teachers' knowledge. Our group's exploration of the possibilities of collaborative and interactive research as one way in which we might "recover our own possibilities" are at the heart of this chronicle. (Miller, 1990, p. 10)

Janet Miller was not the only theorist working with the experience of voice. Jo Anne Pagano asserted: "The task I see for feminist theory in education just now is one of making conversation with our professions and with our history within them. We can theorize our vulnerability as practitioners of our disciplines and as teachers, speak our exile and, in doing so, resettle our disciplinary communities" (p. 14). In such resettlings, however, women do not seek that superiority characteristic of patriarchy. She wrote: "[Women] do not want the power to oppress, to maim, and to silence" (p. 14). The power women seek is to speak women's voices, women's experience: "If we women are to find our voices, we must insist on describing the claiming the difference produced in experience on naming and claiming the original connection denied and forbidden in patriarchal discourse" (pp. 14–15). That connection and difference "open the world to the moral imagination and to humane practice" (p. 156).

In that practice, women resist patriarchal structures and languages. For instance, in "Teaching as 'Women's Work': A Century of Resistant Voices," Petra Munro (1992) noted: "When curricular practice is seen and remembered as fluid and embedded in lived experience, these women [that she studied] not only subvert traditional forms, but deflect the standardization of curriculum which has traditionally functioned as a form of control" (p. 15). In these phases of understanding curriculum as gender and autobiographical text, the concept of voice allowed curricularists to speak their silence, and in so doing, resist patriarchal structures.

In breaking the silence, scholars worked to report and honor the voices of the hitherto marginalized in curriculum research. Paula Salvio (1990) reported undergraduate voices, William Ayers (1990) children's voices, and Bonnie Meath-Lang (1990a, 1990b) deaf students' via dialogue journals. Magda Lewis (1990) has elaborated the gendered, and Lisa Delpit (1988) racialized, complexities of power, pedagogy, and voice. Donald Blumenfeld-Jones has heard the voices of young women dance students, collaborating with Susan Stinson and J. Van Dyke (1990). Working with theater and dance, Margo Figgins devised and performed original forms of pedagogy which explore the politics of voice (Figgins, 1989, 1992; Figgins & Ebeling, 1991; Ebeling & Figgins, 1990, 1992; Figgins & Pinar, 1993). Voice surfaces in certain strands of phenomenological scholarship (Fujita, 1987; see Pinar & Reynolds, 1992). Feminist scholars have labored especially to report the voices of women (Miller, 1990; Grumet, 1988, 1990a, 1990b; Munro, 1992; Ellsworth, 1993; Pagano, 1990; Reiniger, 1982; Doll, 1988a, 1988b, 1996; Casey, 1990, 1991, 1992). Such reporting explores fundamental questions regarding politics, community, and relationality. As Deborah Britzman explains:

> Voice is meaning that resides in the individual and enables that individual to participate in a community. . . . The struggle for voice begins when a person attempts to communicate meaning to someone else. Finding the words, speaking for oneself, and feeling heard by others are all a part of this process. . . . Voice suggests relationships: the individual's relationship to the meaning of

her/his experience and hence, to language, and the individual's
relationship to the other, since understanding is a social process.
(Quoted in Connelly & Clandinin, 1990, p. 4)

Voice is Political

Political scholars observed that teachers' and students' voices have
been silenced as conservatives have attempted to insure curriculum
dissemination without "distortions," a version of so-called "teacher-
proof" curricula. For Peter McLaren and Henry Giroux, critical pedagogy is expressed, in part, through voice, through the stories that teachers and students tell each other. Voice becomes a key element in critical
pedagogy as "it alerts teachers to the fact that all discourse is situated
historically and mediated culturally" (McLaren, 1989, p. 229). Voice is
said to refer to the "cultural grammar" and "background knowledge"
teachers and students employed to understand experience (McLaren,
1989, p. 230). Critical pedagogues distinguished between teacher and
student voice: "A student's voice is not a reflection of the work as much
as it is a constitutive force that both mediates and shapes reality within
historically constructed practices and relationships of power. . . . Teacher
voice reflects the values, ideologies, and structuring principles that
teachers use to understand and mediate the histories, cultures, and subjectivities of their students" (McLaren, 1989, p. 230). Additionally, critical "educators must find a way of making female voices heard in classrooms" (McLaren & Hammer, 1989, p. 46). This apparent solidarity with
feminist theory was just that: apparent.
    In a widely read essay, Elizabeth Ellsworth (1989) pointed out that
critical pedagogy should not be confused with feminist pedagogy,
which "constitutes a separate body of literature with its goals and
assumptions" (p. 298). The key terms of critical pedagogy—"empowerment," "student voice," "dialogue"—represented "code words" and a
"posture of invisibility" (p. 301). Relying upon a decontextualized and
universalistic conception of reason, critical pedagogy led to "repressive
myths that perpetuate relations of domination" (pp. 298, 304). Ellsworth
went on to criticize the concept of "student voice," as it was discussed in
the critical pedagogy literature, relying on her experience in a course she
taught at the University of Wisconsin–Madison to suggest its flaws.
From a gender perspective, for instance, she noted: "the desire by the
mostly White, middle-class men who write the literature on critical
pedagogy to elicit 'full expression' of student voices . . . becomes
voyeuristic when the voice of the pedagogue himself goes unexamined" (p. 312).

Ellsworth concluded that as long as critical pedagogy failed to understand issues of trust, risk, fear and desire, especially as these are expressed through issues of identity and politics in the classroom, its *"rationalistic tools will continue to fail to loosen deep-seated, self-interested investments in unjust relations of, for example, gender, ethnicity, and sexual orientation"* (pp. 313–314; emphasis added). After critiquing critical pedagogy's ahistorical use of "dialogue" and "democracy," Ellsworth suggested a "pedagogy of the unknowable" (p. 318), in which knowledge was understood as "contradictory, partial and irreducible" (p. 321). Ellsworth's criticism provoked considerable comment and controversy, including a response from Giroux (in Aronowitz & Giroux, 1991, p. 132). (For Ellsworth's response, see Ellsworth 1990; for a sample of commentary, see Tierney, 1993, p. 10; Bryson & de Castell, 1993; Edelsky, 1991, p. 5; Stanley, 1992.)

There have been other reservations regarding the use of voice. Madeleine R. Grumet has acknowledged that she is less than comfortable "with voice as a metaphor for feminist theory and pedagogy" (1990a, p. 277). In the 1970s the notion of "voice" enabled Grumet "to differentiate my work from male work and my text from male text" (Grumet, 1990a, p. 278). Grumet observed that voice is gendered: "Drawn from the body and associated with gender, voice splinters the fiction of an androgynous speaker as we hear rhythms, relations, sounds, stories, and style that we identify as male or female" (Grumet, 1990a, p. 278).

Voice may not only express the self-affirmative, self-differentiating complexity that is a woman's voice. Indeed, in the gaze of an objectifying, voyeuristic heterosexual male, voice may be defensive. Grumet explains:

> If the voice is the medium for the projection of meaning, then woman as a meaning maker is undermined by the visual emphasis on her body as an object of display and desire. . . . If he projected the gaze as accuser or interrogator, she receives it, and I suspect, uses speech to deflect it. Teacher talk is then a defensive move deployed to assert her subjectivity in the face of the objectifying gaze. (Grumet, 1990a, p. 279)

Grumet locates this defensiveness in the fantasy of objectification, deflected and reorganized as a projection of maternity. Voice may represent a male narrowing of woman's possibility, a reduction of freedom to social role. She worries: "burdened by nostalgia, the maternal voice in educational discourse is prey to sentimentality and to an audience that consigns its melodies to fantasy, no matter how compelling" (Grumet, 1990a, p. 281). Can women escape the objectifying gaze of male subjectivity? Grumet suggests that a route out may be found in the very same location, the "voice," although understood multivocally. She asserts: "One escape is found in the chorus that is our own voice. . . . We need not dissolve identity in order to acknowledge that identity is a choral and not a solo performance" (Grumet, 1990a, p. 281).

To elaborate such a complex construction of voice, Grumet identifies three elements or parts to educational voice: situation, narrative, and interpretation. She explains:

> The first, situation, acknowledges that we tell our story as a speech event that involves the social, cultural, and political relations in and to which we speak. Narrative, or narratives as I prefer, invites all the spcificity, presence, and power that the symbolic and semiotic registers of our speaking can provide. And interpretation provides another voice, a reflexive and more distant one. (Grumet, 1990a, pp. 281–282)

Janet Miller (1990) also problematizes voice. She rejects a fixed notion that implies that, once "found," one is always able to articulate oneself, to pronounce one's identity, and to be heard:

> However, in openly grappling with the possibility of imposition and in presenting the many voices, the multiple positions and changing perspectives from which each of us speaks, I have tried to point to the ways in which each of us shared in the formation and constant reformation of our collaborative processes. . . . We have begun to hear our multiple voices within the contexts of our sustained collaboration, and thus recognized that "finding voices" is not a definitive event but rather a continuous and relational process. (p. x–xi)

Grumet's and Miller's elucidations of voice are heuristically rich. Understanding the autobiographical voice as the site for society, culture, and politics, a "site" which can be reflexively reconfigured via interpretation of multiple subject positions, hints at both political programs and pedagogical processes. Ellsworth's concern is key: can rationalistic tools associated with modernism possibly reconfigure the politics of voice? How can we speak our minds without losing our bodies to the gaze of the other, becoming categories in the great (white male) chain of being? Can our voices disclose the continuous and relational process of which Miller speaks? Remembering Grumet's advice, let us look at situation, recast here as the regimes of reason in which we speak.

The Power of Reason

There are several explicit uses of reason in American curriculum studies, although I suspect some notion of reason hangs somewhere behind all our scholarship. Scholars speak in the voice of reason. As Robin Barrow (1984) has declared: "Reason lies at the heart of the educational business. Education itself is centrally concerned with the development of reason" (p. 260). This central location is evident in efforts to map curriculum orientations (see also Schubert, 1986; Jackson, 1992; Pinar, Reynolds, Slattery, & Taubman, 1995). For instance, curriculum historian Herbert M. Kliebard (1986) identifies four "interest groups" during the early years of the field, "each with a distinct agenda for action" and each determined to influence the character of "the modern American curriculum" (Kliebard, 1986, p. xi). The first of these Kliebard characterizes as "humanists," whom he describes as "the guardians of an ancient tradition tied to *the power of reason* and the finest elements of the Western cultural heritage" (1986, p. 27; emphasis added). Of course, in our time the status of both reason and the Western cultural heritage is contested however, and a number of efforts to rethink both concepts— from racial theory, postmodernism and poststructuralism, feminist theory, to psychoanalysis—are well underway.

One important advocate of rationality was Joseph Schwab, who promoted deliberation as central to the art of the practical in solving curriculum problems. Schwab's notion of rationality was no simple one; it was informed by diverse sources, although these remain somewhat blurred in his usage of the deceptively self-evident terms "rationality" and "deliberation." Certainly one source was a humanist view of curriculum Kliebard identified as a fundamental curriculum position or orientation. Schwab taught and developed curriculum at the American intellectual center of this view in the twentieth century: the University of Chicago. Schwab was also influenced by Deweyean pragmatism, hermeneutics, and psychoanalysis, although this last influence remains difficult to detect in his published writings. Despite his apparent fidelity to humanist notions of mind and to reason, Schwab did argue that the aim of a liberal education was not to "destroy the mammal within us." Rather, the aim, Schwab (1978) explained, was to harness Eros through reasonableness so to employ its energy for intellectual purposes and, conversely, the capacities for feeling and action Eros makes possible. In so harnessing Eros, Mind remains separate and at the top of the chain of being. In our time, reason has been institutionalized, and at times curriculum specialists have risked becoming bureaucrats of the mind (a phrased suggested by Massumi's [in Deleuze & Guattari, 1987, p. ix] characterization of philosophers as "bureaucrats of pure reason"), as traditional curricularists have been more concerned with principles and procedures than with Eros. Not so in the contemporary field, where reason as well as the character of curriculum have been reconceived (Pinar, Reynolds, Slattery, & Taubman, 1995; Jackson, 1992; Lincoln, 1992; Slattery, 1995).

Right Reason

Contemporary critics point to the historical nature of reason. For scholars intrigued by notions of postmodernism, the concept of reason is linked to modernism and the rise of science. A broad yet succinct summary of these issues is elucidated by William E. Doll Jr. (1993), who employs the concept of cosmology to denote related developments in science, rationality, and the myths by which citizens of the West organized their institutions, and indeed, their lives. Doll (1993) notes that the modern cosmology was characterized by a quest for control and prediction, mathematical and mechanistic models, a belief in progress, a vision of the universe as comprised of dead particles, a Lockean view of the mind, a radical separation of objective and subjective realities, and the personal from the public. On one level, Doll cautions, the modernist paradigm was not a closed vision, for it held out a belief in progress, both politically in terms of human rights, and materially in terms of material well-being:

> But at a deeper level, the [modernist] vision was a closed one. Descartes' methodology for right reason was as certain and dogmatic as the scholastic one it replaced, and Newton's mechanistic science was predicated on a stable, uniform, cosmological order. The centerpiece of this vision, cause-effect determinism measured mathematically, depended on a closed, non-transformative, linearly developmental universe. (p. 21)

The last megaparadigmatic change—postmodernism—Doll sees as occurring in the twentieth century, and as being characterized by open systems, indeterminacy, the discrediting of metanarratives, and a focus on process. Doll goes on to critique Descartes who "bequeathed to modernist thought a method for discovering a pre-existent world, not a method for dealing with an emergent evolutionary one" (p. 32). Doll shows that Descartes and other modernist theorists positioned scientific rationalism as the "wolf," as that reason outside of which nothing existed to which one could appeal for truth claims. Doll critiques Newton's worldview, which regards reality as simple, orderly and observable.

> The real "peculiarity" of Newton's metaphysics, though, lies . . . in our wholesale acceptance of it as the "natural" order of the universe. We consider chaotic or complex order, indeterminacy, transformation, internal direction and self-generation as unusual . . . because they violate our "natural" acceptance of Newton's world view. . . . It is Newton's metaphysical and cosmological views . . . that have dominated modernist thought so long, providing a foundation in the social sciences for causative predictability, linear ordering, and a closed . . . methodology. These . . . are the conceptual underpinnings of . . . scientistic curriculum-making. (p. 34)

The concept of an abstracted uniform order is the dominant organizing principle in the modernist paradigm and it is implicated in the following beliefs: (1) that change is uniform, incremental and follows a linear sequence, (2) for every effect there is an *a priori* cause since we live in a closed mechanistic universe, (3) time is cumulative, linear, and sequenced, and (4) individual atoms are arranged in linear order and form larger building blocks. Arguing that modernism with its emphasis on "right reason" and its concrete embodiment in industrialization gave rise to views of curriculum which have dominated education until recently, Doll critiques the technorationality and scientism of these views, especially the work of Tyler, Bobbitt, and others whose work recapitulates the modernist paradigm. Much of this critique parallels Cleo Cherryholmes's widely read study (1988), although in Doll the target is modernism, while in Cherryholmes it is structuralism. Modernism and structuralism might be portrayed as powerful, still institutionally dominant, "regimes of reason."

Post-Formal Thinking

Another recent characterization of reason, this time usefully linked with political theory, is Joe L. Kincheloe's and Shirley R. Steinberg's (1993) delineation of "post-formal thinking." Kincheloe and Steinberg (1993) begin by stating that: "we have sought a middle ground that attempts to hold the progressive and democratic features of modernism while drawing upon the insights postmodernism provides concerning *the failure of reason*, the tyranny of grand narratives, the limitations of science, and the repositioning of relationships between dominant and sub-ordinate cultural groups" (p. 296; emphasis added). Kincheloe and Steinberg focus upon their impact on what they term "a new zone of cognition—a post-formal thinking" (p. 297). What is postformal think-ing? Kincheloe and Steinberg (1993) answer by outlining its antecedent, that is, formal thinking, which they link with Piaget and with "a Cartesian-Newtonian mechanistic worldview that is caught in a cause-effect, hypothetico-deductive system of reasoning" (p. 297). Here Kincheloe and Steinberg's analysis intersects with Doll's.

Postformal thinking "can change the tenor of schools and the future of teaching" (Kincheloe & Steinberg, 1993, p. 301) by:

1. Supporting an emphasis upon self-reflection for both students and teachers,
2. Ending the privilege of "white male experience as the standard by which all other experiences are measured" (p. 301),
3. Refusing to take for granted the "pronouncements of standardized-test and curriculum makers" (p. 301),
4. Emphasizing understanding rather than memorization and recita-tion.

Postformal thinking emphasizes "the origins of knowledge" (p. 302), "thinking about thinking—exploring the uncertain play of the imagi-nation" (p. 303), "asking unique questions—problem detection" (p. 304), "exploring deep patterns and structures—uncovering the tacit forces, the hidden assumptions that shape perceptions of the world" (p. 305), "seeing relationships between ostensibly different things—metaphoric cognition" (p. 307), "uncovering various levels of connection between mind and ecosystem—revealing larger patterns of life forces" (p. 309), "deconstruction—seeing the world as a text to be read" (p. 310), "con-necting logic and emotion—stretching the boundaries of conscious-ness" (p. 311), a "non-linear holism—transcending simplistic notions of cause-effect process" (p. 313), "contextualization" or "attending to the setting" (p. 314), "understanding the subtle interaction of particularity and generalization" (p. 315), and "uncovering the role of power in shap-ing the way the world is represented" (p. 316). Postformal thinkers, Kincheloe and Steinberg tell us, "are able to understand the way power shapes their own lives" (p. 317). Concluding this synoptic study, Kincheloe and Steinberg acknowledge that the notion of postformal thinking itself is a social construction, "for it also emerges from a par-ticular historical and social location" (p. 317). As a heuristic, the term functions as "mere starting point in our search for what constitutes a higher level of understanding" (p. 317). Formal thinking, it would seem, is a regime of reason in which power is invisible. The white heterosexual male does not realize he is the wolf.

Knowledge Is a Hunt

Following Michel Serres (1983), Jacques Daignault argues that "to know is to kill" (1992, p. 199), "that running after rigorous demonstrations and after confirmations is a hunt: literally" (1992, p. 100). He quotes Serres: "From Plato and a tradition which lasted throughout the classical age, knowledge is a hunt. To know is to put to death. . . . To know is to kill, to rely on death. . . . *The reason of the strongest is reason by itself. Western man is a wolf of science*" (1992, p. 198; emphasis added). Such knowledge—understood poststructurally as the reduction of difference to identity, the many to the one, heterogeneity to homogeneity—is violent. This violence results from competition between ideologies or doctrines, and from "the radical transformation of what exists in conformity with what we believe it ought to be" (quoted in Hwu, 1993, p. 132). For Daignault, as for Serres, to know is to commit murder, to terrorize. Nihilism refers to the abandonment of any attempt to know. It is the attitude that says "anything goes" or "things are what they are." It is to give up, to turn one's ideals into empty fictions or memories, to have no hope. Daignault (1983) calls for us to live in the middle, in spaces that are neither terroristic or nihilistic, neither exclusively political nor exclusively technological. The former leads to terrorism, as it regards education as primarily an opportunity for power. The latter leads to technological manipulation, regarding education as primarily an opportunity for efficiency and manipulation. As Ellsworth and others have noted, political curriculum theory suffers from tendencies toward manipulation, one born in political zeal (which risks terrorism) and informed by a modernist faith in progress and emancipation (Lasch, 1991). Indeed, Marxism in American curriculum studies has functioned as a metanarrative. The metanarratives of the modern age haunt Marxism, like a ghost: "The 'metanarratives' . . . that have marked modernity: *the progressive emancipation of reason and freedom*, the progressive catastrophic emancipation of labor (source of alienated value in capitalism), the enrichment of all humanity through the progress of technoscience" (Lyotard, 1993, p. 17; emphasis added).

We see Lyotard's list embedded in C. A. Bowers's critique of political scholarship. Bowers has concentrated upon the Marxist antipathy toward the past and the uncritical assumption that change is progressive. Bowers appreciates that reason itself is possible only against a denied, perhaps unconscious sphere of "unreason."

The belief that rational thought or theory is the chief means not only of grasping the nature of reality but also for directing the course of change is fundamental to the neo-Marxist educators' modernizing orientation. This stance appears naive when we consider how *reason itself is shaped by the unconscious history embedded in the language through which we derive the cognitive maps that serve as the basis of the rational process,* but it nevertheless provides an important clue to the deep antipathy that Marxist educational theorists feel toward the past. . . . At the center of the new mythology . . . [for the Marxists] is the belief that change is progressive. (Bowers, 1984, pp. 24–25; emphasis added)

Relying upon a decontextualized and universalistic conception of reason, political curriculum theory generally and critical pedagogy specifically have often functioned like "repressive myths that perpetuate relations of domination" (Ellsworth, 1989, pp. 298, 304). As Ellsworth saw, critical pedagogy leaves the structure of domination and authoritarianism in place. Does the modernistic conception of reason that is at work in political theory imply and require a separation between self and other that often leads to domination and authoritarianism? Whose voice is spoken through "reason"?

Regimes of Reason

To move ahead—a political as well as pedagogical agenda associated with political theory—may require passing by Marxian categories. Vincent Leitch (1992) suggests that "regimes of reason" (p. 2) are substitutes for the concepts of ideology and social formation. Why employ substitutes? Leitch (1992) explains:

The notion of regime of reason does not entail commitments to certain problematical Marxian ideas: to the questionable base/superstructure model of social and cultural formation; to the belief that resistance and revolution are uncoded activities; to the vexing view that most socially sanctioned thinking is false consciousness; and to the millenarian certainty about the ultimate direction and victor of history. (p. 3)

As Bowers (1984) has noted, Marxist curriculum studies is a stepchild of modernism, and despite its radical pretensions, carries with it conservative, even reactionary (Wexler, 1987) elements. They are also patriarchal and heterosexist (Pinar, 1983, 1994; Parker, 1993). The notion of "regimes of reason" might preserve the political focus and commitment of contemporary curriculum theory while reformulating the conceptual tools by means of which it elaborates its positions and the means by which it struggles for change. Reason is political and gendered. Reason is the regime in which and through which, our voices are raised, the medium through we are coded as intelligible or not.

We are very familiar with the dominant regimes of reason embedded in mainstream school curriculum practices; these are in large measure borrowed from business and from its sometimes academic employee, educational psychology. In the scholarly field of curriculum, many of these institutional discourses are in disrepute; other regimes are ascendant. Replacing curriculum development discourses have been efforts to understand curriculum as political, racial, gendered, phenomenological, autobiographical/biographical, aesthetic, theological, international, as well as institutional text (Pinar, Reynolds, Slattery, & Taubman, 1995; Castenell & Pinar, 1993; Pinar & Reynolds, 1992). This advance is not without its problems; now we find a "balkanization" of the field. Each discourse "is characterized by a 'regime of rationality.' . . . At issue in any such economy are competing interpretations of the language of truth, assertion, and representation—in short of 'knowledge' and its relation to power" (Goldberg, 1993, p. 52).

Can we be positioned in a regime of reason without being subjected to the currents of power accumulation flowing within that regime? Can we identify with those possibilities excluded by a particular regime, and incorporate them in our narrative voices, without being expelled? Are there strategies we might employ to move toward the margins in whatever regime in which we are positioned, to continually speak from those silent places in order to destabilize the center? Can we crack the hard self-assuredness of the white heterosexual male voice, producing perhaps a falsetto?

Contemporary curriculum discourses tend to deny their relational and historical links with each other, their dependencies upon each other. As Leitch notes in regard to literary discourse (we substitute "curriculum" for "literary"), scholarship and research are rhetorical, implicated in institutions, with their own self-serving and competitive cultures. Discourse is hedged by power, institutions, and society at large. Curriculum balkanization is like the myth of the bourgeois individual, who denies his relatedness to others while believing only in himself. While discursive systems tend to function centrifugally, moving away from the imaginary center toward isolation and a defensive imperialism, their discursive character creates another motion, away from itself, toward the unconscious center. In this movement, discourse provides passages to subjectivity and to the body:

I characterize [curriculum] discourse as at once rhetorical, heteroglot, and intertextual, hedged around by institutions and interests, all rendering the referentiality of language perennially problematic and subject to dispute. About discourse I argue that it
provides the means for entry into subjectivity, initiating the formation of the unconscious, the differentiation of the body, and the
enrollment into regimes of reason. (Leitch, 1992, p. 39)

When we employ a notion of "regimes of reason" we understand
that live in a discursive world, in which material objects as well as psychological realities are coded textually. In such a world, the process of
education requires narrative voices which disclose the political character of language and the rhetorical features of social change. "There must
be some way outta here," and the passage is discursive. As Leitch (1992)
observes: "The hegemonic and counterhegemonic work of culture takes
place in language; the agency of social action and change is rhetoric" (p.
44). To illustrate, let us think for a moment about *écriture féminine*.

Writing identity politically. Identity politics becomes significant,
perhaps essential, for those marginalized groups seeking the center,
problematizing the margins. One problem of the marginalized can be
that of "dual consciousness" (DuBois, 1903; Fanon, 1967; Freire, 1968),
that one's lived space is occupied by others, one's voice inhabited by the
introjected other. (A scholarly field can be occupied as well: see Block,
1995.) Writing identity politically can mean moving around the introjected others, moving across what feels to marginalized to be ice-flows
of reason, moving toward warmer water of self-affirmative complexity.
From the center, identity politics can seem "separatist" and "essentialist," even to the benign, well-wishing and "liberal" elements of the center (Fuss, 1993). Such a view misunderstands the educational challenge,
and political necessity, of writing oneself out of the margin, of creating
a space, finding a voice, in which one is the center. And for those in the
center, movement to the margins is not just downward mobility; it is a
prison-break. The center not only suffocates; it is suffocating. The margins are definitely inconvenient, often dangerous, but at least you can
breathe there.

We can observe these issues in Leitch's (1992) reservations regarding *écriture féminine*. He writes: "The theory of *écriture féminine* has problems as well as strengths. It ontologizes and essentializes 'woman,' link-
ing her firmly with the unconscious, the body, the mother, the
presymbolic—the very imprisoning spaces constructed by patriarchy"
(p. 54). What Leitch appears not to understand is that such "provisional
essentialism" is a political and psychological tactic, a strategy to recover

language conceived by the "other," and make it one's own, self-affir-matively. It brings to mind the projects of theorists such as Mary Daly (1978), who studied the English language for patriarchal distortions, rescued words from misogyny and put them to her own purposes. By employing words used in hatred by others—in Daly's case, for instance, "hag" and in mine, "queer"—one strips these tools of subjugation of their violence and domesticates them, making them objects of play and potential occasions for self-affirmation, political solidarity, and social change.

Revealing an essentialist tendency himself, Leitch (1992) suggests: "Since 'feminine writing' is admittedly written by men like Genet and Joyce as well as by women like Colette and Duras, it is not actually a 'feminist' practice; it celebrates the avant-garde above other writing" (p. 54). True, anatomical males who conceived of themselves as "men" probably cannot engage in such practice; however boys who are (also) girls might. One's hope is that the "subject positions" of the dominant groups—especially middle- and upper-class heterosexual white men—can indeed be changed. Unless subject positions can be changed, we in the margins are doomed to a stalemate at best, maybe condemned to play a loser's game.

And while—returning to the Leitch passage—much "écriture fémi-nine" and other writing associated with identity politics are avant-garde, I would not say that they are avant-gardist. That is, they do not claim an avant-garde status in order to aggrandize their position; indeed, avant-garde is a judgment that can be made only by others. It is our responsi-bility as scholars, teachers, and theoreticians to stake out the future. Perhaps we will be mistaken, but we are obligated to try to clear a path to the next moment. We cannot succumb to nihilism, nor in our political zeal become terrorists. Patiently, rigorously, with all our intelligence, we must study and teach, just beyond reason's reach. It is concerning these issues that Leitch (1992) sees strength:

> What the doctrine of écriture féminine contributes to poststructural cultural criticism, despite its problems, are crucial concepts of the body and the unconscious as genderized (socialized and politi-cized), of writing as both a site of struggle and a utopian arena for social transformation, of language as a producer of differences and of subjectivities, and of grammar and rhetoric as ideological mechanisms. (p. 54)

As self-proclaimed norm, the white straight man speaks as if he were God, with no body. For him, it is women who have bodies. Blacks have bodies. He has reason. What would it mean to write the body, say . . . the white gay male body. In what voice might a gay male body speak?

I might use for a moment the metaphor of the AIDS virus to hint at a male gay version of *écriture féminine* . If I were an infected gay man I imagine I want to locate the virus within me, the virus that destroys my immune system, attaches itself to my cells and changes appearance so I cannot catch it, cannot destroy it. The virus is the political position of the white heterosexual male, who takes himself as "straight," giving the rest of us the "straight stuff," whose psychological semen infects us. He makes me sick. Somehow I must find my way amid the wreckage of dead cells, the violence of my internal struggles, the war zone that is gay male body. Perhaps through speaking, finding voice, and creating space, there is a way out of here.

Can we escape subjugation by/in dominant regimes of reason? Perhaps we do not have to escape. What if we see the spaces between concepts, the traces of knowledge left out or obliterated, might we find the uninfected cells? Maybe we do not have to live the disease: "Since a regime of reason is, in any case, always undergoing processes of formation, having numerous shifting and emergent recesses and margins, it approximates less a monolith than a honeycombed cultural unconscious" (Leitch, 1992, p. 4). And interspersed in the honeycomb are passages away from illness. We might look to these recesses and margins in order to think in educational ways about the problem of being inhabited by others, and the necessity to create our own spaces, to live in uninfected cells. Perhaps this requires separatism, at least for part of the time. Such a separatism is about self-affirmation not isolation, and perhaps we heal self-division by consciously shutting out the other. Through reason we can move to unreason, to the unconscious, from where the imaginary realm speaks silently but loudly, the voice of the body.

Recoding

Speaking from the margins—the articulation of silences—is not without danger, we know. To speak from the margins one's voice moves out toward the center and is there likely recoded. Confession is recoded in the dominant language for the sake of regulation. As Foucault (1980) has shown, speaking about a hitherto silent subject can function in regulatory fashion. We cannot control the political recodings of our discourse. In general, when silences are articulated so that they then circulate in the mainstream public sector—such as, say, confessions on talk-shows do now—they circulate in a regulatory regime. For example, let us imagine a gay man who engages in what may be thought of as his own version of *écriture féminine* by speaking from his own silence. Perhaps he speaks about his love for another man. Suppose he appears on television, that honeycombed center of the state cultural apparatus. When such a confession of love circulates in a homophobic heterosexist regime, it is experienced as an attack. The so-called "Jenny Jones" murder illustrates how a public confession, a confession originating from a male gay body, a private silence, when spoken on mainstream media can circulate in a regulatory, punitive grid. Three days after Scott Amedure disclosed, during a taping of "The Jenny Jones Show," that he was attracted to Jonathan Schmitz, Amedure was killed at his home near Detroit. Schmitz was charged with the murder. The prosecutor was quoted as saying that the program had "ambushed" Schmitz "with humiliation" (Dunlap, 1995, p. E16). Since when is an expression of love an ambush? The answer is: when it circulates in a homophobic regime, where there is a "regime of bodies and the regime of signs" (Deleuze & Guattari, 1987, p. 108). The homosexual body in a homophobic, heterosexist regime is signed "threatening," as "ambushing."

Maybe words move through bodies like pressure building on fault lines. When words are spoken that intensify pressure beyond tolerance, the social surface shifts. The white male ego—the straight white male ego—is in fact fragile . . . a fragile white island we could say. Easily threatened, often threatening, the voice of the white straight guy penetrates the bodies of others. Sometimes people are murdered; lives disappear. In the name of the Father, of universality, of truth and reason, he speaks the "truth." However, as Judith Butler (1993) observes: "These regulatory schemas are not timeless structures, but historically revisable criteria of intelligibility which produce and vanquish bodies that matter" (p. 14). And bodies that are vanquished are not only homosexual, as we know: they are Jewish, they are black, they are female, they are Native Americans. They are the old and the very young. In the dominant regimes of reason the body appears and disappears as subjects are positioned, being is chained, voices are recoded, then silenced.

Self-Division and the Multiplication of Others

Like sex, race is not reasonable. As we know, the notion of race represents not science but fantasy, a strategy of constructing civilization, the invention of savagery. Historically among the most savage peoples on earth (although the competition for this title is keen)— Europeans may have invented the "science" of race, a science requiring reason. Henry Louis Gates Jr. (1993) locates these movements of reason and race historically:

> [T]he Enlightenment . . . used the absence and presence of "reason" to delimit and circumscribe the very humanity of the cultures and people of color which Europeans had been discovering since the Renaissance. . . . [T]he Enlightenment . . . led directly to the relegation of black people to a lower rung on the Great Chain of Being. (pp. 10–11)

Is there something about Western modernist reason that creates such regimes, regimes in which human beings are chained and curved like bells (Hernnstein & Murray, 1994)? Is that the point of reason, to regulate and demarcate? Is reason the panopticon? Why is it that reason in the West gets split off as an instrument of bodily regulation, even imprisonment and slavery? Is there a self-division somewhere in European culture, perhaps linked to and aggravated by Christianity as a cultural and political force, that makes possible this conception of and consequence for reason, that splits off reason from the body and fragments it into the "law," a superegoic regulatory system of desire (Hocquenghem, 1978; in Pinar, 1994, p. 164)? Is the voice of reason the call of the law? Does Althusser's "appellation" call us into reason's jurisdiction?

> And could it not be that the invocation of the "reasonable man" standard in law resembles the way in which the bourgeois white male subject is taken as the "norm" for the human being, and that various oppressions based on race, class, or gender are tied to the ways in which the "human" has been restrictively defined? It should not be forgotten that it is always against humans that human rights need to be defended. (Johnson, 1992, p. 9)

Is empire-building the law turned outward, turned international? Does collective self-division become symbolized as the nation-state, the fatherland, and suspicion of what is "foreign?" As Said (1993) has advised: "we must try to look carefully and integrally at the culture that nurtured the sentiment, rationale, and above all the imagination of empire" (p. 12). That culture is European, and our ambivalent and naive version of it: the European-American. How might we gaze upon European-American culture, particularly the male versions of it, in order to decenter it, and in so doing, change the pitch of its voice? Could we then sing a different tune?

Let us look at the self, in which culture is configured in a singular expression, what Sartre (1981, p. ix) termed the "universal singular." Let us look at a fundamental self-division which seems to occur with the European-American bourgeois male self, with its "divided consciousness, contradictory liberalism, and ironic social alienation—its 'surplus' value of humanness" (Pecora, 1989, p. 25). Capitalism may support bourgeois versions of this self-division, but I suspect that the phenomenon is as much a matter of culture and history as it is of class and the character of the economy. Reason divides and subtracts. Gates (1992) points to the link among European reason and colonization, racism, and slavery.

The Great Chain of Being was a fantasy that chained black bodies, converted them into cargo. The concept materialized and became enslavement. Reason matters. We see reason in the lashes, the scars, as well as in the spiritual and physical strength of the slaves and their descendants. Reason makes masters out of savages, who relocate their own savagery onto others, that is, the creation of "blacks." There are, of course, other "others," including women, Jews, and homosexuals. Reason splits off and relocates onto bodies the denied fragments of the European self. Reason materializes into bodies, like Sorel in the film "Europa, Europa" whose circumcised penis identifies him as Jew while the "rest" of the his body passes, indeed appeals, as Aryan. What is an Aryan? You know the answer: "not a Jew."

> This figuration of masculine reason as disembodied body is one whose imaginary morphology is crafted through the exclusion of other possible bodies. *This is a materialization of reason which operates through the dematerialization of other bodies,* for the feminine, strictly speaking, has no morphe, no morphology, no contour, for it is that which contributes to the contouring of things, but is itself undifferentiated, without boundary. *The body that is reason dematerializes the bodies that may not properly stand for reason or its replicas, and yet this is a figure in crisis, for this body of reason is itself the phantasmatic dematerialization of masculinity, one which requires that women and slaves, children and animals be the body, perform the bodily function, that it will not perform.* (Butler, 1993, pp. 48–49; emphasis added)

Reason creates and destroys, materializes and dematerializes. The European-American man is a living body; he is historical. In his denial, he pretends to be God: bodyless, universal, voiceless, that is, the Word. What happened to him? In order to understand his colonizing, empire-building reason, we turn to language, the realm of the symbolic, the means of positioning on the Chain, the great chain of language.

Can it be that certain forms of literacy aggravate the tendency to create "others," banished from and then sealed off from the tightly bordered body, a separate mind, a fantasy of the isolated individual without relationship to and responsibility for others? Traditional grammar hints at this atomization of lived experience which requires us to postulate as different the "subject," the "object," and the "verb." Who wants to live in a dependent clause? White hetmen pretend they are declarative sentences: "Where the 'self,' as property, resembles a thing, the 'subject,' as reason, resembles a grammatical function. . . . And in the sentence 'I think, therefore I am,' what is posited is that it is thinking that gives the subject being" (Johnson, 1992, p. 3). Whose voice is spoken when these words are declared? Who is this disembodied voice of reason? In what regime does dissociation make sense?

Symbolic Order

Language belongs to the symbolic order, the structure and content of the regimes of reason in which we dwell. Sarup (1992) notes: "The Symbolic order is concerned with the function of symbols and symbolic systems. Language belongs to the Symbolic order and, in Lacan's view, it is through language that the subject can represent desires and feelings. It is through the Symbolic order that subject is constituted" (p. 85). The Symbolic order is not absolute; it is cultural, historical, it exists differently. As we know from object relations theory, the daughter can retain aspects of the symbiotic relation with the mother as she employs her identification with the father, her introjection of paternal language, to separate her from the mother, to create a self that is at once connected to the maternal body, and emotionally charged with the push/pull of the paternal body.

In object relations terms, it is the male who is constituted rather completely in the symbolic, and this constitution requires his repudiation of the (maternal) body, the creation of a Cartesian self, divided. The self does not coincide with itself. The part "left over" allows for reflexivity, a mode of relation to oneself in which one remembers that one has forgotten something. Is this the genesis of desire? Something is not right, something is missing, but what? Is it . . . the "other"? Felman (1987) explains:

> What Lacan thus brings to light is . . . a reflexivity which is thus untotalizable, that is, irreducibly dialogic and in which *what is returned to the self from the Other is, paradoxically, the ignorance or the forgetfulness of its own message*; a reflexivity, herefore, which is a new mode of cognition or information gathering whereby ignorance itself become structurally informative, in *an asymmetrically reflexive dialogue in which the interlocutors—through language—inform each other of what they do not know.* (p. 60; emphasis added)

Here is one succinct formulation of the self-division of the European-American male, a description and fantasy of how white het-men come to be. I think therefore I am; I define myself in relation to Her, in the company of men. The heterosexual male forgets he is a woman [gay men do not: "Hey girl!"—is common in more than a few gay bars]. His reason—is reason only a process of repudiation and dissociation?—is such that it objectifies the other, and not just the woman, but the black and the homosexual as well. Because he sees himself as he is not, as a "man" (not a woman, that is what a man is—not a woman), as white (not black, that is what white is), as heterosexual (not gay, that is what straight is), he circulates through regimes of reason, always chasing the wrong thing, saying the wrong thing, deaf to the message he has heard but forgotten and which he now suppresses in others. He is not happy. Salvation is his imaginary compensation for the life he has lost, and of course, it exists somewhere else, sometime later, when the dead man on the cross climbs down and takes him into his arms: the second coming, as it were. Sleeping beauty awakens with a kiss; kiss him now we might advise, but I am ahead of the story. He (the projected fantasy of the Father) remains limp, dead on the cross: our father who art in heaven.

Murdering the father's son (who is also the father)—nailing him to the cross—we boys become murderous, predatory children, plagued by guilt, driven by desire. Is the fantasy of universal reason compensatory for this essential irrationality, for this essential passion, a tormented race driven to pretend to be what it is not? The asymmetry of the internal self-structure of the European-American male is the infant in the shadow of racial guilt, of a missing, murdered son: infanticide in the name of the Father. For the self haunted by terrorism and nihilism, we worship the corpse on the cross. But the structure of self-reflection reveals the other to be myself. Felman (1987) notes: "Self-reflection is . . . the illusory functioning of symmetrical reflexivity, of reasoning by the illusory principle of symmetry between self and self as well as between self and other; a symmetry that subsumes all difference within a delusion of a unified and homogenous individual identity" (p. 61). The asymmetry of his essential self-division leaves us without balance, stumbling in the shadow of the Other, ruling regimes in which law and order compensate for paradise lost. We are the one on the cross.

In this sense the modernist construction of stability and order represents a compensatory effort to replace what has been sacrificed in a premodern time. Only the most uneven, singular, isolated, and fragile ego could imagine a regime in which reason is identified with logic, in which the body is banished, subjectivity a stain on perception, and women are "other." Only the most subjective, illogical, and unreasonable creature could invent reason. Ah . . . the European! . . . Indeed, I am thinking of the English, that fragile white island busily creating blacks and savages everywhere it traveled, once by ship and now by mind. Civilization: thy name is England.

We begin to see that in order for straight men to speak in a different voice, a different self is required, one not occupying the political and cultural center but occupied by the margins. A self that is not white, not a man, not a heterosexual, and yet one who does banish these as new perversions, who resists becoming unified and self-identical, even in opposition to himself. How can we find our way to heterogeneity? Where is the place of origin for this binary regime of symmetrical conceptual oppositions? Quoting Lacan, Felman (1987) points to the question of origins, a question beginning in mystery and in misunderstanding of the clues:

> The question, first and foremost, for each subject is how to situate *the place from which he himself addresses* the subject presumed to know? . . . Insofar as knowledge is itself a structure of address, cognition is always both motivated and obscured by love; theory, both guided and misguided by an implicit structure. (p. 86)

In the voice is the clue. From where and to whom does the voice of (male) reason speak? Where, when was the moment of self-division?

Perhaps the crime occurred on Calvary. In the imagery of the crucifixion, and in the terms of the resurrection, we might locate historically and culturally the self-division of the European male self which made binary oppositions—most ominously self and other—inevitable. Of course, Christianity is not to blame for the genocidal history of the West; nor, indeed, is all human violence located here. It is our history, however, and we are obligated to understand it. How is it that regimes of reason that legitimated violence against the "other" have developed in the West to such remarkable degrees of systematization? Does this self-divisive, self-repudiating other-producing self-structure have its historical roots in Christianity, rather in the cultural forms Christianity took, and in particular traceable to the political defeat of homosexuality—was it in early Christian Rome? The hooded smooth surface of white supremacy disguises the same divided self who fabricates and then hates homosexuals, women, and children.

A Fragile White Island

England has functioned as the cultural patriarch of the United States, partly thanks to the high-school and college humanities curriculum. An effete patriarch to be sure (a fantasy which allows Americans to feel virile), but historically England is the political "fatherland" of the United States. Now fragile—its colonial, imperialistic past distant indeed—it has become a patient:

> Your fragile white island that with *customs and manners and books and prefects and reason* somehow converted the rest of the world. You stood for precise behaviour. I knew if I lifted a teacup with the wrong finger I'd be banished. If I tied the wrong kind of knot in a tie I was out. Was it just ships that gave you such power? Was it, as my brother said, because you had the histories and printing presses? (Ondaatje, 1992, p. 283; emphasis added)

What drove the occupants of that fragile white island to colonize so much of the world? Did they really imagine themselves as God's ambassadors, epitomizing what is noble and true and civilized? Or was it, simply, greed? Not only teacups were exported, but methods of thinking, structures of language, inflated them into universal reason. The English self became the North American pretense of civilization, the signs of savagery in the New World that had belonged for centuries to others. The solitary individual whose thinking persuades him he exists might well doubt the reality of those around him. Were you, dear England, compensating for your fragility by imagining yourself be the highest expression of what is human?

One legacy of the "fragile white island" in North America is the European-American male. In this sense that island is the isolated ego, obsessed with right manners, with converting customs into "civiliza-tion,' "with empire-building disguised as the missionary's generosity. More than civilization (the Canadians claim that), in the United States the legacy of the English is a self-righteous, moralized imperative for capital accumulation. The English sent their undesirables to the colonies, relocating their cultural unconscious across the water. Of course, the English were greedy—the baser elements of British society were clear about that—and many of those baser elements were exiled here: No taxation without representation! They became slave traders, slave owners, and on the land of natives and backs of Africans, they built the American empire. Ah . . . the Americans . . . and perhaps the crown jewel (as it were) of the Empire is the European-American male. While sometimes more cautious after feminism, he still takes his reality for truth, his private feelings for public policy. His denied desire gets displaced, relocated onto the "other." The structure of the internal self gets enacted in the public sphere:

> Could it not be that governments imprison dissidents for the same
> reasons that the rational, controlling ego attempts to banish
> unwanted impulses from the self? That is, could it not be that the
> rigidity involved in the casting out or denial of anxiety-inducing
> otherness both from the polis and from the self would arise out of
> a similar attempt to become selfsame, unified, without internal
> difference? In that case, a study of the ways in which the ego
> attempts to achieve mastery by projection and repression might be
> of the great interest for defenders of prisoners of conscience.
> (Johnson, 1992, p. 9)

This internal structure of self-division is implicated historically
and structurally in the repudiation of homosexuality. Indeed, one historical origin of this self-division may be linked to the political defeat of
homosexuality, and the systematic, repeated, and vicious attempts at
erasing it from human experience. For the male is the murderer of the
man he loved—the Christ figure—and the hanging of his body on the
cross for two thousand years symbolizes the murder of father-son love,
the creation of the father-wound, the angry young man, the objectified
woman. The creation of "heterosexuality" systematizes and regulates
sexuality so that the self creates its own prisoners, which it relocates
outside, in parks at night, in gay bars.

A politically enforced heterosexuality, one regulated by homophobic masculinities, tends to objectify the woman as he keeps her regulated and available for use. For such men reason is a means to control the
self by objectifying others. Reason makes racism, misogyny, and heterosexism plausible. The structure of these modes of being-with-others recapitulates a self-division, a cognitive structure, that, in classic Cartesian
fashion, divides the world into the (self-dissociated) thinking self, and . . .
everything else! And everything else, as we know, becomes recoded as
"natural resources," available for exploitation . . . I mean development.
Whether the black body as cargo, medium of labor and exchange, the
woman as sexual object, the homosexual as sinful/deviant, or the earth
as raw material, the self-divided, self-alienated hetman sees all as opportunities for gain in a competition with other self-divided, self-alienated
males, striving to defeat the asymmetrical Other he has murdered
already, hanging still on that cross far away inside himself.

Conclusion: A Voice of the Body?

To speak only in voices the institution endorses, which tradition
requires, may support men at the political center, may keep undisturbed

a centuries-old self-division that creates "others," a psychological imaginary and a social field littered with dead and raped bodies. In our academic freedom we have imagined that we can speak the truth detached from others, and from the institutions that support us. To document our subjugation in regimes of reason, one point of which is to create passages out of the center toward the margins and from the margins toward the center, might require being in the body, not as muscled commodity on the sex market, but breathing, desiring bodies moving with others through lived space.

Much as been made of the loss of public intellectuals (Jacoby, 1987), how we are quarantined inside institutions that confer upon us intellectual freedom in exchange for political inconsequentiality. So this is new? Academicians influenced public policy during the Kennedy administration, including the national curriculum reform movement. Was that so great? Probably no intellectual has been more important than John Dewey; did Dewey's support take the United States into World War I (Westbrook, 1991)? Unlikely. What is indisputable is now that the educated, professional classes live their lives in institutions, not just schools, universities, churches, and families, but in heterosexuality and white supremacy as well. There is much work to do where we are; why wring our hands over (imagined) lost influence?

Can regimes be overturned by withdrawing support, by immigrating from the center and speaking from the margins? Should we act up? If the postmodern analysis is at all accurate, we are in the midst of a profound shift in regimes of reason. There is hope that the shift is somehow positive, progressive, that it frees us from regimentation, from subjugation, that we may come to speak in true voices and be heard. Of course, the truth is more complex: "The complicated bottom line is that academic intellectuals are intricately and inescapably implicated in regimes of unreason, that they can more or less unwittingly serve the established order both by attempting to avoid and to criticize it, and that they can, nevertheless, transform it" (Leitch, 1992, p. 168).

The institutional location of university intellectuals is such that "self"-reflection requires multifaceted analysis of the processes of cultural regimentation, the sources of cultural critique, and the possibilities for cultural renewal. What is the location of the body? Lyotard (1993) insists:

The body points to singularity, to difference, to intensities and expressivity. Reason is in principle universally shared. But we have seen that this is not strictly true of the body, and certainly not of the unconscious body (if I can call it that), which imprisons each one of us in an incommunicable secret. (p. 96)

William F. Pinar

The secret of the body might remain a secret, but there are clues everywhere. "The body has a mind of its own," Mary Aswell Doll (1994) said to me one afternoon. When we give voice to the body, we may hear the mind. Severed from the body, Western, logical, official reason divides and multiplies, so that "regimes" are instituted and enforced. Derrida's critique of identity—as self-identical and insular rather than relational—points to "another heading" in which language becomes a passage to the body. Reason needs the body, for its own symbolic and imaginary purposes. Perhaps the body might renegotiate this relationship (Brown, 1959). I am imagining more than "rethinking reason" (Walters, 1994), which possibly risks the expansion of reason, so that it becomes also embedded, racialized, gendered, emotional. This is still reason in the anthropocentric sense (Bowers, 1984). The Empire of Reason has enough territory ceded to it already. Maybe it is 476 for the Reign of Reason, time for the barbarians to enter Rome.

"The term reason is truly vast" (Lyotard, 1993, p. 61). Vast enough to be grafted onto the skin of the body? Why not start with the body? It is vast, too. Maybe we might ask the body to speak? What if I become a speaking body, a thinking body? Would your body call to me? Gay reason abandons the patriarchal position, except as a sexed subject position. Gay reason might reframe the male narrative voice, from the universalistic pretensions of white hetman reason, to that of lover. Think of pillow not podium talk. A gay regime of reason is, of course, no panacea politically or epistemologically. In alliance with lesbians, mothers, and other "others," we might reframe the narrative voice we use to speak with children, with each other, and to "the man." The voice belongs to the body, gay bodies, black bodies, maternal bodies. When the body speaks, what will be said? What will we hear? Will "we" be here? "We are here. We are everywhere. We want everything" (Berlant & Freeman, 1993, p. 193). Is this a voice of the body?

Note

In the introductory sections on voice and reason, I relied on *Understanding Curriculum*, which I wrote with William Reynolds, Patrick Slattery, and Peter Taubman (Peter Lang, 1995).

References

Aronowitz, S., & Giroux, H. (1991). *Postmodern education: Politics, culture and social criticism*. Minneapolis: University of Minnesota Press.

Ayers, W. (1990). Small heroes: In and out of school with 10-year-old city kids. *Cambridge Journal of Education, 20*(3), 269–278.

Barrow, R. (1984). *Giving teaching back to teachers: A critical introduction to curriculum theory.* London, Ontario: Althouse Press.

Berlant, L., & Freeman, E. (1993). Queer nationality. In M. Warner (Ed.), *Fear of a queer planet: Queer politics and social theory* (pp. 193–229). Minneapolis: University of Minnesota Press.

Block, A. (1995). *Occupied reading.* New York: Garland.

Blumenfeld-Jones, D., Stinson, S., & Van Dyke, J. (1990). An interpretive study of meaning in dance: Voices of young women dance students. *Dance Research Journal, 22*(2), 13–22.

Bowers, C. (1984). *The promise of theory: Education and the politics of cultural change.* New York: Longman.

Brown, N. O. (1959). *Life against death: The psychoanalytical meaning of history.* Middletown, CT: Wesleyan University Press.

Bryson, M., & de Castell, S. (1993). En/gendering equity: On some paradoxical consequences of institutionalized programs of emancipation. *Educational Theory, 43*(3), 341–355.

Butler, J. (1993). *Bodies that matter: On the discursive limits of "sex."* New York and London: Routledge.

Capps, D. (1995). *The child's song: The religious abuse of children.* Louisville, KY: Westminster John Knox Press.

Casey, K. (1990). Teacher as mother: Curriculum theorizing in the life histories of contemporary women teachers. *Cambridge Journal of Education, 20*(3), 301–320.

――――. (1991). Teachers and values: The progressive use of religion in education. *JCT, 9*(1), 23–69.

――――. (1992). Why do progressive women activists leave teaching: Theory, methodology and politics in life-history research. In I. Goodson (Ed.), *Studying teachers' lives* (pp. 187–208). New York: Teachers College Press.

Castenell, L. A., Jr., & Pinar, W. F. (Eds.). (1993). *Understanding curriculum as racial text: Representations of identity and difference in education.* Albany: State University of New York Press.

Cherryholmes, C. (1988). *Power and criticism: Poststructural investigations in education.* New York: Teachers College Press.

Clement, C. (1983). *The lives and legends of Jacques Lacan.* (Arthur Goldhammer, Trans.). New York: Columbia University Press.

Connelly, F. M., & Clandinin, D. J. (1990). Stories of experience and narrative inquiry. *Educational Researcher, 19*(4), 2–14.

Daignault, J. (1983). Curriculum and action-research: An artistic activity in a perverse way. *JCT, 5*(3), 4–28.

———. (1992). Traces at work from different places. In W. Pinar & W. Reynolds (Eds.), *Understanding curriculum as phenomenological and deconstructed text* (pp. 195–215). New York: Teachers College Press.

Daly, M. (1978). *Gyn/Ecology: The metaethics of radical feminism.* Boston: Beacon Press.

Deleuze, G. (1989). *Cinema 2.* (H. Tomlinson & R. Galeta, Trans.). Minneapolis: University of Minnesota Press.

———. (1993). *The fold: Leibniz and the Baroque.* (T. Conley, Trans.). Minneapolis: University of Minnesota Press.

Deleuze, G., & Guattari, F. (1987). *A thousand plateaus: Capitalism and schizophrenia.* (Brian Massumi, Trans.). Minneapolis: University of Minnesota Press.

———. (1994). *What is philosophy?* (H. Tomlinson & G. Bruchell, Trans.). New York: Columbia University Press.

Delpit, L. (1988). The silenced dialogue: Power and pedagogy in educating other people's children. *Harvard Educational Review, 38*(3), 280–298.

Doll, M. A. (1988a, Spring). The monster in children's dreams. *JCT, 8*(4), 89–99.

———. (1988b, October). *Connections and disconnections in the classroom: Night thoughts.* Paper presented to the Bergamo Conference, Dayton, OH.

———. (1994). Personal communication. New Orleans: the Doll House.

———. (1996). *To the lighthouse.* New York: Peter Lang.

Doll, W. E., Jr. (1993). *A post-modern perspective on curriculum.* New York: Teachers College Press.

DuBois, W. (1903). *The souls of black folk.* New York: Signet.

Dunlap, D. W. (1995, March 19). Shameless homophobia and the "Jenny Jones" murder. *New York Times,* p. E16.

Ebeling, M., & Figgins, M. (1990, October). *Inside the cage, making love with the beast: A dramatic performance of research into perceptions and experience of first world critical pedagogy.* Presentation to the Bergamo Conference on Curriculum Theory and Classroom Practice, Dayton, OH.

———. (1992, October). *Knowing-in-action: An interactive inquiry into first world critical pedagogy and beyond.* Presentation to the Bergamo Conference on Curriculum Theory and Classroom Practice, Dayton, OH.

Edelsky, C. (1991). *With literacy and justice for all: Rethinking the social in language and education*. London, England: Falmer.

Elbaz, F. (1991). Research on teachers' knowledge: The evolution of a discourse. *Journal of Curriculum Studies, 23*(1), 1–19.

Ellsworth, E. (1989). Why doesn't this feel empowering? Working through the repressive myths of critical pedagogy. *Harvard Educational Review, 59*(3), 297–324.

————. (1990, August). The question remains: How will you hold awareness of the limits of your knowledge. *Harvard Educational Review, 59*(3), 297–324.

————. (1993). Claiming the tenured body. In D. Wear (Ed.), *The center of the web: Women and solitude* (pp. 63–74). Albany: State University of New York Press.

Fanon, F. (1967). *Black skin, white masks*. New York: Grove Press.

Felman, S. (1987). *Jacques Lacan and the adventure of Insight: Psychoanalysis in contemporary culture*. Cambridge, MA: Harvard University Press.

Figgins, M. (1989, October). *Reclamations.* An original theater piece presented to the Bergamo Conference on Curriculum Theory and Classroom Practice, Dayton, OH.

————. (1992). *Autobiography in teacher education: An act of reclamation*. Charlottesville, VA: University of Virginia, Curry Memorial School of Education, unpublished manuscript.

Figgins, M., & Ebeling, M. (1991, October). *Toward a discourse of hard talk: The electronic conference as a means of creating and reflecting on class as a text*. Presentation to the Bergamo Conference on Curriculum Theory and Classroom Practice, Dayton, OH.

Figgins, M., & Pinar, W. (1993, October). *Dancing behind the mirror: A performance of letters*. Presentation to the Bergamo Conference on Curriculum Theory and Classroom Practice, Dayton, OH.

Foucault, M. (1980). *The history of sexuality. Vol. 1: An Introduction*. New York: Vintage.

Freire, P. (1968). *Pedagogy of the oppressed*. New York: Seabury.

Fujita, M. (1987, October). *Dialogical approach to lived meaning*. Paper presented at the Bergamo Conference on Curriculum Theory and Classroom Practice, Dayton, OH.

Fuss, D. (1993). Freud's fallen women: Identification, desire, and "a case of homosexuality in a woman." In M. Warner (Ed.), *Fear of a queer planet: Queer politics and social theory* (pp. 42–68). Minneapolis: University of Minnesota Press.

Gates, H. L., Jr. (1992). *Loose canons: Notes on the culture wars*. New York: Oxford University Press.

———. (1993). James Gronniosaw and the trope of the talking book. In W. L. Andrews (Ed.), *African American autobiography: A collection of critical essays* (pp. 8–25). Englewood Cliffs, NJ: Prentice Hall.

Giroux, H., & McLaren, P. (1986). Teacher education and the politics of engagement: The case for democratic schooling. *Harvard Educational Review, 56*(3), 213–238.

Gitlin, A. (1990). Educative research, voice, and school change. *Harvard Educational Review, 60*(4), 443–466.

Gitlin, A., Siegel, M., & Boru, K. (1988). *Purpose and method: Rethinking the use of ethnography of the educational left*. Paper presented at the annual meeting of the American Educational Research Association, New Orleans, LA.

Golberg, D. T. (1993). *Racist culture: Philosophy and the politics of meaning*. Oxford: Blackwell.

Grumet, M. R. (1988). *Bitter milk: Women and teaching*. Amherst: University of Massachusetts Press.

———. (1990a). Voice: The search for a feminist rhetoric for educational studies. *Cambridge Journal of Education, 20*(3), 277–282.

———. (1990b). Retrospective: Autobiography and the analysis of educational experience. *Cambridge Journal of Education, 20*(3), 321–326.

Hernnstein, R. J., & Murray, C. (1994). *The bell curve: Intelligence and class structure in American life*. New York: Free Press.

Hocquenghem, G. (1978). *Homosexual desire*. London: Allison & Busby.

Hwu, W.-S. (1993). *Toward understanding poststructuralism and curriculum*. Unpublished doctoral dissertation, Louisiana State University, Baton Rouge.

Jackson, P. (1992). Conceptions of curriculum and curriculum specialists. In P. Jackson (Ed.), *Handbook of research on curriculum* (pp. 3–40). New York: Macmillan.

Jacoby, R. (1987). *The last intellectuals*. New York: Basic Books.

Johnson, B. (Ed.). (1992). *Freedom and interpretation: The Oxford Amnest lectures*. New York: Basic Books.

Kincheloe, J., & Steinberg, S. (1993). A tentative description of post-formal thinking: The critical confrontation with cognitive theory. *Harvard Educational Review, 63*(3), 296–320.

Kliebard, H. M. (1986). *The struggle for the American curriculum 1893–1958.* Boston: Routledge & Kegan Paul.

Lasch, C. (1991). *The true and only heaven: Progress and its critics.* New York: Norton.

Leitch, V. B. (1992). *Cultural criticism, literary theory, poststructuralism.* New York: Columbia University Press.

Lewis, M. (1988). The construction of femininity embraced in the work of caring for children—caught between aspirations and reality. *The Journal of Educational Thought, 22*(2A), 259–268.

Lincoln, Y. (1992). Curriculum studies and the traditions of inquiry: The humanistic tradition. In P. Jackson (Ed.), *Handbook of research on curriculum* (pp. 41–78). New York: Macmillan.

Lyotard, J.-F. (1993). *The postmodern explained.* Minneapolis: University of Minnesota Press.

McDowell, D. (1993). In the first place: Making Frederick Douglas and the Afro-American narrative tradition. In W. L. Andrews (Ed.), *African American autobiography: A collection of critical essays* (pp. 36–58). Englewood Cliffs, NJ: Prentice Hall.

McLaren, P. (1989). *Life in schools: An introduction to critical pedagogy in the foundations of education.* New York: Longman.

McLaren, P., & Hammer, R. (1989, Fall). Critical pedagogy and the postmodern challenge: Toward a critical postmodernist pedagogy of liberation. *Educational Foundations,* 29–62.

Meath-Lang, B. (1990a, October). *Teachers responding to the voices of others.* Paper presented at the Bergamo Conference on Curriculum Theory and Classroom Practice, Dayton, OH.

———. (1990b). The dialogue journal: Reconceiving curriculum and teaching. In J. Kreeft-Peton (Ed.), *Students and teachers writing together* (pp. 3–16). Alexandria, VA: TESOL.

Miller, J. L. (1982). The sound of silence breaking: Feminist pedagogy and curriculum theory. *JCT, 4*(1), 5–11.

———. (1990). *Creating spaces and finding voices: Teachers collaborating for empowerment.* Albany: State University of New York Press.

Munro, P. (1992). *Teaching as "women's work": A century of resistant voices.* Paper presented to the annual meeting of the American Educational Research Association, San Francisco.

Ondaatje, M. (1992). *The English patient.* Toronto: McClelland & Stewart.

Pagano, J. A. (1990). *Exiles and communities: Teaching in the patriarchal wilderness.* Albany: State University of New York Press.

Parker, A. (1993). Unthinking sex: Marx, Engels, and the scene of writing. In Michael Warner (Ed.), *Fear of a queer planet: Queer politics and social theory* (pp. 19–41). Minneapolis: University of Minnesota Press.

Pecora, V. P. (1989). *Self and form in modern narrative.* Baltimore: Johns Hopkins University Press, 1989.

Pinar, W. F. (1983). Curriculum as gender text: Notes on reproduction, resistance, and male-male relations. *JCT, 5*(1), 26–52.

————. (1994). *Autobiography, politics, and sexuality: Essays in curriculum theory 1972–1992.* New York: Peter Lang.

Pinar, W. F., & Reynolds, W. M. (Eds.). (1992). *Understanding curriculum as phenomenological and deconstructed text.* New York: Teachers College Press.

Pinar, W. F., Reynolds, W. M., Slattery, P., & Taubman, P. M. (1995). *Understanding curriculum: An introduction to historical and contemporary curriculum discourses.* New York: Peter Lang.

Said, E. W. (1993). *Culture and imperialism.* New York: Knopf.

Salvio, P. (1990). Transgressive daughters: Student autobiography and the project of self-creation. *Cambridge Journal of Education, 20*(3), 283–290.

Sartre, J.-P. (1981). The family idiot: Gustave Flaubert 1821–1857. (Carol Cosman, Trans.). Chicago: University of Chicago Press.

Sarup, M. (1992). *Jacques Lacan.* Toronto: University of Toronto Press.

Schwab, J. (1978). *Science, curriculum and liberal education: Selected essays, Joseph J. Schwab.* (I. Westbury & N. Wilkof, Eds.). Chicago: University of Chicago Press.

Sedgwick, E. K. (1990). *Epistemology of the closet.* Berkeley: University of California Press.

Serres, M. (1983). *Hermes: Literature, science, philosophy.* Baltimore: Johns Hopkins University Press.

Slattery, P. (1995). *Curriculum development in the postmodern era.* New York: Garland.

Stanley, W. (1992). *Curriculum for utopia: Social reconstructionism and critical pedagogy in the postmodern era.* Albany: State University of New York Press.

Tierney, W. (1993). *Building communities of difference.* Westport, CT: Bergin & Garvey.

Walters, K. S. (Ed.). (1994). *Re-thinking reason: New perspectives in critical thinking*. Albany: State University of New York Press.

Westbrook, R. (1991) *John Dewey and American philosophy*. Ithaca, NY: Cornell University Press.

Wexler, P. (1987). *Social analysis of education: After the new sociology*. Boston: Routledge & Kegan Paul.

6

EVOCATIVE AUTOETHNOGRAPHY: WRITING EMOTIONALLY ABOUT OUR LIVES

CAROLYN ELLIS

The crisis of representation provoked by postmodernism challenges some of our most venerable notions about scientific knowledge and truth (Denzin, 1992; Rorty, 1979; Rosenau, 1992). As a consequence, we have lost faith in the theory of language on which orthodox approaches to scientific inquiry are based (Bochner, Ellis, & Tillmann-Healy, 1997), questioned the significance of a social science devoid of intuition and emotions (Ellis, 1991b; Graff, 1979), and raised doubts about the core values of the social sciences (Bochner, 1994; Foucault, 1980; Sampson, 1978) and the usefulness of rigid disciplinary boundaries that separate the humanities, social sciences, natural sciences, and arts (B. Gregory, 1988; D. Gregory & Walford, 1989; Rorty, 1982).

One positive outcome of these criticisms is the opportunity that now exists to connect social science to literature (rather than economics or physics) and thus reconceive the objectives and forms of social science research. To take advantage of this opportunity, social scientists have turned to narrative modes of scholarship that emphasize the goals of human solidarity, community, sense making, coping, and improving life conditions (Bochner, 1994).

Wait a minute. Is this the way I want to tell this story? In an abstract mode, where I describe macro-structural trends and speak as omniscient narrator in the third person voice for and about postmodernist and poststructuralist writers, my words legitimized by the authority of citations? This vocabulary, so familiar and comfortable to scholars, is inaccessible to readers outside the academy. Most people do not speak this way. Even as a member of this tribe, I sometimes feel alienated by this way of talking.

Often this mode of academic discourse camouflages the "I"—the writer herself acting and feeling. Such language often speaks <u>for</u> silenced and marginalized voices, even while it may advocate letting multiple voices be heard; celebrates the usual and the typical while ignoring the possible and exceptional; ignores the emotional and sensuous for the cognitive and visual; privileges theory, concepts, and taxonomies over stories, examples, and cases (Bochner, 1994); generalizations and explanations over details and understanding; the simple and predictable over the complex and ambiguous; telling with authority over coping with our vulnerabilities; and arguments that produce general truth over stories that show lifelikeness (Bruner, 1986, p. 11).

Are there other ways to communicate? I want to talk a different way, not just talk <u>about</u> talking a different way. So let me begin again.

Evocative Autoethnography: Writing Emotionally about Our Lives

I first read Tolstoy's (1886) "The Death of Ivan Ilych" in 1979 when I was a sociology graduate student, assisting in an interdisciplinary course in medical ethics. The story moved me intensely. I have read it at least a dozen times since and assigned it in numerous classes. The story often comes to mind. I cannot forget the evocative dying scene, the servant Gerasim holding up Ivan's feet to comfort him, the talk of his distanced family, the "there but for the grace of God go I" feeling of his friends, and Ilych's search for meaning.

Reading this powerful story made me experience the dilemma of questioning, on one's deathbed, whether a worthwhile life had been lived and meaningful work had been done. The story made me think about how I was living my life and working my work. I thought further about the role of family relationships, career, and social support in one's life, and even more abstractly about mortality, meaning, and life after death. This cognitive awareness was accompanied by emotional, bodily, and spiritual reactions. For a while, I became a part of Ivan Ilych's life and experienced his story in the role of each character in the narrative. Then I rehearsed each scene, only this time the life I rehearsed was mine, the characters my loved ones. I imagined my own life and death in comparison to the way Ilych lived and died his. Then emotionally exhausted, I still began to think about how this experience related to other experiences in which I had played, or would play, a part in others' lives. How had I coped? How would I cope? How did others make it through such meaning shattering experiences of loss? Indeed, how do any of us deal with the human condition?

In 1979, I didn't wonder why sociology, my chosen discipline, couldn't be written more like a Tolstoy story; I couldn't afford to. I had a dissertation on fishing communities to finish, then a book to publish, then a tenure review to pass.

I probably would have continued writing realist ethnography (Van Maanen, 1988) or working on the survey research project I had started, except for what happened in my personal life. In a matter of five years, my brother, father, husband, and dog of fourteen years died. During that period, I read "The Death of Ivan Ilych" a number of times along with many first-person accounts of illness. I sought and found meaning and solace, not in sociology, but in evocative literary and nonfictional stories of loss.

These experiences of loss and the lack of insight and comfort that came from sociology did start me wondering why sociology couldn't be more like literature. I continue to wonder. Now I can afford to. "The Death of Ivan Ilych" and other evocative stories; death and illness and other dramatic life experiences; my continuing passion for sociological imagination, an ethnographic approach, and an engaging story: all have pushed me to follow my "wonderlust" and try to connect social science to literature, academic interests to personal ones, emotions to cognition, and social life to the concrete living of it (Ellis, 1991a,b; 1993; 1995a,b). I find autoethnographic stories, stories that focus on the self in social context, an appropriate form in which to accomplish these goals.

There, that feels better. I am happier and more contented now. This style of writing is so much more connected to my lived experience. Sometimes though I need to show that I can write abstractly; after all, the scholarly community makes up the largest part of my audience and I want them to take me seriously. When I realized that this was part of my motivation for writing the initial "abstract" version of this chapter, I made myself begin again in an autoethnographic voice that concentrates on telling a personal, evocative story to provoke others' stories and adds blood and tissue to the abstract bones of theoretical discourse.

As Lincoln (this volume) warns, this kind of experiment is not easy. There are so many choices to make. I'm not even sure that "The Death of Ivan Ilych" is the best place to start "my story." Did my love of personal storytelling actually begin with the reading of Tolstoy? Or was it set in place long before? Can I even know?

Let me start over again, this time "from the beginning."

Writing Emotionally about Our Lives: Evocative Autoethnography

I grew up in Luray, Virginia, a small town in the middle of the Blue Ridge Mountains. Luray was cut off from the rest of the world by surrounding mountains, and homogeneity was cultivated and demanded. Ours was a working-class community of three thousand people in which telling stories provided an important way to pass the time. The stories I heard and told repeatedly concerned values, feelings, getting through day-to-day life, and deviance or difference. Rarely were abstract theoretical issues discussed, and political economy, culture, or society were never mentioned. Abstract discussion brought the response, "You think you're better than everybody else talking that way. Quit puttin' on airs," while political subjects usually were met with the simple statement, "Politicians and government are crooked." That was all the locals considered necessary to say.

Townspeople often shared stories about their lives—memories of the past, descriptions of present events, and dreams of the future. Illness and health issues always stimulated a lively conversation. Friends and acquaintances compared illness sites, doctor's orders, prescriptions, and home remedies. Frequently we talked about the local environment, especially the weather—how it felt, what was predicted, especially if it called for rain or snow, or was unseasonably hot. Other times we talked about the local lives of others. Day-to-day concerns and crisis events dominated: what the neighbor was doing—where he placed the garbage, how he painted the house, how she dressed when going to town, and when the yard was mowed; who had her hair done this morning, was seen coming out of the liquor store, or driving a new car; and, who died, lost their mind, went broke, found a new love, got engaged, or started a new business. Juicy gossip regarding violation of community norms—who was cheating on a spouse, who got "pissy-assed" drunk and spent the night in jail, lost a job, or had a brawl—was shared with enthusiasm.

Television brought in the outside world, but how much could be learned from game shows, murder mysteries, soap operas, and sitcoms, the shows that most people watched? News programs were usually categorized as being about "those crazy city folk and politicians 'down in the country'." (I never understood, and nobody seemed able to tell me, why Washington, D.C., which was across a mountain range and ninety miles east, was always referred to as "down in the country.") Locals did not think that the national news, which came mainly out of Washington, impacted us, unless the news meant money would be taken out of our pocketbooks in the form of higher taxes. Then some townspeople might complain, but we never thought to try to do anything about the problem. A good complaint was thought to be all regular people could do.

Sometimes while living at home I longed to know what was going on outside the confines of this small town. Now that I've lived outside, sometimes I think fondly of the simplicity of staring out my mom's front window to see that, as she would say, "Indeed, the neighbor is washing his car *again* and he just washed it two days before. Next thing you know, he's gonna' wash the paint right off the fender."

How do I tell my story this time? It depends on what I am ready to learn about myself and the world around me, what my purposes are, and who I think my audience will be. Given that the editors of this book are scholars in the field of education and the book is published by a university press, I imagine readers will consist mostly of academics in education, no matter that the editors make a worthwhile plea for expanding form and readership. Perhaps I'll visualize graduate students while I write. Yes, I think that's a good idea. I'll write to stimulate and entertain them. Hopefully, the style will engage readers outside our academic tribe as well, maybe even my mother.

How I tell my current story depends on how I've told my story before, and the responses each version received (Ellis, 1996). The telling also is affected by the kind of week I had, what mood I'm in, if the flowers are blooming, or my colleagues are acting up. It is impacted by what I last read and studied, which you should know were Nathan McCall's (1994) evocative, frighteningly honest and powerful autobiography, Makes Me Wanna Holler, *about living as an African American male in a racist society, and Denzin and Lincoln's (1994)* The Handbook of Qualitative Research. *Very different, these two books. Both had a powerful effect on me. I tried to write the first introduction to this article in the cognitively engaging style of the Denzin and Lincoln text. As I write this version, I hold in my mind the emotionally evocative style of McCall. I want to write an evocative autoethnographic account about writing autoethnographic accounts.*

I accept Lincoln's (this volume) invitation to consider the means we choose to tell our stories reflexively. In this chapter, I speak in several voices, which represent some of the multiple selves Lincoln says feed into the writing of our texts. Connecting personal and scholarly details, my autoethnographic voice takes readers through my experience of writing autoethnographic texts, examines the writing process and the cultural context, shows how I moved from writing realist tales to evocative stories, and discusses the goals of evocative autoethnographic texts.

A second voice lurks in the background, sometimes breaking into my story, other times blending with the autoethnographic tale. Sometimes this voice will be contrary, playfully willing to violate canons of writing social science; other times, it will be vulnerable and self-conscious; and, on other occasions, it will be "deadly serious," seeking to claim authority as it connects my autoethnographic story more directly to some of the issues of reframing the narrative discussed in this volume. In commenting on the story I tell, this voice will be both more personal and more academic than the voice telling the main story. Sometimes this voice will call on authorities (i.e., citations), and sometimes it will call on thoughts and feelings I'm having as I write (i.e., experience). Voices from other texts, representing the extraneous happening and distractions of everyday life (Carr, 1986; Polkinghorne, this volume), also may intrude occasionally. This dialogic, multivocal narrative decenters my authority by holding it up for readers to inspect (see Kinchloe, this volume; *or experience your own reading of the text.*)

How did I get to a place where I write autoethnographic stories for social science readers, to a place where I think that sociology can be emotional, personal, therapeutic, interesting, engaging, evocative, reflexive, helpful, concrete, and connected to the world of everyday experience? Certainly I did not learn this in my own graduate education. Yet the ideas grew and flourished nevertheless. How did this happen? What were the forces that allowed me to hold on to and develop my love for evocative storytelling?

That's more introduction and guidance than I had planned to write. Even so, some readers may complain that the author didn't lay out what she was doing until page five. Ah, social science writing conventions are powerful, hard to shake off (Richardson, 1994). Now I'm afraid if I don't guide you, you won't stay with me. I resist the temptation to write more. (To be honest, one of my editorial voices—Art Bochner—crossed out in an earlier draft the "more" I did write, giving me courage to continue without giving more direction. Thanks, Art. What would we do without our silent co-authors and respondents?)

> *A member of the Sociological Chorus,[1] a gray-bearded, balding, white male, interrupts: "What is this? You don't thank people in the middle of an article." The author smiles confidently and says nothing.*
>
> *A second member of the chorus, also a balding, gray-bearded, white male (somewhat shorter than the first speaker) can't help but speak up to the rest of the Sociology Chorus: "That's nothing. She hasn't even defined her terms yet. What is autoethnography? And what about the people who have used the term before? She doesn't cite them. How can we consider her an authority?"*
>
> *Author, trying to be helpful: "See if you can figure out what the term means from the story I tell." (All chorus members frown.)*
>
> *Growing impatient, the author continues: "Do you have to be told everything? I have a limited number of pages. You're not supposed to be*

in my text anyway. I'm not addressing this to you. Do you always have
to have a voice? I think I'll make you a subject in my story so you can see
how that feels. (The author's last comment brings forth gasps of indig-
nation and horror from chorus members.)

Transition to College

In college, at first I held onto my small-town values, went to
church every Sunday, and kept "deviant" activities to a bare minimum.
By the time I was a senior, I had stopped believing in God (and
announced it to my family), tried out a number of relationships, exper-
imented with drugs, and took seriously the social construction of reality
I learned in sociology classes. Thus I reconstructed myself, taking on a
new appearance and, in many cases, new values.

By the time I got to graduate school, I had made a break from
small-town life. I became an "experience junky," wanting to try everything that had been unavailable to me in Luray. I collected other people's life experiences as comparison points. In contrast to trying to be
like everyone else in my small town, now I celebrated being different
from those in my home town community, who became "other" to me
(Ellis, 1995b). The social and political climate of the 1970s made "being
different" a relatively easy task.

I wanted to blend in with other students, who came from many
locations and had led different lives than I. Like them, I wore the outfit
of the day—faded, tight, bell-bottomed (the more belled the better) blue
jeans, preferably bought from an Army/Navy store; accentuated by my
long, straight, stringy hair with a paisley bandana around the forehead;
the image completed with a drab tee-shirt or nondescript sweatshirt,
army-green cloth backpack, and, of course, work boots. We formed a
subculture and, for the most part, shared values as well, values that
were not always consistent—the importance of education and career,
living a meaningful and authentic life, doing one's thing and letting it
all hang out, telling it like it was, and participating in the youth movement.

Upset by my changes, my mother viewed my unshaven armpits
and hairy legs as signs of my final demise. After reprimanding me for
my "unclean" ways, she told me, "You're just like that Patty Hearst."
Her comment signifies the different worlds we inhabited then better
than a description could ever depict.

Skeptic 1 (They can come out of nowhere. This one is a middle-aged
male dressed in a nondescript gray sportscoat and tie retrieved from his

father's closet): "What does this have to do with reframing the narrative voice in terms of an autoethnographic approach? This is just a story." (He looks to Sociological Chorus for approval, which he gets.)

Author (taking on her undergraduate class lecturing voice and belaboring the obvious): "All phases of our lives prepare us for who we become. While growing up in a small town led to an appreciation of local stories, being in college in the seventies fed my desire to find relevance and meaning in what I did, and supported rebelling against the status quo. The changes I went through in college stimulated my interest in studying personal transition and in rewriting and reconstructing identity."

Skeptic 1 (now unsure how he should respond): "Oh."

Before graduate school, I spent a year as a social worker. The contrast between this worldly experience and the abstract discourse I encountered in my graduate classes in 1974 was hard to assimilate. I learned early on that my sentiment that sociology should "help people" was best left unexpressed publicly. My socialization "took," and soon I shared the hierarchical notion that it was important to separate sociologists (the knowers) from social workers (the doers). Still I continued to wonder whether sociology shouldn't strive to open peoples' eyes to the world they lived in and assist us in living our lives. For the most part, I could not connect my life to what was being taught in classes. How could those outside this tribe connect their lives to what we were doing? The reality was that few scholars included connection to lived life as one of their goals.

Do you think I'm being self-indulgent now? Wasn't it self-indulgent to think we could white out or separate self from our studies, as we did for years (Mykhalovskiy, 1996)? How self-adoring was it to make sure our writing practices protected the self of the ethnographic author from close and critical scrutiny? How self-protective is it to write for only ourselves and our small tribe or to spend our time writing articles that don't seem to make a difference to "anything but the author's career" (Richardson, 1994, p. 517)?

Okay, I admit I'm being defensive and talking down to you now. And I doubt that saying everybody else has been self-indulgent too is a persuasive way to make an argument. I don't want to dismiss your charge, especially if it means you don't read any farther. Before you skip to the next chapter, at least give me a chance to explain my position.

I want to reclaim self-absorption, not explain it away, or cop out by saying all of us are self-absorbed. Autoethnography should be self-absorbed. If you're not absorbed with the topic of your research, how can you write well

about it? Of course, a person writing autoethnography also needs to be absorbed
with the world she inhabits and the processes she finds herself a part of, which
also work their way into one's identity.

If we accept the argument that ethnography should be reflexive and
include the self/selves of the writer, as Kinchloe and Lincoln (this volume)
argue, writing about the self is a logical extension. We don't want to squeeze
out the other (Bruner, 1993, p. 6), but as Jackson (1989, p. 17) argues, "our
understanding of others can only proceed from within our own experience,
and this experience involves our personalities and histories as much as our
field research."

Now back to the story. I don't want the telling of it to get lost in my
argumentative voice.

Finding Connection in Isolated Fishing Communities

In search of a real world connection, I worked in graduate school
on a comparative ethnographic study of two isolated fishing communities (Ellis, 1986), during which I lived and participated with the people
whose lives I was studying. While in the communities, I often experienced conflict between remaining uninvolved and distant, as I had been
trained, and participating fully, which was my impulse; between recording only my "objective" observations of fisher folks' actions and speech,
and noting my experience of their emotional lives. When I began to
write my dissertation, I felt constrained by the detached and abstract
social science prose and the authoritative and uninvolved voice in
which I was asked to write. It was difficult to capture the complexity of
the lives of the fisher folk using social science categories, and I often felt
unsure of the conceptual distinctions I was forced to make.

Mostly I was invisible in the writing of the story. Any effects I
might have had on what the fisher folk said and did, or what I might
have learned through their reactions to me, took a back seat. I never
admitted how much my own emotional experiences in the communities
influenced what I saw and wrote.

I did, however, insist on inserting vignettes of specific incidents
and people acting, which breathed some life into my more passive
telling and categorizing of the fisher folks' lives. In these stories, I was
occasionally present, though I rarely let myself speak as a participant or
presented myself as feeling like one.

Not until later would I recognize how important it was to give
more voice to community members, show myself in interaction, and
confront how these conventional strategies may have disempowered
those I studied. Not until later would I realize that the situation of the

fisher folk—who lived largely apart from mainstream society and had begun having more and more contact with the outside world—paralleled my own transition from a small southern town to the metropolitan northeast (Ellis, 1995b). As a sociologist governed by orthodox writing practices, I did not understand how to connect my work and life to my research and writing.

> *Skeptic 2 (middle-aged woman, dressed in a suit and high heels, and wearing an SWS button): "But . . . is this sociology?"*
> *Author: "Shouldn't real life have a place in sociology?"*
> *Skeptic 2: "Well, yes, but don't we have to define and protect our boundaries?"*

Life Intersects Work

In the early 1980s, Gene Weinstein, one of my professors, and I began a project that involved a direct examination of jealousy. Although we administered a survey about jealousy experience, our main source of information consisted of our own episodes of jealousy buttressed by friends' descriptions of their experiences. When we submitted our work for publication, we played down our introspective method and instead emphasized informal interviews and written descriptions that we had collected from students. When the reviewers rejected our paper saying we needed numerical data, we inserted a few statistics from a survey we were working on, and the article was published (Ellis & Weinstein, 1986).

Why did our introspective data have to be hidden in our published article? After all, I knew some things from my own jealousy experiences that I would never know from surveys or interviews of others, such as what it felt like when the jealousy flash took me over physically and emotionally in spite of my rational intentions. Why did social science have to be written in such a way that detailed lived experience was secondary to abstraction? Even though our jealousy paper was based on people's stories, the final version was written abstractly, camouflaging informants' everyday experiences. Wasn't there something worthy about showing in evocative detail how they lived and felt jealousy? Couldn't we use our informants' own metaphors to get our message across? Didn't "like a dentist's drill hitting a nerve" tell readers more about the jealous flash and get more reaction than "extreme, intense pain" or "blended emotion" (Ellis & Weinstein, 1986)? Wasn't there something valuable in provoking readers to see themselves in our work and react emotionally to what we wrote?

Although I present this story linearly (see Tierney, this volume), I have to remind myself that we do not live life linearly. Thoughts and feelings circle around us, play back, then forward (Ronai, 1992). Life is "lived through the subject's eye, and that eye, like a camera's, is always reflexive, nonlinear, subjective, filled with flashbacks, after-images, dream sequences, faces merging into one another, masks dropping, and new masks being put on" (Denzin, 1992, p. 27).

Let me circle back, and drop another mask, a very important one.

Work Intersects Life

While a graduate student at Stony Brook, I began a romantic relationship with one of my professors, Gene Weinstein (*yes, the same one I wrote with*), that lasted until he died nine years later from emphysema. Gene and I spent many hours each week talking about his illness, our relationship, and their intersection, as well as probing emotions and other aspects of sociological inquiry. In our conversations around the kitchen table, I learned more sociology than I ever learned in classes. But when we left the kitchen table, the only knowledge that seemed respected was the abstract conclusions we had drawn, not the stories we had told. "You're so perceptive about what people are feeling, thinking, and what motivates them," Gene once said. "Too bad there isn't a way to turn that into sociology" (which for him meant abstraction).

I was intimidated by the elite intellectual repartee I encountered in graduate school, which celebrated abstract thinking and knowledge of macro-political issues. I also was not accustomed to calling on higher authorities as I talked. ("Marx said . . ." "According to Weber . . . or Durkheim . . . or Simmel. . . ." "In *The New York Review of Books* . . ."), and it seemed similar to quoting baseball scores and listing football team players. Nor did I have a developed abstract vocabulary in which to express myself. The only higher authority we had called on as I was growing up had been God (in church), and occasionally my father (when I was in trouble). Instead, I was accustomed to calling on my feelings and everyday experiences, and comparing them to the experiences of those around me, whom I always watched carefully, especially if they were different from me. Given my background, people around me often seemed very different, so I never lacked for things to watch. I felt I had to learn to think and talk like other academics if I wanted to be a full member of this tribe. Parallel to trying to fit in with my peer group and rebel against those "over thirty," I now tried desperately to become like other successful professors—all over thirty—whom I admired. Most students experienced this contradiction to some extent; because of my romantic involvement with one of my professors, my contradictions may have been even more poignant.

In 1981, I got an academic appointment at University of South Florida. A few months later, my younger brother was killed in an airplane crash on his way to visit me (see Ellis, 1993). At the same time, Gene entered the final stages of chronic emphysema. Mocking my fears and hopes, flashbacks of live TV footage of passengers from my brother's plane floundering in the Potomac River were interrupted in real life by Gene choking and yelling for me to untangle his oxygen hose. Suddenly, the scientifically respectable survey of jealousy I was working on seemed insignificant.

Instead, I wanted to understand and cope with the intense emotion I felt about the sudden loss of my brother, and the excruciating pain I experienced as Gene deteriorated. I wanted to tell my stories to others because it would be therapeutic for me and evocative for them. I knew how much we yearn for companionship when we are going through disastrous experiences (Mairs, 1994), and I felt these stories contained rich sociological insights.

In early 1985 I was promoted to Associate Professor. Now it felt less risky to write something other than traditional social science, something that would be engaging, therapeutic, and sociologically useful. Now I could better afford to challenge the boundaries of what counted as legitimate sociology, an endeavor that became a passion after Gene died a few weeks later.

The advent of a section in the *American Sociological Association* called "Sociology of Emotions" legitimated the study of emotions as a proper arena of research. Though I thought I now had an opportunity to broaden the scope of sociological writing, I was soon disappointed to see many colleagues follow a "rational actor" approach to emotions research, busily handing out surveys, counting and predicting emotional reactions, observing facial muscles contracting on videotapes, categorizing people, and abstracting generalizations from lived experience. Emotion was in danger of becoming simply another variable to add to rational models of social life. What about emotion as lived experience and interaction? I vowed to resist the rationalist tendency to portray people exclusively as spiritless, empty husks with programmed, managed, predictable, and patterned emotions (Ellis, 1991b).

In this context, I began writing *Final Negotiations: A Story of Love, Loss, and Chronic Illness* (1995), an autobiographical account of the interplay of illness and my relationship with Gene. I based my story on fieldnotes I kept during Gene's illness and on notes I systematically reconstructed after he died.

Writing *Final Negotiations*

It took nine years to construct and reconstruct the story of my relationship with Gene (Ellis, 1995a), to work out satisfactorily a version of what this relationship had been and had meant to me, and to tell a story that cohered both with what I remembered and what my life had become (Crites, 1971). During this time, I moved from conceiving of my project as science to viewing it as interpretive human studies and narrative inquiry (Bochner, 1994), transforming the process of writing the text from realist ethnography to a narrative story, and my primary goal from representation to evocation.

Writing about this relationship was so difficult that I kept notes on the writing process in the same way I had written fieldnotes on the actual relationship and illness process. These notes eventually became the basis for telling how I transformed ethnographic fieldwork into a story that I hoped would speak therapeutically and meaningfully to a mass audience and sociologically to an academic one.

Writing sociology as an intimate conversation about the intricacies of feeling, relating, and working confronted me with the deficiencies of traditional social science research for dealing with day-to-day realities of chronic illness and relational processes. From the beginning, I violated many taken-for-granted notions in social science research: making myself the object of my research and writing in the first person infringed upon the separation of subject and researcher (Jackson, 1989); writing about a single case breached the traditional concerns of research with generalization across cases and focused instead on generalization within a case (Geertz, 1973); the mode of storytelling fractured the boundaries that normally separated social science from literature; the episodic portrayal of the ebb and flow of relationship experience dramatized the motion of connected lives across the curve of time and thus resisted the standard practice of portraying social life as a snapshot; and the disclosure of normally hidden details of private life highlighted an emotional experience and thus challenged the rational actor model of social performance that dominates social science. Many times during the nine years it took to finish this story, I stopped writing in order to work out for myself, and try to make respectable to other social scientists, the breaches of convention that were occurring in this work (for example, Ellis, 1991a,b).

As I wrote and rewrote, I moved closer to telling an evocative and dramatic story and farther away from trying to get all the ethnographic details "right." I *showed* interaction so that the reader might participate more fully in the emotional process, not merely observe the resolution.

This meant moving from generalizing about a kind of event that took place to showing one event in particular, such as a doctor's visit, often by condensing a number of scenes into evocative composites. I reconstructed conversations Gene and I might have had, even when I had not recorded them, reading and rereading them aloud until I heard the ring of authenticity, continually questioning my mode of presentation and my motives.

I began to concentrate more on being true to the feelings that seemed to apply in each situation I described than to getting all the "facts" in the exact order and time sequence. More and more I moved away from trying to make my tale a mirror representation of chronologically ordered events and toward telling a story, where the events and feelings cohered, where questions of meaning and interpretation were emphasized, and where readers could grasp the main points and feel some of what I felt. Now I was tying the past to the future in the present, much as we all do narratively to understand our experiences and work out our identities (Crites, 1971).

Along the way, more canons of social science research were called into question. I began to advocate research and scholarly writing as healing; being emotionally involved with what we study; writing social science as creative nonfiction with scene setting, dialogue, and unfolding dramatic action; showing details instead of telling abstractly; and, evoking readers' experiences and feelings in addition to analytic closure as a proper goal of research (Ellis, 1995b).

One goal I continued to share with traditional social science was a commitment to writing a truthful account. But my means of achieving this goal—systematic introspection (Ellis, 1991a) and writing from the heart as well as the head—meant my project differed considerably from the "truth" of most social science.

> *Sociological Chorus (speaking at the same time, loudly and bois-*
> *terously):* **"That's for damn sure!"**
> *Yvonna Lincoln and William Tierney (facing the chorus and whis-*
> *pering softly through index fingers poised at lips):* "Shhh." *Chorus mem-*
> *bers roll their eyes, but say nothing. The author smiles and nods thank-*
> *fully toward the editors.*

In *Final Negotiations*, I worked not from an assumption of "fiction" but rather than an assumption of "truth" (Webster, 1982) in which I strove to tell a story that cohered with the details of personal experience, my notes, and recollections of others (Krieger, 1984). Especially in the beginning I tried to tell a story that was "faithful to the facts," and stayed close to what I recall happened (Richardson, 1992).

The first version of the text poured out of me, uncensored. It seemed important to get it "all" down and contextualized, so that I might have some sense of "what had been." I wrote with the confidence that I could delete anything at any time. The notes that I kept during the eight months prior to Gene's death and for two years afterward guided my writing. I interacted constantly with them to recall the way events had happened and how I had felt, adding details that came to memory.

As soon as I began to write from these notes, it became apparent that I needed to show the first years of our relationship as well, since attachment and loss are so intricately interwoven. This led to recreating my chronological history with Gene by first recording major events during the relationship and then connecting them. Interviews with family and friends; physicians' records and nurses' notes; tape recordings of conversations; diaries, calendars, and travel logs contributed to my systematic recollection of this period. I also had the advantage of many sociological conversations over the years with Gene about our relationship and the illness process.

Gradually I allowed myself dramatic license to tell a good story, since it was not so much the "facts" that I wanted to redeem but rather an articulation of the significance and meaning of my experiences. I came to feel that while personal narratives should be based on facts, they cannot be completely determined by them (Bochner, Ellis, & Tillmann-Healy, 1997).

I became less concerned with "historical truth" and more involved with "narrative truth," which Spence (1982, p. 28) describes as "the criterion we use to decide when a certain experience has been captured to our satisfaction." It is "what we have in mind when we say that such and such is a good story, that a given explanation carries conviction, that one solution to a mystery must be true." Narrative truth seeks to keep the past alive in the present; through narrative we learn to understand the meanings and significance of the past as incomplete, tentative, and revisable according to contingencies of present life circumstances and our projection of our lives into the future (Bochner, Ellis, & Tillmann-Healy, 1997). I wanted to incorporate alternative versions of what happened as well as revised senses of the self that were generated with each reflection on the experience (Rosenwald, 1992, p. 275). As Merleau-Ponty (1964, p. 59) says, I tried "to give the past not a survival, which is the hypocritical form of forgetfulness, but a new life, which is the noble form of memory." I was concerned that the story be both horizontally coherent—that the events were cohesive enough to warrant their meaningfulness—and vertically coherent—that the episodes were warranted by an honest depiction of feelings and thoughts of the characters (Rosenwald, 1992, p. 285).

In addition to telling what took place, I was intent on probing my psychic defenses and emotional complexities of this experience, although I understood that my attempts would be limited by what is possible to know and admit to oneself about oneself. To explore these psychological processes, I used a practice of "emotional recall," similar to the "method acting" of Lee Strasberg at the Actors' Studio (Bruner, 1986, p. 28). To give a convincing and authentic performance, the actor relives in detail a situation in which she previously had felt the emotion she wants to enact. I placed myself back into situations, conjuring up details until I was immersed in the event emotionally. Because recall increases when the emotional content at the time of retrieval resembles that of the experience to be retrieved (Bower, 1981; Ellis & Weinstein, 1986), this process enhanced the recollection of more details.

More intent on showing ambivalences and contradictions that occurred along the way than on declaring an outcome, I wanted to let the reader in on the emotional process. As Virginia Woolf (1953, p. 66) states about de Montaigne's essays, I attempted "to communicate a soul . . . to go down boldly and bring to light those hidden thoughts which are the most diseased; to conceal nothing; to pretend nothing."

My hope was that readers would see my "self-absorption" as an avenue to learn from exposure to candor and vulnerability (Lopate, 1994, p. xxvi). Necessarily, the exposure had to include betrayals, uncertainties, and self doubt, including doubt about what I had written. I wanted readers to trust that I had started with what I didn't know and discovered what I did know through the process of writing. I never pretended to have it all worked out, nor to suggest that the finished product disclosed the bare truth.

The moves in and out of these emotional situations were painful yet therapeutic. They allowed me to experience emotionality safely in my office, often reminded by a phone call or a click of the computer key that I was not actually in this situation. If the emotionality became too intense, I could stop and return to current time, a safety valve I did not have while engulfed by the epiphany of the initial experience. This "safety" gave me confidence to explore each incident as fully as I could, and to pay attention to what was most upsetting and least resolved.

I concentrated on the singular loud voice screaming inside my head or the raw fear gnarling within my gut. Then, embracing the multiplicity of selves that all human beings harbor, I tried to bring to my consciousness the contradictory and ambiguous thoughts and feelings that I also had felt. Whenever possible, I wrote down what the many competing voices in my head were saying. The experience was similar to a conference call in which I interacted with many speakers at one time.

This introspective homework (Ellis, 1991a) allowed me to enter into dialogues and disputes with myself before creating a discourse with which others could interact. The "plot" of my story, its drama and suspense, consisted of inviting readers to move with me through my defenses toward deeper levels of examination (Lopate, 1994, pp. xxv-xxvi). I wanted my story to "grasp" readers, pull them into its world, and persuade them that they were "in the reality of the story" (Parry, 1991, p. 42).

My open text consciously permitted readers to move back and forth between being in my story and being in theirs, where they could fill in or compare their experiences and provide their own sensitivities about what was going on. I attempted to write in a way that allows readers to feel the specificity of my situation, yet sense the unity of human experience as well (Lapate, 1994, xxiii), in which they can connect to what happened to me, remember what happened to them, or anticipate what might happen in the future. I wanted readers to feel that in describing my experience I had penetrated their heads and hearts. I hoped they would grapple with the ways they were different from and similar to me. Along with Mairs (1994, p. 120), I shared the sense that if "I do my job, the books I write vanish before your eyes," and I invited the reader into "the house of my past," hoping the "threshold" crossed would lead them into their own homes.

Returning to each event time and again, I felt that it was my responsibility, as a writer of sociology, not only to probe feelings but to try to make sense of the experiences, to find concepts and patterns that might explain how certain actions, even contradictory ones, fit together. Similar to the grounded theory approach (Glaser & Strauss, 1967), I looked for larger schemes within which these events might be contained.

*Sociological Chorus: "**About time!**" Involved in the telling of my story now, I ignore them and continue:*

Sometimes I could explain situationally or historically why seemingly contradictory details had occurred. Often features of culture and social structure, gender and socialization patterns, and structural constraints had impacted my experience, and social conventions and commitments had narrowed my vision and understanding of myself (Rosenwald, 1992, pp. 276, 280).

*Shaking their heads up and down, chorus members are getting
excited now.*

I tried to give readers enough clues about these macro-social forces that
they could see the impact and draw their own conclusions.

Sometimes, unlike grounded theory, I let contradictions and seemingly random events stand, willing to admit, after deep exploration,
that no explanatory scheme or pattern was readily apparent and that
understanding is never complete.

Chorus members return to half-fetal position.

I hoped that this stance would resonate with readers whom, I had to
assume, also experienced a similar lack of resolution in or explanation
for their thoughts and feelings. All of us must learn to live with contingency; to attempt to explain all of it away would be an illusion (see
Becker, 1994).

"As far as I'm concerned," states Mairs (1994), "my text is flawed
not when it is ambiguous or even contradictory, but only when it leaves
you no room for stories of your own. I keep my tale as wide open as I
can" (p. 74). Coles (1989, p. 47) similarly suggests, "The beauty of a
good story is its openness," how readers "takes it in" and use it for
themselves.

The question for me now is not whether narratives convey precisely the way things actually were, but rather what narratives do, what
consequences they have, and to what uses they can be put (Bochner,
Ellis, & Tillmann-Healy, 1997; see also Kinchloe, Lincoln, and Pinar, all
in this volume).

Evocative Autoethnography:
Crossing Boundaries, Reframing, and Connecting

This essay presents one way to reframe the narrative voice.
Evocative autoethnography connects the autobiographical impulse with
the ethnographic impulse. The ethnographic impulse has been characterized by "the gaze outward," as Neumann (1996) says, "at worlds
beyond [our] own, as a means of marking the social coordinates of a
self." The autobiographical impulse "gazes inward for a story of self,
but ultimately retrieves a vantage point for interpreting culture" (p. 173).

Autoethnography fluently moves back and forth, first looking
inward, then outward, then backward, and forward (Clandinin &
Connelly, 1994, p. 417), until the distinctions between the individual

and social are blurred beyond recognition and the past, present, and future become continuous (Crites, 1971). The inner workings of the self must be investigated in reciprocal relationship with the other: concrete action, dialogue, emotion, and thinking are featured, but they are represented within relationships and institutions, very much impacted by history, social structure, and culture, which themselves are dialectically revealed through action, thought, and language.

A story's "validity" can be judged by whether it evokes in readers a feeling that the experience described is authentic and lifelike, believable and possible; the story's generalizability can be judged by whether it speaks to readers about their experience.

Whoops! I slipped again into speaking in a generalized, abstracted mode that provides no concrete examples of what I'm talking about. I thought you would expect this in the conclusion.

Let me tell you a short story instead.

Evocative Autoethnography:
Crossing Boundaries, Reframing, and Connecting

At a Society for the Study of Symbolic Interaction Stone Symposium in 1991, Art Bochner and I performed a play we had co-constructed on our personal experience of an abortion (Ellis & Bochner, 1992). This was highly emotionally charged for us, both as an experience we had lived through and as a drama we would perform publicly and dialogically for a professional social science audience. After our performance, we whispered to each other that finally we felt finished with this epiphany that had dominated our lives for eight months. Emotionally drained, we barely heard the two conventional conference presentations that followed.

Afterwards, the first point raised from the audience was directed at our presentation. The speaker said something like: "It seems to me that telling stories about your own experience is a strategy that permits intellectual elites to control the stories that get told. It is a form that permits the telling of your stories but silences all voices not in the position of power to tell theirs—members of other ethnic groups, poor and uneducated people, for example. In contrast, traditional research practices recover other peoples' experiences. If we follow what you are doing, our research will only be about elite academics who can write narratively, nothing more. This is not a method that will allow silenced voices to speak or allow us to know about the life of others."

Some agreement sounds murmured through the crowd. Initially Art and I sat silently, caring more in that moment about the deepened emotional closeness and understanding that had come through our performance than we did about academic debate. Then, for another moment, I feared rejecting the politically correct sentiment that had been expressed.

Suddenly I said something like, "I doubt that people whose voices have been silenced identify with the talk of statistical tests and hypothesis testing. Do you think that people find their stories among the statistical analyses of large databases about social minutiae?"

(Actually I doubt I have ever spoken the word "minutiae," but it fits perfectly in the story I'm telling here. Nor, probably, was I or the questioner this articulate. Remember that stories told are always partial and reinterpreted from our present circumstances. This story is told from the perspective of trying to be true to the feelings that I remember having in that circumstance. Written from my perspective, the story might not be completely true to the feelings the questioner was having.)

I continue: "Do you think poor, uneducated people understand that language well enough to use it to tell their own stories or to understand the ones we tell for them?"

Catching myself pointing out the limitations of other approaches to defend my own, I changed my tack: "You are making an interesting point—that we have to figure out how to open up spaces for others to tell about their lives, but at least this method—storytelling about life epiphanies—is a strategy that most people employ in their everyday lives. It's a familiar form. Perhaps telling our stories might encourage others to speak their silences as well."

After hearing our story, many people at the symposium did share with us their stories about abortion. Friends, colleagues, relatives, and students continue telling us and each other their stories of abortion. The telling and retelling, as Clandinin and Connelly (1994, p. 418) point out, are reflexively related to living and reliving a story, and provide opportunities for growth, change, and resistance to our culture's canonical narratives.

This vignette highlights why I have told this personal autobiographical tale here and how it fits with the rest of the chapters in this volume. Similar to other authors in this collection, I want to reframe the narrative voice in ways that open up social science discourse to a larger and more varied audience, that make social science more useful, that allow for the silenced voices of others and the silenced parts of ourselves to speak themselves, and that challenge the "oppressive structures that create the conditions for silencing" (Tierney, 1993, p. 4; Pinar, this volume).

Social science education did not prepare me to write from the heart, touch other people, or improve social conditions. My education taught me to write in a way that would bring respect from a small, elite group of colleagues. If I had not suffered losses early in my life, losses that traditional social science did not help me understand or cope with, then I might never have explored writing in other ways for other purposes.

Perhaps all of us should go back to why we were attracted to higher education in the first place, to our dreams and hopes of what we could do with a Ph.D., to a place we inhabited before our creativity and imagination were discouraged by our professional socialization. How satisfied are we now with our scholarship? The goals of our research? The audiences we reach? The lack of connection of our work to the rest of our lives?

Writing this piece makes me feel that I have connected many of my voices. I feel like I have returned home and considered again the stories of the people in Luray. "Yes, the neighbor is washing his car again. I wonder why he does it so often?" I respond to my mother in my fantasy, repeating the same conversation we have had many times, and understanding that these exchanges contribute to the bond between us, and that they are neither inferior nor superior to the conversations I have repeatedly with colleagues at my university about the problems in our departments, only different. "Good sociology should help make people's lives better," I adamantly respond in my imagination to a professor I had during graduate school, realizing that the goal of knowledge for knowledge's sake represents only one possible goal for research.

Contemplating now how my life and work are connected and worthwhile gives me hope that I might not have to ponder these issues for the first time on my deathbed, as Ivan Ilych did. I don't need to wait that long.

Reframing the Narrative Voice: In Conclusion

Author: Once

upon a

time, Do, re,

me, fa . . .

Sociological Chorus (to other authors in this volume): "WHAT is she doing now?"

Tierney: "Expanding the range of her voices."

Pinar: "She's trying to find her voice, speak from her body, not from the body of the paper."

> *Polkinghorne: "Telling a story of do, re, me, and fa."*
> *Lincoln: "Can't you see? She's writing from the margins."*
> *Kinchloe: "And fashioning her voice in negotiation with her environment."*
> *Naive Reader (rolling her eyes, unable to hold back): "She's just making a joke."*
> *A dissident member of the Sociological Chorus, joining in quietly, hoping for approval: "Oh, she's teaching the Sociological Chorus how to sing an old song in a new key." All the authors laugh.*
> *Rest of Sociological Chorus: "Jokes don't belong in serious social science research, especially not in the conclusion where you're supposed to tell us what all this means."*

No one responds. Exasperated, the chorus members (minus the one dissident who is now dancing exuberantly on his desk) go off to interrogate yet another new social science text. In the table of contents, they find not only sections on reflexive ethnography and autoethnography, but also a unit called sociopoetics as well (Ellis & Bochner, 1996). "Of all things. Where will it end?" the leaders wonder aloud, and turn immediately to generate a conversation about mathematical modeling, their old standby topic. Unbeknownst to the chorus leaders, several members have slipped away to experience this new book. Those who remain keep looking over their shoulders to try to figure out what is going on.

Notes

Thanks To Arthur Bochner for permission to use our co-constructed ideas, to Laurel Richardson for letting me borrow her "sociological chorus," and to the editors of this volume for the opportunity to write this way.

1. See Richardson (1996) to learn more about the sociological chorus.

References

Becker, H. (1994). "FOI POR ACASO": Conceptualizing coincidence. *The Sociological Quarterly, 35,* 183–194.

Bochner, A. P. (1994). Perspectives on inquiry II: Theories and stories. In M. Knapp & G. R. Miller (Eds.), *Handbook of interpersonal communication* (pp. 21–41). 2nd ed. Newbury Park. CA: Sage.

Bochner, A. P., Ellis, C., & Tillman-Healy, L. (1997). Relationships as stories. In S. Duck (Ed.), *Handbook of personal relationships,* 2nd ed. New York: Wiley.

Bower, G. H. (1981). Mood and memory. *American Psychologist, 36,* 129–148.

Bruner, E. (1986). Experience and its expressions. In V. Turner & E. Bruner (Eds.), *The anthropology of experience* (pp. 3–30). Urbana: University of Illinois Press.

———. (1993). Introduction: The ethnographic self and the personal self. In P. Benson (Ed.), *Anthropology and literature.* Urbana: University of Illinois Press.

Carr, D. (1986). *Time, narrative, and history.* Bloomington: Indiana University Press.

Clandinin, D. J., & Connelly, F. M. (1994). Personal experience methods. In N. Denzin & Y. Lincoln (Eds.), *Handbook of qualitative research* (pp. 413–427). Thousand Oaks, CA: Sage.

Coles, R. (1989). *The call of stories: Teaching and the moral imagination.* Boston: Houghton Mifflin.

Crites, S. (1971). The narrative quality of experience. *Journal of the American Academy of Religion, 39,* 291–311.

Denzin, N. (1992). The many faces of emotionality: Reading 'Persona.' In C. Ellis & M. Flaherty (Eds.), *Investigating subjectivity: Research on lived experience* (pp. 17–30). Newbury Park, CA: Sage.

Denzin, N., & Lincoln, Y. (Eds.). (1994). *Handbook of qualitative research.* Thousand Oaks, CA: Sage.

Ellis, C. (1986). *Fisher folk: Two communities on Chesapeake Bay.* Lexington: University Press of Kentucky.

———. (1991a). Sociological introspection and emotional experience. *Symbolic Interaction, 14,* 23–50.

———. (1991b). Emotional sociology. In N. Denzin (Ed.), *Studies in symbolic interaction* (Vol. 12, pp. 123–145). Greenwich, CT: JAI Press.

———. (1993). "There are survivors": Telling a story of sudden death. *Sociological Quarterly, 34,* 711–730.

———. (1995a). *Final negotiations: A story of love, loss, and chronic illness.* Philadelphia: Template University Press.

———. (1995b). Emotional and ethical quagmires in returning to the field. *Journal of Contemporary Ethnography, 24,* 68–96.

———. (1996). On the demands of truthfulness in writing personal loss narratives. *Journal of Personal and Interpersonal Loss, 1,* 151–177.

Ellis, C., & Bochner, A. P. (1992). Telling and performing personal stories: The constraints of choice in abortion. In C. Ellis & M. Flaherty (Eds.), *Investigating subjectivity: Research on lived experience* (pp. 79–101). Newbury Park, CA: Sage.

————. (1996). Composing ethnography: Alternative forms of qualitative writing. Walnut Creek, CA: Altamira Press.

Ellis, C., & Weinstein, E. (1986). Jealousy and the social psychology of emotional experience. *Journal of Social and Personal Relationships, 3,* 337–357.

Foucault, M. (1980). *Power/knowledge.* New York: Pantheon.

Geertz, C. (1973). *The interpretation of cultures.* New York: Basic Books.

Glaser, B., & Strauss, A. (1967). *The discovery of grounded theory.* Chicago: Aldine.

Graff, G. (1979). *Literature against itself.* Chicago: University of Chicago Press.

Gregory, B. (1988). *Inventing reality: Physics as language.* New York: Wiley.

Gregory, D., & Walford, R. (Eds.). (1989). *Horizons in human geography.* London: Macmillan.

Jackson, M. (1989). *Paths toward a clearing: Radical empiricism and ethnographic inquiry.* Bloomington: Indiana University Press.

Krieger, S. (1984). Fiction and social science. In N. Denzin (Ed.), *Studies in symbolic interaction* (Vol. 12, 269–287). Greenwich, CT: JAI Press.

Lopate, P. (1994). *The art of the personal essay: An anthology from the classical era to the present.* Garden City, NY: Doubleday/Anchor Books.

Mairs, N. (1994). *Voice lessons: On becoming a (woman) writer.* Boston: Beacon Press.

McCall, N. (1994). *Makes me wanna holler: A young black man in America.* New York: Vintage.

Merleau-Ponty, M. 1964. *Signs.* (R. C. McCleary, Trans.). Evanston, IL: Northwestern University Press.

Montaigne, M. de. (1973). *Selections from the essays.* (D. M. Frame, Ed. and Trans.). Arlington Heights, IL: AHM Publishing.

Mykhalovskiy, E. 1996. "Reconsidering table talk: Critical thoughts on the relationship between sociology, autobiography and self-indulgence." *Qualitative Sociology, 19,* 131–151.

Neumann, M. (1996). Collecting ourselves at the end of the century. In C. Ellis & A. Bochner (Eds.), *Composing ethnography: Alternative forms of qualitative writing.* Walnut Creek, CA: Altamira Press.

Parry, A. (1991). A universe of stories. *Family Process, 30*, 37–54.

Richardson, L. (1992). The consequences of poetic representation: Writing the other, rewriting the self. In C. Ellis & M. Flaherty (Eds.), *Investigating subjectivity: Research on lived experience* (pp. 125–137). Newbury Park, CA: Sage.

————. (1994). Writing as a method of inquiry. In N. Denzin & Y. Lincoln (Eds.), *Handbook of qualitative research* (pp. 516–529). Thousand Oaks, CA: Sage.

————. (1996). Educational birds. *Journal of Contemporary Ethnography, 25*, 6–15.

Ronai, C. R. (1992). The reflexive self through narrative: A night in the life of an erotic dancer/researcher. In C. Ellis & M. Flaherty (Eds.), *Investigating subjectivity: Research on lived experience* (pp. 102–124). Newbury Park, CA: Sage.

Rorty, R. (1979). *Philosophy and the mirror of nature*. Princeton, NJ: Princeton University Press.

————. (1982). *Consequences of pragmatism: Essays 1972–1980*. Minneapolis: University of Minnesota Press.

Rosenau, P. (1992). *Postmodernism and the social sciences: Insights, inroads, and intrusions*. Princeton, NJ: Princeton University Press.

Rosenwald, G. (1992). Conclusion: Reflections on narrative understanding. In G. Rosenwald & R. Ochberg (Eds.), *Stories lives: The cultural politics of self-understanding* (pp. 265–289). New Haven, CT: Yale University Press.

Sampson, E. (1978). Scientific paradigms and social values: Wanted—a scientific revolution. *Journal of Personality and Social Psychology, 36*, 1332–1343.

Spence, D. (1982). *Narrative truth and historical truth: Meaning and interpretation in psychoanalysis*. New York: Norton.

Tierney, W. (1993). Developing archives of resistance: Speak, memory. In D. McLaughlin & W. Tierney (Eds.), *Naming silenced lives: Personal narratives and processes of educational change* (pp. 1–5). New York: Routledge.

Tolstoy, L. (1886/1960). *The death of Ivan Ilych and other stories*. New York: New American Library.

Van Mannen, J. (1988). *Tales of the field: On writing ethnography*. Chicago: University of Chicago Press.

Webster, S. (1982). Dialogue and fiction in ethnography. *Dialectical anthropology, 7*, 91–114.

Woolf, V. (1953). *The common reader*. New York: Harcourt Brace and World.

PART II

EXPERIMENTS IN VOICE, FRAME, TIME, AND TEXT

7

THE ETHNOGRAPHER AS POSTMODERN *FLÂNEUR*: CRITICAL REFLEXIVITY AND POSTHYBRIDITY AS NARRATIVE ENGAGEMENT

PETER MCLAREN

I knew that when the great guiding spirit cleaves humanity into two antagonistic halves, I will be with the people. And I know it because I see it imprinted on the night that I, the eclectic dissector of doctrines and psychoanalyst of dogmas, howling like a man possessed, will assail the barricades and trenches, will stain my weapon with blood and, consumed with rage, will slaughter any enemy I lay hands on. And then, as if an immense weariness were consuming my recent exhilaration, I see myself being sacrificed to the authentic revolution, the great leveler of individual will, pronouncing the exemplary *mea culpa*. I feel my nostrils dilate, savoring the acrid smell of gunpowder and blood, of the enemy's death; I brace my body, ready for combat, and prepare myself to be a sacred precinct within which the bestial howl of the victorious proletariat can resound with new vigor and new hope.

—Ernesto Ché Guevara, *The Motorcycle Diaries*

This is the paradox never to be resolved: the endemic in determination renders man free to choose, yet this freedom is invariably deployed in frenzied efforts to foreclose the choice.

—Zygmunt Bauman, "Searching for a Centre that Holds"

The central theme of this collection of reflections is that both the world of academic science and that of everyday life need the agency required of the self-reflexive *flâneur*. This short essay—originally developed as a type of discursive montage—was provoked by reflecting upon my own location as *flâneur* in both academic settings and those of the mundane world of popular culture. It developed out of the social

trajectory of my own formation as an ethnographer and the social historical conditions of possibility that enable me to exist within the structured spaces and struggles of academia yet which provoke me *flagrante
bello*, to remain, for the most part, outside of such spaces. Yet being
"outside" the academy while remaining "officially" within it carries
with it certain risks surrounding the *rapports de force* within university
life, most notably the risk of being ambushed by the world, being sub-
jectivized by it as one seeks to escape the crippling banality and sterility
of formal institutions of higher learning. A theme that repeats itself
throughout this paper is that the professional *flâneur* as an outsider-
within is trapped between an identification with the bloom and buzz of
the popular and a perverse loyalty to the strident strictures of academic
science yet frequently fails to understand how she is positioned simultaneously in both social spaces.

I take as my primary object of investigation the situatedness of
the *flâneur/flâneuse*—the primordial ethnographer—within postmodern, postorganized, late capitalist culture, since for me the figure of the
flâneur/flâneuse embodies an attempt in urban settings to live within the
blurred and vertiginous strategies of representation and the shifting
discourses of capitalism's marketing strategies and mechanisms and
merge with them. This merging is strategic and should not be confused
with fusion (this will be made clearer in the final section of the chapter)
since the *flâneur/flâneuse* still tries to (albeit often in vain) retain some
form of detachment by setting "a pace that is out of step with the rapid
circulations of the modern metropolis" (Tester, 1994, p. 15). The
flâneur/flâneuse seeks out the mystery of daily life, unaware that such
seeking can surreptitiously fuse with the very logic of commodity that
fascinates, thrills, and repulses with equal force.

More specifically, I seek to problematize the reflective gaze of the
ethnographer and the reading of ethnographies. In doing so, I will
describe the formation of the reader and writer of ethnography who
lives the dual role of *flâneur/flâneuse* and critical theorist, as incompatible as these roles might appear at first glance. I wish to shed some light
on the dilemma faced by the urban ethnographer who lives in the in-
between spaces of the city, who cannot escape his or her memories and
who, in his or her creatively charged strolling, always already occupies
the existential geography of his or her own desire and fear as one who
lives in the thrall of metropolitan existence and the postmodern hybridity of cosmopolitan public spaces. While seeking asylum in the crowd
(Benjamin, 1973), in what Morawski (1994, p. 189) calls "the homogenized heterogeneity of the surrounding world," the *flâneur/flâneuse* is the

prototype of the urban ethnographer. How the ethnographer's location in space by way of speed technology (e.g., a computer terminal, flights to many different places around the globe), moral technology (a commitment to a revolutionary praxis of liberation), and the textual and discursive economy of academic work together impinge upon his or her *flâneurism* will be touched upon but not systematically developed. In this regard, my journal entries are to be considered anti-texts in which private memories shape formal thought through both necessity and disposition and in ways that outrun my conscious intention. Such anti-textual reflections betray a necessary partiality. They become events that rupture the continuity of my theoretical understanding as well as its formal logic. The diary excerpts illustrate moments when I recognize the need to interrogate the discourses of self/other that locate me as gringocentric, as informed by guero consciousness.

Saturday, August 6, 1995, West Hollywood

I think only of the open road, and yearn to get a bike and join my *compas*. One of my co-authors and co-editors once died momentarily in a motorcycle accident. Since his death we have written a number of articles and co-edited several books. He was pronounced as having been dead for several minutes; today he can't recall if he had any visions of angels, and continues to ride his Triumph. I have always wanted a Norton 500—which is what Ché rode across Latin America. The thought of his Poderosa II inspires me. Yet I am haunted by the feeling that my spirit has already died with Ché's. A trip to Havana in 1987 in search of his memory only left me frustrated, ready to abandon academia altogether. They say Ché's remains are buried under an airport runway. If his sandals are discovered with his remains, maybe they will be put up for auction by the Lloyds of London.

My position as author will reflect the figure of the ethnographer as *flâneur/flâneuse*, the image of urban spectators who dwell in prohibitive spaces both inside and outside of academia, losing themselves in their incognito observations, who indulge in the thrill of public spaces, whose identity, personal and professional, depends upon acts of *flânerie*, who are the mirror image of postmodern culture, and who are emptied of all modern practices of the self in order to make way for the creation of new postmodern subjectivities. This perspective is meant to be suggestive and heuristic rather than definitive as a means of unmooring ethnography from some of its debilitating modernist discourses and of demoting the epistemological certainty that surrounds them.

Of course, the figure of the *flâneur* is most often associated with the writings of Baudelaire, Zola, Balzac, Benjamin, Dumas, Kracauer, and Sartre—a transitory, solitary bohemian figure who strolls the streets and boulevards of the city in the thrall of violent urban dislocations (usually Paris but also London and Berlin); who seeks incognito the meaning of modernity; who searches for the eternal in the fleeting and transitory and who discovers a unity between the transient and the timeless; and who discovers both the particular in the universal and the universal in the particular—what David Frisby (1994, p. 98) refers to as "the ever-same in the new; antiquity in modernity; representation of the profane in the mythical, the past in the present." What I wish to emphasize—thematically at least—is the idea that as ethnographic readers and writers of texts, and as the authors and subjects of the texts of our own lives, we experience *flânerie* as being at the root of all the intellectual and political work that we do. According to Elizabeth Wilson, the *flâneur* replaced the bohemian during the decline of bohemia during France's Second Empire. In this case, the *flâneur* "appears as the ultimate ironic, detached observer, skimming across the surface of the city and tasting all its pleasures with curiosity and interest" (1992, p. 97). Rob Shields notes: "the *flâneur*, like the prostitute, risks being swallowed up by the goods in the stores and becoming little more than a commodity or a mannequin: 'the sandwich man' whose identity is hidden by the large advertising sign carried front and back" (1994, p. 75).

Monday, August 7, 1995, Westwood, Los Angeles

I am trying to reflect on my feelings about the Gypsy Cafe. Before moving to West Hollywood, I came here almost every evening to write. My apartment was so small, I became claustrophobic. A large number of U.C.L.A. students frequent at the Gypsy, mostly the undergraduate crowd. They annoyingly chatter to their friends and pretentiously smoke their American Spirit cigarettes. I am unable to feel serious about what I do in such an atmosphere. My work suffers but this is the only cafe in Westwood that I find tolerable. Here I become the *flâneur* peering at the world from the margins "like the ragpicker assembling the refuse, like the detective seeking to bring insignificant details and seemingly fortuitous events into meaning constellation" (Frisby, 1994, p. 99). I savor the narcotic impressions from the rag and bone shop of my sociological imagination. I think of my *compañeros y compañeras* in Mexico, Argentina, Brasil and wonder if their revolutionary praxis is purer, more real. How can anyone take anything seriously in this city, in this world of fluff and tinsel, of murder, hopelessness, poverty, and ostentatious wealth—all thrust in your face (which you are constantly urged to have "lifted" in Beverly Hills).

Whereas historically the *flâneur*, the nineteenth-century stroller of the turbulent streets of the industrial city, who rubbed shoulders with the bohemians, dandies, courtesans, workers, grisettes, soldiers, drunkards, and ragpickers confronted "the space-time dislocation and disorientation due to the expanding scale of social relations" (Shields, 1994, p. 77) and lived a life of "space-time psychosis" in a futile search for individuality and agency, the late-twentieth-century *flâneur* of the postmodern present confronts a world where nature has been almost eclipsed by the commodity form. Shields rightly notes that "the *flâneur's* problems are as timely for us at the close of the twentieth century as they were for the Parisian dandy of the nineteenth century" (1994, p. 77). The success of mass production of "the look" through media advertising need not be rehearsed here. Suffice it to say that here in the West we are constantly seduced by the tantalizingly empty commodities and their fatal strategies that have penetrated our structures of thinking and feeling, acquiring their own logic.

Commenting upon Benjamin's depiction of the *flâneur*, Eagleton describes the *flâneur* as a "drifting relic of a decaying petty bourgeoisie" who is something of an allegorist (1981, p. 25). "Strolling self-composedly through the city, loitering without intent, languid yet secretly vigilant" the *flâneur* becomes an expression of the contradictory nature of the commodity form "as both the *flâneur* and the commodity tart themselves up in dandyish dress" (pp. 25, 26). According to Eagleton, "The *flâneur* at once spiritually pre-dates commodity production—he strays through the bazaars but prices nothing—and is himself the prototypical commodity, not least because his relationship to the masses is one of simultaneous complicity and contempt. In this, indeed, the *flâneur* resembles the allegorist, for both dip randomly into the ruck of objects to single out for consecration certain ones that they know to be in themselves arbitrary and ephemeral" (p. 26).

Tuesday, August 8, 1995, East Los Angeles

East L.A. is busy as usual. I'm thinking of all the *pinche gringos cabrones* who voted for Proposition 187. I'm imagining Ron Prince,

initiator of the proposition, deported out of the U.S., or locked
up in the county jail. *Vale cacahuate.* Too bad it's just a fantasy.
But it is hard to swallow that 23% of Latinos, 36% of Democrats,
and 54% of first generation immigrants also voted for this
insidious measure. The answer to this lies in the secret of capitalism's success. *"Andale, ya ves,"* I can hear Marx whispering
from the grave. My eye catches a group of what the locals call
"cha-cha goddesses" with penciled eyebrows, matte burgundy
lips, and brown lipliner, whom I'm told are probably on their
way to the Eastside clubs like Baby Doe's or Florentine Gardens
in Hollywood. I find my reaction to be uncomfortably conditioned by the media and public discourse about East L.A. and
Latinas as the exotic Other, as the object of male desire. Here is
where I am trapped by the very discourse of sexism I struggle
against. I'm thinking about what it takes to be a citizen in the
white metaculture known as Gringolandia. For this Canuck
gabacho from El Norte del Norte (Canada) thrown into the identity politics of academic struggles over the possibility of critical
agency in a postmodern culture, I'm depressed by such a focus
on cultural politics at the level of the superstructure. I'm not
that interested anymore in shopping retro in the second-hand
stores of Venice Beach or Boyle Heights as a way of subverting
the high fashion doyens of the metropole who serve us up
bulimia and anorexia as *de rigeur* taste. The issue for me is to
question my role as a professor as an adjunct of the state, as a
legitimator of patriarchal capitalist cultural capital and sovereign epistemological languages, of research models and the
imperialist values inscribed in them. I want to pluck out these
guero eyes and cut out this gringo tongue. I want to see the
world through an imagination purged of whiteness. I worry
about the essay that's going to come out of these fieldnotes—
about the *flâneur/flâneuse.* I worry about not only the textual
politics of deconstruction, but also the politics of resource allo-
cation and political economy. I want to move beyond helping
students adjust to Gringolandia. I want to help them malad-
just to *gabacho* injustice. For white people this means becoming a race traitor.

   I can see the extraordinary expanse of my own Anglo-
centrism, sentimentalizing the effects of capitalism, derealizing it,
turning it into the empire of the gaze. This was supposed to be the
afternoon that I would start to read *In the Realm of the Diamond*

Queen but I'm too interested in a group of homeboys heading south on Lincoln Avenue and the park bench I'm sitting on is burning up in the hot L.A. sun.

What is important to emphasize is that the figure of the *flâneur* "the detective of street life" (Shields, 1994, p. 61) who is "caught between creativity and commodification" (p. 35), who carefully and scrupulously observes the sights and sounds of metropolitan life, thereby calling the world's bluff of civilized existence, and who engages in a "discernment of the subtle pleasures of urban life"—a type of "pedestrian connoisseurship and consumption of the urban environment" (p. 61)—is not a monadic subject or detached, autonomous voyeur of the world of asphalt and brick, but a situated observer, located in material relations of power and privilege. Ethnographers as *flâneurs* cannot escape their positionality as both subjects and objects of the gaze. They are not transcendentally removed from the messy web of social relations that shapes both themselves as observers and those whom they choose to observe. They do not live in some *post-histoire* moral universe where value judgments cease to exist.

The *flâneur* or dandy whose aim is to be aimless, to shun any *idée fixe*, to master the intellectual poker face, must negotiate the everyday scene of postmodern hybridity. He must bring some semblance of meaning to intercultural social relations within the frenetic narratives and signs that are available, without the gaze of the *flâneur* assimilating the other. At the micropolitical level of hegemonic social relations, the *flâneur* is an agent of the empire. *Flânerie*, notes Shields, is "an attempt to appropriate and reinvigorate the position of spectator to transform the display of empire into a spectacle which (it is hoped) can be 'mastered'" (1994, p. 75). Rob Shields makes the following important observation:

> the *flâneur* reimagines the world and rebuilds a cognitive mapping of newly expanded socio-economic relations. Once again we find ourselves faced with the chiasmus of the imaginary *flâneur* (in the sense of being a literary figure) as an active "imaginer." Benjamin draws a close link between *flânerie*, imagination and dreaming. This process takes place first via a reconstruction of the situation from collecting the evidence or "traces" of social relations in commodities. However, a more ambiguous process of consumption and self-implication is also involved. An interpretive attempt to grasp the totality of social relations through a *verste-*

hen—like experiencing of the "aura" of the sense of commodity consumption in the arcades requires the *flâneur* to become part of the process of commodity exchange as a "participant observer." (1994, p. 75)

To what extent does the city, bathed in all of its commercialism and philistinism, take possession of the *flâneur*; to what extent does the condition of postmodernity force the *flâneur* to turn more and more inward yet become more and more ethically disabled in terms of acquiring an ability to effect change, to apprise himself of responsibility? Priscilla Parkhurst Ferguson astutely observes that political and social transformation and the incertitude and confusion brought on by "a changed and changing population" makes it difficult if not impossible for the *flâneurs* "to narrate the connections among the several parts [of the city]" (1994, p. 39). They are obliged to advance "the cult of *nouveauté* or ritual of fashion" as the bacillus through which history becomes homogenized (Eagleton, 1981, p. 28). Postmodern *flâneur* and *flâneuses*, or ethnographers of everyday urban life, find little to establish coherent narratives that can fuse together the warring contingencies of everyday existence under late capitalism. They are obliged through their willing participation in semiotic guerrilla warfare to uncover the deep narratives that remain buried within schemes of representation that occur in contemporary urban spaces. They are motivated to understand how such schemes of representation are linked to regimes of discourse and patterns of social relations and regulations not only locally but also globally through the development and proliferation of new technologies.

In other words, postmodern *flâneurs/flâneuses* negotiate spatial and temporal narratives, in private, public and hybridized spheres, and wrestle with the tension between the contingent and the universal, between presence and absence, between utopias and heterotopias, between temporal disjunctions and historical trajectories, and between implosions and explosions of subjectivity.

Thursday, August 10, 1995, East Berlin

Sitting at the next table to us are these pathetic Euro-kids eating their flan desserts and speaking in German and French interchangeably and with pronounced bourgeois gestures. Just like the kids I've read about in European newspapers. Possibly the children of parents working at the European Commission in Brussels or of *fonctionnaires* in West Berlin. I wonder how their education— in their respective *lycée* or gymnasium or comprehensive school—

might have shaped their view of East Germany. How different were their high schools from the barrio high schools of Los Angeles Unified, which many of my doctoral students attended. I am repulsed by the wealthy classes and find it hard to observe them. *Flânerie* fails me.

Ethnographic *flâneurs* are prohibited from intersubjective exchange yet they often learn something from their failed attempts. As Shields remarks "As a consumer of sights and goods, the *flâneur* is a vicarious conqueror, self-confirmed in his mastery of the empire of their gaze while losing his own self in the commodified network of popular imperialism" (Shields, 1994, p. 78).

David Frisby notes in the work of Benjamin that the *flâneur* as a strolling sightseer, as a conceptual detective suggests a methodology. *Flânerie*, in this sense, refers to both consuming and producing texts detachedly and actively. *Flânerie* consists, therefore, of

activities of observation (including listening), reading (of metro-politan life and of texts) and producing texts. *Flânerie*, in other words, can be associated with a form of *looking*, observing (of peo-ple, social types, social contexts and constellations), a form of *read-ing the city* and its population (its spatial images, its architecture, its human configurations), and a form of *reading written texts* (in Benjamin's case both of the city and the nineteenth century—*as texts* and of *texts on the city*, even texts as urban labyrinths). The *flâneur*, and the activity of *flânerie*, is also associated in Benjamin's work not merely with observation and reading but also with *pro-duction*—the production of distinctive kinds of texts. The *flâneur* may therefore not merely be an observer or even a decipherer, the *flâneur* can also be a producer. . . . Thus, the *flâneur* as producer of texts should be explored. (1994, pp. 82–83)

It is important to consider that postmodern urban *flâneurs* and *flâneuses*, often enmeshed in a world of enthroned meaninglessness, are also producers of ethnographic texts. It is virtually impossible to pro-duce such texts impartially, in isolation, uncontaminated by the giddy buzz and blur of discursive formations and practices, since the act of reading itself is ideological. In fact, such texts are often contingent on the terms according to which the European observer of the streets was invented. David Frisby underscores the concept of the *flâneur* as the producer of narrative texts: "[T]he activity of the *flâneur* is not exhausted in strolling, observing or reading the signifiers of the modern metropolis. Benjamin's own activity in producing the hitherto most illuminating account of the *flâneur* involved the *reading* of texts *on* metropolitan modernity and the production of texts on that modernity" (p. 96).

Friday, August 11, 1995, East Berlin—
Former Gestapo Headquarters

I've never seen so many photographs of Himmler in one place. Because of the playful fiction of *flânerie*, I can leave the scene I am observing by creating a border, the crossing of which will take me away from the site of my observation and the role of observer. It's all a play—and to play "is to rehearse eternity." Only inside the play of the assignment, to engage in and write about ethnography as *flânerie*, do I commit myself to academic convention, do I confine the freedom of my choice to a framework or narrative not of my making but inflicted on me by other players. But the scene itself is a player—and a formidable one because it is mostly made up of memory. Not my memory both those of torturers and their victims. If this event is textual play, it is a hideous discursive adventure. My *flânerie* brings me into a space where I am dialogized by the screams that were heard fifty years ago. Later that evening in a hotel conference room, they echo in my lecture and choke my words into tiny pebbles that seem to roll off the podium.

According to Bauman, the goal of the *flâneur* is "to rehearse contingency of meaning" (1994, 142). It is to rehearse the unrehearsable. The *flâneuse*; is in tacit agreement with herself to live the fiction of her emptiness as the empty fullness of the real. What is known in the qualitative literature as grounded theory is built on *flânerie*; it is the hope for openness to the world, an openness untainted by prejudice, to enter a state of receptive innocence. The *flâneur*, notes Bauman, seeks the aim of his wanderings, the reason for his gaze. He seeks new narratives while purging himself of those that have already come, even those that inform his desire to free himself from them. But the gaze always already has narrative intentionally, a motivated way of seeing, even as the *flâneur's* gaze seeks to escape from the fixity of time. Bauman describes the *flâneur* as on vacation from reality, as reproducing the "contingency of life instead of confining it" (1994, 141). As a stranger in the crowd, the *flâneur* is able to control the strangeness of the scene by choosing to ignore it.

The difficulty of enticing students to pay greater attention to their *flânerie* has to do with postmodern life as *flâneurisme*, with the fact that our exterior lives have become managed by larger narratives linked to production and consumption; we are forced to play at *flâneurisme* in a world in which fiction has made reality disappear. We are living in the panoptic fortresses of our cities (L.A. seems worse than Paris or Berlin) where identities are always already structured in dominance in the form of capitalist dependency. Bauman describes this as:

> The body drill of modern places of confinement and centralized surveillance turned into post-modern—thoroughly individual-ized and freely exercised—passions for jogging and dieting. The sexual drill of modern moral guardians turned into post-modern frantic search for the advice of sexual experts and counsellors of partnership. The modern assignment of social identities-tied-to-the-class turned into post-modern individual assembly and dis-assembly and reassembly of market-supplied lifestyle-tied identity kits. The modern medicalization and psychiatrization of social problems rebounded in post-modern horror of disease and toxic substances that cause it by entering the body or touching the skin. Central supply, individual consumption. Dependence that condi-tions freedom and depends on it for it reproduction; freedom that reinforces and rejuvenates dependence and depends on it for its exercise. (1994, 154)

If, as Bauman notes, "The post-modern *flâneur* cannot but see the world (as far as he can see it) as the site of past or potential nomadic expeditions" (155), and if the *flâneur*, whose nomadic desire is now manufactured by rented dreams on videotape, and who constitutes the entire world as a consumer expedition, allows us to live more comfort-ably, harbored in our alienation, then we need to question those forms of subjectivity that structure us as *interpreters*, as *ethnographers* who have been raised as *flâneur/flâneuse*—poets amidst the city streets of the post-modern metropolis and the guardianship of the postmodern state. If we wish a *flânerie* to dethrone consumer hegemony and to adopt a *crit-ical flânerie*, are we seeking a contradiction in terms? Can we create a *flânerie* capable of resisting the swindle of civilization?

What motivates the *flâneur/flâneuse* is not some primal narrative linked to desire but is rather what Jean Baudrillard calls "the vertigo of seduction" (1990, 139). To be seduced is to be lifted out of oneself and into the "play of the world." The world is composed of sovereign, fatal eruptions. The play of the world tears us from our narrative of instinc-tual belonging, from those narratives born of a libidinal economy, from our Oedipal history, from our fantasies and repressions. Seduction takes us to the realm of appearance and away from the realm of meaning and interpretation. It is anti-narrative. It takes us to the realm of pure objects, to the world of kind and cruel illusions, to the antitheater of destiny. Theory, like ceremony, notes Baudrillard, is the initiator of violence, since it acts in order to discriminate, in order to connect according to the rules. Postmodern *flâneurs* create violence when they defend us from the seduction of the world, when they wrench us back to the world of metaphor and meaning through the violence of theory-building, when they assign to the world the vocation of a symptom and when they assign to appearances the reign of hidden motives.

Towards a Reflexive *Flânerie*

According to Lash and Urry (1995), the spacialization and semiotization of contemporary political economies opens up new possibilities for critical self-reflexivity and social relations at the level of everyday life, in both cognitive and aesthetic-expressive dimensions. The authors are referring to forms of self-reflexivity that are both constitutive of and constituted by changes in social structures and personal biographical narratives brought about by late capitalism. High modernity has now superseded the discourses of objectivity of earlier modernity with more personalized, subjective temporalities in the form of new, self-created narratives. The advanced differentiation of social relations and institutions of modernity has given way to a high modernity of hyperdifferentiation into internally-referential or auto-poetic systems of "pure relationship" (Lash & Urry, 1994). Viewed from this perspective, a larger role is given to agency as the abstract systems that serve as sources of reflexivity change from political institutions to cultural, media and education institutions. Lash and Urry develop the important concept of aesthetic *reflexivity* based on the work of Charles Taylor, Alasdair MacIntyre, and Michael Waltzer. Lash and Urry claim that the Cartesian and Enlightenment tradition that dealt with "disengaged reason" primarily stressed cognition whereas the romantic—aesthetic high modernist tradition stressed aesthetic knowledge. They further argue that the latter tradition dealt primarily with symbol and the former with allegory. Romantic expressionism developed by Goethe, Hegel and Schiller saw symbol presuming a natural order comprising the unity of the sensual and spiritual and a compatibility between aesthetic life and morality. The tradition of allegory founded in Baudelaire and Nietzsche rejected the unity of the sensual and spiritual and aesthetic life was seen as incompatible with moral life. In this case, symbol is grounded in the assumption of a unity of form and content outside of the conceptual order of language where as allegory separates form and content, privileging the signifier and denying a separate order of meaning. Allegory's shift away from transcendence and toward the immediacy of *local* contexts ruptures the notion of expressive unity and views the subject as decentered. Allegory speaks to a reflexivity built on the notion of cultural hybridity. Critical hermeneutics best fits as a means of exploring such hybridity. We will visit briefly the concept of cultural hybridity as it relates to the construction of identity in the section that follows.

Sunday, August 13, 1995, East Berlin

Checkpoint Charlie, Gestapo Headquarters, the site of the train station that transported Jews out of Berlin to the camps, walls everywhere riddled with bullet holes from World War II battles. Photo exhibits of Nazi execution squads. I wanted to urinate on Hitler's bunker site but I couldn't locate where it once stood. I can't relax in this city. Police vans are everywhere as the authorities anticipated violence surrounding the Kurdish hunger strikers. An East Berlin artists' colony in an old abandoned building. Young people with shaved heads, black boots and nose rings. The Reichstag unwrapped. A *flânerie* haunted by history's silences.

The question of identity is a nagging one for our postindustrial, postmodern *flâneur/flâneuse*. It is a nagging issue because of the disappearance of the unitary, self-directed subject and the stress on the decentered subject that has been encouraged to celebrate its *"mestizaje"* or border-crossing characteristics (McLaren, 1995). For hybridity or border-crossing dimensions of identity formation may be structural (pluralization of the available modes of organization both locally and globally) and could include, for instance, urbanization as the fusion of precapitalist and capitalist modes of production in border zones of, say, Latin America; hybridity may also be cultural in terms of the production of multiple identities and the decentering of the social subject (Pieterse, 1995). Hybridity also refers to the reflexiveness of *global consciousness*. As Pieterse notes:

How do we come to terms with phenomena such as Thai boxing by Moroccan girls in Amsterdam, Asian rap in London, Irish bagels, Chinese tacos and Mardi Gras Indians in the United States, or "Mexican schoolgirls dressed in Greek togas dancing in the style of Isadora Duncan?" How do we interpret Peter Brook directing the Mahabharata, or Ariane Mânouchkine staging a Shakespeare play in Japanese Kabuki style for a Paris audience in the Théâtre Soleil? (p. 53)

How do we make sense of this hybridization, what Pieterse claims is "foregrounding the *mestizo* factor," and creolization "which highlights what has been hidden and valorizes boundary crossing" (1995, p. 54)? And what about the neoimperialistic undercurrents of global intercultural exchange. Is it enough to say that we all are better social agents because of the multiple forms of cultural contact we experience in postindustrial urban contexts? While *mestizaje* identity as articulated by McLaren, Anzaldúa, and others refers to a *counternarrative* that builds community within the margins of culture; it also has an assimilationist inflection in Latin America (referring to a gradual "whitening" of the population and culture and the reproduction of elite European ideologies; see Pieterse, 1995, p. 54). According to Valle and Torres (1995), Mexico's ruling Partido Revolucionario Institucional "invokes the term to maintain the hegemony of a one-party state" (p. 148). Further, Valle and Torres note that "Where in Mexico, the term has been co-opted to legitimize and integrate the nation's mestizo middle class and peripheral regional cultures, here in the United States its lived experience occurs beyond official sanction. Valle and Torres argue that on this side of the border, *mestizaje* refers to a refusal to prefer one national culture at the expense of others. It is inclusive and can have transgressive features that are adaptive and strategic. The border crosser "willfully blurs political, racial, or cultural borders in order to better adapt to the world as it is actually in constructed" (pp. 148–149). It is both transnational and postnational. As an adaptive strategy, it can be threatening even amidst the decline of the imperial West. Valle and Torres note that "the border crosser *que se amestiza* in the act of transgression, inevitably undermines the discourses of the nation-state while, paradoxically, contributing to the same state's economic well-being by providing cheap surplus labor" (p. 149).

While viewing identity as *mestizaje* ushers in important ways of unsettling the isolationist narratives of nationalism, racism, and cultural chauvinism and religious triumphism, it also opposes the challenge of new forms of sociality based on cooperation, imagination, translocal cultural expressions and new forms of competition (p. 64). Consequently, Pieterse remarks that when discussing hybridity we need always to pay attention to the *terms* of the mixture, and the conditions surrounding the mixture and cultural mélange. This mandates for the critically reflexive *flâneur/flâneuse* an understanding of the means by which hegemony is both reproduced and refigured in the process of hybridization. It also emphasizes the close attention that must be paid to similarities and transcultural historical affinities as well as to differences. The idea of translocal cultures and the politics of hybridity deals with more than difference as mixture but also, as Pieterse notes, with the process of similarities across differences (see also Kanpol & McLaren, 1995). It also has important implications for new forms of narrative hybridity in terms of biotechnology and information technologies such as the notion of cyborg identity (see McLaren, 1995). The central question is: How productive is it to work with the notion of hybrid cultures/identities if all cultures result from mixtures (Pieterse, 1995). It appears productive in the way hybridity is able to counter essentialism (Pieterse, 1995).

Valle and Torres emphasize that the "aggressive disregard for boundaries and unexpected inclusions" of mestizaje identity needs to be understood within the context of global transformation, including the unequal development resulting from the emerging conditions of post-industrial society. *Mestizaje* consciousness cannot ignore the neocolonial present and its own deformation in the cauldron of virtual capitalism. Syncretism, hybridity, *creolité*, and *mestizaje* need to be understood with respect to postcolonial diasporic movements of peoples and the global circulation of mass-mediated commodities. This point is underscored by Shohat and Stam (1994):

Hybridity is an unending, unfinalizable process which preceded colonialism and will continue after it. Hybridity is dynamic, mobile, less an achieved synthesis or prescribed formula than an unstable constellation of discourses. (p. 42)

Postcolonial hybrid identities with their multilayered displacements and diasporic histories, are forms of problematic agency. According to Shohat and Stam (1994):

A celebration of syncretism and hybridity per se, if not articulated with questions of historical hegemonies, risks sanctifying the *fait accompli* of colonial violence. For oppressed people, even artistic syncretism is not a game but a sublimated form of historical pain, which is why Jimi Hendrix played the "Star Spangled Banner" in a dissonant mode, and why even a politically conservative performer like Ray Charles renders "America the Beautiful" as a moan and a cry. As a descriptive catch-all term, "hybridity" fails to discriminate between the diverse modalities of hybridity: colonial imposition, obligatory assimilation, political cooptation, cultural mimicry, and so forth. Elites have always made cooptive top-down raids on subaltern cultures, while the dominated have always "signified" and parodied as well as emulated elite practice. Hybridity, in other words, is power-laden and asymmetrical. Whereas historically assimilation by the "native" into a European culture was celebrated as part of the civilizing mission, assimilation in the opposite direction was derided as "going native," a reversion to savagery. Hybridity is also cooptable. In Latin America, national identity has often been officially articulated as hybrid and syncretic, through hypocritically integrationist ideologies that have glossed over subtle racial hegemonies. (p. 43)

George Lipsitz argues that the notion of hybridity—articulated by Gloria Anzaldúa and others as *mestizaje* sensibility—has often been misunderstood as meaning that one can simply construct whatever identity that one pleases. Lipsitz maintains, rightly in my view, that

some postmodern critics have wrongly understood Anzaldúa and other intellectuals from aggrieved racial communities to be saying that we can choose any identities we want. But the *mestizaje* consciousness articulated by Anzaldúa depends upon situated knowledge, on her identity as a woman, a worker, a Chicana, and (in Anzaldúa's case) a lesbian. Her concept entails appreciation of the things that people learn through struggle. Members of embattled communities have to "theorize" about identity everyday; they have to calculated how they are viewed by others and how they want to view themselves. (1994, 142)

For the postmodern *flâneur/flâneuse*, identity must take into account the recognition of one's site of enunciation, and this often means abandoning the ventriloquistic illusions of speaking from where one is not and directing ethnographers to examine their own local terrains of identity formation. Equally important is preventing local knowledges and standpoints from becoming conscripted into the service of the universal everywhere (i.e., the space of the white Anglo Protestant heterosexual male). Kamala Visweswaran, after Chow, notes the importance of the coalitional subject, that is, of using subject positions and positioning as a means of forging alliances with other subjects. This is, of course, an important means of dismantling the unified, autonomous, self-determining subject of modernity. It is also important to remember, notes Visweswaran, that subject positions often arise from a series of displacements—especially in the case of women of color. Visweswaran is here speaking about multiple-voiced subjectivity that is "lived in the resistance to competing notions for one's allegiance or self-identification" (1994, pp. 91–92). Of course, how the mobile constellation of race, class, gender, caste, and nation come to be articulated in relation to each other poses many questions since relations of power are so various and multiple.

The question that must be raised at this point is: How do we articulate new identities in the United States that meet the conditions of dignity and freedom? How do we include in the universal those groups placed below its threshold—African Americans, Latino/as, gays, and lesbians? In this regard, William Connolly calls for a "participation in the ambiguous politics of enactment" (1995, p. 185). For Connolly, inclusion in a universal right paradoxically creates a barrier to further attempts at pluralization because it leads to closure in the structure of universals. Each pluralizing move toward justice migrates from an abject other. The politics of enactment is a dialectical movement that works best retrospectively—because it exposes absences in the practice of justice. When, for instance, you invoke the universal, you must also invoke the injuries of those practices not considered to be part of the universal. We can never reach the point of justice without absence. There will always be a missing fullness. When democracy ceases to be restless it will have transmuted into fascism. According to Connolly, difference always exceeds universal justice. Justice, therefore, is always a form of constitutive uncertainty. We need, as Connolly puts it, a maintenance of dissonant interdependence between the practice of justice and the ethos of critical responsiveness. When a new group shifts the operational constellation of identities and difference, the practice of justice becomes fundamentally important. Justice and critical responsiveness must bind together in what Connolly refers to as "a relation of dissonant interdependence." However, the ethos of critical responsiveness is more fundamental, and therefore exceeds the codes of justice nourished by it since it does not rely on the universal ground invoked by conventional theorists of justice. The ethos of critical responsiveness means coming to terms with the relational and contingent aspects of one's identity and responding to the injuries that occur when universal justice is put into practice. It means, too, acknowledging the reciprocal contestability of competing discourses of justice.

Also important in the discussion of hybridity in the making of the postmodern *flâneur/flâneuse*, is to acknowledge M. M. Bakhtin's notion of dialogized hybridity. Bakhtin wrote that "only a dialogic participatory orientation takes another person's discourse seriously. . . . Only through such an inner dialogic orientation can my discourse find itself in intimate contact with someone else's discourse, and yet at the same time not fuse with it, not swallow it up, not dissolve in itself the other's power to mean" (cited in Schultz, 1990, p. 142). This sentiment on the part of Bakhtin echos the critical responsiveness spoken by Connolly and takes up the position that the categories used to explain one's meaning should not digest that meaning and make it one's own in the sense of dissolving such meaning or repressing such meaning or fusing such meaning with one's own expressed ideology. In this sense the *flâneur/flâneuse* "strove with extraordinary dedication and artistry to take as little from the world as possible, and to restore what he did take away as best he could" (Schultz, 1990, p. 143). It is true that when considering our individual voices in relation to the voices of others, there exists an inevitable gap between interlocutors precisely because no two speakers fully understands what the other means. Yet we still can form an agreement with the perspectives of others—and this enables cultures to exist as assemblages of heteroglot elements that form what Bahktin calls an "open unity" (cited in Schultz, 1990). Agreement is not the same thing as a fusion of perspectives since agreement is always dialogic, which means that it does not result in a monologic fusion of voices into an overarching impersonal truth. Discussions of hybridity must take into account the shifting of fixed boundaries and this cannot occur with abstract or rational forms of dialogue. Dialogized hybridity has more in common with the carnival in which boundaries are interrogated, challenged, and overcome, yet new and different boundaries come into being. Hybridity in the sense that I am using it, after Bakhtin, suggests the development of a hybrid, multilingual and multicultural consciousness in order to maintain a surplus of vision, a liberating perspective. This has little, if anything, to do with establishing a uniform or unitary cohesiveness of views but rather "a dialogic *concordance* of unmerged twos or multiples" (Bakhtin, cited in Schultz, 1990, p. 147).

A more measured and sustained exploration of dialogized hybridity would entail the further development of a theory of dialogue through an engagement with the works of Levinas, Buber, and Freire, a task that is precluded by the space allotted here. Suffice it to say that dialogized hybridity with respect to consciousness refers to a *critical consciousness*, a consciousness that rejects both the giddy whirl of mindless relativism and the inscrutable force of biological determinism or epistemological monomania. As Schultz warns, such hybridity renounces all monologic premises: "To resist in this way the temptation to epistemological monomania should make the critic, and the ethnographer, more sensitive to the ground of diversity and dialogue out of which social and linguistic change arises. Linguistic and cultural freedom is discerned in the way people reaccent and mix the generic forms they inherit from the past or borrow from contemporaries. We never begin with a clean slate, but this does not mean that we cannot attain, with effort, a significant degree of expressive liberty" (1994, p. 141).

Monday, August 14, 1995, East Berlin

We met Wolfgang Haug at Brecht's former house, now a restaurant. During dinner, my back rested on the wall of a cemetery. The graves of Brecht and Engels were nearby. Perhaps the good conversation—if not the pungent aroma of the sauerkraut—aroused their spirits. I'm not sure why I have spent so many days visiting cafés visited by famous figures in history. Perhaps to be closer to a time that was prior to its own simulacra, a real time, a time that was felt to be—dare I say it?—original. Is it possible to engage in *flânerie* today—or just a parody of it. Can criticism, and social analysis even exist in hyperreality? Has authenticity ever existed?

In Search of the Self-Reflexive Flâneur/Flâneuse

A theme emphasized throughout this paper is that *flânerie* constitutes the precondition of sociological reflection (Tester, 1994, p. 18) and that the current conditions of the postmodern popular (not to mention the popularity of postmodernity) necessitate that an effort be made at critical reflexivity. Sadly, it is all too often the case today that ethnographic agency either has been unable to recognize itself outside of its preconstituted and precarious unity in language or else it has lapsed into a narcissistic infatuation with uncovering the subjectivity of the *ethnographer-flâneur/flâneuse* herself. This concluding section argues that in order to transform itself into an emancipatory political practice, ethnography as postmodern *flânerie* needs to be conjugated with the contingency of historical struggle and in terms of establishing a post-hybrid dialogism.

Like his counterpart in the nineteenth century, the *flâneur* is "a man of pleasure," a man "who takes visual possession of the city" and a man who is the embodiment of the "male gaze" (Wilson, 1992, p. 98). Public space is still largely masculine, organized largely for the convenience and recreation of men. Within postmodern urban spaces, the sexual economy of the postmodern *flâneur* still privileges the male's freedom to look, to evaluate, and to possess (Wilson, 1992). The *flâneuse* of the nineteenth century (primarily writers and journalists) did not have the same opportunities as men to wander the streets. The postmodern *flâneuse* has considerably more opportunity to stroll than her earlier counterpart but cannot match the opportunities that patriarchal capitalism provides the male.

Anthony Giddens (1991) has written that the self-constitution of identity is a "reflexively organized endeavor" and that relations of race, class, and gender need to be understood in light of providing differential access to forms of self-actualization and empowerment. Postmodern society offers disillusionment and hope in reanimating the possibilities for narrative identities that will enable new forms of critical reflexivity. In a postmodern political economy, time and space become emptied out and more abstract since space is constructed not primarily to live in but to move through (Lash & Urry, 1994). This disembedding and increasing abstraction of time and space that have spread into international market economies privileges utility and functionalism at the expense of affectively charged symbols. We are witnessing postmodern sign value replacing modernist use value and exchange value, and deterritorializing almost completely the object of meaning. Time is reduced to a series of "disconnected and contingent events, as exemplified in the rock video and the advent of 'three minute culture'" (p. 16). Identity is easily mutated through video narratives and operates not through affectively charged symbols such as equality of opportunity and socialism but rather through postmodern "spectacular events of violence and cultural flamboyance" (16). Our culture is one of zero tolerance, not simply for drugs that cross the border but for human border-crossers known as immigrants. It is an era of the politics of purity. I have rehearsed this argument in detail elsewhere (most notably in McLaren, 1995), and my aim here is to briefly explore not only the disabling aspects of postmodern cultures but also some enabling aspects.

According to Lash and Urry (1994), the spatialization and semiotization of contemporary (disorganized or postorganized) political economies opens up new possibilities for critical self-reflexivity and social relations at the level of everyday life, both in cognitive and aesthetic-expressive dimensions. They are referring to novel forms of self-reflexivity that enable—for instance, in the case of the postmodern *flâneur/flâneuse*—different ways of organizing subjectivity and cultural identity in light of the changes in political institutions and social formations brought about by economic restructuring at a global level. Here, the postmodern *flâneur/flâneuse* as political agent can be traced to the nineteenth-century Réfractaires. The question uncoils: Can we use new ways of organizing subjectivity to create a self-reflexive social agent capable of dismantling capitalist exploitation and domination?

Thursday, August 17, 1995, Paris

Again, the dead live during this visit. The Cimetiére du Montparnasse became a day of meditating at the graves of Baudelaire—the father of the *flâneur*—Jean-Paul Sartre, Simone de Beauvoir. The conversation that I had with Baudelaire's ghost should have been taped. I could have sold it to *Hard Copy*. The day before we paid our respects at the graves of Truffaut and Nijinsky, in Montmartre. We tried for almost an hour to find Man Ray but he eluded us. And the day before that we had discovered the graves of Proust, Schindler, Simon Signoret, Yves Montand, Edith Piaf, Oscar Wilde, Chopin, Kardac, and yes, Jim Morrison at the Cimetière du Père Lachaise. Kardac's teachings are popular in Brasil, I've noticed. Today we visited the tombs of Rousseau and Voltaire at the Panthéon. Perhaps the greatest gnostic kinship we have with others is the kinship of the grave. We will all be brothers and sisters there. I read today that the ailing former French president, Mitterand, has just purchased his cemetery plot. Nowhere near Sartre's and Beauvoir's. I am not surprised.

The question can now be raised: If the postmodern *flâneur/flâneuse* as ethnographic agent has assumed a narrative identity built upon cultural hybridity in a world undergoing a process of structural hybridity on a global basis, then in what sense does this call for a new kind of reflexivity with respect to both global and local contexts and concerns? What would such a self-reflexivity look like as a form of dialogized ethnographic *flânerie*? To answer such questions we will need to visit some of the recent perspectives of Pierre Bourdieu.

Thursday, August 17, 1995, Paris

Luckily I chose the Dali Museum over the Arc de Triomphe for Thursday's excursion, saving us the minor embarrassment of being killed by a terrorist bomb that exploded today. We went to the bomb site and I found a piece of metal that was perhaps part of the bomb. Since the bomb was in an empty trash can and trash cans are everywhere in Paris, it made for nervous *flânerie*. Fear motivates your faculties of observation. Furtive glances take on new meaning. After listening to the French news reports, which demonized Muslims, I should be taking notice of who might be

Algerian. I should become uncomfortable around Arab men in dark glasses and with chin stubble. How has the culture of imperialism been written on me, in me, through me?

Flânerie as Political Praxis

A crucial question that emerges in relation to the development of the postmodern *flâneur/flâneuse* (the prototype of the critical ethnographer) has to do with the question of reflexivity as sociological praxis. For instance, in their engagement with the oppressed and in their connection to certain populist exhaltations of popular culture, do postmodern *flâneurs* simply reproduce the dominated in their subordination and the dominant in their relations of superordination, as they confuse acts of resistance with a playful inversion of social hierarchies—acts that actually reconfirm such hierarchies at the most basic level? Following our discussion of the *flâneur/flâneuse* as ethnographic agent, as a sociologist *par excellence*, what does it mean to take part in self-reflexive praxis? Over the previous decade, the practice of self-reflexivity has become *de rigeur* in the salons of postmodern anthropology. Yet I would argue, along with Bourdieu, that the fashionable forms of ethnographic apostasy practiced among the avant-garde bourgeoisie that have developed out of postmodern interpretive skepticism, textual reflexiveness, and (neoformalist) hermeneutic cultural interpretation based on *différance*, or out of (an often frivolous) infatuation with the unconscious of the researcher (as in the confessional diaries popularized by postmodern ethnographers) need to be reconsidered in light of their lack of potential for sociological transformation. According to Bourdieu, critical reflexivity directs itself to the epistemological unconscious of sociological practice—to the "unthought categories of thought" in relation to the organizational and cognitive structure of the discipline. Further, it gestures towards the study of the very act of construction of the object—that is, the work of the objectivation of the objectivating subject (Wacquant, cited in Bourdieu & Wacquant, 1992, p. 41). This means distinguishing between anthropological practice informed by abstract logic and that informed by practical logic. Wacquant states it thus:

> Sociological reflexivity instantly raises hackles because it represents a frontal attack on the sacred sense of individuality that is so dear to all of us Westerners, and particularly on the charismatic self conception of intellectuals who like to think of themselves as undetermined, "free-floating," and endowed with a form of symbolic grace. For Bourdieu, reflexivity is precisely what enables us

to escape such delusions by uncovering the social at the heart of the individual, the impersonal beneath the intimate, the universal buried deep within the most particular. (Bourdieu & Wacquant, 1992, p. 44)

Mainstream sociology, for the most part, is impertinent to this form of sociological reflexivity. Bourdieu is able to uncoil a series of concerns that have been compressed by the weight of everyday sociological routine. What might seem among sociologists as a narcissistic concern with the personal narrative of the ethnographer (e.g., biographical narrative, personal intellectual history) can be transformed, in Bourdieu's view, into a form of epistemic reflexivity. I sign my agreement with Wacquant when he writes:

Far from encouraging narcissism and solipsism, epistemic reflexivity invites intellectuals to recognize and to work to neutralize the specific determinisms to which their innermost thoughts are subjected and it informs a conception of the craft of research designed to strengthen its epistemological moorings. (Bourdieu & Wacquant, 1992, p. 46)

Epistemic reflexivity as articulated by Bourdieu fashions itself as an approach that is able to *"safeguard the institutional bases for rational thought"* (Bourdieu & Wacquant, p. 48), grounding rationality in history and producing a self-reflexive rational subject. Finally, epistemic reflexivity attempts to overcome the nihilistic relativism of deconstruction (e.g., Derrida) and the scientistic absolutism of modernist rationalism (e.g., Habermas). According to Wacquant, historical rationalism enables Bourdieu to reconcile deconstruction with universality and reason with relativity by anchoring sociological practice in the historically constructed structures of the scientific field. In doing so, Bourdieu affirms the possibility of scientific truth yet argues against the transcendentalist illusion of transhistoric structures of consciousness or language. He affirms the contingency of social categories and their political embeddedness. Yet he still believes that, in some cases, universally valid truths still hold and this is evident in his examination of the historical conditions of possibility for the deconstructive enterprise itself. In Bourdieu's view, the final goal of epistemic reflexivity is to "denaturalize and defatalize the social world; that is, to destroy the myths that cloak the exercise of power and the perpetuation of domination" (Bourdieu & Wacquant, p. 50).

The postmodern *flâneur/flâneuse* rejects the strong claim of relativism that beliefs held within different cultures are completely incommensurable since, if we accept this to be the case, we would not even possess the background of consensus necessary to recognize cultural difference. The problem resides with the epistemic privilege given to the West in which history enjoys ethnic privilege: the superiority of European people and culture (Chatterjee, 1986). Consequently, the post-modern *flâneur/flâneuse* must question the moral and political consequences of representing social life within post-Enlightenment theories of progress. This calls for a certain type of epistemic reflexivity that I characterize as postmodern Marxist reflexivity.

Kamala Visweswaran (1994) makes a distinction between deconstructive ethnography and reflexive ethnography that I find particulalry instructive. According to Visweswaran, reflexive ethnography, like normative ethnography, rests on the "declarative mode" of imparting knowledge to a reader whose identity is anchored in a shared discourse. Deconstructive ethnography, in contrast, enacts the interrogative mode through constant deferral or a refusal to explain or interpret. Within deconstructive ethnography, the identity of the reader with a unified subject of enunciation is discouraged. Whereas reflexive ethnography argues that the ethnographer is not separate from the object of investigation, the ethnographer is still viewed as a unified subject of knowledge that can make hermeneutic efforts to establish identification between the observer and the observed. Deconstructive ethnography, in contrast, often disrupts such identification in favor of articulating a fractured, destabalized, multiply positioned subjectivity. Whereas reflexive anthropology questions its authority, deconstructive anthropology forfeits its authority. Both forms of anthropological practice are useful in developing a critical sociological self-reflexivity. In fact, both forms of ethnographic critique have been used to uncover the deep strata of western cultures of schooling and expose the predicates which make possible certain species of Eurocentrism (McLaren, 1993).

Friday, August 18, 1995, Paris

There's a bench not far from the Louvre and it seems like a good time to get started on *In the Realm of Diamond Queen*. But I can't help feeling discomfort at the thought of how all Parisian museums make me think of last month's visit to the Getty Museum after an uncommonly lousy fish dinner in Malibu. I feel vulgarized, as though L.A. is forcing me to stain the purified traces of History's most aesthetic moments. Is it possible to enjoy historical Paris once you've been to the Getty Museum?

Self-reflexivity as a political project requires a certain degree of essentialist strategy. I identify my own *flânerie* as essentialist—as that of a Marxist social theorist, cultural critic, and critical ethnographic theorist—if by the term "essentialist" I am able to critically reenvision my conception of ethnographic agency, while living a posthybrid identity (posthybridity here refers to hybrid consciousness inflected towards a postnational critical reflexivity). For instance, I consider my own understanding of what constitutes the political identity of a subject in relation to ethnographic practice to be different from a non-Marxist reading of the subject. I am an essentialist in the sense that I approach the narrativity of ethnographic *flânerie* and agency in specific ways: Through the historically diverse traditions of Marxist theory and their political, critical, and textual practices; through the social and cultural specificity of Marxist forms of address; and, most importantly, through attempting to live in the world as a Marxist.

Further, I take as axiomatic that all experiences of the *flâneur/flâneuse* be historicized, and be treated as gendered and racialized practices. From a Marxist standpoint, the critical ethnographer as *flâneur/flâneuse* must seek to do more than de-fetishize, displace, and unsettle oppressive reading and writing practices by challenging their frameworks and presuppositions in terms of their links to patriarchal practices and capitalist social relations. Rather, the critically self-reflexive *flâneur/flâneuse* needs to transform the very social relations and cultural and institutional practices out of which oppressive reading and writing practices (ideologies) develop. The critically self-reflexive *flâneur/flâneuse* is not a subject position that is easily assumed since it is an emergent *clustering* of positions, and as such is untotalizable; it is not grounded in a fixed and intractable notion of difference but in a different way of provisionally "fixing" acts of reading and writing the world so that they both free the object of analysis from the tyranny of fixed, unassailable categories and reenvision subjectivity itself as a permanently unclosed, always partial, narrative engagement with text and context, a narrative engagement whose conditions of possibility are always *mediated*, for instance, by relations of class, gender, sexuality, and ethnicity, and whose effects are always multiple and are played out in numerous and often contradictory ways. This mandates a social theory that is attentive to both a political economy and a cultural politics. Consider Michael Keith's recent remarks in his discussion of the sociology of the street:

> The spaces of the street are, in other words and a familiar language, contradictory. And a language of contradiction usefully returns us to the agenda of political economy, not in search of

Hegelian resolution but for bearings. Paul Gilroy has recently argued forcefully "that the problem with the cultural left" is that they have never been cultural enough. It is worth echoing this with the comment that cultural politics without political economy will be equally rudderless. (1995, p. 309)

What would some of the guiding conceptions of the postmodern Marxist *flâneur/flâneuse* look like? Recently, Jack Amariglio and David Ruccio (1994) have articulated some characteristics of what they describe as "postmodern Marxism" that I believe are worth summarizing as a means of locating the *flâneur/flâneuse* in an emergent tradition of self-reflexivity that combines Marxian imperatives with new postmodern insights. According to Amarglio and Ruccio, postmodern Marxian assumptions include, among others, the following: Needs are not exogenous and do not exist prior to and independent of the social context in which such needs are expressed; all patterns of capitalist consumption involve differentiation within and across social groups; needs are only partly determined by markets or planning and are also determined by subjectiveness informed by race, class, ethnic and gender relations; disorder, decentering, and uncertainty constitute key aspects of Marxian economic discourse, replacing the modernist Marxian emphasis on economic laws of motion; the concepts of historical conjuncture and contingency as well as that of overdetermination (à la Althusser) help to explain economic value as something that depends on a concatenation of economic and noneconomic forces; economic processes are not essences of laws that causally determine their effects; there exists "no inexorable or preordained trajectory for the capitalist economy" (1994, p. 28); and in addition to eliminating the preordained historical subject, postmodern Marxism rejects any teleological historical process and asserts that there is "no necessary end to any process of change and/or transition" (1994, p. 28). Further, postmodern Marxists assert that no special class has been granted a privileged status in constructing the plot of history, that the subject is always open, and that forms of subjectivity—despite being overdetermined—never coalesce or become unified. Knowledge that may be categorized as Marxist eschews "the premises and logical consequences of classical—empiricist and rationalist—epistemology" (1994 , p. 30).

Friday, September 29, 1995, Halle, East Germany

Ever since they closed down the chemical plant here in Halle, unemployment has been at a record high. My presentations to the educators are over, and now I've hit the mean streets of Halle with my comrade, Mike Cole, a working-class Marxist professor from Brighton, England. Mike just took me to task in an article he co-wrote for the *British Journal of Sociology of Education* (Cole & Hill, 1995). He thinks I've given up my Marxist roots. We drank beer in the pubs, and he kept on questioning my Marxist credentials. I don't know what I have to do short of tattooing a hammer and sickle on my forehead to get him to shift the topic. My position—that you can still be a Marxist and incorporate ideas from poststructuralism—doesn't sit well with him. We disagreed but remained comrades. We asked dozens of pubcrawlers what they thought of the FGR in comparison to the former GDR. Nearly everybody wanted the old GDR back since at the very least they had steady jobs in those days. While people are now permitted to travel outside of Germany, who could afford to do it? And according to the residents of Halle to whom we spoke, the West Germans almost seemed to wish that the wall would go back up. We ended up jumping in a cab with a bunch of blokes at a pub, thinking we were going to another seedy pub, and found ourselves at a brothel. The beer was good, and Mike and I decided to interview some of the prostitutes about working conditions in the FDR. It was getting late, and the young men who came into the bar at about 4 a.m. looked pretty mean and angry in their short cropped hair and black boots. Since we both are foul-mouthed louts, I encouraged Mike to leave with me before we made any unfriendly comments to the new arrivals. As we got up to leave, Mike slipped on a patch of water on the cement floor, and went crashing through a table, splitting open his head. The brothel keeper and bartender, a man no more than three-and-a-half feet tall, helped me drag Mike—whose head was pulsing arches of blood—to a taxi. The cab driver refused to take Mike in his car because of the blood squirting (rather impressively, I thought) from between Mike's eyes. I rushed into the brothel and, since there were no towels available, I was given some sanitary napkins from two women and used them to stem the bleeding; another cab driver found my efforts acceptable and I poured Mike into the back seat, where I kept putting pressure on his head. We made it back to the hotel. The next day Mike took the train to Prague. I tried to read *In the Realm of the Diamond Queen* again but just couldn't concentrate on anything. The cold wind and dampness were too depressing.

If all knowledge is discursive and if all events are overdetermined then can we ever arrive at the truth of an idea? As postmodern Marxist *flâneurs/flâneuses* of urban spaces and places, is the best that we can do merely to accept the incommensurability of discourses and reject the search for some "interdiscursive form" that can help us adjudicate among the wild plurality of discourses that we find in cosmopolitan settings? Must we accept the fact that all truths are contingent and that we can judge based only upon the social effects of such truths? To the extent that the reading practices of the postmodern Marxist *flâneur/flâneuse* are embedded in webs and networks of interrelated social practices can we hope for critical discourses that can create alternative ways of world-making, shaping history as they are shaped by history? In response to such questions, I am arguing for a *theoria* of praxis, that is, purposeful practice and action guided by critical reflection and a commitment to revolutionary praxis. What is important to emphasize is that the critical rationality that guides our praxis as critical ethnographers of contemporary social texts and that assists us in adjudicating the narratives of those who have been marginalized and excluded must reject the historical logic in which their exclusion and marginality is inevitable. This is certainly in keeping with Bourdieu's emphasis on epistemic reflexivity and commitment to a rational, scientific approach to truth rather than to revealing a transcendental or transhistorical structure of consciousness. It is in this light that the *flâneuse* of contemporary cosmopolitan spaces and places can avoid fusing with the object of the gaze and resist the commodification of both her senses and her commonsense.

Friday, December 29, 1995, East Los Angeles

Here in Baby Doe's in East L.A. I catch myself thinking about the role of the church. Earlier I stopped by a Herbería on Cesar Chavez Ave. to buy a figure of Saint Simon of Guatemala and Jesús Malverde. I like the way the saints are syncretized to produce particular indigenous inflections of Santería. Jesús Malverde is a saint of the *vato locos*. He protects *vato locos* from the law and I've been told that here in East L.A. criminals pray to him for protection from the LAPD. I think this vato loco saint could easily be the patron of all the *gabachos* in Pete Wilson's government and is definitely on the altar of Newt Gingrich's office. How else can you explain why Newt is still pontificating on Capitol Hill and making *Time* magazine's "Man of the Year" instead of resting behind bars where he belongs. Suddenly the strobe lights join the car lights outside in a dance on the window across from where I am sitting. Through the window I notice that the highways are filled with streams of cars and my mind follows them off the ramps and into the streets where they disappear into the night sky.

Sunday, January 7, 1996, West Hollywood

Diana Ross looks good. So does RuPaul. So do the West Hollywood Cheerleaders and so do the Dykes on Bikes. I'm watching them make a video just a few minutes away from my place, near the clubs on Santa Monica Ave. Something about the whole scene is weird and wonderful. The evening is in high gear. Tonight I'm going to start *In the Realm of the Diamond Queen*.

Friday, January 26, 1996, Juarez, Mexico

Another border town. As I look through my guero eyes, the bridge from Pasiente is crowded with lean looking cars and Wheel of Fortune dreams. My Mexicano colleague remarks that the *pollero* on the side of the road with the Dallas Cowboys hat is trying to figure a new angle on getting a family past the guards and into El Paso. The drug dogs sniff around our jeep. There's a long wait into the other zone.

I love to work the border. To walk past the bars, restaurants, and vatos on their cellular phones, the *policia* pulling a *movida chueca*, the parking generals in 1950s New York cab driver hats, the near brushes with *vatos locos* who are *buscando putazos*, the next day *cruda*, and eating *menudo* at Sanborns in the morning. As I look around I see the invisible hands of Euro-American colonization, I see the USA sneezing and this town getting pneumonia. I see the results of gringo economic injustice. From this place you can look north and stare right into the sphincter of Gringolandia. Met with some professors from Mexico City and shared some ideas about qualitative research. Fell asleep in a bar, dreaming of Cabbagetown, Toronto, and the smell of fish and poultry at Kensington Market. When I awoke, I saw a dog in the back alley and wondered if it could lick my conscience clean. Maybe tonight I'll start to read *In the Realm of the Diamond Queen*. Or maybe I'll just walk the streets instead.

Thursday, May 9, 1996, Florianopolis, Brasil

Each time I give a speech here I realize how partial my knowledge is compared to the students or the workers. Today during my visit with Father Wilson, I was reminded of the terrible beauty among the people in the *favela*. Father Wilson looks the same, perhaps thinner. He made me a wonderful fish stew. The tires of his car had recently been slashed, the windows broken. The note on the broken windshield read: You see what we have done to your car. We can do this to you. Father Wilson is not popular with the *favela*'s drug dealers. During my talk at the university, I wondered how culpable North American educators were in depicting marginal outsiders of Latin America as people devoid of history. What is the role of the university educator? Words are revolutionary tools when they critique systems of thought and not merely other words. It is true that words do not take to the streets, but when used to criticize and transcend structures of domination they can serve as vehicles of liberating praxis.

Friday, May 10, 1996, Rio de Janeiro

The steps of Candelaria are quiet. There are no flowers, candles or monuments to the street children massacred by the police for the crime of being poor and destitute. I was careful not to disturb the Macumba offerings on the street corners of Copacabana near my hotel. There was an enormous chandelier dominating the room where I lectured. In the evening I bought some plaster figures of some Orixás at a shop that keeps local Umbanda practitioners well supplied.

Monday, May 13, 1996, Rio de Janeiro

Closing comments.
Dear brother and sister educators. We are living at a time of intense upheaval. The trajectory of international capital that begins in the cunning boardrooms of national conglomerates and ends in the suffering faces of the inhabitants of places such as Rocinha, appears to be unassailable and invincible. And yet I believe that the fragile vibrations of hope that I see in the eyes of the dispossessed will one day bring forward victory's gaze. I say this knowing full well that the conditions of emergence of victory are shifting perilously and that unions and strikes and revolutions are fast being reinvented as historical fictions. Yet I say to you that in our shackled voices we will yet find new ways to struggle. If we

remain silent we shall surely perish and if we rise up as a collective spirit to challenge injustice we shall perish still. Yet it is better to perish alongside one's *compañeros y compañeras* than to perish standing alone in cynical solidarity and mutated longing with the new barons of postindustrialism who offer nothing to the people but empty dreams and fleeting intimations of plenitude. So, brothers and sisters, let us rise up to meet our destiny, our arms locked together and our fists raised defiantly. If the contours of such an invocation seem rendered in nostalgia, then I stand willingly accused. I would rather the nostalgia of modernist hope than the false fulfillment of contemporary society.

Tuesday, May 14, 1996, Rio de Janeiro

I was removed from the rest of the line at the airport terminal and taken to a private room to be searched by airport security. I thought it might be a strip search but they just checked under my clothes and emptied my pockets. A minor indignity when compared to the daily lives of the people in the *favelas*. During the flight to São Paulo I wondered about many things. What kinds of coordination among the left will be necessary to put an end to the deceit of capital? Is this thought perhaps even a ruse of capital itself?

Friday, June 7, 1996, South Central Los Angeles

The acoustics under the freeway made the gunshot blast deafening. Carlos, my student, grimaced with a sharp pain in his left ear as he slammed on the brakes. Juan, another of my students and a former marine, quickly located the smoke through his window on the passenger side and told Carlos to hit the gas pedal. I was crouched in the back seat. With the smell of gunpowder in the air we peeled out of there. South Central can occasionally be unkind to motorists. We were driving back to East L.A. after a failed attempt to get a ticket for the De La Hoya versus Chavez fight for the electrician who does some work for Carlos. At Carlos's house we switched from the car to Carlos's van and took about ten of Carlos's relatives and friends with us to the fight. I spent the evening cheering with a Mexican flag in one hand. It was a great evening until we got back to the van and noticed that half of the bumper had been peeled back from the body. On the way back to East L.A. I wondered what the city might have been like in better times, for instance, when the lowriders used to cruise Whittier Boulevard on Saturday nights in their chrome-lined, chop-topped *ramflas*, resplendent with suicide doors, micro-flake paint jobs, hydraulic lifts and with titanium plates under their frames. In those days when car clubs like the Imperials, Sons of Soul and the Dukes would form caravans along the streets with "Angel Baby" by Rosie and the Originals wafting from the speakers of their '57 Chevys. Should I be romanticizing a past that wasn't mine to experience? I know I'm in trouble when that happens. How has the Anglocentric dream factory of Hollywood shaped the direction of my desiring? How is my own formation within gabacho myths of self/other fatalizing and naturalizing forms of Otherness? At Carlos's house we feast on tacos and listen to the die-hard Chavez fans whine.

Tuesday, June 11, 1996, West Hollywood

Today the *Los Angeles Times* carried a front-page photograph of Boris Yeltsin doing a Russian version of the "jerk" on a stage with two females in mini-skirts during a rock concert in Rostov. Less prominently positioned on the page was a story about the fire-bombings of southern African-American churches. If these had been churches populated by whites, the National Guard would have been called out months ago. Tomorrow I leave for Argentina, having been invited to give a series of talks to coincide with Che's birthday.

Is it possible that a scrap of memory, a figural trace, or fading afterimage can reinvent itself as the perverse totality of theory? Ethnographers would do well to remain suspicious of their professional loyalties in as much as their academic identifications foreclose a stepping out of those systematic dimensions that preclude them from analyzing the broader narratives of imperialism and from sharing the collective responsibility to understand the multiple spaces that map us tactically and strategically as agents of change. Critical ethnographers recognize the arrogance of speaking for others, and also the presumptuousness that feeds the notion that men and women can speak for themselves. Knowledge is never transparent to the speaking subject so we can never be sure who is really served by our words, or whom we nourish and fortify with our criticisms. We begin speaking for ourselves only when we step outside of ourselves—only by becoming other. It is in recognizing ourselves in the suffering of others that we become ourselves.

Note

An expanded version of this paper will appear in Peter McLaren, *Revolutionary multiculturalism: Pedagogies of dissent for the new millenium* (Boulder, CO: Westview Press). Thanks to Lauren Langman for his insights on the *flâneur*.

References

Amariglio, J., and Ruccio, D. F. (1994). Postmodernism, Marxism, and the critique of modern economic thought. *Rethinking Marxism, 7*(3), 7–35.

Baudrillard, J. (1990). *Fatal strategies.* New York: Semiotext(e).

Bauman, Z. (1994). Desert spectacular. In K. Tester (Ed.), *The flâneur* (pp. 138–157). London and New York: Routledge.

———. (1995). Searching for a centre that holds. In M. Featherstone, S. Lash, & R. Robertson (Eds.), *Global modernities* (pp. 140–154). London: SAGE.

Benjamin, W. (1983). *Charles Baudelaire: A lyric poet in the era of high capitalism,* trans. H. Zohn. London: Verso.

Bourdieu, P. (1988). *Homo academicus.* Cambridge: Polity Press; Stanford: Stanford University Press.

Bourdieu, P., & Wacquant, L. (1992). *An invitation to reflexive sociology.* Chicago: University of Chicago Press.

Chattergee, P. (1986). *Nationalist thought and the colonial world.* Minneapolis: University of Minnesota Press.

Cole, M., & Hill, D. (1995). Games of despair and rhetorics of resistance: Postmodernism, education, and reaction. *British Journal of Sociology of Education, 16*(2), 165–182.

Eagleton, T. (1981). *Walter Benjamin: Or towards a revolutionary criticism.* London and New York: Verso.

Connolly, W. E. (1995). *The ethos of pluralization.* Minneapolis: University of Minnesota Press.

Ferguson, P. P. (1994). The *flâneur* on and off the streets of Paris. In K. Tester (Ed.), *The flâneur* (22–42). London and New York: Routledge.

Frisby, D. (1994). The flâneur in social theory. In K. Tester (Ed.), *The flâneur* (pp. 81–110). London and New York: Routledge.

Giddens, A. (1991). *Modernity and self-identity*. Cambridge: Polity Press.

Jessop, B. (1996). Interpetive sociology and the dialectic of structure and agency. *Theory, culture, and society 13*(1), pp. 119–128.

John, M. (1989). Postcolonial feminisms in the Western intellectual field: Anthropologists and native informants.

Guevara, C. (1995). *The motocycle diaries: A journey around South America* (Ann Wright, Trans.). London and New York: Verso.

Kanpol, B., & McLaren, P. (1995). *Critical multiculturalism*. Westport, CT: Greenwood Press.

Keith, M. (1995). Shouts of the street: Identify and the spaces of authenticity. *Social Identities, 1*(2), 297–315.

Kincheloe, J. (1993). *Toward a critical politics of teacher thinking*. Westport, CT: Bergin & Garvey.

Lash, S., & Urry, J. (1995). *Economics of signs and space*. London: SAGE.

Lipsitz, G. (1994). The bands of tomorrow are here today: The proud, progressive, and postmodern sounds of Las Tres and Goddess 13. In S. Loza (Ed.), *Musical aesthetics and multiculturalism in Los Angeles*. Selected Reports in Ethnomusicaology, vol. X. Department of Ethnomusicology and Systematic Musicology, University of California, Los Angeles (pp. 139–147).

McLaren, P. (1993). *Schooling as a ritual performance: Towards a political economy of educational symbols and gestures*. London and New York: Routledge.

————— . (1995). *Critical pedagogy and predatory culture*. London and New York: Routledge.

Morawski, S. (1994). The hopeless game of flânerie. In K. Tester, (Ed.), *The flâneur* (pp. 181–197). London and New York: Routledge.

Pieterse, J. N. (1995). Globalization as hybridization. In M. Featherstone, S. Lash, & R. Robertson (Eds.), *Global modernities* (pp. 45–68). London: SAGE.

Schultz, E. A. (1990). *Dialogue at the margins: Whorf, Bakhtin and linguistic relativity*. Madison: University of Wisconsin Press.

Shields, R. (1994). Fancy footwork: Walter Benjamin's notes on *flânerie*. In K. Tester (Ed.), *The flâneur* (61–80). London and New York: Routledge.

Shohat, E., & Stam, R. (1994). *Unthinking Eurocentrism: Multiculturalism and the media*. New York and London: Routledge.

Tester, K. (1994). Introduction. In K. (Ed.), *The flâneur* (pp. 1–21). New York: Routledge.

Tsing, A. L. (1993). *In the realm of the diamond queen.* Princeton, NJ: Princeton University Press.

Valle, V., & Torres, R. D. (1995). "The idea of *mestizaje* and the 'race' problematic: Racialized media discourse in a post-Fordist landscape." In Antonia Darder (Ed.), *Culture and difference: Critical perspectives on the bicultural experience in the United States* (pp. 139–153). Westport, CT: Bergin and Garvey.

Visweswaran, K. (1994). *Fictions of feminist ethnography.* Minneapolis: University of Minnesota Press.

Wilson, E. (1992). The invisible flâneur. *New Left Review, 191,* 90–111.

8

PERFORMANCE TEXTS

NORMAN K. DENZIN

Borrowing from Turner (1986b), Turner and Turner (1982), Conquergood (1991), and extending Trinh (1991), my topic is performing ethnography, the performance text. I examine ethnographic and cultural texts turned into poems, scripts, short stories, dramas that are read, and performed before audiences (see Mienczakowski, 1995, 1992; Mienczakowski & Morgan, 1993; Paget, 1993, pp. 24–25; Loseke, 1995; Richardson, 1995; Conquergood, 1992; Becker, McCall, & Morris, 1989; McCall & Becker, 1990; Hilbert, 1990; Kapferer, 1986; Schechner, 1986; V. Turner, 1986a, b; Bruner, 1986; Bochner, 1994; Bauman, 1986; Tedlock, 1983). Performed texts have narrators, drama, action, shifting points of view. Performance texts make experience, concrete, anchoring it in the here and now (Paget, 1993, p. 40). They are dramaturgical, they create spaces for the merger of multiple voices and experiences (Conquergood, 1985a, p. 10).

The performance text is a genre within ethnography, what Paget calls ethnoperformance (1993, p. 42), Mienczakowski (1994) labels ethnodrama, and Turner and Turner (1982, p. 40) term performance and reflexive anthropology, the rendering "of ethnography in a kind of instructional theater" (1982, p. 41).[1] I connect this textual form to the narrative turn in the human disciplines (Bochner, 1994, p. 30; Rorty, 1980), the move that sees culture as a performance, as theater (Burke, 1989; Goffman, 1959; Geertz, 1973, 1995; Bruner, 1984). Performance texts are messy, they exist in what Conquergood calls "the borderlands" (1992, p. 80), the spaces where rhetoric, performance, ethnography and cultural studies come together (Conquergood, 1992, p. 80).

I will critically read this genre, offering a vocabulary of performance text terms, while tracing the genre's genealogy in sociology and anthropology, locating it within the field of performance studies (Strine, Long, & Hopkins, 1990). I will give special attention to performance science texts (Becker, McCall, & Morris, 1989; McCall & Becker, 1990), while discussing the main strengths and weaknesses of other contemporary performance approaches. Guidelines for constructing these texts will be addressed.

I will privilege those performance texts that focus on the co-construction and co-audience performance of critical, improvised "mystories" (Ulmer, 1989, p. 209). Mystories are reflexive, critical, multimedia tales and tellings. They begin with the writer's biography and body, epiphanic moments, turning-point experiences, times of personal trouble and turmoil, Turner's (1986b, pp. 34–35) liminal experiences.[2] Performed mystories move from epiphanic moments to those larger cultural and scientific texts that purport to interpret and make sense of such personal experience, public explanations of private troubles (Mills, 1959). When performed, mystories critique these larger systems of personal, popular and expert knowledge (Ulmer, 1989, pp. 209–211). I conclude with a discussion of politics and ethics and their place in a performative cultural studies.

Interpretive Assumptions

The following assumptions and arguments organize my readings of this textual form. In the beginning is the field, arenas of ongoing dramatic experience entered by the fieldworker. This arena may be known and already familiar, or it may be foreign and strange. The interpretive ethnographer enters those strange and familiar situations which connect critical biographical experiences (epiphanies) with culture, history, and social structure. He or she seeks out those narratives and stories people tell one another as they attempt to make sense of the epiphanies, or existential turning-point moments, in their lives.

The postmodern world stages existential crises. Following Victor Turner (1986b, p. 34) the ethnographer gravitates to these narratively structured, liminal, existential spaces in the culture. In these dramaturgical sites people take sides, forcing, threatening, inducing, seducing, cajoling, nudging, loving, living, abusing, and killing one another (see Turner, 1986b, p. 34). In these sites ongoing social dramas occur. These dramas have a temporal or chronological order (Turner, 1986b, p. 35), multiple beginnings, middles and ends. They are also storied events, narratives which rearrange chronology into multiple, and differing, forms of meaningful experience (Turner, 1986b, p. 35). The storied nature of these experiences continually raises the following questions: "Whose story is being told (and made) here? Who is doing the telling? Who has the authority to make their telling stick?" (Smith, 1990a). As soon as a chronological event is told in the form of a story it enters a text-mediated system of discourse where larger issues of power and control come into play (Smith, 1990a). In this text-mediated system new tellings occur. The interpretations of original experience are now fitted to this larger interpretive structure (Smith, 1990b).

This larger, text-based interpretive system reproduces the cultural logics of Western naturalism. This is realism writ large, the attempt to accurately reproduce a real, external world of objects, to accurately map and represent that world with a high degree of verisimilitude. But this is a socially constructed world, with multiple points of view operating. Kurosawa's (1950) *Rashomon*'s effects are always present. This is the space entered by the performance text, for it attempts to expose and challenge these larger systems of realistic interpretation and meaning.

Performance ethnography enters a postmodern culture "with nearly invisible boundaries separating theatre performance from dance, music, film, television, video, and the various performance art 'disciplines'" (Birringer, 1993, p. 182). This means the performance text is situated in a complex system of discourse, where traditional, and avant-garde meanings of theatre, film, video, ethnography, performance, text, and audience all circulate and inform one another. Aesthetic theories (naturalism, realism, modernism, postmodernism) collide with positivist, postpositivist, and poststructural epistemologies, and hypertexts interact with traditional print and performance forms of representation.

The reflexive performance text must contest the pull of traditional "realist" theater, "method" acting, (and ethnography) wherein performers, performances and texts solely, or primarily reenact and recreate a "recognizable verisimilitude of setting, character and dialogue" (Cohn, 1988, p. 815), where dramatic action reproduces a linear sequence, a "mimetic representation of cause and effect" (Birringer, 1993, p. 196). A postmodern performance aesthetic, and evocative epistemology must be developed, an aesthetic that goes beyond "the already-seen and already-heard" (Birringer, 1993, p. 186). This aesthetic will venture into those undefined, taboo spaces where the unpresentable in the culture is felt and made visible, seeking a performance sublime for postmodernism (Birringer, 1993, p. 197).

This means there will be a continual rediscovery of the body; that is the performance text always works outward from the body. The bodies theatrical presence is "a site and pretext for . . . debates about representation and gender, about history and postmodern culture, and about theory and its vanishing point or referent" (Birringer, 1993, p. 203; also

Conquergood, 1991, p. 180). The postmodern body, and the discourses that surround it, must be presented, from the AIDS body, to the over-sized, and the undersized anorexic body, to the pornographic, or the sporting body, to Haraway's (1985) cyborg, and the bombed, mutilated bodies of little children. Accordingly, performance texts should be dia-logical, critical of the structures of experience they enact (see Conquergood, 1985, p. 4). They should not be mere commodified exten-sions of a theater (and ethnography) that reproduces the ideological and technological requirements of late-capitalist social realism and hyperrealism (Birringer, 1993, p. 175).

These texts-as-performances will challenge the meanings of lived experience as simulated performance. They will interrogate the con-cepts of specularity, reconceptualizing the framing features which define the visual apparatus of the stage, including sound and lighting. Traditional understandings of costume, directors, actors, performers, the spectator, spectatorship and the audience, voyeurism, and perfor-mance space will also be questioned, as will conventional notions of the theatre and what goes on in a performance, in a night at the opera, to invoke the Marx Brother's film (see Birringer, 1993, p. 186)

The performance text enters that world opened by the standpoint episte-mologies. These works potentially answer to Trinh's call for the produc-tion of texts that seek the truth of life's fictions where experiences are evoked, not explained (1991, p. 162). As dramatic theater, with connec-tions back to Brecht (Epic Theater) and Artaud (Theater of Cruelty) they turn tales of suffering, loss, pain, and victory into evocative perfor-mances that have the ability to move audiences to reflective, critical action, not just emotional catharsis (see Coger & White, 1973, pp. 29–31; Maclay, 1971, pp. 37–38).

In the moment of performance, these texts have the potential of overcoming the biases of an ocular, visual epistemology. They can undo the voyeuristic, gazing eye of the ethnographer, bringing audiences and performers into a jointly felt and shared field of experience. These works also unsettle the writer's place in the text, freeing the text and the writer to become interactional productions. The performance text is the single, most powerful way for ethnography to recover yet interrogate the meanings of lived experience. The performed text is a lived experience, and this in two senses. The performance doubles back on the experi-ences previously represented in the ethnographer's text. It then re-pre-sents those experiences as embodied performance to and with the audi-ence. It thus privileges experience, the evocative moment when another's experiences come alive for the self. But there are many ways to present lived experience. If performance is interpretation, then performance texts have the ability to criticize and deconstruct taken-for-granted understandings concerning how lived experience is to be represented.

As ethnographic stagings, performances are always "enmeshed in moral matters . . . [they] enact a moral stance (Conquergood, 1985a, pp. 2, 4), asking the audience to take a stand on the performance and its meanings. In these productions, the performer becomes a cultural critic (Bowman, 1988, p. 4). If culture is an ongoing performance (Bruner, 1986), then performers critically bring the spaces, meanings, ambiguities and contradictions of culture alive in their performances (Conquergood, 1986, p. 56). The performed text is one of the last frontiers for ethnography to enter, Victor Turner's (1986b, p. 25) liminal space, a new, but old border to be crossed.[3] When fully embraced, this crossing will forever transform ethnography and cultural studies. It will serve, at the same time, to redefine the meanings of ethnography in its other moments and formations.

A Performance Text Vocabulary

A family of contested concepts and terms (see figure 8.1), including theater, dramatic script, editing reality, interpretation, performance syntax, performance, performer, performance text, and audience, define the ethnographic performance perspective (see Strine, Long, & Hopkins, 1990). These terms blur into one another.

Dramatic performances occur within the spaces of *ethnographic theater*, an aesthetic place and space where texts, performers, performances, and audiences come together. The theater may be a stage organized for performances, or it may be an improvised space, such as a classroom, or a lecture hall. A performance is marked as theatre when a dramatic script with delineated characters in plotted dramatic action is performed. *Dramatic scripts* are crafted from fieldnotes what McCall and Becker (1990, p. 118), call editing reality. They have a performance syntax, a theoretical, interpretive vocabulary that articulates the drama of the field situation (see below). Scripts can be based on composite experiences and characters, be fragmentary, personal, autobiographical, and incomplete. Good ethnographic theater stirs the critical, emotional imagination of the audience.

A *performance* is an interpretive event, a rehearsed, or improvised creative set of activities, with a beginning, middle, and end, performed for the benefit of an audience and the performers. Performance is interpretation. *A performance is simultaneously a text and an interpretive process* (see Strine, Long, & Hopkins, 1990, p. 184).

FIGURE 8.1

A Performance Text Vocabulary

Concept	Variations
Audience:	Interactive structure; *types:* professional, participatory-interactional, co-participants, lay, aesthetic, electronic, cinematic, postmodern
Dramatic script:	Evocative text, "delineated characters in a plotted dramatic action capable of stirring the imagination/and or emotions of an audience, bringing it to a state of awareness" (Coger & White, 1973, p. 6); fragmentary, composite, messy, natural, autobiographical
Editing reality:	Turning a field text into a dramatic, reflexive script (performance syntax, McCall & Becker, 1990, p. 118) that is then rehearsed, staged, and performed;
Interpretation:	As performance, text vs. performance-centered
Performer:	*Types:* solo, group, natural, professional, ensemble, readers chamber, interactional theater
Performance:	As interpretive event; *meanings:* aesthetic, intellectual, emotional, participatory, political, commemorative; *types:* natural, dramatic, improvised
Performance syntax:	A text's theoretical, interpretive vocabulary that is embedded in the script, giving a connection and shape to the field text (Jackson, 1993, p. 29); directions for performing, and presenting, including publication
Performance text:	*Types:* dramatic, natural, performance science, ethnodrama, staged readings; realist, postmodern
Theater:	An aesthetic place and space where text, performers, performances, and audiences come together to participate in an embodied, evocative, reflective experience. Contemporary types: readers, chamber, of the mind, community, regional, Cruelty, absurd, Epic, forum or oppressed (Boal), realist, postmodern, Third World, feminist, ethnographic (see also types of performance texts).

Three types of performances can be distinguished:

1. A natural performance is the reperformance of ordinary interaction, a staged version of a recorded conversation (Stucky, 1993, p. 168).

2. A dramatic performance is organized in terms of the aesthetics of performance or oral interpretation theory (see Bacon, 1980). Traditionally, dramatic performances have been text-based, drawing on existing drama, or literature for the text that is performed (i.e. Chamber or Reader's Theatre; see McClay, 1972).
3. More recently (Conquergood, 1992), ethnographers have performed rituals and stories drawn from fieldwork sites. An improvised performance seeks its own organization and structure in the process of performance.

A performance is a public act, a way of knowing, a form of embodied interpretation. Performances are contextual, situated productions that mediate and define ongoing relationships between texts, readers, interpreters, performers, and audiences (Loxley, 1983, p. 42). Any given performance event is shaped by an aesthetics of experience (theories of performance, audience expectations), and by the social experience of bearing witness to the performance itself (Loxley, 1983, p. 42).

Two generic performance aesthetics can be identified, presentational, and representational theater (see Donmoyer & Yennie-Donmoyer, 1995). Representational theater enacts the logics of naturalistic realism. It recreates an on-stage verisimilitude. Through realistic, method acting, a faithful rendering of everyday interaction and conversation is produced, complete with slurred speech, mumbles, hesitations, repetitions, scratches, slouches, and other personal mannerisms. In representational theater, method actors bring their inner experiences to the character, action and emotion being portrayed, submerging themselves in the character, Marlon Brando in *Street Car Named Desire*. Thus the audience does not see the performer playing a character, they see only the character.

In contrast, presentational theater is the stylized and individual display of the part and character in question, there is no attempt to dissolve the performer into the role, the emphasis is on stylization, not realism. Performers might read from scripts, "assume a variety of roles . . . interact with imaginary characters, and manipulate non-existent or partial props in the process of presenting literary works" (Donmoyer & Yennie-Donmoyer, 1995, p. 7). Presentational theatre asks the audience to create meaning from "what is suggested, rather than from what is literally shown" (Donmoyer & Yennie-Donmoyer, 1995, p. 7). Representational theater employs a performance-based aesthetic, while presentational theater creates the spaces for an audience-based aesthetic that works to uncut the logic of strict realistic theater. This aesthetic allows audience members to separate their emotional reactions to a performance from the text (and the performance).[4]

The *performed text* interacts with a prior text, fieldnotes, interviews, a literary work.[5] This interaction produces the performance, the interpretive event. Multiple meanings and pleasures can be brought to the performance site, including those that are aesthetic, intellectual, emotional, participatory, political, and commemorative of various forms of cultural memory (Strine, Long, & Hopkins, 1990, pp. 185–188). The performance text reports upon (brings news from), dramatizes, and critiques some segment of ongoing cultural life (Strine, Long, & Hopkins, 1990, pp. 188–189).

The *performance text* can take one of five forms: (1) dramatic texts such as rituals, poems, and plays meant to be performed (see Bacon, 1980; Turner, 1986b); (2) natural texts, transcriptions of everyday conversations turned into natural performances (see Stucky, 1993); (3) performance science texts, fieldwork notes, and interviews turned into performance texts (see Paget, 1993; McCall & Becker, 1990; Becker, McCall, & Morris, 1989); and (4) improvisational, critical ethnodramas that merge natural script dialogues with dramatized scenes and the use of composite characters. (See Mienczakowski, 1995, 1994, 1992; Mienczakowski & Morgan, 1993)

These four dramatic forms must be distinguished from (5) "staged readings," where one or more persons holds a script, the text, and reads from it (see Paget, 1993, p. 27). Staged readings are text-centered productions, and may involve rehearsals by readers-as-performers. Improvised staged readings call for the stage director (the author of the paper) to hand out parts of the script to members of the audience, who then read on cue. Performance texts attempt to move away from the written text, although some may preserve "its content on stage" (Paget, 1993, p. 27). Finally, these five forms have different performance syntaxes and semantic structures.[6]

Nondramatic, natural performance scripts recount events, tellings, and interpretations from the field. They do not necessarily move the audience through a dramatic structure of events, such as is found in the many variations (absurd, German Epic, cruelty) on the traditional (Elizabethan, Stuart, Restoration, realism, neoclassical, romanticism, comedy, etc.) theater model (see Turner, 1986b, pp. 27–31). They may have only a few speaking parts. They use a scholarly performance syntax, invoking terms and theories that resonate within the intended scholarly community.

Dramatic natural performance texts, in contrast, conform, in some fashion to this traditional theater model, and its variations (as well as those found in Chamber, Story, and Readers and Peoples Theater; see discussion below). They have multiple speakers, protagonists and antagonists, and they move action through to a dramatic resolution. Audience-centered, dramatic performances make the audience part of the performance, attempting to break down the wall between performer and audience. A scholarly performance syntax is often woven into the script (see Jackson, 1993, p. 29).

Improvisational, and critical ethnodramas draw on field texts (interviews and conversations), while combining multiple narratives within a single performance which may have many dramatic beginnings, middles, and endings (see Mienczakowski, 1995). Audiences may be co-performers in these productions. If the postproduction method of forum theater (Boal, 1985, 1995) is used, discussions with audience members and performers will occur, and scripts and performances will be modified, on the basis of these conversations. The text's syntax draws primarily from the worlds studied, with a minimum emphasis on scholarly, theoretical terms.

Each of these performance variations (which of course blur) may focus (respectively) on reporting, dramatizing, or critiquing that which is being presented. However, critical ethnodrama explicitly focuses on cultural critique (Mienczakowski (1994, p. 48).

Dramatic and nondramatic texts, based on the performance science model, will utilize scripts taken from the literal translation of field-notes and field texts. These scripts can be turned into dramatic performances, for example, Stucky's (1993) natural performances, or Jackson's (1993) and Paget's (1993) plays. Or they can be nondramatic readings such as Becker, McCall, and Morris's (1989) scripts with speaking parts for researchers and informants. Dramatic, improvisational, ethnodrama alters and changes the field text, producing composite characters, emphasizing multiple tellings of the same event, shifting concern away from verisimilitude toward dramatic reinterpretation and cultural critique (but see Mienczakowski, 1994, pp. 50–51).

Varying degrees of text-centeredness define these styles. While the performance is a transformative process for each, those that emphasize natural performances are more text-centered, keying on the actual words that were spoken and transcribed. The closer the text moves to an audience-centered production, the less text-centered and more improvisational it becomes. Of course, all performances are based on texts. The issue here is the status of the text as it refers back to the field experience and the field text. Improvisational, ethnodrama texts fundamentally transform that experience. Dramatic and nondramatic natural performances maintain a deeper commitment to that site and its "original" meanings.

Audiences are neither pure voyeurs, nor passive recipients, of performance events (Peterson, 1983, p. 33). Audiences are organized around performance events, witnesses to an oral interpretation of a text (Langellier, 1983, p. 36). Audiences interpret and live through performances, they are performers of their own interpretations, and witnesses of the performed text (Langellier, 1983, p. 34; Dufrene, 1973; Iser, 1978). Audiences complete performances by being there for the performance, they participate in mute dialogue, offering also "a background of pure silence that allows other voices to emerge" (Langellier, 1983, p. 34). They also clap, laugh, cough, weep, perceive, listen, appreciate, respond, evaluate, and perform (Loxley, 1983, p. 43).

The audience is an interactive structure. While members bring their own interpretive frameworks as audience members to a performance, the audience-as-a-performer can also enact its own performance aesthetic. In this way the audience is both inside the performance text, and observer of its performance (Langellier, 1983, p. 36). *The audience both creates a text and is created by the text as a performance.* Hence the audience "may be more or less competent, equal to or unqualified" (Langellier, 1983, p. 37) to interpret the performance in question.

Every audience, like any performance, is different, any audience "simultaneously participates in an unrepeatable creation as well as within a history of performances that precede and succeed it" (Langellier, 1983, p. 37). Unable to see the text as a totality, the audience is an ongoing witness to the text as it is performed. This moving viewpoint means that audiences (and their members) are always in interpretive motion, continually moving in and out of the performed text as performer, witness, and interpreter (Langellier, 1983, p. 38).

There are four types of ethnographic performance audiences: professional, participatory, lay, and aesthetic. A professional audience is a group of scholars at a professional meeting, hearing a text performed, rather than read (Becker, McCall, & Morris, 1989). A participatory audience is an audience involved as co-performers, or critics (in the post performance phase) of the performance. Participatory audiences are often lay groups, whose experiences are being performed by fellow performers (see Mienczakowski, 1995, 1994, 1992; Mienczakowski & Morgan, 1993). A lay audience is distinct from the aesthetic audience, the audience who comes to enjoy a work for its performance values, its ability to recreate experiences and interpretations connected to a performance tradition (i.e., classic Shakespearean theater).

Performers may be solo performers, or members of a theater, ensemble, readers, peoples, or chamber performance group (Bacon, 1980). Performers may be natural actors, scholars or persons from everyday life performing their own or other's texts. Performers use props, including manuscripts, lecterns, lighting, and music for their performances (Bacon, 1980, p. 5). Performers interpret texts, bringing them alive. A performer creates a living space for a text, locating the performance in some form of direct, or indirect contact with the audience (Bacon, 1980, p. 4).

Performers or actors may perform their own, or someone else's, work. In the first instance they are writers who are also performers, artists doing a narrative text, in which case they are in doing an interpretation of a text they have produced. In the second case, they are interpreters of another's text. In both performative contexts, performers bring their interpretations to bear on this work, connecting a performative self to a performance that brings the work alive (see Van Oosting, 1981, p. 68). Method actors work from the outer edges of a work, the printed text, moving into its inner meanings, fitting those meanings to their own interpretations of the event, or character in question (see Van Oosting, 1981, p. 68). They attempt a realistic rendering of the text and character in question, folding themselves into the character. Such performers move through three interpretive stages in their performance work. They begin as readers of the text, moving to interpreters who become translators able to move from print to performance, "from imaginative vision to structured articulation" (Van Oosting, 1981, p. 74). In contrast, non–method actors are more concerned with presentation, not representation. They draw, accordingly, on their noncharacter experiences, as they improvise an interpretation of the sitaution and part in question.

A Genealogy of the Performance Text

The origins of the alliance between ethnography and performance can be traced to many sources, told in many different ways (Conquergood, 1992, p. 80; Jackson, 1993). In 1959 Erving Goffman proposed to read society dramaturgically, to look at those parts of daily life that were staged, and to place an emphasis on the difference between reality and appearance. In 1969 Kenneth Burke (1969, p. 43) suggested that anthropologists examine the rhetorical nature of their own field, that anthropology be imported (in part) into rhetoric. Victor Turner called (1986b) for an anthropology of performance. At the same time Richard Bauman (1986) was formulating a model for connecting narrative texts, and oral performances, and Dennis Tedlock (1983, pp. 300, 304) examined the problems involved in joining the spoken word with the printed text, situating the anthropoplogist in the center of the performances being recorded. Richard Harvey Brown (1989) contended that society be read rhetorically, and Stanford Lyman (1990, p. 221) suggested that the metaphor of a dramaturgical society had become an interactional reality in America. Today Debord's (1983) "society of the spectacle" has been realized, we understand everyday life through the mass-mediated performances that make the hyperreal more real than the real (Baudrillard, 1983; see also Denzin, 1992a, p. 138).

Turner's call to perform ethnographic narratives is anticipated by Paget's (1987) concept of "verbatim theater" which Mienczakowski (1995, p. 5) connects to the BBC documentary radio ballads of the 1950s, which culminated in Joan Littlewood's "Oh What a Lovely Way," a musical play that used verbatim accounts and "documentary evidence as a basis for it depiction of class-attitudes towards the First World War" (Mienczakowski, 1995, p. 5). Chessman (1971) extended this approach, using oral history techniques to develop realistic narratives then presented on stage (Mienczakowski, 1995, p. 5). The concept of performance science, scholars performing ethnogaphic texts, was introduced by Becker, McCall, and Morris in 1989 and elaborated by McCall and Becker in 1990. In 1991 Laurel Richardson and Ernest Lockridge presented "The Sea Monster: An Ethnographic Novel," a further extension of this form, now using the dramatic form to deconstruct the traditional ethnography (see also Richardson, 1993). In a parallel vein, Mienczakowski (1995, 1994, 1992; Mienczakowski & Morgan, 1993) has been experimenting with Boal's (1979, 1995) forum theater techniques, using postperformance discussions with informants and audience members as a way of modifying scripts and performances. Mienczakowski's performance scripts (see discussion below) are based on verbatim accounts of field materials gathered via grounded theory, case study, and ethnographic methods of inquiry.

Over the last decade Conquergood and his students have continued to rethink ethnography in terms of a performance rhetoric, doing fieldwork in order to have new texts to perform (see Conquergood, 1985a, 1986, 1989, 1991, 1992; also Jackson, 1993).[7] In this framework, building on Goffman, Burke, Geertz, Turner, and Bakhtin, the world is understood to be a performance, culture is a verb, not a noun, fieldwork is a collaborative process, a performance, and knowledge is performative, not informative (Conquergood, 1991, p. 190). This model assesses the ethics and politics of the performed text, arguing that it should exist alongside the published text as a scholarly work in its own right (1991, p. 190). The performance text thus complements the narrative, storytelling approach to ethnographic practice, that approach which problematizes the place of the other in the messy, layered text (Marcus, 1994; Ronai, 1995), while encouraging the reflexive, autobiographical voice that is aware of of its own historical contingencies (Bochner, 1994, pp. 32–33).

Conquergood's arguments for the performance text are embedded in a deep history connected to theater, rhetoric, and oral interpretation (see Bacon, 1979, 1980; Strine, Long, & Hopkins, 1990, pp. 181–183; Sayre, 1990).[8] This history revolves around the meanings brought to the terms discussed above (texts, performers, and performances). From the 1950s to the 1970s the field of performance studies was text-centered, seeing texts as repositories of latent meaning, focusing on performances and oral interpretations as the methods for making these latent meanings manifest (Strine, Long, & Hopkins, 1990, p. 182).

Chamber and Readers Theater

Text-centered performance studies extended the traditional dramatic theater model (where plays were performed by a group of actors), to Chamber and Readers Theater. Chamber Theater was defined as a "technique for staging prose fiction, retaining the text of the story or novel being performed, but locating the scenes of the story onstage" (Bacon, 1979, p. 466). Chamber Theater often used a narrator. Readers Theater, embodies the same elements as Chamber Theater, but may not use a narrator, and the locus of the drama is not onstage with the readers (as it is for Chamber Theater), but "off stage in the imagination of the audience" (Bacon, 1979, p. 457). Readers Theater is a technique for "staging literary texts in such a way that the text is featured in the performance" Maclay, 1971, p. 7). Chamber Theater is representational, attempting to reproduce the illusion of reality on stage. Readers Theater is presentational, the emphasis is less on realism, more on action that occurs in the audience's critical imagination (see Donmoyer & Donmoyer, 1995).

Chamber and Reader's Theater (also called Theater of the Mind, or the Theater of the Imagination) used a grammar of practice that modified the traditional theater model, while giving special meanings to scripts, casting, rehearsals, directing, stage design (the arrangement of readers on stage), props (lecterns, stools, chairs), costumes (ordinary clothes), lighting, dialogue, performance standards, and specific guidelines for relating performances to texts (see Maclay, 1971; Pickering, 1975; Coger & White, 1973, p. 31).

Readers Theater has three essential elements. First, it must have a script with delineated characters in a plotted dramatic, often conflictual, action. The materials in the script may be a collation of materials (poems, diary entries, excerpts from short stories), but they must interact, functioning as a gestalt, a dramatic whole (Coger & White, 1973, p. 6), producing a sense of drama for the audience. Thus a reading of a poem, or a group reading of a text is not Readers Theater. Second,

Readers Theater must be embodied, through vocal intonations and bodily tensions (and movements), characters must be evoked and brought alive, "effective performance is the second essential element in Readers Theater" (Coger & White, 1973, p. 7). Third, a willing and participatory audience must be present. In Readers and Chamber Theater the audience is asked to imagine their way into the characters and story that is being staged, to ignore the fact that the actors are readers, not characters in a play. This is called double-vision (Coger & White, 1973, p. 7). The audience is asked to give itself over to the performance, to suspend literary analysis and literary criticism. These criticisms may come later, after the performance, but if present during the performance, they interfere with the audience member's "contribution to the work, and lacking [this] participation, the performance will be incomplete" (Coger & White, 1973, p. 7).

In certain versions (Maclay, 1971, pp. 37; 99; Coger & White, 1973, pp. 29–31), Readers Theater, attempted to break from traditional staging procedures in order to develop new relationships with the audience. Many Readers Theater directors drew upon Bertolt Brecht's concept of Epic Theater, which used the method of actor alienation to make the audience aware of the "simultaneous presence of actor and actor" (Maclay, 1971, p. 37). Brecht's alienating devices included direct speeches to the audience, avoidance of the concept of the fourth wall,[9] actors shifting roles, and playing more than one character, or more than one actor playing the same character, actors singing to the audience in a way that commented on ongoing action, the projection of pictures and printed comments on background screens, bare stage walls, minimal props, successions of independent scenes and segments, and the use of narrators who tied sequences together (Coger & White, 1973, pp. 29–31).

While Readers Theater seeks emotional involvement on the part of the audience, Brecht's experiments were intended to create a thinking audience, an audience with detachment, an audience who could think and act critically. Brecht's was not a theater of emotional catharsis, rather "it was to be a stimulus for social action and social criticism" (Maclay, 1971, p. 37). In contrast to conventional Reader's Theater, which is representational and realistic, Brecht's Epic, or Dialectical Theater is deliberately disruptive and political, and thus anticipates the more radical forms of contemporary postmodern, political theater that has connections back to Artaud's concepts of a pure theater (Birringer, 1993, p. 217).

Third World popular theater, "theater used by oppressed Third World people to achieve justice and development for themselves"

(Etherton, 1988, p. 991), extends these critical views of what theater (and ethnography) can do politically. The International Popular Theater Alliance, organized in the 1980s, uses existing forms of cultural expression to fashion improvised dramatic productions that analyze situations of poverty and oppression. This grassroots approach uses agit-prop and sloganizing theater[10] to create collective awareness and collective action at the local level. This form of theater has been popular in Latin America, in Africa, in parts of Asia, in India, and among Native American populations in the Americas (Etherton, 1988, p. 992).

The crisis of representation in ethnography's fourth and fifth moments challenged the text-centered approach of Chamber and Readers Theater. The work to be performed could no longer be viewed as a stable entity with inherent meanings that a performance would reveal (Strine, Long, & Hopkins, 1990, p. 182). The performance of a text was now redefined, no longer confined to the single performance of a "repeatable and preexistent text" (Sayre, 1990, p. 91). Texts were now understood to be subject to multiple interpretations and meanings[11] Thus a text could neither authorize, nor transcend, its own performance (Sayre, 1990, p. 91). This is the space that Conquergood and Turner's work enters and defines.

Performance Art

Thus emerged performance art, a movement that predates, while running alongside, the crisis of representation in the human disciplines. It is traced (Sayre, 1990, pp. 92–93) to the futurists in the 1910s and the dada cabaret movement of the 1920s, Brecht's experiments with a theater of the mind (Capo, 1983, p. 35), culminating in the mid-1960s in an "interdisciplinary, often multimedia kind of production which has come to be labeled 'performance art'" (Sayre, 1990, p. 93).[12] Transformations of this movement focused on the gendered body, dissolving, fragmenting, blurring, and displacing its centered presence in performance (Birringer, 1993, pp. 220–221). The literal body was challenged, replaced by a gendered, autobiographical, confessional body text, cries and whispers on stage, gyrations and repetitions, a body in motion working against itself and its culture (Birringer, 1993, p. 221). This body was soon supplemented by a globalizing, electronic, postmodern video technology. Laurie Anderson's multitrack, audiovisual choreographies are key here. Her electronic body, represents a "kind of electronic closed-circuit transvestism" (Birringer, 1993, p. 222), awaiting only on-line movement into cyberspace, her own hypermedia site on the World Wide Web, video theater on the computer. Montage and mise-en-scène will never be the same again.

In performance art, a performance becomes a dialogical, often improvisational work that takes authority away from the text; the emphasis is on the performance, not the work per se. The concept of an original, against which the performance can be measured, is questioned (Sayre, 1990, p. 94). The world outside the text, including the audience, is brought into the performance. The performance becomes a transformative process, where performers are no longer locked into fixed characters in a text. Audiences may become active participants, or co-performers in the performance. The performer creates a field or aesthetic situation in which audience and performer together "face, as a group, a common dilemma" (Sayre, 1990, p. 101). This may be called participatory theater, together audience members and performers co-produce a performance text (Capo, 1983, p. 33; also Langellier, 1983, p. 34; Dufrenne, 1973; Iser, 1978). At the same time, performance artists maintain their own identities, and "distinguish themselves from actors and actresses . . . because the latter 'pretend' to be someone else in a time different from the real time of the event" (Sayre, 1990, p. 96).[13]

Enter the Social Sciences: Performance Science Texts

Becker, McCall and Morris introduced in 1989 the concept of performance science, a play on performance art (McCall & Becker, 1990, p. 119). Instead of reading scientific papers aloud at professional meetings, they began performing them, first writing, and then reading scripts in which they played themselves, while also reading the parts given to their informants. A quasi-storytelling format, unlike the argumentative structure of the scientific article, was adopted. This format allowed them to present their work as a collaborative project, without privileging a single authorial voice. The script format permitted the presentation of emotion and mood. Through the use of intonation and pacing they could alter the meanings of their text, thereby highlighting, and openly acknowledging the constructed nature of their social science data (1989, pp. 94–95).[14] As performers they felt as if they were having the experiences they were describing. Performances made the research process more visible and alive to outsiders, voices became real people.

Here is a sample text. It is from the prologue of their play *Theatres and Communities: Three Scenes* (Becker, McCall, & Morris, 1989, p. 100).

(A meeting room at an academic conference. On a raised platform at the front of the room are three circles in a semi-circle. Three sociologists center, carrying scripts).

Lori: Everyone says Chicago is so hot now. Well, it's because of the
            Non-Equity Theaters.
Michal: Minneapolis/St. Paul was a very fat theater town in 1978.
            There was a good crowd for everything.
Howie: San Francisco has a problem that we share with a lot of smaller
            centers, smaller cities, which is that we have a lot of talented,
            really fine actors.

These script fragments define the problem analyzed in the play, the
interconnection between theaters, workers, groups, communities, plays,
and productions, and a shrinking national theater scene.

The performance science script, as analyzed by Becker, McCall,
and Morris, presents certain problems of formating and syntax, including how to mark speakers, how to indicate shifts in headings, how to
indent quotes, what to leave in and what to leave out, whether to give
stage directions, or not (1989, pp. 95–96; 1990, pp. 122–123; see also
Jackson, 1993, pp. 26–31).[15] These scripts represent a mixed genre, part
theater and part social science, and standards for reading them are yet to
be fully developed (see Hilbert, 1990).[16]

Jackson (1993, p. 28) addresses some of the problems identified by
Hilbert (1990) in the McCall and Becker project, namely the absence of a
theoretical framework for understanding the quotes from the field.
Drawing on Strine, Long, and Hopkins (1990, p. 189), Jackson's script (and
performance) combined three types of performance scholarship: reporting,
dramatizing, and critiquing. She simultaneously reported on and dramatized the world of the audition, by evoking that world and its tensions.
Within her script she inserted critiques of the structures of domination
that impinge on actors and actresses in these arenas, using in several places
lines from the works of Michel Foucault (1993, p. 30). Her performance text
became an ideological critique of objectivist ethnography and that brand of
objectivism that is reified in the audition process (p. 21).

In the following lines she offers a critique (using Foucault) of the
auditioning process (Jackson, 1993, p. 30):
Theorist: . . . each subject finds himself caught in a punishable, pun-
            ishing university.
Actor 1:   Don't give a big introduction to your piece.
Director: Act like you want to be there.
Actor 1:   But don't brown-nose
Actor 2:   Be real.

Jackson (1993, p. 31) describes her efforts with this script-segment, " I
was representing more than information gleaned from the interviews.

The attempt was to dramatize the actor's dilemma within the audition structure." She elaborates (1993, p. 126), "During the editing process, decisions about what to include and exclude, how many characters to have, in what order to place the accounts, how to stage the piece—all were made . . . and remade in tandem. . . . Eventually, I would decide on a cast of two actors, two actresses, one director, and a director's assistant. The words of each character were not the words of a single respondent. . . . I clustered the words of several individuals around each figure." Jackson's text dramatizes action and moves it forward, in contrast to the nondramatic, Becker, McCall, and Morris script.

Stucky (1993) takes the performance science project to another level, what he terms the aesthetics of natural performances. Natural performances are reperformances of "something which was, at first performance, an ordinary event" (1993, p. 168), for example, natural conversational interaction. Stucky distinguishes two types of natural performances, staged natural performances that resemble dramatic monologues (personal narratives of a single speaker), and those natural performances that are drawn from conversational settings (interviews, telephone talk). These performances resemble dramatic dialogue (p. 169).

Here is fragment from a longer scene in a fully staged theatrical production called *Naturally Speaking* (Stucky, 1993, p. 169). The words are taken from a recorded conversation between a counselor (Pat), and a client (Liz):

Liz: And when, uh: the abuse started it didn't start like he would just
       come in and beat me up of something it was
Pat: U: m hmmm::
Liz: like a slap in the face=
Pat: =started slow
Liz: Uh::: b'cause i remember that slap in the face real hh w(h)ell

Stucky's performers listen to tapes of texts like this, gleaning an understanding of paralinguistic details such as intonation and voice quality (Stucky 1993, p. 170).

The texts for natural performances, which include interviews, stories and personal narratives, are based on audiovisual recordings of "real" conversations that are rich in "first-order performance details" (p. 170). Performances then draw on these texts, a second body does what a "prior body has already done" (p. 171). The goal is a mix of mimesis and verisimilitude, understanding that there is no "original" against which the performance is to be judged. Performers use natural speech to create the impression that they are reenacting the experiences and actions of ordinary people in the world.[17]

This natural world is, however, privileged, it describes what Stucky calls the first-order performance source of the text (p. 173). It is different from the world of fiction, recordings of speeches, stories, and conversations reference how things actually happened. Performers base their performances on these texts, taking them in, learning them, modifying them, making the performance a theatrical event (p. 173). A distinction is maintained between the original source, or text, and the performance, the real and its fictional representation. (An example would be Dana Carvey, late of the TV show "Saturday Night Life," imitating former President Bush. See Stucky, 1993, p. 174.)

Paget (1993) clarifies this distinction between the real text from the performed text, referring back to her play, *The Work of Talk*. The real text, the written version of the performed text, was "a version of a series of conversations/encounters/exchanges on the problems of a woman seeking medical care. The 'real' text was the text from life. . . . The performed text was another version of the text" (1993, p. 32), but in the performed text Paget was no longer the narrator of her story. Paget's real text was moved directly to the stage, it was a "a piece of science on stage" (p. 25), hence the use of words like discourse, microparadigm, and speaking practices (p. 25). The play had seven characters, the narrator, the doctor, the patient and a panel of four experts (p. 25). The doctor and the patient enacted the dialogue taken from her transcribed interviews.

Finally, an excerpt from Mienczakowski and Morgan's (1993) *Busting: The Challenge of the Drought Spirit*, a two-act, ten-scene play with eighteen characters. Part of a larger project, the play is set in a detoxification unit, and is intended to present "audiences with validated experiential ideas in regard to alcohol and drug use and abuse" (Mienczakowski & Morgan, 1993, p. 1). After each performance audience members are invited to critically reflect upon the play and to inspect their understandings of the issues involved. The dialogue in the script is based on verbatim interview transcriptions, the characters are composite figures, symbolic persons drawn from the field setting. The text is dramatically performed by nursing and theater students, who take a Stanislavskian (method acting) approach to their performances, including being paired with staff members who acted as their mentors (Mienczakowski, 1995).

The play opens this way:

A teenage girl, Maria, lit by a solitary spot light, stands centre stage. She has a half bottle of bourbon in her hand. . . . [T]he cyclorama (a curved background on the stage set) is suddenly littered with several slide images of the girl. . . . Gradually the slides change to Maria in a variety of "street drinking" situations.

The play quickly moves to an exchange between Maria and two nurses:

Nurse # 1:   Can you tell me your name?
Maria: Maria . . .
Nurse # 1:   How old were you when you began drinking?
Nurse # 2:   When did drinking first become a problem for you?

Mienczakowski calls this ethnodrama, turning ethnographic narratives into a dramatized form. Ethnodrama methodology, based on interviews and participant observation, attempts to create texts with a high degree of verisimilitude; that is, texts which are plausible and realistic, containing validated accounts that evoke commonly understood perceptions and beliefs about the phenomenon in question (1995, p. 6). A complex interpretive process occurs, wherein informants, audience members, and health care professionals engage the drama and its performance in a reflective discourse, struggling to create and share meaning, coming to agreement on the authentic nature of the language in the text.

This form of writing and performance brings a new, public voice to science, placing it in the hands of consumers who validate its authenticity as well as its potential for practical, political, therapeutic, and pedagogical purposes. Ethnodramas are written, then, for public consumption, and are often distributed to audiences prior to performances (1995, p. 9).

Reading Performance Science and Ethnodrama Texts

These several examples of the performance science, ethnodrama text open the spaces where I want to go. To repeat, I seek a critical postmodern, performance aesthetic for a performative cultural studies. This aesthetic will work against the realist impulse that organizes the logic of the natural performance text, an impulse not unlike the one that can be found in *America's Funniest Home Videos* and *Court Television* (Stucky, 1993, p. 177). This impulse valorizes real, lived experience, ordinary life, arguing that the recent emphasis on performance in anthropology (Turner, 1986b) requires serious consideration of "the ways people perform their everyday lives" (p. 177). But the reproduction of realist texts often fails to untangle and expose the very structures that make any situated version of reality a historical fiction.

Return to Trinh's (1991, p. 39) criticisms of the documentary film style. Like documentary film, natural science performance texts seek to re-create the circumstances and authentic experiences of real people in real life situations. Natural science texts invoke real time and its passage. They attempt to capture objective reality, to dramatize the truth, to always maintain a naturalistic connection between the moving image and the spoken word. They relentlessly remind the spectator that actual facts are being presented in a truthful way, that the words spoken and heard here are ones spoken by common, ordinary people.

Thus, despite their many virtues, natural performance texts remain dangerously close to those forms of ethnography that dominated ethnography in its golden age, that moment when the ethnographer remained committed to coming back from the field with an authorized telling of what had been found.[18] Authentic tales, with high verisimilitude, reproduce the pull of realism and run the risk of not criticizing what they reproduce. They remain confined within the spaces of a modernist aesthetic and a postpositivist (at best) epistemology. There is, accordingly, a tension between representational and presentational theater (Donmoyer & Yennie-Donmoyer, 1995). The field is caught between those who produce ethnographic performances that report on and reproduce reality on stage, and those who critique reality and its representations. Preoccupations with the syntax of the text, recordings, transcriptions, analysis, rehearsals, the structure of the printed text, and its directions to the reader, reveal an unwillingness to fully enter the improvisionational spaces created by postmodern, performance studies.

These texts do not always contest the body as a site of resistance. They thereby fail to make problematic how identity, gender, race, and sexual orientation are socially constructed on the postmodern cultural terrain. By emphasizing the recovery of lived experience these works falter at that moment when they could interrogate those cultural apparatuses that valorize specularity, and simulated, hyperreal reproductions of the real. This means they do not exploit the insights of the standpoint epistemologies, especially the arguments of Collins and Trinh that explore the facades of realism, and examine the truth of fictional texts. With the exception of the work of Richardson and Mienczakowski, there are few attempts to explore a form of theater that moves an audience to critical, reflective action. Finally, there is a tendency to remain within the confines of either a traditional Readers theater model, or to produce solo, dramatized, text-centered readings. These readings entangle the performance with its text. In their celebration of performance, readers may fail to critique the autoethnographic text being performed.

While performance science and ethnodrama texts dramatize field-notes, and destabilize the teller's place in the story that is told, they do not take the next step, which is entry into that space where full impro-visation, audience-co-participation, and cultural critique operate. It is this space that I next explore. I return to the mystory, and the study and performance of those cultural moments that leave indelible marks on people, their bodies, and their biographies. Aesthetics and episte-mology first.

The Mystory Text and Its Performance

A critical, performative cultural studies attempts to put in place subversive performance texts that carry forward Trinh's agenda for the retelling of stories that the sciences of the human disciplines have reduced to fiction, minor literature, or have marginalized, stigmatized, and paternalized as politically correct multicultural performances. These works interrogate the realities they represent, locate the teller's story in the history that is presented, make the audience responsible for their own interpretations, foreground difference, not conflict, oppose dichotomies, and use multiple voices in their tellings. These texts resist the temptation to turn actors into objects of the voyeuristic gaze, desta-bilizing common methods of establishing verisimilitude. Performance texts are messy productions. They presume an evocative epistemology that performs, rather than represents the world.

These texts invoke and then criticize standard social science meth-ods of research, including doing parodies of the interview as a tool for gathering objective data about the world of the other. The scientific article as a vehicle for presenting knowledge about the world is also mocked, and the objective ethnographer is criticized for his or so-called objective methods of truth-seeking. Following Trinh, there is an attempt to create a distance between the written and the performed text. Critiques of the notion of any kind of unified subject are offered. These works open a space for the audience as co-performers to constantly create new under-standings of the experiences being described and interpreted.

Writers and performers attempt to avoid Trinh's Lady Painter and Quiller-Couch syndromes, neither scribbling masculine texts, or over indulging the personal, confessional style of presentation. A form of writing and performing that opens new ways of presenting the plural self in its multiple situations is sought. The goal is to create texts that produce a sudden awakening on the part of the viewer who as audience member is also a performer. This means the performed text will be ever-changing. It will constantly work against those textual strategies (verbatim transcriptions, etc.) that would allow readers and listeners to assimilate the performance as a realist text.

These are the aesthetic and epistemological features that partially define a postmodern performance sublime.

Mystory as Montage

The mystory is simultaneously a personal mythology, a public story, and a performance that critiques. It is an interactive, dramatic performance. It is a variation on Readers Theater, a participatory theater of the mind, a version of one of Brecht's learning plays (Ulmer, 1989, p. 210), presentational, not representational theater (Donmoyer & Yennie-Donmoyer, 1995). A mystory performance has parallels with a staged reading. However, these are performance- not text-centered interpretive events. The emphasis is on performance, presentation, and improvisation, and not just a reading of the fixed text.

The mystory is a montage text, cinematic, and multimedia in shape, filled with sounds, music, and images taken from the writer's personal history. This personal text (script) is grafted into discourses from popular cultural, and locates itself against the specialized knowledges that circulate in the larger society. The audience co-performs the text, and the writer, as narrator, functions as a guide, a commentator on what is occurring.

The mystory performance event is improvised, each member of the audience brings his or her biography and voice to the lines that are read and spoken. A stage per se is not used, the wall between performers and audience disappears because all parties to the performance are also performers. The script is fashioned from the imagined and puts into words experiences, actions, and words that were, or could have been, and will be spoken here. The script brings this world and its ethnodramas alive (Rose, 1995), reports on it, in some fashion, and then criticizes the structures of power that operate therein. It delineates specific characters and these characters are caught up in dramatic conflict, which moves to some degree of resolution at the end of the script. However, simplistic characterizations based on traditional oppositions (male/female, etc.) are avoided, difference, not conflict, is privileged (Trinh, 1991, p. 188). There can be as many characters as there are readers available to do readings. The same reader can read the parts of the same and different characters. Every performance is different, different readers, different lines, different meanings and interpretations, yet in every instance, a story is told and performed.

Of course, the mystory text is not easily constructed. It involves the hard interpretive work of editing personal, biographical reality

(McCall & Becker, 1990, p. 118; Jackson, 1993, p. 26). Editing biographical reality produces a dramatic re-interpretation of what has felt and lived by the person, moments of crisis and pain. What will be edited is determined by what has been remembered, collected, and written down, notes to the self, the "Rashomon" effect turned inside out. From the several layers and versions of the biographical fieldtext, the writer aims to tell a story, with some degree of dramatic power. Editing, or crafting the text will involve many decisions, These include: what words to put in the mouths of which characters, who the characters will be, and how many readers there will be. The focus is always on showing not telling. Minimal interpretation is favored.

The mystory text begins with those moments that define the crisis in question, a turning point in the person's life. Ulmer (1989, p. 209; 1994, pp. xii, 139) suggests the following starting point, "Write a mystory bringing into relation your experience with three levels of discourse—personal (autobiography), popular (community stories, oral history or popular culture), [and] expert (disciplines of knowledge). In each case use the punctum or sting of memory to locate items significant to you" (p. 209). The sting of memory locates the moment, the beginning, once located this moment is dramatically described, fashioned into a text to be performed. This moment is then surrounded by those cultural representations and voices that define the experience in question.

Here is an excerpt from a poetic, mystory play (Sanmiguel, 1995), entitled *Re-Defining Endometriosis/Re-Defining Me*. The play has parts for Dad, Lisa, family/society, the voices of physicians, medicine, psychiatry, self-help, first love, lasting love, Mom, Grandma, and the popular media. The text is meant to be read, not staged, and has been performed several times by and to classes of communication graduate students at the University of Illinois.

Dad:	My daughter doesn't worry about boys and all that shit.
Lisa:	She was supposed to be a boy. That's what her daddy always said. . . . Her Aunt said, "You're a woman now." A woman at age 10?
Family/Society:	It's just a woman's lot. . . . It's just a female thing.
Physicians:	So What have you been up to? Good girls don't come to see me this young. Who've you been having sex with?
Lisa:	I'm a good girl. . . . I haven't even kissed a boy!
Physicians:	They all say that.

Mom:	When a doctor finally did exploratory surgery and told us she had endometriosis, I was so relieved and happy to know what was wrong.
Medicine:	Endometriosis is . . . the presence of endometrial glands and stroma outside the endometrial cavity.
Lisa:	Endometriosis is defined as the thief that stole my life.

The play continues. Sanmiguel has psychiatrists, self-help groups, first loves, and members of her family comment on her condition. The play ends with the following lines:

| Lisa: | A new definition for endometriosis: A condition that empowers as it strengthens character and makes one reevaluate the gendered self as constructed by society.
Individual solutions become collective action.
No more victims of categorization.
No more labels.
No more good girls. . . . |
| Family/Society: | She's never been like the other girls. |

This text, when performed, powerfully and critically moves the audience into the position of co-creating a female subject defined as having endometriosis. The text unsettles and criticizes medicine, psychiatry, and those popular culture texts that urge women to accept this condition as their fate.

Sanmiguel's play gives the audience lines to perform, an alternative textual form allows the audience to create its own response to a prior text. Allan Northcott's (1995) "New Woman" is a song written as a critical and participatory performance text. About women's magazines and their discourses, the audience is asked to compare the lines of this song to the words found in *Playboy* or *Penthouse*.[19]

> The magazines at the check-out stand
> Made a thousand things go running thru my head
> The cover girl was as cute as can be
> Lyle Lovett can do it so why not me. . . .
> So take your Glamour and your Vanity Fair
> Take your silicone parts and your perfect hair
> Pack your magazines and say good-bye
> You're Cosmo baby but you're not my style

Upon hearing the song performed by Northcott and Martin Srajek, with a moderate blues shuffle, in the key of G, audience members were asked to write their own lines for the song. Individuals responded to "New Woman" with the following sample verses:

> What to tell your psychiatrist
> 15 days to sexual bliss
> natural perfumes and aphrodisiacs
> silk dresses to enhance your bare back

> A New Man is who I'd like to be
> Sensitive, aware and fancy-free
> So me and my New-Age spiritual pals
> Could make it with all those feminist gals.

These verses were then incorporated into the original song, which became a new song when it was performed again. Thus the audience as co-participants and co-song writers, created their version of the New Woman.

Finally, a natural performance text assembled out of multiple posts from the Internet, in this case from a newsgroup for persons with eating disorders (Walstrom, 1995). The performance text is guided by the author's personal experience with an eating disorder, and a desire to use this experience of her "self" to analyze and critique the limits of social understandings of those disorders (Foucault, 1984; Rabinow, 1984). The researcher fills the performance text with excerpts from postings to the newsgroup, along with experiences stemming from her own experience of anorexia. This juxtapostion of the newsgroup excerpts and the researcher's mystories (Ulmer, 1989) aims to offer "shocks of recognition" (Probyn, 1993) of the experience of eating disorders to the audience members. The performance begins with audience members' reading of introductions, as women post for the first time on the newgroup.

> I hope it is okay that I have come here. One thing that many of us have in common is that to a greater or lesser extent our bodies, how we deal with them, and how we feed them are the expression of how we feel in relation to the world. . . . Thanks, and I wish you all peace and healing.

An introduction of the author to the newsgroup is read by the author, as well.

Next, are text-fragments given to audience members to be read:

One: I always hate my body. It never looks good enough to me. I
        don't think it ever will.
Two: I think if I could stop hating my body, it would be a good step.
Three: Can you ever get over hating your body? I look at pictures of
        models, and wish I looked like them. I remember a lot of peo-
        ple commenting on how horrible Kate Moss looked. Part of me
        agreed, but another part would whisper "Why can't I look like
        that?"

The performed elextronic text restores a voice and new embodied emotion to the silent screen. This text offers a view of women are struggling to find a mystory that will help them make sense of the new troubling situations they find themselves in. These writers conceivably react
to the New Woman described in Northcott's song, and could add their
lines to his, just as their words could exist alongside those written by
Sanmiguel.

        Three performance texts that take up Birringer's challenge (1993,
pp. xi–xii) to accomodate and integrate the impact of women's experiences into postmodern, performance cultural studies.[20] Three texts
which work back and forth between private troubles and public discourse, texts that trouble the body and its meanings, texts that take the
truth of fiction as a starting point for social criticism.

Ethics for a Performative Cultural Studies

        Every time a text is performed, a performance ethics is enacted.
Performers, as Stucky (1993, p. 176) argues, need to take responsibility
for their interpretations of another's life experiences. These interpretations will be shaped by a variety of factors, including who the audience is, rehearsal histories, what is selected to be performed, whose
point of view is represented, what is revealed about the other in the
performance, and the ranges of actions that are attributed to another
individual (Stucky, 1993, pp. 176–177).

        In each of these texts there remains a tension between the writers'
and the performers' identity and their ability to recognize and understand the differences that define another person's world. In every
instance the researcher must ask and answer the question raised by
Prattis, "Just what are we doing in other people's culture?" (1985b, p.
277). This question (and its answer) are doubly problematic in performance work. As Conquergood (1985, p. 2) observes, the performer is
unable to maintain aesthetic distance from the experiences being performed and interpreted. Empathetic performances intensify the par-

ticipatory nature of fieldwork. They challenge attempts to create intellectual, or epistemological barriers that would separate the writer from those studied (Conquergood, 1985, p. 2). Performances do not "proceed in ideological innocence and axiological purity (Conquergood, 1985, p. 2). Performers must avoid four ethical pitfalls, morally problematic stances towards the representation of the other's experiences (Conquergood, 1985, p. 4). Conquergood (1985, p. 4) gives the following labels to these four pitfalls: "The Custodian's Rip-Off," "The Enthusiast's Infatuation," "The Curator's Exhibitionism," and "The Skeptic's Cop-Out." Cultural custodians or cultural imperialists enter the field looking for good texts to perform, and then perform them for a fee, often denigrating the cultural group which regards its texts as sacred.[21] The enthusiast's stance occurs when the writer (and the performer) fail to become deeply involved in the cultural setting that they reperform. Conquergood (1985, p. 6) says this trivializes the other. The skeptic, or cynic values detachment and cultural differences, taking the position, for example, that "only blacks can understand and perform black literature [and] only white males [can perform] John Cheever's short stories" (Conquergood, 1985, p. 8). This position refuses to face up to the "ethical tensions and moral ambiguities of performing culturally sensitive materials" (p. 8). Finally, the curator, or sensationalist, is a performer who sensationalizes the cultural differences that supposedly define the world of the other. He or she stages performances for the tourist's gaze. This is "the Wild Kingdom approach to performance that grows out of a fascination with the exotic, primitive, culturally remote . . . the Noble Savage" (Conquergood, 1985, p. 7).

These four stances make problematic the questions of "How far into the other's world can the performer and the audience go? Can the differences that define the other's world be respected? Is their a null point in the moral universe?" (Conquergood, 1985, pp. 8–9). Or does the other always exist, as Trinh would argue, in the spaces on each side of the hyphen (Conquergood, 1985, p. 9)? If so, the performance text can only ever be dialogic, a text which does not speak about or for the other, but which "speaks to and with them" (Conquergood, 1985, p. 10). The dialogic text attempts to keep the dialogue, the conversation, between text, performer and audience ongoing and open-ended (p. 9). This text does more than invoke empathy, it interrogates, criticizes, and empowers. This is dialogical criticism. The dialogical performance is the means for "honest intercultural understanding" (Conquergood, 1985, p. 10).

If this understanding is to be created, the following elements need to be present. Scholars must have the energy, imagination, courage and commitment to create these texts (see Conquergood, 1985, p. 10). Audiences must be drawn to the sites where these performances take place, and they must be willing to suspend normal aesthetic frameworks, so that co-participatory performances can be produced. In these sites a shared field of emotional experience is created, and in these moments of sharing, critical, cultural awareness is awakened.

The co-performed cultural studies text aims to enact the feminist, communitarian moral ethic. As argued there, this ethic presumes a dialogical view of the self and its performances. It seeks narratives that ennoble human experience, performances that facilitate civic transformations in the public and private spheres. This ethic ratifies the dignities of the self and honors personal struggle. It understands cultural criticism to be a form of empowerment, arguing that empowerment begins in that ethical moment when individuals are lead into the troubling spaces occupied by others. In the moment of co-performance, lives are joined and struggle beings anew.

Conclusion

Of course, there are more ways to do a text then to just read it to an audience. The text can be performed, the writer reads a poem, for example. Or, the written text can be supplemented by other devices. The author can use pictures, slides, photographs, show a film, use audiovisual aides, bring in music and a sound track, lip-synch words set to a musical text, create a scholarly version of a Merle Haggard MTV text. The author can even bring the audience into the performance, do a sing-along, hand out a script, give audience members speaking parts, make a communal performance out of the scholarly text. Within the performance the author can assume multiple places, be the ethnographer, the subject in the field, the audience member, a representative from a scholarly community, who asks, "What is going on here?"

This chapter has attempted to answer this question. What is going here is something new, ethnography has crossed that liminal space that separates the scholarly text from its performance. The text is now given back to those to whom it has always belonged, the reader, the other, who finds in these texts parts of themselves, parts of others just like them. We are all co-performers in our own and others' lives. This is what the performance text does. But a fear lingers. Ethnographers of performance must produce texts that are accessible and performable. If they can not do this "the ethnographic movement in performance studies will die" (Conquergood, 1985, p. 11).

Notes

1. A performance-conception of oral literature (and folklore), with an emphasis on the performance event (the telling of a story, or myth) is also an important part of this tradition (see Bauman, 1986, p 3; Tedlock, 1983, pp. 3–6).

2. Turner's (1986b, pp 34–35) liminal experience is always part of a larger, processually structured social drama. They are bracketed by public action on both sides, beginning with a breach of an everyday code of conduct, moving to a crisis (where the liminal experience occurs), with people taking sides, applying redressive or remedial pressures on the person, culminating in the social reintegration or exclusion of the person from the social group.

3. Recall the discussion in the Preface on the long history of performance texts (poetry and short story readings) within anthropology (see Turner, 1986b).

4. A confusion in such response is often termed the affective fallacy (Bacon, 1979, p 196), being taken in by the performance, neglecting to critique the text on which the performance is based. Of course this relationship is always dialectical (see Tedlock, 1983, p. 236).

5. There are at least five texts embedded in every performed text: notes from the field, research texts, and interpretive documents (memos), which become public texts (drafts of articles) These public texts are then transformed into a performance text. Then, fifth, there is the performance, the *mise-en-scène* itself (Paget, 1993, p. 27), the live event. And behind all of this stands the dramatic field experience, which the performance aims to recreate, or relate back to in an evocative fashion. These textual forms stand in a complex relationship to one another.

6. These two terms refer to the ways in which the text uses everyday and scientific language, as well as how it articulates that language, for the printed, as opposed to the performed text (see Becker, McCall, & Morris, 1989) In the following section, I omit a discussion of staged readings and the performance of preexisting dramatic texts. They appear to have less relevance for performance ethnography, at this stage of its development.

7. Conquergood's work is located on the boundaries between speech communications, communication and performance studies, and urban ethnography See also his two documentary films (Conquergood, 1985b, 1990).

8. Of course, there is a large literature on performance texts, especially in the field of speech communication, where the oral and performance interpretation of classic, folk and native literatures has a long history (see Hamera, 1986; also Strine, 1988) The interpretive move in anthropology opened the way for these practionners to take an ethnographic turn, producing texts that could then be performed (see Conquergood, 1985, 1986, 1991, 1992). This lead to inter-

actions with Bakhtin, Geertz, Victor Turner, poststructuralism, the Frankfurt School, feminism , postmodernism, language poetry, and performance art (see Park-Fuller, 1986; Hamera, 1986; Pace, 1987; Tallant, 1988; Bowman, 1988; Pollock, 1988; Capo, 1988; Strine, 1988; Conquergood, 1992).

9. *Fourth wall:* In Readers Theater, an imaginary barrier between performers and audience which the audience crosses (looking in upon the actors), but the actors do not look out at the audience (Coger & White, 1973, p 28).

10. *Agit-prop* and *sloganizing theater*: theater pieces devised to ferment political action and agitation.

11. A case in point is Richardson (1993, p 699), who skipped a line when she read a poem which was based on a transcribed interview. Audience members charged her with changing the poem's meaning, with violating the original text and endangering its reliability and validity. Some said her findings were no longer accurate. One audience member even asked if it was all fiction, "Did you actually do an interview?" (p. 700).

12. The rise of performance art corresponds to the politicization of art and culture associated with the Vietnam War and Watergate, as well as with the women's movement (Sayre, 1990, p 98). It would be co-opted in the 1980s with the New Wave movement (see Birringer, 1993, p. 173).

13. The concept of a group (ensemble) of performers who performed the same dramatic work over and over again was also challenged ("traditional" theater) Peoples' theater also emerged, where (in some versions) members of the local community, previously denied power, including the elderly, ethnic minorities, women, the handicapped, and the imprisoned (Capo, 1983, p. 34) become performers of their own stories of oppression (see also Boal, 1985, 1995; Bacon, 1979; Pickering, 1975; Liggett, 1970).

14. They called this "editing reality (1990, pp 117–118), contending that the script method created spaces for the inclusion of large chunks of verbatim quotes, while letting many different voices be heard.

15. They offer a series of rules: If the performance is to be documented, then stage directions should be included in the published script, if not, they can be left out If the script is formatted for publication, when sociologists speak they can treated like a theater chorus, giving the audience interpretations of what is going on. When members of the audience speak, their speeches are indented and their characters are given names. When the sociologist speaks to other characters, the dialogue format is used, and the names of real people are not used in the script (1989, p. 86).

16. Hilbert (1990, p 134)) argued that the McCall and Becker had not given sufficient reasons to support their new form of reporting social science data. He suggested that that there is no inherent advantage in presenting large chunks of verbatim quotations, and wondered what happened to the sociolo-

gist's goal of analyzing ethnographic materials, fearing that McCall and Becker leave the analyst with no guidelines for what to do with their scripts and performances.

17. Stucky (p 178) argues that the staging of natural performances involves five steps: recording, transcribing, analyzing, rehearsing, performing.

18. Mienczakowski's project is less subject to these criticisms

19. The song's title "refers not only to a magazine but also to a feminine ideal from the 1920s that glamorized women by making them equal in position to men" (Northcott, 1995, p 3).

20. Limitations of space prohibit the presentation and discussion of another co-performance text which uses quilting, and the arrangement of fabric squares with text-fragments which are held and spoken by audience members (see Page, 1995)

21. Conquergood cites a cultural preservation group who performed (over the objections of Hopi elders) the sacred Hopi Snake Dance, and sold trinkets for $750, all in the name of preserving a dying culture (Conquergood, 1985, p. 5).

References

Bacon, W. A. (1979). *The art of interpretation*, 3rd ed. New York: Holt, Rinehart and Winston.

————. (1980). An aesthetics of performance. *Literature in Performance, 1,* 1–9.

Bakhtin, M. M. (1968). *Rabelais and his world*. Cambridge, MA: MIT Press.

————. (1981). *The dialogical imagination*. Austin: University of Texas Press.

————. (1986). *Speech genres and other late essays*. Austin: University of Texas Press.

Bauman, R. (1986). *Story, performance, event: Contextual studies of oral narratives.* Cambridge: Cambridge University Press.

Becker, H. S., Michal, M. M., & Morris, L. V. (1989). Theaters and communities: Three scenes. *Social Problems, 36,* 93–116.

Birringer, J. (1993). *Theater, theory, postmodernism.* Bloomington: Indiana University Press.

Boal, A. (1985/1979). *Theater of the oppressed.* New York: Theater Communications Group.

————. (1995). *The rainbow of desire: The boal method of theater and therapy.* (Adrian Jackson, Trans.). New York: Routledge.

Bochner, A. P. (1994). Perspectives on inquiry II: Theories and stories. In M. Knapp & G. R. Miller (Eds.), *The handbook of interpersonal communication* (pp. 21–41). Thousand Oaks, CA: Sage.

Bowman, M. S. (1988). Cultural critique as performance: The example of Walter Benjamin. *Literature in Performance, 8,* 4–11.

Brown, E. B. (1989). African-American women's quilting: A framework for conceptualizing and teaching African-American women's history. *Signs, 14,* 921–929.

Brown, R. H. (1987). *Society as text.* Chicago: University of Chicago Press.

Bruner, E. M. (1984). The opening up of anthropology. E. M. Bruner (Ed.), *Text, play, and story: The construction and reconstruction of self and society* (pp. 1–18). Washington, DC: American Ethnological Society.

————. (1986). Experience and its expressions. In V. M. Turner & E. M. Bruner (Eds.), *The anthropology of experience* (pp. 3–30). Urbana: University of Illinois Press.

————. (1993). Introduction: The ethnographic self and the personal self. In P. Benson (ed.), *Anthropology and Literature* (pp. 1–26). Urbana: University of Illinois Press.

Burke, K. (1969). *Rhetoric of motives.* Berkeley, CA: University of California Press.

Capo, K. E. (1983). Performance of literature as social dialect. *Literature in Performance.* 4: 31–36.

————. (1988). Presence, aura, and memory: Implications of Walter Benjamin and the Frankfurt School for performance theory. *Literature in Performance, 8,* 28–34.

Coger, L. I., & White, M. R. 1973. *Readers theater handbook.* Glenview, IL: Scott, Foresman and Company.

Cohn, R. (1988). Realism. In M. Banham (Ed.), *The Cambridge guide to theater* (p. 815). Cambridge: Cambridge University Press.

Conquergood, D. (1985a). Performing as a moral act: Ethical dimenstions of the ethnography of performance. *Literature in Performance, 5,* 1–13.

————. (1985b). *Between two worlds,: The Hmong shaman in America* (Documentary Film). Chicago: Siegel Productions.

————. (1986). Performing cultures: Ethnography, epistemology, and ethics. In E. Slembek (Ed.), *Miteinander sprechen and handeln: Festschrift für Hellmut Geissner.* Frankfurt: Scriptor.

————. (1989). Poetics, play, process and power: The performance turn in anthropology. *Text and Performance Quarterly, 9,* 82–88.

————. (1990). *The heart broken in half* (Documentary Film). Chicago: Siegel Productions.

————. (1991). Rethinking ethnography: Towards a critical cultural politics. *Communication Monographs, 58,* 179–194.

————. (1992). Ethnography, rhetoric and performance. *Quarterly Journal of Speech, 78,* 80–97.

Debord, G. (1983). *Society of the spectacle.* Detroit: Black and Red.

Denzin, N. K. (1992). *Symbolic interactionism and cultural studies.* Cambridge, MA: Blackwell.

————. (1996). *Interpretive ethnography.* Newbury Park, CA: Sage.

Diamond, S. (Ed.). (1986a). A special issue on poetry and anthropology. *Dialectical Anthropology, 11,* 2–4.

————. (1986b). Preface. A special issue on poetry and anthropology. *Dialectical Anthropology, 11*(2–4), 131–132.

Donmoyer, R., & Yennie-Donmoyer, J. (1995). Data as drama: Reflections on the use of readers theatre as an artistic mode of data display. *Qualitative Inquiry, 1*(4), 402–428.

Dufrenne, M. (1973). *The phenomenology of aesthetic experience.* Evanston, IL: Northwestern University Press.

Ellis, C. (1993). Telling a story of sudden death. *Sociological Quarterly, 34,* 711–773

————. (1994). Between social science and literature: What are our options? *Symbolic Interaction, 17,* 325–330.

————. (1995). *Final negotiations.* Philadelphia: Temple University Press.

Ellis, C., & Bochner, A. P. (1992a). Telling and performing personal stories: The constraints of choice in abortion. In C. Ellis & M. G. Flaherty (Eds.), *Investigating subjectivity: Research on lived experience* (pp. 79–101). Newbury Park, CA: Sage.

Ellis, C., & Flaherty, M. G. (1992a). An agenda for the interpretation of lived experience. In C. Ellis & M. G. Flaherty (Eds.), *Investigating subjectivity: Research on lived experience* (pp. 1–16). Newbury Park, CA: Sage.

Etherton, M. (1988). Third world popular theater. In M. Banham (Ed.), *The Cambridge guide to theater* (pp. 991–992). Cambridge: Cambridge University Press.

Fabian, J. (1990). *Power and performance: Ethnographic explorations through proverbial wisdom and theater in Shaba, Zaire.* Madison: University of Wisconsin Press.

Foucault, M. (1984). What is enlightenment? In P. Rabinow (Ed.), *The Foucault reader* (pp. 32–50). New York: Pantheon

Geertz, C. (1973). *The interpretation of culture*. New York: Basic Books.

———. (1983). *Local knowledge*. New York: Basic Books.

———. (1988). *Words and lives*. Stanford: Stanford University Press.

———. (1995). *After the fact*. Cambridge, MA: Harvard University Press.

Goffman, E. (1959). *The presentation of self in everyday life*. New York: Doubleday.

Gottlieb, A., & Graham, P. (1993). *Parallel worlds: An anthropologist and a writer encounter Africa*. Chicago: University of Chicago Press.

Grindal, B. T., & Shephard, W. H. (1993). Redneck girl: From experience to performance. In P. Benson (Ed.), *Anthropology and Literature* (pp. 151–172). Urbana: University of Illinois Press.

Hamera, J. (1986). Postmodern performance, postmodern criticism. *Literature in Performance, 7*, 13–20.

Haraway, D. (1985). A manifesto for cyborgs: Science, technology and socialist feminism in the 1980s. *Socialist Review, 80*, 65–107.

Hilbert, R. A. (1990). The efficacy of performance science: Comment on McCall and Becker. *Social Problems, 37*, 133–135.

Hymes, D. (1980). Educational ethnology. *Anthropology and Education Quarterly, 11*, 3–8.

———. (1985). Foreword. In J. I. Prattis (Ed.), *Reflections: The anthropological muse* (pp. 11–13). Washington DC: American Anthropological Association.

Iser, W. (1978). *The act of reading: A theory of aesthetic response*. Baltimore: Johns Hopkins University Press.

Jackson, M. (1989). *Paths toward a clearing: Radical empiricism and ethnographic inquiry*. Bloomington: Indiana University Press.

Jackson, S. (1993). Ethnography and the audition: Performance as ideological critique. *Text and Performance Quarterly, 13*, 21–43.

Kapferer, B. (1986). Performance, and the structuring of meaning and experience. In V. M. Turner & E. M. Bruner (Eds.), *The Anthropology of Experience* (pp. 188–203). Urbana: University of Illinois Press.

Kurosawa, A. (Director). (1950). *Rashomon*.

Langellier, K. M. (1983). A phenomenological approach to audience. *Literature in Performance, 3*, 34–39.

Lavie, S. (1990). *The poetics of military occupation: Mzeina allegories of identity under Israeli and Egyptian rule*. Berkeley, CA: University of California Press.

Lefebvre, H. (1971/1984). *Everyday life in the modern world*: New Brunswick, NJ: Transaction Books.

Liggett, C. E. (1970). *The theater student: Concert theater*. New York: Richard Rosen Press.

Loseke, D. R. (1995). Homelessness and involuntary commitent: Constructing persons, writing rights. Presented to the 1995 Annual Meeting of the Midwest Sociological Society, Chicago.

Loxley, R. B. (1983). Roles of the audience: Aesthetic and social dimensions of the performance event. *Literature in Performance, 3*, 40–44.

Lyman, S. (1990). *Civilizatation: Contents, discontents, malcontents and other essays in social theory*. Fayetteville: University of Arkansas Press.

Maclay, J. H. (1971). *Readers theater: Toward a grammar of practice*. New York: Random House.

Madison, D. S. (1993). "That was myoccupation": Oral narrative, performance, and black feminist thought. *Text and Performance Quarterly, 13*, 213–232.

Marcus, G. E. (1994). What comes (just) after "post"? The case of ethnography. In N. K. Denzin & Y. S. Lincoln (Eds.), *The handbook of qualitative research* (pp. 563–574). Newbury Park, CA: Sage.

McCall, M., & Becker, H. S. (1990). Performance science. *Social Problems, 32*, 117–132.

Mienczkowski, J. (1992). *Synching out loud: A Journey into illness*. Brisbane: Griffth University, Reprographics.

————. (1994). Reading and writing research. *NADIE Journal, 18*, 45–54.

————. (1995). The theater of ethnography: The reconstruction of ethnography into theater with emancipatory potential. *Qualitative Inquiry, 1*(3), 360–375.

Mienczkowski, J., & Morgan, S. (1993). *Busting: The challenge of the drought spirit*. Brisbane: Griffth University, Reprographics.

Mills, C. W. (1963). *Power, politics, and people: The collected essays of C. Wright Mills* (I. L. Horowitz, Ed.). New York: Ballantine.

Minister, K. (1983). Doing deconstruction: The extra-institutional Performance of Literature. *Literature in Performance, 4*, 51–55.

Northcott, A. (1995). New woman. Unpublished song. Institute of Communications Research, University of Illinois, Urbana.

Pace, P. (1987). Language poetry: The radical writing project. *Literature in Performance, 7,* 23–33.

Page, B. (1995). Parkland College instructor mom/student son co-performance text. Performance Text, Department of Special Education, University of Illinois, Urbana. *Literature in Performance, 7,* 23–33.

Paget, M. (1990a). Performing the text. *Journal of Contemporary Ethnography, 19,* 136–155.

———. (1990b). Life mirrors work mirrors text mirrors life . . . *Social Problems, 37,* 137–148.

Park-Fuller, L. M. (1986). Voices: Bakhtin's heterglossia and polyphony, and the performance of narrative literature. *Literature in Performance, 7,* 1–12.

Peterson, E. E. (1983). Symposium: The audience in interpretation theory: Introduction. *Literature in Performance, 3,* 33.

Pickering, J. V. (1975). *Readers theater.* Belmont, CA: Dickenson.

Pollock, D. (1988). Aesthetic negation after WWII: Mediating Bertolt Brecht and Theodor Adorno. *Literature in Performance, 8,* 12–20.

Prattis, J. I. (Ed.). (1985a). *Reflections: The anthropological muse.* Washington DC: American Anthropological Association.

———. (1985b.) Dialectics and experience in fieldwork: The poetic dimension. In J. I. Prattis (Ed.), *Reflections: The anthropological muse* (pp. 266–283). Washington DC: American Anthropological Association.

Probyn, E. (1993). *Sexing the self: Gendered positions in cultural studies.* London: Routledge.

Rabinow, P. (Ed). (1984). *The Foucault reader.* New York: Pantheon.

Richardson, L. (1991). Postmodern social theory. *Sociological Theory, 9,* 173–79.

———. (1992). The consequences of poetic representation: Writing the other, rewriting the self. In C. Ellis & M. G. Flaherty (Eds.), *Investigating subjectivity: Research on lived experience* (pp. 125–137). Newbury park, CA: Sage.

———. (1993). Poetic representation, Ethnographic representation and transgressive validity: The case of the skipped line. *Sociological Quarterly, 34,* 695–710.

———. (1994). Writing as a method of inquiry. In N. K. Denzin & Y. S. Lincoln (Eds.), *The Handbook of Qualitative Research* (pp. 516–529). Newbury Park: Sage.

———. (1995). But is it sociology? *Journal of Contemporary Ethnography:* in press.

Richardson, L., & Lockridge, E. (1991). The sea monster: An ethnographic drama. *Symbolic Interaction, 14*, 335–340.

Ronai, C. R. (1992). The reflexive self through narrative: A night in the life of an erotic dancer/researcher. In C. Ellis & M. G. Flaherty (Eds.), *Investigating subjectivity: Research on lived experience* (pp. 102–124). Newbury Park, CA: Sage.

————. (1995). Multiple reflections of child sex abuse: An argument for a lay-ered account. *Journal of Contemporary Ethnography, 23*, 395–426.

Rorty, R. (1980). *Philosophy and the mirror of nature*. Princeton: Princeton University Press.

————. (1989). *Contingency, irony, and solidarity*. Cambridge: Cambridge University Press.

————. (1991). *Objectivity, relativism, and truth*. New York: Cambridge University Press.

Rose, E. (1995). The wearld. *Studies in Symbolic Interaction, 17*, 110–135.

Sanmiguel, L. M. (1995). Re-defining endometriosis/re-defining me. *Cultural Studies: A Research Annual, 1*, 101–106.

Sayre, H. (1990). Performance. In F. Lentricchia & T. McLaughlin (Eds.), *Critical terms for literary study* (pp. 91–104). Chicago: Univesity of Chicago Press.

Schechner, R. (1986). Magnitudes of performance." In V. M. Turner & E. M. Bruner (Eds.), *The anthropology of experience* (pp. 344–369). Urbana: University of Illinois Press.

Smith, D. E. (1990a). *The conceptual practices of power: A feminist sociology of knowl-edge*. Boston: Northeastern University Press.

————. (1990b). *Texts, facts, and femininity: Exploring the relations of ruling*. New York: Routledge.

Strine, M. S. (1988). Response: Negotiating the tensions between art and every-day life. *Literature in Performance, 8*, 35–38.

Strine, M. S., Long, B., & Hopkins, M. F. (1990). Research in interpretation and performance studies. In G. M. Phillips & J. T. Wood (Eds.), *Speech commu-nication: Essays to commemorate the seventy-fifth anniversary of the Speech Communication Association* (pp. 181–204). Carbondale, IL: Southern Illinois University Press.

Stucky, N. (1993). Toward an aesthetics of natural performance. *Text and Performance Quarterly, 13*, 168–80.

Tallant, C. (1988). Editor's introduction. Symposium: Performance and Critical Theory—The Frankfurt School. *Literature in Performance, 8*, 1–3.

Tedlock, D. (1983). *The spoken word and the word of interpretation.* Philadelphia: University of Pennsylvania Press.

Trinh, T. M. (1989). *Woman, native, other: Writing postcoloniality and feminism.* Bloomington: Indiana University Press.

————. (1991). *When the moon waxes red: Representation, gender and cultural politics.* New York: Routledge.

————. (1992). *Framer framed.* New York: Routledge.

Turner, V. (1981). Social dramas and stories about them. In W. Mitchell (Ed.), *On narrative* (pp. 141–168). Chicago: University of Chicago Press.

————. (1982). *From ritual to theater.* New York: Performing Arts Journal Publications.

————. (1986a). Dewey, Dilthey, and drama: An essay in the anthropology of experience. In V. M. Turner & E. M. Bruner (Eds.), *The anthropology of experience* (pp. 33–44). Urbana: University of Illinois Press.

————. (1986b). *The anthropology of performance.* New York: Performing Arts Journal Publications.

————. (with E. Turner). (1982). Performing ethnography. *The Drama Review, 26,* 33–50.

Turner, V., & Bruner, E. (Eds.). (1986). *The anthropology of experience.* Urbana: University of Illinois Press.

Ulmer, G. (1989). *Teletheory.* New York: Routledge.

Van Oosting, J. (1981). Some observations upon the common aesthetics of story writing and the solo performance of prose fiction. *Literature in Performance, 2,* 66–75.

Walstrom, M. (1995). "Mystory" of anorexia nervosa: New discourses for change and recovery. *Cultural Studies: A Research Annual, 1,* 67–100.

9

PERFORMING BETWEEN THE POSTS: AUTHORITY, POSTURE, AND CONTEMPORARY FEMINIST SCHOLARSHIP

ERICA McWILLIAM

All academic writers and teachers claim authority, including those who seek to disrupt modernist mechanisms of authorial or pedagogical power. Academics enact this claim through particular textual and corporeal performances. As textual and material "bodies of knowledge," we pose and gesture what it means to be in authority for a range of audiences, from undergraduates to editors. The strategic use of authoritative citations in an academic paper, for example, is a gesture that may serve the same symbolic function that a lecturer's body does when it grasps both sides of the lectern, leans forward, and utters measured and resonant sounds in a mass lecture. In both of these instances, the scholarly performance functions to shore up the authority of the writer/speaker. A "disruptive" or transgressive scholastic performance is not a refusal of academic authority. It is simply a different posturing of authority, whether it is the thesis which has departed from the traditional print format or the teacher who signals the start of a pedagogical event by creating a diversion in the back of the lecture hall.

There are rules about what constitutes an authoritative posturing of academic scholarship. This flies in the face of the myth that eccentricity and academic genius operate outside rules. The (gendered) rules about what it means to perform as a "mad professor," for instance, are well understood and rehearsed by many academics, as are the rules for being an "enfant terrible." These rules govern strategic use of quirky humour, style of personal presentation, use of obscene or sexually explicit language, and the like.

The authoritative textual performance of a poststructural, postcritical, or postpositivist research project also follows rules. These are the rules for transgressing modernist writing strategies and formats. These rules may (or may not) become available to researchers as they engage for extended periods in the careful and close reading of the theoretical texts which will inform their postfoundational work. This comes as a disappointment, of course, to those who hope for a quick fix on postmodernism or any other set of "post" ideas, or those who hope to avoid their own dose of PMT (Post Modernist Tension: see McWilliam, 1993). As a supervisor of "post" projects, I require my dissertation students to be able to make explicit what their writing rules are, and often this involves a long process that begins with understanding what they are *not*. Like their positivist sisters, "post" researchers must generate a cogent and integrated textual performance. The difference is that "post" research projects effectively engage with, in order to *disrupt*, orthodox representations of reality as integrated and cogent. They will therefore be most unlikely to involve a linear, one-off treatment of theory/method/findings.

In speaking of the "post" rules, I am not referring to the imperative to produce "socially recognisable data" (Ladwig, 1995)—although this might be a reasonable expectation from any piece of educational research. I am talking about the fact that epistemological and theoretical shifts mean *new* textual forms rather than *no* textual form. The sort of multi-layered research that "post" scholarship tends to generate is a conscious and visible performance of theorising in a way that foundational research rarely enacts. Thus nothing is more deadly to any "post" research project than a researcher who has confused performing the "posts" with serendipity, idiosyncrasy, or mere pluralism. It is just as fatal as the instrumentalist call for a little empirical moment to make what is apparently flaccid data "harder." The result is certainly a performance, but one that is untrustworthy in its lack of potential to disseminate valid knowledge.

New Feminist Scholarship as a Performance

As demonstrated above, I frequently write and speak below the belt as feminist "post" writer and teacher. Contributing to this collection gives me the opportunity to reflect openly on the way feminist scholars in particular have performed "post" scholarship in education, including two of my own performances to date. My purpose is to indicate how "re/membering the body" (Shapiro, 1994) of feminist scholarship might extend the range of narrative possibilities for feminist educational writers and teachers. To do this, I am extending the metaphor of narrative "voice" by trying to foreground the "bodies of knowledge," both material and figurative, which produce written and spoken language as a stylised and performative *utterance*.

In the dual domains of teaching and research, feminists, as material and textual bodies of knowing, have demanded authority through our performances in the halls of academe. Our "post" performances in education have been very seductive for some (including myself) and very off-putting for others. This has to do with the way "post" scholarship has been "postured" in our writing and speaking. While this will come as no surprise to the academic reader, there are particular aspects of this that demand closer scrutiny. I will not take up here issues that are to do with the way women scholars may be read doubly as women and as scholars (unlike male academics), nor will I deal with issues around the construction of the female student/reader, although these topics continue to be fleshed out by other feminist writers (e.g., Gibbs, 1995). Rather, I want to squeeze the thespian metaphor for what it might offer up in terms of a more robust enactment of feminist scholarship in the academy.

I am aware of the prevailing antitheatrical impetus that cautions against moving education too predictably toward the metaphor of theater—with the scholar performing for the pleasure of hearing "author!" For a feminist readership, the metaphor of "performing" teaching and research may well be doubly worrying as narcissistic and ignorant. Given the huge volume of work devoted to critiquing "personality cult" teaching as pedagogical arrogance, and related deconstructive research about male patriarchal gaze, this is understandable. However, I am proceeding in this way in order to signal the importance of the relationship between the issue of how feminists perform as "authorities," and the matter of how pleasure is at work in such performances. I want to heed the challenge of Gamman and Marshment (1993), who argue:

> What we need is an analysis which can begin to explain in more specific ways the relationships between our *pleasures* and their ideological grounding, and how we might go about changing these relationships. (p. 6, emphasis mine)

Much feminist research has insisted on a direct relationship between the authority that ought to be accorded to a text and the degree to which it engages with women's lived experiences in the context of oppressive power relations. This has been enacted, with justification, through a preoccupation with women's pain as the most compelling catalyst for feminist research. We are much less practiced in textual performances that interrogate pleasure, including the pleasure of our own research, writing, and teaching. As a result, many opportunities to perform disruptively as "women dancing back" (Gotfrit, 1988) have been missed. As feminists, we have at times positioned ourselves narrowly in relation to educational scholarship, striking mawkish poses that deny "our passion for power in learning, our delight in the flirtatiousness of intellectual debate, in the game of competing, in the sexiness of winning" (Kirby, 1994, p. 19). The appeal to the abstract principles of a socially transformative project has relegated pleasure to a problematic "lower order" status as a theme for research. The desire of women to be pleasured (especially heterosexual women) is uncomfortably bound up with issues around the eroticisation of women's subordination (Jackson, 1995). Fortunately, there is now an increasing tendency for feminists to display *the pleasure of ethical identities* rather than to perform ethics *as the antithesis of* pleasure (e.g., Stinson, 1995; Grant, 1993; Gamman & Marshment, 1993; Gotfrit, 1988).

The caution remains justified that *performing pleasure* runs a big risk of sliding feminist scholarship into artifice—passive entertainment or mere showing off. But I insist on it because it connects our work as feminists to ancient traditions of performative instruction among women. Women were once powerful scholars and instructors, particularly in the erotic arts, through which they revealed the art of pleasuring the body to other women, giving quite specific instruction about female bodily pleasure and what it meant to be pleasured as a woman. In this ancient tradition, knowledge was transmitted typically through a strict procedure whereby the disciple followed step by step a woman who was "keeper of the secrets" (Cryle, 1994, p. 77). Cryle cites the work of Nicolas Chorier who, writing in 1655 about ancient representations of the figures of Venus, depicted erotic art as a set of tableaux, setting out a range of venereal positions in such a way as to allow them to be taught by women to women. Cryle (1994) elaborates:

> They set out all they knew, and conceivably all there was to know, so that it could be understood and followed by others. . . . [T]he nature and number of those skills appeared quite finite (pp. 12–13) . . . the set of postures is likely to be numerically precise—as is the space of effort available to the learner. . . . (pp. 12–13)

> [T]he examples . . . to be imitated . . . continue[d] to be made present by the on-going practice of postural modeling as erotic learning. Later when the originals [were] lost, this procedure . . . continue[d] of itself. (p. 18)

What is interesting to me here is that certain women occupied unproblematically the position of "instructor" of other women, and insisted on being very closely read and imitated by others. In a modernist scholastic world where men have claimed "to know" and women have claimed that something "is known" (Le Doeuff, 1977), there may be much to gain from feminists' speaking as instructors and keepers of secrets of erotic pleasure. The metaphor of "postural modeling" certainly allows a way of reflecting on the specific ways feminist "post" authors and teachers have displayed our disciplines at work in the culture of education. Clearly we have rehearsed and enacted particular poses or authoritative "positions" in relation to knowledge and performed these for the gaze of others. I want to move in closer to examine feminist "post" scholarship as a "sight/site of authoritative display" (Angel, 1994, p. 61).

Below are my reflections on two performances of my own academic work as a "post" scholar and feminist. The first was the process of changing my "postpositivist" thesis into a book. This was important inasmuch as it required a significant change of textual "posture" in which much loss was suffered, and a few small gains made, by the book over the thesis as a site of feminist scholarship. The second is to do with a much earlier confrontation over the issue of language use. It is a reflection upon public arguments among women scholars and the implications of this sight of feminist knowledge performance.

Performing from Thesis to Book

I was told in my doctoral days that my Ph.D. would serve as a kind of driver's licence, permitting me to steer around the twists and turns of scholarship as an academic, an insider. For the overwhelming bulk of the population, including academics, a doctoral thesis certainly has something in common with a driver's licence in that it is about as interesting a read as a driver's licence, with the disadvantage that reading it takes a lot longer. Moreover, a driver's licence at least has someone literally "in the picture." (Could this mean, you may ask, that in doctoral texts it is the rest of us who have been framed?) To sustain the metaphor of driving and being driven just a little longer, I negotiated a number of postmodern turns and more than a few jump starts, about which I have written in an earlier cathartic paper, "Post Haste: Plodding Research and Galloping Theory" (1993).

Given the legendary status of the doctorate as necessarily and perversely unreadable, the issue of whether to embark on a very different sort of textual performance, that is, to publish the doctoral thesis as a book, in part or whole, can be a tricky and demanding one for any postdoctoral scholar. Already such a scholar will have passed through a number of phases. At the beginning, there were enthusiasms in the area of endeavor—an idea that might well save/enlighten/empower a world. That idea—perhaps despite resistance—was turned into a smaller and more sober project that was actually doable, through hours of time spent with supervisors and others "in the know." There was the shock of finding that "the literature" was an inappropriately tidy term for a disparate array of ideas that must be turned into a coherent conceptual map. There was the venture into the seductive and depressing domain of "qualitative" research, and the agony of feeling that the center was not holding, things were falling apart—that interpreting an already interpreted world was all very well as a guiding principle, but, as a set of operations, it had all the structural qualities of a blancmange. There was then the horror of being advised in the "final week" that it looked as though there were only two months of really hard work left to generate the absolutely final draft.

In my own case, having survived the loneliness of the long-distance thesis—mine was a longitudinal study (McWilliam, 1992)—it remained for me to consider whether and how to publish what I had produced. This meant a considerable reworking of the text from its fairly close approximation to the predictable linear form of literature-theory-method-findings. There were a number of matters that must be attended to. These matters derived from the inescapable fact that my erstwhile audience of three picky, knowledgeable, academic examiners had become, potentially at least, a fair percentage of the print-literate world. The issue for me as actor/writer here was: What sort of textual performance is now appropriate?

While there are a host of issues I could comment on in terms of "performing" the published thesis, I want to select two issues here—both of which pertain to the matter of "troubling clarity" (Lather, 1995) in initial teacher education. The first is the extent to which publishing forces an ironing out of "rhizomatic" methodology (Lather, 1993). The second is to do with plain and simple truths.

The thesis contains three research "moments"—the first, "Making Semiotic Space: The Researcher as Subject," is a "corrective" moment in which I brought forward my own prejudgments of pre-service teachers for scrutiny. The second "moment," "Producing and Contesting Needs Talk: The Pre-service Teacher as Subject," analyses the texts produced by a group of pre-service teachers over their three-year course of professional preparation, while the third "moment," "Playing out Critique in the Real: The Researcher and the Researched as Co-theorists," is a reciprocal, negotiated phase of the research, a period of collective reflection-in-action on the texts produced by both the students and myself.

What I was finally unable to do in the book (McWilliam, 1994a) was to include the quite complex process by which I brought forward my own "liberatory" assumptions and was forced to question them. While my deconstruction of a liberatory text was included, an editorial decision was made to omit the empirical study of over 350 pre-service students through which I looked again at the allegation of student teachers' "ideological conservatism." Not only was it considered irrelevant for the American reader, but it disrupted the flow of the text with its empirical disciplining of the data. The fact that a discourse-theoretical reading of that data was provided in order to abide by the writing rules of my postpositivist dissertation, was immaterial. Now it is a strange thing for me to find myself being an advocate for empirical work of the statistical kind, but in this case the important issue in terms of methodology was the kind of strategic intervention I was making here. I was wanting to disrupt the quantitative-as-hard/masculine versus qualitative-as-soft/feminine binary formulation of research methodology as much as I wanted to disrupt the liberal/conservative binary formulation used to "judge" student teachers. The book, while much more readable than the thesis, is less than satisfactory as a "performance" of the "journey among intersections, nodes and regionalisations" (Lather, 1993, p. 680) that characterized the research project.

In the book, I took up Michael Apple's (1988) dictum that "clarity begins at home," reworking it from a caution against obscurity in critical scholarship into a caution to guard against the "blissful clarity" that results from keeping our familiar discourses intact. Perhaps predictably, however, the editors kept insisting that the simple stories I was determined to overthrow were the best part of my writing. "This bit is nice and clear," they said, "why can't you write the rest like this?" For me, the very simplicity of the cause/effect story or conspiracy theory was the problem—for the editors it was the highlight of the performance. I was as dramatist delivering the carefully crafted soliloquy about new life while a spent but still twitching corpse upstaged me, and the critics raved. I have since tried to perform my written text more simply, but not simplistically. This is because I do want to give others entree to the "post" ideas that I find pleasurable, pragmatic, and overdue in education. I do not wish to seem perversely determined to be misunderstood. At the same time, I reject the view that all complexity can be represented through plain language and that this should be the perennial criterion of the good textual performance.

Performing for the "Anti-Post" Industry

Of course, not everyone feels this way. That is, not everyone sees "post" theoretical developments as pleasurable or pragmatic, much less overdue for educators. Nor does every "post" writer really want to give entree into "an increasingly small and precious world" of scholars, as Maxine Greene (1993) has named "post" academic communities. At times it has seemed to me that access to the "post" agenda is like purchasing the item with the Gucchi label. If you have to ask about what's written on the ticket, then you simply won't be buying any of it.

Part of the problem here is that New French Theory, which permeates so much of the poststructural and postcritical literature, insists on making the familiar strange. The implications of this for researchers is that they may not use a pinch of poststructuralism to add contemporary spice to a pre- and post-attitudinal survey. Nor may a researcher claim to be using "postcritical" theorizing and still speak unproblematically of an emancipatory or transformative project. A postpositivist research project will not be produced out of writing that gestures toward pluralism as "multi-methods" but never troubles the binary formulation of quantitative *versus* qualitative research by addressing it as an epistemological problem. A lack of clarity about discourse, language, vocabulary, rhetoric, text—or the elision of the lot—will spell disaster for the disciplining of the data, and so on. The possibilities remain seductive, but the rigor required in getting the transgressive performance *right*, as well as written, is extremely demanding.

That feminist writing "between the posts" has been a bearer of this academic "news" means that it constantly suffers the fate of the unwelcome messenger as a result. Performing this telling for audiences of academics and other educators runs the grave risk of inciting anxiety, even downright animosity, in the reader/listener, academic or otherwise. While postmodern scholarship may be seductive to those among them who love to play with words—a theoretical cocktail for playing with and giggling over, for slashing and burning, for bracketing and bucketing—it is galling for the many others who take their writing neat.

For the uninitiated, "post" may well have all the allure of a completely foreign dialect. I remember well my anguish years ago, when sitting at a dinner table of guffawing French academics, one of whom had told what was apparently a screamingly funny joke which, with my own French limited to "Merci, tres gentil," I could not understand. When I asked for a translation I was told, "It's actually hilarious but untranslatable!" My feelings at that moment I have seen again in the reactions of many "modernist" scholars to New French Theory and all those who cherish it. "Post" comes to them as a judgment, condemning their own work as either facile or past its use-by date. While this might be understood to misconstrue the post agenda's insistence on "post" as necessarily "engaged with," it is an understandable response by those who feel condemned to the ranks of the Neanderthal.

As writers we are also "post" teachers, and we must struggle against not so much a lack of knowledge but resistance to knowledge—what Lacan calls *the passion for ignorance* (Lacan, cited in Felman, 1986, p. 30). Because ignorance is not passive but an active and radical condition, that is, "the desire to ignore" (Felman, 1986, p. 30), an active dynamic is needed to counter its power, a performance that is more seductive than we have been able to achieve in feminist post scholarship thus far. Seduced ourselves by the idea of the new analytical tools to be shaped out of the rich resource of New Theory, we underestimate the radical desire in others to ignore those same resources, and the strength of their passion to defend familiar, even sacred ground. Such anti-post arguments may be cast as an extension of the perennial "relevance" debate—that "post" scholarship is theoretical work so remote from the lived experience of mortals as to be mere academic dillentantism. In the same way that undergraduates will give the reason of "presumed irrelevance" for not attending lectures, the more pressing and understandable reason may be the overwhelming desire to ignore the message altogether.

As I have argued elsewhere (McWilliam, 1995), it is increasingly necessary for university teachers to be *seductive* and to claim the power to seduce, particularly in those discipline areas that have been damned with the label "theory." Here I want to rescue the notion of "seductive power" from any radically subjective connotation by drawing on the work of Ross Chambers (1984), who states:

> [T]he claim to seductive power [is] . . . a claim of perlocutionary force, another *kind* of power. It is not self-directed but other-directed; and it is definable as the power to achieve authority and to produce involvement . . . within a situation from which power is itself absent. If such a power can be called seduction, it is because seduction is, by definition, a phenomenon of persuasion: it cannot rely on force or institutional authority ("power"), for it is, precisely, a means of achieving mastery in the absence of such means of control. It is the instrument available to the situationally weak against the situationally strong. (pp. 211–212)

In Chambers terms, "theory" teachers and writers have become the "situationally weak." The power that institutional authority and social deference once made available to the academic as philosopher/guru has been lost in the rush to pragmatism observable in the restructuring of tertiary institutions, as *praxis* becomes elevated over *theoria*. In broad terms, "theory" teachers have increasingly been unable to "occupy the symbolic position of subject supposed to know" (Deutscher, 1994, p. 40). It is for this reason that my insistence on the legitimacy of the seductive power in new feminist teaching and writing is not mere scholarly indulgence, but pragmatic and overdue.

To be more seductive first means recognising that seductive textual and pedagogical performances are duplicitous, that is, they conform to the reader/learner's desires while also having the function of satisfying other desires (e.g., the desire to instruct) in the writer/teacher. This recognition does not have to imply that the imperative to seduction is demeaning or unscholarly. It is simply necessary. Where once "erudite" or "complex" was a compliment to scholarship, quite the reverse is now true. With the halls of academe filled with new dialects producing new knowledges, there is nothing gained and much to lose from insisting that all objections to "post" performances must be motivated by "anti-intellectualism."

Having said that, I would nevertheless reject the implication that scholars can change "real life" practices and leave shared language in tact. There is a form of inverted intellectual snobbery that insists that a spade be called a spade and never a groundbreaking, earthmoving, agricultural implement. While I have understand the usefulness to which brevity can be put, I find myself perversely agreeing with Oscar Wilde in his insistence that those who call a spade a spade should be made to use one because it is all they are good for. I think history has shown us that language refuses paralysis, and this, indeed, would be evidenced by the racist overtones that might now be attributed to this very aphorism so long after Wilde's death.

For feminists, the "post" performance can be doubly problematic. Our poses may look like lack of political will to many who continue with the deconstructive project of ideology critique. Meanwhile, we are as implicated in the politics of the backlash as any other feminist writer. I am constantly hearing about the supposed hegemony of "post" writing and feminist agendas in general, while at the same time noting that our education library's periodical section, as a site of educational knowledge, is almost entirely given over to "modernist" educational psychology and cognitive science, in which the majority of the authors are still men.

To probe the issue of feminist "bodies of knowledge" as the literal "sight" of authoritative display, I want to recall a debate/argument around the issue of language use in which I became embroiled at an international symposium for teacher educators. I had been described by an early keynote speaker as "an expert on action research," a frame that I was unhappy with, given that I was concerned about how issues of advocacy were *not* being met by the models of action research I was interrogating. Nevertheless, my "action research" paper was urged upon the final speaker by a participant who thought that she might find it helpful. In delivering her keynote address the next day, this speaker performed as pragmatist—someone who, as she put it, "calls a spade a spade and has her feet on the ground." She insisted on the need for change but had no truck with big words. And she insisted that she could cut it with the students in a way that these other "big word" users wouldn't begin to be able to emulate. By "big" words, the speaker seemed to mean *unfamiliar* words. It became clear that my "action research" paper was to be held up as an exemplar of "big word" use, which must be lampooned in the service of plain speaking. I was increasingly annoyed by the assumption that my scholarship was designed not to be understood and that it could therefore be assumed that my skills as a teacher educator were nonexistent.

My students, undergraduate or postgraduate, rarely if ever have expressed a problem with my language or a concern about my rarefied theorizing—on the contrary, they have often thanked me for my "pragmatism." I am aware, however, that a number of academic peers have from time to time expressed the view that students must find my work unfathomable, given the nature of my "post" scholarship. Ego to the fore, I pointed out, possibly unkindly, that a word like "semiotics" has no more syllables than "quantitative," and that, as teacher educators, all of the conference participants should be as open to new ideas in new forms as we expect our students to be. I argued that some ideas in "post" work—for instance, Foucault's dictum that "everything is dangerous"—are not expressed in big words, but are extremely useful as corrective moments in our own practice.

What followed from the keynote speaker was a refusal to engage and an expression of both hurt and anger. Later that day I saw the problem of this binary formulation "for or against the post," with the symposium becoming divided around the issue of "big [post] words." I was later approached by a female conference participant who expressed sympathy with my position but lamented the fact that a woman [me] had taken on another woman in a public forum in full view of "the chaps." Whatever objections I had, she said, I might have held them over to a more private moment. I was made quite annoyed by what I perceived to be her mawkishness about feminist/female public debate, but I was also not happy about the fallout from the event either. I enjoyed neither the demonising of my work nor my own preparedness to take on the role of public defender of "the posts." It is, of course, just an galling to be told, as I often have, that what you have just expressed is "the feminist point of view" as though "feminist" ideas are prescribed and proscribed—and thus so much simpler to dismiss.

Future Posting?

I am aware that a recent book chapter (Morgan & McWilliam, 1995) of mine is in a collected work called *Post postmodernism: Politics, Identity and Education* (Smith & Wexler, 1995), which begs the question "Where to from here?" in terms of a title (strike three posts and you're out). I am also aware that I am not at all seduced by most of the textual performances I can observe and be engaged in through the World Wide Web. As a voyeur on the Internet, a lurker on networks, I am both underwhelmed and limp when it comes to textual intercourse on the Net. And yet I see many of my colleagues mobilized by the potential thrill of surfing the Net. I can recognize this as profound desire, but I cannot share it. Netizens' dialects are at times as annoying to me as my writing has no doubt been to others. I am too easily distracted by numerical codes, incorrect spelling, and sloppy prose. I continue to be seduced by the certainty of print, the materiality of the crafting of words, the elegant substance of a leather-bound book.

What then of future "post" performances, with or without the Net? If increasingly the seductive power of our texts and utterances is to be enacted, it will not happen by reigning in our analyses or by excessive throat-clearing and textual gesturing toward ideological safety. It is not more timid or paralyzed performances we need but more adventurous ones. We need adventures that are allow us to perform knowing in ways that are pleasurable to ourselves and a larger audience of others. I have found, for example, that by making a lateral shift into engaging with eighteenth-century literary criticism, I have been able to draw on premodernist practices in the erotic arts to write about how feminist pedagogues might push past the modernist binary formulation of "being Sir or staying Mum" (McWilliam, 1994b). This has been a much more pleasurable and "practical" endeavor for my work as a teacher educator than reploughing the familiar fields of learning theory and/or critical pedagogy.

In performing our scholarly narratives, nothing will succeed like *excess*. However, this is not excess as a "spillover" of unruly thinking, nor excess as a rarefied retreat from the "pragmatic" demands of others. It is excess as a seductive display of feminist authority, in all the ways that new terrains of theory may make possible.

References

Angel, M. (1994). Pedagogies of the obscene: The specular body and demonstration. In J. J. Matthews (Ed.), *Jane Gallop seminar papers: Proceedings of the Jane Gallop seminar and public lecture "The teacher's breasts," June 1993* (pp. 61–72). Canberra, Australia: Humanities Research Centre.

Apple, M. (1988). *Teachers and texts: A political economy of class and gender relations in education.* New York: Routledge and Kegan Paul.

Chambers, R. (1984). *Story and situation: Narrative seduction and the power of fiction.* Minneapolis: University of Minnesota Press.

Cryle, P. (1994). *Geometry in the boudoir: Configurations of a French erotic narrative.* Ithaca, NY: Cornell University Press.

Deutscher, P. (1994). Eating the words of the other—Ethics, erotics and cannibalism in pedagogy. In J. J. Matthews (Ed.), *Jane Gallop seminar papers: Proceedings of the Jane Gallop seminar and public lecture "The teacher's breasts," June 1993* (pp. 31–46). Canberra, Australia: Humanities Research Centre.

Felman, S. (1986). Psychoanalysis and education: Teaching terminable and interminable. The Pedagogical Imperative: Teaching as a Literary Genre. *Yale French Studies, 63,* 21–44.

Gamman, L., & Marshment, M. (1994). *The female gaze: Women as viewers of popular culture.* Aylesbury, UK: The Women's Press.

Gibbs, A. (1995). Writing/eroticism/transgression: Gertrude Stein and the experience of the other. In B. Caine & R. Pringle (Eds.), *New Australian feminisms* (pp. 134–146). Sydney: Allen and Unwin.

Gotfrit, L. (1988). Women dancing back: Disruption and the politics of pleasure. *Journal of Education, 170*(3), 122–141.

Grant, L. (1993). *Sexing the millenium: A political history of the sexual revolution.* London: HarperCollins.

Greene, M. (1993). Reflections on postmodernism and education: Review essay. *Educational Policy, 7*(2), 206–211.

Jackson, S. (1995). Heterosexuality, power and pleasure. *Feminism and Psychology, 5*(1), 131–135.

Kirby, V. (1994). Response to Jane Gallop's "The Teacher's Breasts." In J. J. Matthews (Ed.), *Jane Gallop seminar papers: Proceedings of the Jane Gallop seminar and public lecture "The teachers breast's," June 1993* (pp. 17–22). Canberra: Humanities Research Centre.

Ladwig, J. (1995). Science, rhetoric and the construction of socially recognisable evidence in Eeducational research. *The Australian Educational Researcher, 21*(3), 77–96.

Lather, P. (1993). Fertile obsession: Validity after poststructuralism. *The Sociological Quarterly, 34*(4), 673–693.

———. (1995). *Troubling clarity*. Paper presented at the Annual Meeting of the American Educational Research Association, San Francisco, April 8–22.

Le Doeuff, M. (1977). Women and philosophy. *Radical Philosophy, 17*, 2–12.

McWilliam, E. (1992). *In broken images: A postpositivist analysis of student needs talk in pre-service teacher education*. Unpublished doctoral dissertation, University of Queensland, Department of Education, Brisbane.

———. (1993). Post haste: Plodding research and galloping theory. *British Journal of Sociology of Education, 14*(1), 199–205.

———. (1994a). *In broken images: Feminist tales for a different teacher education*. New York: Teachers College Press.

———. (1994b). *Seductress or schoolmarm: On the improbability of the great female teacher*. Paper presented at the Annual Meeting of the Australian Education Research Association, Newcastle.

———. (1995). (S)education: A risky inquiry into pleasurable teaching. *Education and Society, 13*(1), 15–24.

Morgan, W., & McWilliam, E. (1995). Keeping an untidy house: A dis/jointed paper about academic space, work and bodies. In R. Smith & P. Wexler (Eds.), *After postmodernism: Education, politics and identity*. London: Falmer Press.

Shapiro, S. (1994). Re-membering the body in critical pedagogy. *Education and Society, 12*(1), 61–79.

Stinson, S. (1995). Body of knowledge. *Educational Theory, 45*(1), 43–54.

10

CREATING A MULTILAYERED TEXT: WOMEN, AIDS, AND ANGELS

PATTI LATHER

[T]o be of use to cultural studies it would be necessary . . . to remember the value of experimentation, the importance of interdisciplinarity, the breaking down of the distinctions not just between philosophy, history, literary criticism and cultural analysis, but also between art and criticism, not for the sake of the new, but for social change and transformation.

—Angela McRobbie, *Postmodernism and Modern Culture*

"Science is a performance" (Fine, 1986, p. 148) and this chapter is about practices that register a possibility and mark a provisional space in which a different science might take form, a science that takes the crisis of representation into account. This chapter is also about science as a contested site and the contributions of feminist research to seeking our answers toward a different science in inquiry as it is lived. Exploring what it means to rehearse other practices in an effort to change the social imaginary about research in the human sciences, the chapter is situated in writing a "text of responsibility" (Spivak, 1994; Derrida, 1994) about women living with HIV/AIDS, what the women in the interview study call a K-Mart book, widely accessible to a general audience.

In what follows, I delineate the interpretive and textual moves of my co-researcher, Chris Smithies, and myself in writing up the results of this study of twenty-five women in women and HIV/AIDS support groups in four Ohio cities. Given the situated urgency of delivering copies to the women in a timely fashion, we desktop-published the manuscript in late 1995. In early 1996 we met with many of the women in their HIV/AIDS support groups in order to gather their reactions to the book, *Troubling Angels: Women Living With HIV/AIDS.*[1]

In probing the instructive complications of this study, my particular interest is in the difficulties and limitations of the categories within which I as a feminist do my work, situated at the site of ethnography and the postmodern. At such an intersection, what is made possible when normatively fixed categories and identities are disrupted? What does it mean to create a different space in which to undertake other performances, other thinking, power, and pleasures, to create new lines of flight, fragments of other possibilities, to experiment differently with meanings, practices and our own confoundings? Such questions owe much to Foucault, Deleuze, and Irigaray and their suggestions of routes of escape, moments, and practices to refuse what we are, to get our identities as social researchers all wrong. This is about working within/against the dominant, contesting normalized borders, tracing our complicity, moving toward some place that might be called feminist imaginaries of a double science, both science and not science, a version of what Nietzsche has called the "unnatural sciences" (1967, p. 155).[2]

Situated in the problematics of data analysis and text construction, this chapter records the web of paradoxes from within which feminist researchers work, given the indignity of being studied, the violence of objectification (Karamcheti, 1992). It also probes the inescapability of being placed in a position of speaking with, of, and for others from partial, situated, densely invested positions (Alcoff, 1992). "Invited in" as a feminist qualitative researcher, my primary interest has been "to be of use" (Piercy, 1973) to the women's goal of producing a K-Mart book, widely accessible to a broad audience that often assumes too much and knows too little about the work of living with HIV/AIDS. This desire to be of use is in tension with my desire to position this project as a Gramscian historical laboratory in which to explore a science marked by practices of productive ambiguity that cultivate a taste for complexity.

The interpretive and textual strategies of *Troubling Angels* arise out of that tension. Our aim was a broadly accessible multilayered weaving of method, the politics of interpretation, data, and analysis that fosters brooding about the issues involved in telling other people's stories and living in the shadow places of history as loss. In what follows, textual decisions will be analyzed in Chris and my move toward a mosaic, multilayered text designed to interrupt the reductiveness of the restricted economies of representation that characterize mainstream social science. After introducing the concept of feminist imaginaries of a double science, the "performance" of the chapter entails displaying sections of the data along with Chris and my interpretive and textual

moves. This is followed by discussion of what such practices might
mean within the concept of a feminist double science, particularly the
idea of situated methodology.

Ethnography and the Postmodern:
Feminist Imaginaries of a Double Science

> Deconstruction can only help in the big talk here in the academic arena.
> More specifically, in the production of the performance of the discipline of
> philosophy. Like I said, disciplines are performed. But the stuff that I'm
> talking about, outside of the academic arena, it will not come from the
> consolidation of systemic talk or systemic change. Derrida is not my
> prophet. It seems to me that here you must go into the field.
>
> —Gayatri Spivak

I have wanted to never be an armchair methodologist. While
unabashedly theoretical, I have long believed that practice always
exceeds theory's grasp. Hence, my goal throughout my academic work
has been to ground my projects in a theory of knowledge where praxis
"does not put itself in place of theory; it would be theory itself becoming
practical—the opposite of pragmatism" (Tiedemann, 1989, p. 202).
While I am not exactly sure what that means, it has something to do
with a deconstruction of the theory-practice binary that gestures toward
a third space of both/and and neither/nor of theory and practice, a
space I presently call a theory of situated methodology.

Before turning to my study of women living with HIV/AIDS for
what it might contribute to a theory of situated methodology, I focus
briefly on the implications of the postmodern turn for the doing of what
I am loosely calling ethnography, although I really mean the more inclusive term of qualitative research that includes sociological fieldwork as
well as anthropological ethnography. In terms of what I am loosely calling the postmodern, I find arguments about the nihilism and relativism
presumed attendant upon the loss of foundations (e.g., Anyon, 1994) to
be much less interesting than efforts like Butler and Scott's 1992 edited
collection, *Feminists Theorize the Political*. There both feminism and postmodernism are put under the pressure of a conjunction as they reuse,
rethink, reinscribe, and redeploy poststructuralism as "a field of critical
practices which cannot be totalized" (p. xiii). With both feminism and the
postmodern positioned as "discourses on the move," the conjunction is
both "an awkward pairing" and "a name for the way we live now"
(Wicke & Ferguson, 1992, pp. 1, 2, 4). In sum, Baudrillardian apocalypse,

Foucauldian limit-attitude, Deleuzean nomadology, Lyotardian language games, Lacanian Imaginaries, Derridean "play" and excessiveness—all of these are intersecting with feminist commitments to praxis in ways that position Jamesonian nostalgia and despair and Habermasian concerns about irrationalism as panic discourses that mark the displacement of Enlightenment hegemony over cultural theory.

Poised at the end of the twentieth century, the human sciences are in search of a discourse to help chart the journey from the present to the future. Withering critiques of realism, universalism, and individualism take us into the millennium (Borgmann, 1992). Conferences are held to explore the End of Science;[3] others argue for science as rhetoric (Nelson, Megill, & McCloskey, 1987; Simons, 1989), narrative (Polkinghorne, 1988), and/or social practice (Woolgar, 1988). Regardless of terms, each is part of an antifoundational era characterized by the loss of certainties and absolute frames of reference (Fine, 1986). As a poststructural feminist in pursuit of a less comfortable social science, the concept of feminist imaginaries of a double science helps me to think my way into such a moment.

Double Science

When I began thinking about the idea of a double science, I knew it involved a material turn that endorsed neither the collapse of the referent nor its transparency. In the context of my project on women living with HIV/AIDS, I knew it had to do with a gesture toward bodies that exceed social constructions, a referent that is there but is not speakable within present frames of intelligibility. In such a place, I, as researcher, become a poststructuralist "material girl," anxious in Donna Haraway's words to "'give up mastery but keep searching for fidelity'" (in Stockton, 1994, p. 18), some "suggestive tension" (Gallop, in Kirby, 1991, p. 11) about the limits and possibilities of the referent as "the body outside quotation marks . . . real bodies and political rage" (Stockton, 1994, pp. 4, 6).

Brantlinger and Ulin (1993) discuss genealogy and nomadology as double practices, both/and science and antiscience, both obvious examples of disciplinary discourse of the human sciences and wanderers outside of the scientific paradigm they purport to follow. Noting that such a character has historically defined ethnography (p. 35), they gesture toward a double science as that which is "as much nomadology as sociology," both antiscience, deconstruction of positive knowledges (p. 60), *and* the vitality of the deviations that elude taxonomies. The concept of a double science, then, argues the need for a proliferation of eccentric kinds of science to address the question of practice in postfoundational discourse theory.

Heidegger's insistence on the double necessity of working from within a tradition, from within the institutional constraints of a tradition even while trying to expose what that tradition has ignored or forgotten underscores the kind of double gesture that might recapture science, make it new, reappropriate it (Nealon, 1993, p. 237). In this effort I find invaluable Walter Benjamin's idea of history as a constant state of emergency where "those without a name" work the scenes of fragmentation and repression to reinvest history out of the debris and waste material of an epoch. Benjamin captured his philosophy of history in the image of the Angel of History.

Ironically excessive, the Angel of History is a return of the forgotten that "messes a situation up, yet it is the only hopeful thing about it" (Benjamin, 1968, p. 132), an antihumanism that opens up for thought a humanity that affirms itself in destruction. As "Angel of the Odd," "new angel," and "terrible angel," it marks a century of political secularization, scientific ideologies, and revolutions without precedent (Buci-Glucksmann, 1994, p. 58). Messing up "an economistic Marxism in thrall to a social-democratic conception of linear progress" (p. 60), Benjamin's detour into the arcana of Western history sketched a "logic of bodies, feeling, life and death [that] does not coincide with the logic of Power, nor with that of the Concept" (p. 71). This is an imaginary of the nonvisible or unconscious of modernity, that which is outside a victory narrative and the mediations of conscious intentionality, an "unreconciled history" (p. 89), the now-time of a crisis of otherness. Here, the task is to rethink "materialist" politics by engagement with the imaginary via images that capture "'what is already at work in the future'" (p. 113). The Angel, then, is a staging of otherness, of the divine, the feminine, and death, which makes the invisible visible, an enchanted illusion in a disenchanted world, an untimely understanding of history. All of this is to evoke a reason other to that created by the modern state that encroaches on the lifeworld. This reason appeals "to the 'sentimental'" (p. 160), foregoing wholly verifiable knowledge in order to construct a different subjectivity for different times.

Benjamin's interest in the interstices of reason and feeling maps onto a talk at Ohio State University[4] where Gregory Ulmer posited that the analytical, argumentative, dialectical reasoning invented by Plato to deal with alphabetic writing is exhausted in the face of a culture of images, graphics, and computer/human interfaces. Terming himself "still modern in the post-sense," Ulmer called on Benjamin's concept of the dialectical image that displaces the concept and hostile interrogation as ways of knowing with logics that are more about the economy of the unconscious, juxtaposition, paradox, montage, palimpsest, the structure of emotions, the logic of sense.

This can be layered onto Kathryn Bond Stockton's (1994) literary study of correspondences between Victorian and postmodern periods in terms of female desire where she traces the return of expressive forms long dismissed as "Victorian": "sentiment and sobs" (p. xxii). In the age of AIDS, she suggests, "emotional extravagance" might seem fitting to academic cultural critics. As a way to join public sentiment, "teasing out sobs" is about learning how to visit loss via a risk of the personal form that is transgressive in its sentiment. Her caution is that such ardor not sacrifice shadow for sense (p. xxiii) as she endorses a kind of opaque personal confession outside formulas, personal writing that is scandalous, excessive, and leaky but based in lack and ruin rather than plenitude, "investing in failure for the sake of our future . . . the failure of who we are as 'women' and 'men'" (10–11).[5]

Hence Benjamin's baroque imaginary of ruin and dislocation, not a plenitude but a loss of meaning, a loss of aura, is layered with Ulmer's economy of pathos and Stockton's evocation of female potential for otherness and transgression. Here, according to Buci-Glucksmann (1994), historical praxis is fed via the feminization of culture, its values and imaginaries, undermining from within, exploding certainties, topologies of excess to address an imaginary in the continued throes of secularization where the commodity-aura of the ever-new replaces theology (p. 109). How to proceed in such a time is precisely Benjamin's investment in what Buci-Glucksmann terms a "methodology of the imaginary" (p. 72).

In a methodology of the imaginary, metaphysical images are transmuted into dialectical images in a postsubjective, socially engaged form of thinking and writing, a "grammatopraxis" poised at the frontier of the sayable and the unsayable: "here is the site of the magic spark between word and deed" (Pensky, 1993, p. 38). The three stages of this move are: (1) fragment material, (2) brood over liberated fragments, and (3) construct constellations of new meaning (p. 137). This is an interruptive process which produces an image that works as an uninterpreted flash of recognition, a beholding that does justice to the material and the meaning of meanings in a Now loaded to the bursting point with time. Nonarbitrary in its historic indexicality, the archaic wish image is rescued as a dialectical image. The specific moment of its legibility is its ability to foreground the absence of truth; it is, hence, the truth which denies its essence. At its moment of recognizability, this tension becomes productive. The task of the critic is to work the mythic-alienating force of the fragmenting motion of the commodity economy in which the image operates so that a fragile, transient image can spring forth as legible, graspable, politically useful. In an alchemy beyond conscious intentionality, neither entirely knowable nor manipulable, the dialectical image gains a new and unsettling relevance, an ethical force that is directed at the heart of the present. Via such a path of detours and delays, the inquiry effects a diffracted magnification of its subject/object through a tension between modes of appropriation that vacillate between love and use, being done justice to in the only way possible, by being used for the sake of the imperiled present.

Here, the cultural critic assumes an intermediary position between artist and scientist, "combining the immediacy of representation of the artist and the rigorous conceptuality of the philosopher with the scientist's engagement with the plenitude of the empirical" (Pensky, 1993, p. 68). "The task is to bring fragments (all we have) into a critical constellation so precise that truth will allow itself to appear, however fleetingly, in the mosaic representation itself" (p. 93). Such a process yields a nonrepeatable graphics of thought which is based in historical specificity (p. 102), a situated methodology. To explore what this might look like, I turn to Chris and my project on women living with HIV/AIDS.

An Ache of Wings: Women Living with HIV/AIDS

There are many levels in this theater of AIDS. Its excess, illusion, disillusion, returns, and leave-takings create "a sense of the abyss which motivates thought to persevere" (Buci-Glucksmann, 1994, p. 172). In such a place, a methodology of the imaginary fosters writing that overflows the linguistic order, proceeding via figuration where the dialectical image is a fragment, a rune, a multiplicity of meaning. Benjamin combined an "ontological distaste for subjectivity" with a "fixation on the historical object" (Pensky, 1993, p. 63). Here subjectivity was a kind of entrapment that clouded the "receptive capacity whereby the messianic moments of historical experience could disclose themselves in the medium of critical thinking" (ibid). Risking the abyssal, endless descent into inner recesses of speculation, he became, to quote Adorno, "'an arena of movement in which a certain content forced its way, through him, into language'" (ibid). Intensely inward without being subjectivist in showing how knowledge and experience were thoroughly historical, his capacity for a "critical subjectivity" that flies in the face of idealist/materialist dualisms is produced by a double practice. This practice sifts through the fragments, fixing them conceptually in place next to apparently heterogeneous fragments as an ensemble, so that an idea may be momentarily represented (p. 67). I turn now to some of my own efforts toward such a practice.

Decisions about the textual format of *Troubling Angels* grew out of many factors: my interest in nonlinear, many-layered textuality, the practical need for a format that would allow Chris and me to write separately and then combine parts, our desire to include whatever the women themselves wanted to contribute in the way of writing, and, finally, my interest in the angel as a means of addressing what Rilke terms the "Too Big" in an accessible way to a broad-based audience. In what follows, I present an excerpt from Story Series 4, "Living with/Dying of AIDS," and an experimental format that was designed for but not used in Story Series 5, Support Groups.

Story Series 4: Living/Dying with AIDS

"We Are the Teachers"

Lila:	When they told Janice she had PCP [a rare form of pneumonia common in AIDS patients], she said "count me out." She was so tired. The intestinal diarrhea had absolutely destroyed her strength. When they told her she had PCP, she refused treatment. She'd tell doctors exactly what they could do. I mean, she'd get up in their face. One night at 3 AM I was talking to her on the phone. They came in to draw blood, and she looked at this doctor and she said, "Motherfucker, I can't believe you're in here at 3 o'clock in the morning poking me with a needle, now you get your fucking ass out of here, I'm on the phone." Now that's exactly the way Janice was, but then she got to the point where that didn't work. She was just tired. She told me, I'm going to leave. And she just left.
Chris:	What did that do to you in terms of living your own life?
Lila:	Oh man, it's been really hard. I miss her. I miss her really really bad. Because no matter how bad it got, we would laugh. She was this magical little outlet for me and I was the same thing for her. But then after a while the magic was gone. She was too tired. When Janice went that way, it strengthened my belief that this is a journey, a series of experiences. I will be back. Life is a collection of experiences and there has to be a reason for it.
Patti:	What is that reason?
Lila:	It is *not* punishment. It is *not* an individual lesson, but a collective lesson; *we are the teachers.*

--- — — ---

From Patti's research journal, May 16, 1994

Chris invited me to go with her tonight to visit Darla, whom I don't know beyond an introduction at the 1993 retreat. I am thankful for the opportunity to once again confront my too comfortable distance in all of this. Chris is

Sharon: I for some reason did not realize I was going to die before I got infected, and now I think about it—"I was going to die before I got HIV." I mean, you know; for some reason it reassures me, knowing that you're gonna die, and you're gonna die. Sometimes you feel like you are the only one and that everyone else goes on and is gonna have this wonderful life forever. But life isn't really so wonderful, even if you're not positive, you know what I mean. I don't remember my life being wonderful before, you know. But when you first find out you're HIV positive, it seems like everything was wonderful before that. It did to me, anyway. I think it's a lot like death. When I read the things you go through with death: I went through the bargaining, the grieving, the anger, the isolation, the loneliness, all those things. I must have bargained with God for months and months and then I was angry with him. I think I am finally at a full circle.

Chris: What would you name that stage?

Sharon: Maybe content, being content. I am at peace with it. I am not happy with it, but I have genuinely accepted it. Even before I was diagnosed, death was never a scary thing for me. I wasn't brought up to be scared of people dying. I've always believed that if I died tomorrow, there is still something better where I am going. I mean it has to be better than here.

---

out there daily, on the front lines. I sit in my office, writing away, immersed in the data and the storytelling. It's too easy to forget the human cost and how arbitrary are the made versus the lost stories, e.g., Darla's story is largely absent in this book due to her intermittent involvement in the support group. Also lost is any elaboration of Donna's choosing this moment to come out to her family as HIV+, as Darla lies dying at home, caught up in PML, a galloping virus in the brain that plunges this 32-year old from relative health to death's door in a matter of weeks. [Darla died on June 13, 1994.]

In the car on the way to visit Darla in her hospital bed at home, Donna tells her story of coming out as HIV+ to her mom and aunt. Carefully choosing the scene so that the aunt would be there to buffer the mother, they want to know why she didn't tell them sooner. Fearing her imminent death, they have to learn to live with this as Donna has over the last two and one-half years. Wanting to know who she got it from, filling in holes in what they know of illnesses of Donna's friends, now identified as AIDS, they decide to go ahead with telling the rest of the family and parcel out the doing. Making clear how

Patti: Is this a religious belief?

Sharon: Right. So death isn't scary for me and I still actually believe
           that everybody else is going to die before me. I believe in
           God; I am not scared of death.

Sarah: I am not worried about dying, I just don't want to die from
           AIDS. If I could die from cancer—I don't want to die from AIDS.

Chris: Can you explain?

Sarah: I have a stigma of it. I can't—there are people discussing their
           illnesses at work and what medications they take—not that I
           am looking for that. I can't say, hey by the way, I am dying
           from AIDS.

Chris: Other women describe it as a double life. Does that fit for
           you?

Sarah: Very much so. I have to go to work, deal with the public; I get
           asked out by people who say, you want to go out, I know
           you don't have AIDS. I have people joking about it in my
           face. I absorb it and I think that I am not going to let it bother
           me. And it might not bother me for two-three days and then
           I will just fall apart and I won't be able to go to work. My
           boss, he goes what is wrong with you, god damn it, you are
           intolerable. If I could just tell him. This is why—I get to work
           somehow, I don't know, but I have to deal with it in public. I
           actually work at a sales counter, talk to people, I get asked
           out.

---

*she wanted to be dealt with at the end, "if it comes to that," Donna does not
want to be in their homes; she wants a nursing home or hospice. Chris says,
"Get it written down." We listen to Reba McEntire sing a song about women
and AIDS, "She Thinks His Name Was John," and talk about blame and
shame.*

Next day, May 17

*As we walk in, Darla is sleeping in a hospital bed in her son's room,
now transformed into a sick room. Three children, a husband and a mother-in-
law, taking care of her. Walking into the room, it is hard to tell her from a
corpse at first, the stillness, the drawn face, the pallor. She wakes; she attends
some, but mostly there are her eyes—intense, a Rorschach test for those in the
room. Is she pissed? scared? zoned out? She speaks but once, to joke with her
youngest daughter about the daughter's hair. She blinks when Chris says, if you
want us to come back, blink once. She throws her bedclothes off twice to pull the*

Chris: Danelle, you said you think you might die this year?
Danelle: I feel that way because the media says that if you have no T4 cells, you are probably gonna die. So, it still impacts the way I think about the disease. I mean, obviously I am still doing alright but everyone thinks if you have no more T4's, you don't have anything to fight anything, you are gonna be dead.
Chris: How do you prepare for that?
Danelle: I don't know.
Tracy: I think this disease has made us sort of obsessed with living and we just think that our success is if you make it. A friend of mine died about four weeks ago, and my friend did fight. I saw a TV show with cancer women and some of them did die, but they died empowered, you know. And I think right now some of us are trying to find some strength, something about finding death or maybe some people are more religious, some are looking for the spirituality to fit in that gap. We want to fight this possibility that we won't live that long, but death should not be regarded as a failure. People are talking about living fourteen years, but there are some people who live three years. Look at Doreen, she died in May and the woman fought like a little dragon. She never gave up, she was always trying to empower other people during the retreats. I don't think Doreen failed. I guess, maybe, for women, or for all of us, we need people who can help us

---

catheter out. I witness this with the horror of my not knowing her, witnessing something so private. Like my in-coma brother's nakedness in the hospital bed when I unexpectedly came outside of visiting hours, but there I was family. Here I am a stranger, riding Chris' coattails as she lets the family know that she is there if they need her, listening to the mother-in-law speak of the last few weeks. Chris tells them how she touted them at a conference on families and HIV that she just attended where they were the counter story to people being deserted by their families: a family rallying from the beginning, coming to the support group en masse, children speaking out publicly as children of an HIV mom, now bringing her home to care for as she dies, attending as she wanders in and out of consciousness, a "chatty-Cathy" now silent, in the words of her friend, Donna. Only the eyes, the restlessness and the pulling out of the catheter.

I think of James Agee's words: "What is it, profound behind the outward windows of each one of you, beneath touch even of your own suspecting . . . so that the eyes shine of their own angry glory, but the eyes of a trapped animal, or

with that ultimate side. Instead of just physical healing we need to hear how to heal ourselves. I think there are not enough resources. Danelle and I were talking about it the other day and she was telling me that her parents had never gone to church. She doesn't have that religious belief, whether there is God. I don't believe in Christianity per se, I believe in god, but where are those resources?

Patti: Have you found anything to help in that search?

Tracy: Yes, I joined this interesting church. To other people it might seem like a cult, but the only thing we believe in is god and people in this church are comfortable with death. They believe they are going to come back, reincarnation. That keeps them going. Tomorrow I am going to the library to do some readings like my friend who researched lots and lots of religions until he found what gave him groundings. So when he died he was not miserable although he was in pain.

Patti: Is this part of what you mean when you say empowered?

Tracy: Yeah. Like for me now, I am starting to think about death more, I'm trying to find something to be comfortable with. I want it to be a positive experience, because a lot of people who have had those near-death experiences and come back have said it is really wonderful and there is no fear involved. So I want to try to set myself up thinking maybe it won't be

---

of a furious angel nailed to the ground by his wings, or however else one may faintly designate the human 'soul.' . . . [H]ow, looking thus into your eyes and seeing thus, how each of you is a creature which has never in all time existed before and which shall never in all time exist again and which is not quite like any other and which has the grand stature and natural warmth of every other and whose existence is all measured upon a still mad and incurable time; how am I to speak of you as . . . 'representatives' of your 'class,' as social integers in a criminal economy, or as individuals, . . . wives, . . . daughters, and as my friends and as I 'know' you?" (Let Us Now Praise Famous Men, 1941, pp. 99–100)

Bonnie: *I talked to Deanne and she said she was depressed and didn't want to talk about it, that's why she's not coming.*

Kathryn: *There's a couple of things we're talking about. One is people's response to what happened last week; people seemed pretty stunned by it and we didn't get a chance to process it. And I think what Lisa*

so bad and not thinking that I am just going to go in the ground and then nothing. I need to feel that there is going to be something positive there so I am gonna research, find that out and empower myself. I want to be passing away, like gone, and say I lived a good life. You know? That kind of feeling, not miserable.

Patti: That death itself is not a failure?

Tracy: What else can I do?

Pre-text to Story Series 5 of *Troubling Angels*

Background

What follows is an experimental formatting of data from a gathering of the longest-running of the four support groups with whom Chris and I met, where the group is wrestling with issues of difference. The goal is to present the data in a way that is respectful of the complexity of the hard work of living across layers of sedimented differences, in this case, of race and class. While the following textual experiment was of use in coming to some understanding of the dynamics at work in this meeting of the support group, we eventually decided not to use it in *Troubling Angels*. It functions, then, as a sort of pretext or palimpsest, an earlier form that was erased but upon which the later form is layered.

---

has brought up is critically important to the group. I mean we need to look at what is it that you want this group to be and why is it that there's a lot of women out there and they're not getting referred here and it really worries me. So I want to ask people to talk about your own feelings about what happened last week.

Chris: *When you said you weren't a psychologist—give yourself a bit of a break. It makes sense that your buttons got pushed. You're in this group as members and you have needs and your buttons are going to get pushed sometimes. If that happens so much that people are feeling excluded from the group, then I guess that's what we're here to talk about. But many people I've worked with are where Lola is, whether they're victims of sexual abuse or battering or AIDS or whatever. In our society, it's typical for women to blame ourselves. It's a tribute to all of you that that's not the norm in this group, that's one of the wonderful things that this group has to offer that, over time, you all rub off.*

February 1994

Lisa has requested that the group discuss an incident at last week's meeting where a black woman, Lola, who was new to the group confronted them with how they were to blame for their HIV status because of their lifestyle choices. This evoked anger from many directions, including how the group consistently runs from dealing with hard issues. The crisis was so great that Chris was asked to attend, although she had turned facilitation of the group over to Kathryn the previous year. In what follows, the subtext is what I excised from the "main" story which unfolds in big font on the top of the page. Within the detours of the split page, the text unfolds in "real time" where sequence is unchanged.

"We're Supposed to Be a Support Group": Differences

Kathryn: We need to begin with what happened last week and people's feelings about it, especially the way we reacted to Lola's charge that we're here because of our lifestyles which violated the one rule of this group, that we don't blame one another for being HIV+.

Lisa: It's the same old story with this group; it happens with everybody who isn't in the little group that's been here from the beginning. And I felt so guilty that this woman

---

Lisa: *I don't think we do, Chris. Look at all the women who haven't come back.*

Chris: *So maybe there's something to look at as to why that isn't happening and what's so painful for you all going through that period of time before that person can kind of catch up or change or, maybe in some cases, not change.*

Kathryn: *Can we accept people where they are, even if you don't like it and not require them to change?*

Bonnie: *I've seen us do that. Remember that woman who came who was pregnant. None of us was comfortable with what she said about wanting a healthy baby because she wanted some money, but no one ridiculed her. I never told her she was wrong. I mean I think, for the most part, people choose not to come for their own needs. When I don't come it's because I don't want to talk.*

Kathryn: *Did she stay?*

Bonnie: *No.*

was so desperate, the only two times I've ever seen her, the only thing she's ever talked about is how she had no friends, no support, no one to turn to, and we're supposed to be a support group and we spend our time in these meetings talking about what we did last weekend, and not what people really need. So I decided I'm done. I don't want to come here and have a social group and ignore people in the community that need us. Since then, I've talked to someone very involved in the AIDS community and found out that there's a perception that this group is a little clique, that we don't want anybody here. So the case workers aren't referring people here anymore. We either need to fix it or just disband it and start over. If people need to walk in that door, then they need to walk in that door. This isn't just about Lola. It's about all the other women who stopped coming here.

Cara: I'd like to speak somewhat in defense of Lola. I've seen her outside of the group more than I think anyone else has and I've talked to her on the phone. She has to go two blocks to use the phone and she visited me once and Kathryn and I visited her once. I won't go into too much detail, but a lot of her pain and anger come from her husband. She says every day it's like, bitch you've got it, you're gonna die and I'm gonna bury you. And with that kind of feelings being said to

---

Chris: *I don't think collectively we did extend out to her. I mean she had a terrible body odor and it was hard to sit by her.*

Lisa: *Plus it's out in the community not to come here. I think it's kind of vibes, we sit around and chit-chat and we don't know them and it's quite obvious that we all know each other well.*

Bonnie: *But that's part of coming to a new group. When I came, I remember, people were standing in the hallway talking and I just stood there and didn't know what to do and felt very uncomfortable and I said, is this Dr. Chris Smithies' group? They said yeah and just kept on talking. So I went in and I gave it a shot and it's the best thing I ever had. The times I've talked to my doctor, she feels that the women who don't come to groups, they don't want to deal with it, they don't take care of themselves. That's sad to me, because I had the same kind of experience at first, but I gave it a shot and it worked for me.*

Kathryn: *But things may be different now, it's a different group than it was then and it may not be the experience for a new person coming in*

her, I thought about it after that episode, she came here and she lashed out at us. She couldn't lash out at him. I don't know if he ever hit her or beat her. I just had the feeling she was saying to us what he says to her, that she can't say back to him. I knew what Lola was going through at home, and I didn't express it to anyone else, but I felt she was crying out for help, so I wasn't angry. I mean what she said was disturbing and later me and Lila jokingly said, oh it's our lifestyle, but it's just a kidding between us. I felt I knew where she was coming from. We get positive strokes during the day, I mean we can pick up the phone and call someone, or go to a movie, but she is in that house, and that's where she is. When you say about the perception that's out there about that we're this little clicky group, some of it may be true.

Chris: Each of you had some degree, in some cases a lot, of positive self-esteem before this happened. It's a lot easier to not think of oneself as a victim if you have some positive self-esteem. I don't know Lola, but the impression I get is that she's had a rough past and very little has been positive or reinforcing so it's very easy for her to absorp this idea, so different from how we usually approach it, that she's to blame.

Lisa: I got the feeling that she was trying to gather us like we're all scum together, she didn't want to be scum alone. After I got

---

now that it's as welcoming a group as it was. Since I've been with you the two women I referred haven't returned and I think that's troubling and it worries me a lot. I think some people aren't going to come but there are at least 300 HIV+ women in this area, why aren't they coming?

Chris: *I think one thing that's changed, I mean all of you have been living with this for quite a while now and it's hard to in addition to all that you have to do to keep yourselves healthy, to also have the leftover love and energy and time to really respond to someone. And some of these women coming in are really needy. I mean they deserve help, but they're really needy. And the reality is that as this goes on over time, the epidemic is changing. The women getting this are often IV drug users, living on the streets at some time, who are in many cases going to be African American women or other minorities, in many cases who don't have formal education. It's not just here or because this group is doing something wrong or*

over my initial anger, I thought that she really wanted to come here and have a group because she sits in that hell-hole alone.

Kathryn: Part of what concerned me is that I didn't see anyone respond to Lola. I mean I understood that it was felt that it was real aggressive what she had to say, but I was concerned that no one said what you're saying now.

Cara: I was embarrassed. I felt awful.

Lisa: It still makes me sick, I mean I'm not a psychologist, but it was such an obvious cry for help and, again, we just shoved it aside.

Chris: What happens when a woman is African American? Not to put it all on you, Cara, but why has this group worked for you, and how can it work for all women who don't have formal education being that most of us are white and middle class?

Cara: About being African American and about Lola, for me it was women like you before the virus who helped me to see my self worth. I went to workshops and I read and went to conferences that made available to me other resources that women like Lola never had. And I have to say for a fact that if I hadn't had some of the previous experiences that I did years ago, I would not be here today. I would not feel that I could be a part of this group.

---

gotten off on the wrong footing. It's very difficult to always have a lot of love and energy and kindness for someone else, and to keep that up is challenging. It's so hard for women to go to the groups for so many reasons, like childcare and work schedules, but from what I heard, the problem is not so much getting women to come for the first time, but what happens when they get here. Once a woman gets here, how is she made to feel that this could work for her over time and can the group still work for you all with those kinds of changes?

Lisa: *It's a drag to tell the same story. I'm going on five years now and I don't want to keep telling the same story, but on the other hand, I really have a desire to help people over that hump and besides, who really is alike though? I mean none of us are really alike in this room.*

Kathryn: *But the differences are, there's not discomfort or fear about the differences, the differences don't disturb our sensibilities.*

Chris: I think it's because you knew, I mean some of the women who
            come to this group don't even know how to participate in
            this kind of talk and you knew all that. You made it easy for
            us to embrace you. Besides just being the beautiful person
            that you are, you could be what the group needed you to be,
            not that any of that was explicit. I don't think it even has stuff
            to do about racism, it's simply you're from a different place
            than a lot of the people and you have bridged it so then we
            could love you. Once you came here, fine, of course, you were
            accepted as much as anyone else. But a lot of people with
            your background, with how you've lived, haven't kind of fig-
            ured their way.

Cara: I'm a Lola.

Lisa: I'm in the other women's volunteer group and we go around
            and speak and blah blah blah about how there's this won-
            derful support group and there's not, there hasn't been.

Cara: This is the safest place I have that I can relate to other women.
            So I generally get what I need. I have a great friend in Lila, so I
            feel like I'm just tagging along until the dam breaks. With Lola,
            I felt bad and I was embarrassed but I had this urge to go and
            sit next to her, even when she was blaspheming us. And then I
            just, it was bad, I mean sick inside me and in my head, I don't
            know, she was a woman and she was a black woman, and I
            relate to her. And I feel like a traitor that I didn't.

--- — ---

Lisa: *This group has a problem dealing with the tough issues, the dis-*
            tasteful things. When [my husband] died, I was really glad to have
            everybody and I know I lost some time there, but I don't remember
            any grieving sessions.

Kathryn: *I was surprised hardly anyone showed up after Bonnie's husband*
            died. I said something and Lisa said that's what we do, when some-
            one dies, we scatter. So it never really got talked about and people's
            feelings never got expressed.

Chris: *And maybe the meeting right after a death isn't the time. It may be*
            too soon, but it needs to happen; we have to find some way to talk
            about loss.

Chris: *There does need to be some frank discussion, even among the regu-*
            lars here. And what about Lola, is there some way to attempt to cor-
            rect that situation? I hear a lot of regret about how that went and I
            think we have some understanding now of why it went that way.
            How could you make peace with yourself about it?

Kathryn: I think what that says is that we can make mistakes in this group, that it doesn't matter, if we reach out, we're not gonna lose somebody. We can say something, or not say something, as long as we call up later and say, gee, I felt like such an ass. I wanted to come over and put my arms around you and I felt bad that I didn't. There's room to make mistakes.

Enacting a Methodology of the Imaginary

In the preceding experiment with format, the text was shaped as I took it apart and put it together. First I grouped all the pieces by the categories of facilitators/black woman/white women. Wanting at first to tell a victory narrative of the group's admirable wrestling with these difficult issues, splitting the text into fragments yielded some learnings about the way racism and classism work in a context where AIDS brings unexpected groups together. Differences get homogenized and deflected and contestations get constructed against these leveling effects. Putting the text together again, I formatted it so that my original success story stands, but now I put that that I had originally left out into the split text on the bottom, in a smaller font, as a kind of outburst of the repressed in a context where, while 75% of HIV+ women are women of color, there is only one woman of color present at this support group for women living with HIV/AIDS. My guiding principles were four:

1. To instantiate a topology of excess that foregrounds the absence of truth and the loss of aura via a mode of representation that alters the standard frames of reference and visibility.
2. To effect an economy of the unconscious via juxtaposition, paradox, montage, and palimpsest in an effort to work the scene of fragmentation toward the construction of difference-aware subjectivities.

Lisa: *I was going to drop her a line.*
Bonnie: *What if some of us asked her if we could come over and bring her some dinner and just talk?*
Cara: *It would probably be better to take her away, out of the house, away from that husband.*
Lisa: *Whoever plans it, count me in. I have some things I want to say to her. The argument was between her and me because I was the one who responded.*
Kathryn: *I think you were saying what others were feeling, you weren't speaking alone. You were the courageous one to speak up.*

3. To work against the concept of the researcher as Great Liberator, origin of what can be known and done, "master of truth and justice," to use Foucault's devastating words.
4. To deny the "comfort text" in the hope of opening up possibilities for displaying complexities, a "sur/realist tale" (Meiners, 1994) that is respectful of its source.

This experimental textual and interpretive strategy is not included in *Troubling Angels*. Too complicating and complicated, it was useful in leading to the format we did use where the top portion of the split text presents the women's efforts to deal with differences in the support groups in "real time," while the bottom text consists of Chris writing about support group dynamics. This gesture toward a more traditional interpretive move is interrupted by my two concluding sections in the subtext of the book. "Conclusion 1: Out of Place," speaks out of my desire for meaning, activism and community. "Conclusion 2: The Book as Ruin," interrupts the first, refusing to contain AIDS in familiar frameworks, putting at risk readers and writers presumed to know about worlds presumed to be knowable. What I was searching for in both formats was an experimental approach where I could turn away from the conventional move of researchers positioned "behind [the] backs [of informants] to point out what they could not see, would not do, and could not have said" (Britzman, 1995, p. 237).

What is my resistance to theorizing and/or interpreting their words? Why did I not use my concluding subtextual commentary to probe how these women deal with the hard work of living across layers of sedimented differences of race and class in their support groups? As Spivak (1994) asked of her "fieldwork" with Bangladesh villagers fighting World Bank policy around flood control, "What would it be to learn otherwise, here?" against easy reading and easy generalities of the subaltern as transparent? "I was adrift," she writes, in "the silent gnawing of such a betrayal" (pp. 62–63). Trying to learn otherwise, my struggle against making sense of participant efforts to make sense of their experiences of HIV/AIDS troubles the ethics of reducing the fear, pain, joy, and urgency of people's lives to analytic categories.

Both formats explore the textual possibilities for telling stories that situate researchers not so much as experts "saying what things mean" in terms of "data," but rather as witnesses giving testimony to the lives of others, with subtextual and intertextual practices that displace direct commentary on such testimony. Britzman (1995) raises the dangers of the posture of researcher as witness: the reification of experience and identity, agency and voice, and unmediated access to some "real." There is no exit from the lack of innocence in discursive stagings of knowledge, she notes.

Poststructural anthropologist, George Marcus, writes of this as a moment where "the need to chronicle the world seem[s] to outstrip the capacity to theorize it. . . . What we're saying . . . is kind of old-fashioned: that it is possible to present the voices of others in a more or less unmediated way" via evocative portraits, a type of data reporting that "emphasizes a direct exposure to other 'voices' . . . unassimilated to given concepts, theories, and analytic frames" (1993, pp. 13–15). Such words help me to locate myself both within and against conventional notions of social science research, taking the crisis of representation into account, but I remain haunted by the task of doing justice to the women's words.

"Easy to spot the problem, hard to supply the ethic!" Serres writes, in addressing a code of practice for messengers (1995, p. 101). His answer is quite useful here, in all its density: that the task of the trans-lator is to fade out behind the message, once the incomprehensibility of the message is communicated, once philosophy herself appears, in the flesh. Becoming visible as an intermediary, the task becomes to empty out the channel while still foregrounding the productive and distorting effects of the channel, a kind of presence, and absence, and presence again (p. 104). The only way to break free from this is to invent new channels that will soon become blocked again as messengers derive importance from the channels created, but the goal is to disappear in delivering the word of the something else that the word signals and gestures toward.

Present and absent and present again, working a Benjaminian sort of "circumspect, convoluted and sometimes seemingly perverse mode of analysis . . . [a] fragmented 'montage' method of argument" (McRobbie, 1994, pp. 106–107), *Troubling Angels* addresses the question of practice in postfoundational times out of its very precise location in a very particular situated inquiry. Nietzsche writes, "My 'theory' grows from my 'practice'—oh, from a practice that is not by any means harm-less or unproblematic!" (1967, p. 340). Within such a situated practice, the work of methodology becomes to negotiate the instructive compli-cations that knowledge projects engender regarding the politics of knowing and being known. Here method is resituated as a way *into* the messy doings of science via risky practices that both travel across contexts and are remade in each situated inquiry.

Interested in the grounds of science and the attachment to its pro-cedures, the experiments of *Troubling Angels* are premised on the use-fulness of the intructive complications of situated inquiries regarding the possibilities as well as limits of our knowing. Rubbing against the sort of stubborn materiality in which Benjamin's interest was a rescuing of philosophy from abstraction, the practices that Chris and I developed in our study of women living with HIV/AIDS grew out of our effort to write a K-Mart book that assembled fragments through which one could read and then reread one's way into some understanding that keeps shifting regarding the work of living with HIV/AIDS.

Conclusion: Insisting (on) Angels

I don't think angels should have the last word. . . . They're only angels.

—Ellen McLaughlin

I've invented a novel that is so hard to write I often think I'm not the one to write it. I had the idea for it, but I can't do it.

—Fran Lebowitz

Refusing textual innocence and an untroubled realism, I have moved to what Britzman terms ethnography as "a site of doubt" where the focus is on how poststructuralism fashions interpretive efforts (1995, p. 236). Here, as Britzman notes, representation is practiced as a way to intervene, even while one's confidence is troubled. Here the task becomes to operate from a textual rather than a referential notion of representation, working the ruins of a confident social science as the very ground from which new practices of research might take shape.

The textual and interpretive practices delineated in this chapter work toward a multiplicity and complexity of layers that unfold an event which exceeds our frames of reference, evoking insight into what not knowing means. Like Rilke's *Duino Elegies*, in a text that accumulates meaning as it progresses, a reader must move across the different registers of the text's ebbs and flows of different subject positions, as well as shifts among meditations, facts, personal reminiscences, reporting, quotations, and epiphanies that cannot be frozen "but must constantly be recaptured, re-earned" (Komar, 1987, pp. 199–204). Backtracking to issues that cannot be settled for long, "ruminations [that] dramatize the construction of a poetics as well as an ontology," the form of the book cancels the distance between subject and object, reader and writer and written about (ibid, p. 1). Here, the text turns back on itself, putting the authority of its own affirmations in doubt, an undercutting that causes a doubling of meanings that adds to a sense of multivalence and fluidities.

In searching for a textual form adequate to the task of portraying the work of women living with HIV/AIDS, Chris and I have designed a book that defies a reader's narrative urge to make sense of, to impose order on the discontinuity and otherness of historical experience. In a space where untroubled witnessing won't do, the text undercuts any immediate or total grasp via layers of point-of-view patterns. Working the limits of intelligibility, we mix the women's stories of living with HIV/AIDS, researcher interpretive moves and retraction of such moves, and "factoid" boxes, all juxtaposed with angel intertexts that bring moments of sociology, history, poetry, popular culture, and "determined policy talk" into a network of levels and orders in constructing an audience with ears to hear.[6]

For those invested in expanding our map of possible occupiable sites in the name of a feminist double science, our job, I posit, is to live out the ambivalent failures of research intended to contribute to social justice toward something more productive of its disciplining effects. Inhabiting the practices of its rearticulation, "citing, twisting, queering," to use Judith Butler's words (1993, p. 237), we occupy the very space opened up by the ruins of ethnographic representation and a more innocent moment in feminist research toward a future that is unforseeable from the perspective of what is either given or even conceivable within our present categories. Here the angels function somewhere "between theory and embarassment" (Ellison, 1996, p. 368) as we live out a complexity of "the pure too little, the empty too much" (Komar, 1987, p. 89), an ache of wings.

Notes

1. Westview/HarperCollins, in press.

2. "Unnatural" science is that "which I call the self-critique of knowledge." A revaluation of feminism and Nietzsche is well underway, spurred, perhaps, by Luce Irigaray, *Marine Lover of Friedrich Nietzsche* (Columbia University Press, 1991), including edited collections such as *Nietzsche and the Feminine*, edited by Peter J. Burgard (University Press of Virginia, 1994) and *Nietzsche, Feminism and Political Theory*, edited by Paul Patton (Allen and Unwin, 1993).

3. At the Twenthy-fifth Nobel Conference at Gustavus Adolphous College in St. Peter, Minnesota, in 1989 on the End of Science, feminist philosopher Sandra Harding put it this way: "As we study our world today, there is an uneasy feeling that we have come to the end of science, that science, as a unified, objective endeavor is over. . . . This leads to grave epistemological concerns. If

science does not speak about extrahistorical, universal laws, but is instead social, temporaral and local, then there is no way of speaking of something real beyond science that science merely reflects" (quoted in Kiziltan, Bain, & Canizares, 1990, p. 354).

4. November 3, 1993.

5. In *Epistemology of the Closet*, Eve Sedgwick does this well in Axiom 7 where she positions auto-identification as strange, impossible, and necessary: strange in its assumption that such things are clear to the self, impossible because such practices "entail a hidden underpinning of the categorical imperative" in the very ways they reify identity, and necessary as lived experiments toward countervailing "the terrible one-directionality of the culture's spectacularizing" of its objects of study (1990, pp. 59–63). See, also, chapter 3 for Sedgwick's tracking of "the strange career of 'sentimentality'" and her argument that reinvesting this stigmatized but potent problematic in terms of audience relation, thinking sentimentality outside of ressentiment, entails facing its discrediting as kitsch and its partial rehabilitation as "camp." Thanks to Deborah Britzman for alerting me to this.

6. The issue of audience for such a text, particularly the Nietzschean concept of a text that constructs its audience, is dealt with in Lather, "Troubling Clarity: The Politics of Accessible Language," *Harvard Educational Review*, vol. 66, no. 3, fall 1996, 525–545. In that article, I draw heavily on the "response data" that is beginning to emerge in reaction to *Troubling Angels*.

References

Alcoff, L. (1992). On speaking for others. *Cultural Critique, 20*, 5–32.

Anyon, J. (1994). The retreat of Marxism and socialist feminism: Postmodern and poststructural theories in education. *Curriculum Inquiry, 24*(2), 115–134.

Benjamin, W. (1968). *Illuminations: Essays and reflections* (H. Arendt, Ed., H. Zohn, Trans.). New York: Schocken Books.

Borgmann, A. (1992). *Crossing the postmodern divide*. Chicago: University of Chicago Press.

Brantlinger, P., & Ulin, D. (1993). Policing nomads: Discourse and social control in early Victorian England. *Cultural Critique, 25*, 33–64.

Britzman, D. (1995). "The question of belief": Writing poststructural ethnography. *Qualitative Studies in Education, 8*(3), 233–242.

Buci-Glucksmann, C. (1984/1994). *Baroque reason: The aesthetics of modernity* (P. Camiller, Trans.). Thousand Oaks, CA: Sage.

Butler, J. (1993). *Bodies that matter: On the discursive limits of "sex."* New York: Routledge.

Butler, J., & Scott, J. (Eds.). (1992). *Feminists theorize the political.* New York: Routledge.

Derrida, J. (1994) *Spectres of Marx.* New York: Routledge.

Ellison, J. (1996). A short history of liberal guilt. *Critical Inquiry, 22*(2), 344–371.

Fine, A. (1986). *The shaky game: Einstein, realism and the quantum theory.* Chicago: University of Chicago Press.

Genova, J. (1994). Tiptree and Haraway: The reinvention of nature. *Cultural Critique, 27,* 5–28.

Karamachi, I. (1992, September). The business of friendship (Review of *Friends, brothers and informants: Fieldwork memoirs of Banaras,* by Nita Kumar). *Women's Review of Books, 9*(12), 16–17.

Kirby, V. (1991). Corporal habits. *Hypatia, 6*(3), 4–24.

Kiziltan, M., Bain, W., & Canizares, A. (1990). Postmodern conditions: Rethinking public education. *Eduational Theory, 40*(3), 351–370.

Komar, K. (1987). *Transcending angels: Rainer Maria Rilke's Duino Elegies.* Lincoln: University of Nebraska Press.

Marcus, G. (1993). Interview, in Inside Publishing. *Lingua Franca,* July/August, 13–15.

McRobbie, A. (1994). *Postmodernism and popular culture.* New York: Routledge.

Meiners, E. (1994). *Course writing for Education 508B: Data analysis in the crisis of representation.* University of British Columbia.

Nealon, J. (1993). Thinking/writing the postmodern: Representation, end, ground, sending. *Boundary 2,20*(1), 221–241.

Nelson, J., Megill, A., & McCloskey, D. (Eds.). (1987). *The rhetoric of the human sciences: Language and argument in scholarship and public affairs.* Madison: University of Wisconsin Press.

Nietzsche, F. (1974). *On the genealogy of morals/Ecce Homo* (W. Kaufmann, Trans.). New York: Vintage.

Pensky, M. (1993). *Melancholy dialectics: Walter Benjamin and the play of mourning.* Amherst: University of Massachusetts Press.

Piercy, M. (1973). *To be of use.* Garden City, NY: Doubleday.

Polkinghorne, D. (1988). *Narrative knowing and the human sciences.* Albany: State University of New York Press.

Ropars-Wuilleumier, M.-C. (1994). The cinema, reader of Gilles Deleuze. In C. Boundas & D. Olkowski (Eds.), *Gilles Deleuze and the Theatre of Philosophy*. New York: Routledge.

Sedgwick, E. (1990). *Epistemology of the closet*. Berkeley: University of California Press.

Serres, M. (1995/1993). *Angels a modern myth* (F. Cowper, Trans.). Paris/New York: Flammarion.

Simons, H. (1989). *Rhetoric in the human sciences*. Beverly Hills, CA: Sage.

Spivak, G. (1994). Responsibility. *Boundary 2, 21(3)*, 19–64.

Stockton, K. B. (1994). *God between their lips: Desire between women in Irigaray, Bronte, and Eliot*. Stanford, CA: Stanford University Press.

Tiedemann, R. (1989). Historical materialism or political messianism? An interpretation of the theses "On the concept of history." In G. Smith (Ed.), *Benjamin: Philosophy, history, aesthetics*. Chicago: University of Chicago Press.

Wicke, J., & Ferguson, M. (1992). Introduction: Feminism and postmodernism; or, the way we live now. *Boundary 2,19(2)*, 1–9.

Winant, H. (1990). Gayatri Spivak on the politics of the subaltern. *Socialist Review, 20(3)*, 81–97.

Woolgar, S. (1988). *Science: The very idea*. London: Tavistock.

11

PICO COLLEGE

GREG TANAKA

Reason is only reason, and it only satisfies man's rational requirements.
Desire, on the other hand, is the manifestation of life itself.

—Fyodor Dostoyevsky, *Notes from the Underground*

Story	Sidenotes

Story

A middle-aged man of medium height looked down from his second-story office and saw a pink rose garden lining a long walkway—just as lights at an airport might line a night runway, guiding planes home to safety or directing them to a faraway place. **(1)** From his window in the pristine white building at the top of the hill, he could see young men and women moving with purpose under the bright sunshine, some hailing others as they walked, others stopping to talk in animated voices. They must be animated voices. That was what this business was all about, wasn't it? Voices. And passion.

A long row of California oaks ran along the walkway. Gnarled

Sidenotes

1. Theoretical Framework. The theoretical basis of this narrative is Mikhail M. Bakhtin's critique of Fyodor Dostoyevsky's "polyphonic" novel, found in *Problems of Dostoevsky's Poetics* (1929/1984). A polyphonic style rejects the author's authority to make all characters and events contribute to a plot that is prefixed in the author's mind. Under a polyphonic approach, narration is no longer "subordinated to the hegemony of a single, unified consciousness" (Gardiner, 1992, p. 26) and no "single point of view dominates all the presented material" (Fanger, 1965, pp. 95–96). Instead, each character is given the authority to speak for him or herself. What matters is "the hero's discourse about himself

and thinned, they bravely withstood the smog at the edge of the city and gave shade to those in need. And there, at the very bottom of the hill, a spectacular fountain with flying shiny steel arcs reached frantically in all directions for something unstated. For what, an emotion? An understanding beyond the reach of calculated certainty? Some say the fountain served tribute to the liberating joy of space age technology; others saw the imperceptible waning of human spirit.

The man of medium height had a broad nose and big bushy eyebrows. When he smiled, crowsfeet spread from the corners of narrow, sensitive eyes, highlighting the warmth and intelligence of his gaze. His mustache was prematurely thinned and grayed, and his hands were too large for his body.

The man seemed more like a soft-spoken traveling salesman than the leader of a highly prestigious institution. But he was nonetheless a man who met challenge with wisdom and gentle words. His aura was that of a person who thought carefully—about both people and ideas—before making a decision.

Gazing out the window, the dark man with graying close-cropped hair and smiling eyes knew the bucolic peacefulness was deceiving.

and his world"—not a character type or temperament or "objectified image of the hero" (Bakhtin, 1929/1984, p. 53).

Refusing to see life as finished entity, the writer is free to represent reality "as developing idea" (Emerson in Bakhtin, 1929/1984, p. xxxix). It is this emphasis on "unfinalizability" (Bakhtin, 1929/1984, p. 53) that gives the writer new power to see *relationships* (Emerson in Bakhtin, 1929/1984). Characters are no longer objects in the author's eye but subjects who can be autonomous (Bakhtin, 1929/1984, p. 5), contradict themselves (p. 18), act fully in the present (p. 29), and experience the multiple ambiguities of human existence (p. 30). (Ong, 1987, p. 216, notes the study of cultural change in Malay society is "incomplete, fraught with ambiguity and shifting perceptions.") Under a schema of polyphony, characters and plots can be seen in musical terms as "modulations and counter-positions" (Bakhtin, 1929/1984, p. 40). Together, these traits give the author the ability to represent *interaction*.

In this maelstrom, Dostoyevsky avoids closure—and thus reaches a vantage point from which to appreciate "subtle shifts of meaning . . . the smaller shapes: voice zones, shifts in speakers, the overlapping boundaries between various characters' fields of vision" (Emerson in

Bakhtin, 1929/1984, p. xxxviii). Here, contradictions and ambiguities do not merge but stand alongside each other in "an eternal harmony of unmerged voices" (Bakhtin, 1929/1984, p. 30). It is this coexistence of different voices with harmony that makes Bakhtin's critique of Dostoyevsky so fecund in today's world of social science research, where it seems that difference has shattered all unity.

In the basement of the same building a tall, thin man with sandy brown hair stood and stretched as high as his six foot two frame would take him. He let out a long, slow whispered breath. It was not very long ago that students from the Black Students Alliance had engaged in a pitched battle with white students from Sigma Alpha Epsilon. The melee had not lasted long, but it would remain etched forever in the memory of the institution. **(2)**

"Why?" he asked himself. It started when a white student used racial slurs to say that blacks would not be welcome at a fraternity party. So what happens next? A group of black students attack two fraternity members standing nearby. Well, that was it. Free for all. In one crazed, unthinking, destructive moment, our grand experiment was about to end. Everything we had

2. The Debate. The onset of racial and ethnic fragmentation has become increasingly worrisome at U.S. colleges and universities. Of their own volition, students of color are sitting at segregated tables in student unions across the country. White students have been caught yelling "Water buffaloes!" at large black women students. At the University of Massachusetts at Amherst, there was a violent fight between whites and blacks following a World Series baseball game which some saw as a confrontation between a predominately black team and a predominately white team. Last October at the UCLA Graduate School of Education, someone put a letter in student mailboxes demanding that the emphasis on multiculturalism come to an end and that faculty of color be asked to leave since "we prefer white professors who have had similar

worked for, ready to go down the drain! Hey, *we* were the ones who brought all these different races together in one place. Wasn't it our fault?

No, that can't be right! We meant for this to work out right. If some students came with preconceived notions about minorities that were bound to cause trouble—would that be our fault? A deep furrow formed on his forehead. The spark in his eyes flickered—and for one moment longer he willed the ideals not to die.

"We were always about positive change here," he heard himself say. "The road was bumpy but we were willing to take our problems head on." The tall, thin man wanted to tell himself that this was also about who he was, too, and why his life would make a difference.

Taking a seat, Dean Wilder clasped his hands behind his head and closed his eyes. Some students were yelling outside his window. Students were always getting excited about the slightest thing when spring arrived. And the BSU-fraternity riot? It will become a distant memory. Then we will start over. Right?

Opening his eyes, the tallish, sandy-haired man shook his head as if to clear it. His office was neat and his round "dialogue table" was spotless. He was dressed in a long sleeve pastel cotton dress shirt, opened at

life experiences to ours."

Most recently, someone placed hate mail in the mailboxes of African American first year law students at the University of California at Berkeley—the day before final examinations. The note accused black students of being inferior and admitted only because of affirmative action requirements—this overlooking the fact that black graduates of Boalt Law School outperform white graduates on bar exams. Similar hate speech and fights have broken out over issues of sexual identity, class difference and gender. Meanness of spirit is occurring at a time when many campuses are experiencing large influxes of students of color and there is rising cultural pride among many identities.

Against this backdrop, many universities seem caught in a double bind of monocultural past—and fragmenting cultural future. Some commentators bemoan the loss of simpler times (A. Bloom, 1987; Bennett, 1988, 1992; L. Cheney, 1989; Kimball, 1990; D'Souza, 1991; Schlesinger, 1991; and Hughes, 1993). But that nostalgia for a Western based view of what counts as knowledge conjures only a superficial reassurance: white students can see with their own eyes that they are associating with large numbers of students of color and they find it impossi-

the top. No tie. His thin eye-brows twitched and he knew this day would bring something unexpected.

Well, it was five years ago that we planned the move to "multi-culturalize" this campus, he heard himself saying. And I was in on the planning. So where are we now—five years later? And what will we tell the trustees? That change doesn't move in a straight line?

The tall dean stood and went over to the window. He had kind, intelligent eyes. A few strands of light brown hair fell down over his forehead. He remembered how it had been in the beginning—when things were so promising. We were going to achieve something no other college in the United States had achieved!

ble to reconcile what their eyes see with that one culture tradi-tion.

The attempt to sustain a Western worldview also gives students and faculty of color no real purchase in the university. Perhaps worst of all, by leaving out large numbers of the campus population, university policy-makers leave themselves with no real opportunity to build a new sense of community. By the same token, tribalistic tendencies have proven equally divisive as they promote one ethnic passion over all others (e.g. Deloria champi-oning Native Americans, 1988, and Jeffries on Afrocentrism). This can lead to a cacophony of "separate" cultures.

The two views of Western retrenchment and ethnic sepa-ratism seem worlds apart yet share the same debilitating effect on policymakers by providing no clear way out of the dilemma (see e.g., West, 1993; Gates, 1992; McLaren, 1993; cf. Myrdal, 1944). This forces people to choose arti-ficially between a unity that is available only to whites—and the multicultural worship of dif-ference at the expense of unity.

We were going to be a test case. (3) Pico would be the first college to bring diversity into the curriculum. It was in 1978 that we voted *as a faculty* to establish a "core program" with two

3. Research Questions. Follow-ing this debate over how to end the social fragmentation on our campuses, one question is *whether a polyphonic novelistic style lends itself to the representa-*

world cultures courses, two European cultures courses *and two American minority cultures courses* required of all entering students. That put us ahead of Stanford—and U.C. Berkeley, too!

But there was one thing none of us anticipated. It wasn't enough for us just to change the curriculum. We had to change the professors, students—and administrative staff. There had to be an *interconnectedness.*

That's it. Our vote to have cultural diversity in the curriculum wasn't enough. We forgot to allow for retraining—of everyone!

Well, I was right in there with everyone else who thought the new president would give us the impetus we needed. Impressive record. In 1987, he promised right up front to make race diversity a major thrust in student admissions. And he did.

But did he move too fast? That was another step, a good step—to change the face of the student body from historically white to 50 percent of color. But was the decline in number of white students too sudden? Would this come back to haunt?

Well, the student body has a new face. We have a visionary for a president. What more could we ask for? He heard people yelling outside and paused.

There is this little feeling inside me, it's true. I can't deny

tion of swirling cultural stories and competing racial agendas. Here I am testing Bakhtin's belief that a writing which moves away from the author's controlling, authorial voice—and lets each character have his or her own voice— will be *more* able to represent the feelings and ideas of those characters. For example, will a polyphonic orientation let us see the person from his or her own point of view—and give voice to that person's own cultural tensions and identities?

How about where one event is perceived differently by different people? Or where there is a serious inconsistency between the statements of two characters—or between two statements by the same person? This study explores whether a polyphonic approach is *better* than a more authoritative style at showing the highly layered, multiplexed, nuanced, shifting, contradictory and often ambiguous findings that current campus conditions reflect.

This inquiry raises a follow-up question. Assuming for the moment that a new social arrangement might be possible—the second issue presented is *whether a polyphonic novelistic approach will give social scientists a new capability for studying how social unity and cultural difference might come to coexist in a society which is becoming increasingly heterogeneous.* This is where:

it. A voice is telling me the younger professors—who never went through the sixties and only know material wealth—are forming a faction with very senior white faculty. Will they try to repeal our efforts to multi-culturalize the campus?

The dean of students knew then that he was no longer a "young buck" hell-bent on changing the system. Cruelly, he had become suspended some-where in between an idealistic youth and the tempered period of generativity yet to come. In this in-between space of produc-tivity and achievement, he had begun to harbor a tiny suspicion. Have I *become* the establishment?

We thought it would be easy, he heard himself saying. I helped lead the charge. But then came the sacrifices. Were we ready to change *ourselves?* I mean "us," the faculty? Were we willing to examine who *we* were?

Institutional research says we are getting better. In 1982, we had only six professors of color out of a faculty of 150. By 1992, that number had reached 29. That's 20 percent!

Are the trustees still behind us? Anders Fine has been lead-ing the way and I will continue to support him. But maybe we should have been working to add more pieces. I just wish we had more women and people of color on that board. It all takes

Unity = a sense of shared, pos-itive sentiment that comes from interrelat-ing, and

Difference = an appreciation of dis-tinct cultural identi-ties centering on race or ethnicity, gender, sexuality, class, age, etc.

The question of whether and how unity and difference might coexist is not new (D. H. Hwang, 1994; W. G. Tierney, 1993a; G. R. Daniel, 1992; Burbeles and Rice, 1991; R. Rosaldo, 1989; S. A. Tyler, 1987; T. T. Minh-ha, 1987; C. Sandoval, 1982; A. Lorde, 1979; and Bakhtin, 1924/1984). In his later writings, Bakhtin expanded his discussion of the novel to encompass the idea of multiple languages, the end of reliance upon valorized tempo-ral categories, and a new zone of "maximal contact with the pre-sent" (Bakhtin, 1930s/1981, p. 11). In doing this, he may have foreshadowed the emergence of the United States as a multicul-tural society, stating it was not coincidence that the new novel should appear in Russia at a time of

rupture in the history of European civilization; its emer-gence from a socially isolated and culturally deaf semipatriar-chal society, and its entrance into international and interlingual contacts and relationships. (p. 10)

time. Time. And now what *is* all that racket outside? At the window, the tall professor looked out to see what the commotion was and immediately saw the large group of students milling about.

Michael Holquist describes Bakhtin's ability to contemplate the dual existence of difference and unity as a "Manichean sense of opposition and struggle . . . a ceaseless battle between centrifugal forces that seek to keep things apart, and centripetal forces that strive to make things cohere" (p. xviii). Bakhtin had earlier described these opposites in a context of hope:

> This disintegration (of the epic wholeness of an individual) combines in the novel with the necessary preparatory steps toward a new, complex wholeness on a higher level of human development. (pp. 37–38)

Wholeness. I can think of no better way to describe the hope I have for humanity when I contemplate the possible coexistence of social unity and cultural difference. But the question of *how* unity and difference might come to coexist at a campus that has long championed one cultural history is an issue of first impression.

My hunch is that Bakhtin's celebration of Dostoyevsky's writing *mirrors* G. Reginald Daniel's (1993) projection of a third place beyond the extreme poles of ethnic tribalism and Western retrenchment. What Daniel and Bakhtin hold in common is a fundamental view that one must never stop affirming the autonomy of the person—especially when people from different positions of power and different ethnic cultures are interacting with each other.

I did encounter one particular problem here in crafting. While it might appear to the reader that all the characters were interviewed on the same day, in fact, these interviews were spread out over a period of many months. The timing of the stories in this text is therefore "fictionalized" for the purpose of bringing them together under one expression.

This raises the question of whether polyphonic writing can ever truly be adapted to social science research, where interviews of so many different informants are typically conducted separately and over a long period of time. Is it possible to tie this all together in an "essential, irreducible multi-centeredness, or 'polyphony,' of human life" (Booth, in Bakhtin, 1929/1984, p. xx)—without resorting to fiction? If expressing the "super real" now becomes possible for my research—then at what cost?

From high atop the hill, the middle-aged man with large hands could see the cracked plaster and chipped paint on the exterior walls of the buildings that rimmed the long walkway below. **(4)** The brown patches of

4. Novelistic Writing of Fieldnotes. Novelistic writing of fieldnotes is not new. Zora Neale Hurston, who studied under Boas, wrote authentically if not poetically in *Mules and Men* (1935):

sun-dried grass and hard dirt appeared more obvious now. Like sentinels, the delicate pink roses stood as if in defiance of the encroaching decay around them. There were no other plants in the quad. Instead, red-tiled roofs drooped over tired buildings. It was then that Marcel Godot recalled when he was first hired to lead Pico College.

To his surprise, first one then another member of the search committee had expressed a desire to make Pico the first highly ranked liberal arts college to "multiculturalize" itself. They did not want a token minority applicant. They wanted a leader of color to take them to a new place.

One member of the faculty, a tall man with sandy brown hair, added that Pico needed a leader who could help make the campus reflect the community of the urban sprawl to the south. Walter Wilder would become one of his staunchest allies on the faculty.

Another man, aging and feisty, said that the city was fast becoming cosmopolitan with almost half the population from non-Western cultures. This man said that Pico would become a model for how to build a sense of community among diverse cultures. Anders Fine would become his best supporter on Pico's board of trustees.

But that was then. Today, the

Lemme tell you 'bout John and dis frog: It was night and Ole Massa sent John, his favorite slave, down to the spring to get him a cool drink of water. He called John to him.

"John!"

"What you want, Massa?" (Hurston, 1935, p. 9)

While some might be shocked by her vernacular style— Hurston's storytelling about a southern black community *was* storytelling, and in a Bakhtinian sense, it was among the first narratives to give the authority to speak to "ordinary" people (see Hernandez, 1995).

In *Under the Mountain Wall*, Peter Matthieson (1962) took the art of storytelling one step further by effectively merging art with the formality of ethnographic detail. The problem was that Matthieson too obviously read his own worldview into the writing:

The food in the valley forests was plentiful, and he had brought with him—or there came soon after—the sweet potato, dog, and pig. The jungle and mountain, the wall of clouds, the centuries, secured him from the navigators and explorers who touched the coasts and went away again; he remained in his stone culture. In the last corners of the valley, he remains there still, under the mountain wall. (Matthieson, 1962, p. 5)

dark complected Marcel Godot wondered how much longer they all would support him.

He watched the students below moving with spirit and chatting excitedly. Many were walking up the hill, toward the administration building. So why am I doing this, he asked himself? Has this idea already become bigger than me—or am *I* the idea?

I know exactly what it was then, what we all wanted. It was supposed to be about something bigger than the things that separate us. If there is no core that holds people together—and we are only a collection of different identities—then there is no community.

Tortoise shell glasses framed Godot's soft, doleful eyes, making him seem like the favorite grandfather or uncle of your youth. With his heavy eyebrows and slow manner, he was the epitome of deliberation and reflection. But there was much more to this president than his calm demeanor. The outward appearance hid an inner history of swirling emotions.

At a small school like Pico, he thought, it should be possible for every student to interact with every other student at some point during the four years— and with every faculty member and even me. This is a college where it is possible to communicate—to establish values and

This passage demonstrates an exoticism about the people of New Guinea and an all too frequent Western penchant for wanting to discover "the last aboriginal culture." Still, there is no denying Matthieson's mastery of the art of writing nonfiction as literature (see e.g. Zinsser, 1988, p. 53ff.). He gives me confidence to proceed with this project.

More recently, John Langston Gwaltney published *Drylongso* (1993) which expresses in narrative style the fieldwork he had completed in the 1970's. In this writing, Gwaltney gives his informants real voice by naming them and representing their narratives verbatim:

> Hannah Nelson: I am a colored woman sixty-one years of age. I was born in Boston and grew up right here. I came to Harlem when I was about six or seven. . . . My maiden name is Nelson and I married a man named Nelson, too. Anyone who would see me would say, "There goes a colored woman in her early sixties who could afford to lose a few pounds."

But while Gwaltney achieved the goal of giving each character his or her own authority to speak, he did not *combine* their voices into a unified, novelistic experience. With each story standing on its own, the total expression was not polyphonic

principles and discuss them and abide by those that make sense.

So maybe it doesn't matter if I have become the idea or not. It's too late to worry about that. What I do know is this: my stomach is telling me there's something going on. I know I should listen. I know I should listen.

in a Bakhtinian sense.

James Clifford (1986) was one of the first to urge ethnographers to write a polyphonic text that could account for multiple perspectives (Park, 1993), and in 1988 he lauded the rich novelistic detail expressed by some earlier ethnographers (Michel Leiris in 1946, and Barbara Tedlock in 1984).

Then, in 1994, Kamala Visweswaran published *Fictions of Feminist Ethnography*. A powerful and well researched piece about the use of narrative in qualitative research, this work successfully interwove theory with autobiographical storytelling:

> Somehow, during the course of that first year in India, I accumulated a lot of saris . . . old ones, new ones, cotton ones, and silk; torn, but still lovely ones; others in colors so gaudy I dared not wear them. The logic was, if I looked Indian, surely in a sari, I must be Indian. . . . I soon discovered, however, that the wearing of saris was coded by factors such as age and class. (Visweswaran, 1994, p. 166)

Effective at deconstructing the power and gender relations imbricated in a storytelling, Visweswaran's piece nonetheless remains authorial. Visweswaran arguably sacrifices contradiction, nuance and multiplicity in order to reaffirm the authority of her own voice—and falls short of attaining a truly polyphonic novelistic expression.

What is new in the present paper is its attempt at making a novelistic writing of fieldnotes "polyphonic"—and secondly, to engage that narrative in a dialogue with (what I shall call) "sidenotes" that allow for ratiocination and critique.

In attempting to represent findings through story, I draw further courage from Patricia J. Williams' *Alchemy of Race and Rights*, Michael Taussig's "Montage," Renato Rosaldo's "Grief and A Headhunter's Rage," James Clifford's "Identity in Mashpee," Simon Schama's *Dead Certainties*, Dorinne Kondo's *Crafting Selves*, and Anna Lowenhaupt Tsing's *In the Realm of the Diamond Queen*. I am especially encouraged by the work of Kirin Narayan (1993) who urges ethnographers to continue to combine both narrative and analysis in one text, and Ruth Behar and Deborah Gordon (1995) whose edited volume uses fiction, memoir, plays and other non-traditional forms to redefine the contours of ethnographic writing.

On the outskirts of campus, a young man sat in a dark room composing his thoughts. **(5)** Dressed in a dark coat and tie, he was short, with straight dark

5. The Setting. Pico College (fictitious name) is a small, highly ranked private liberal arts college on the west coast. The setting was picked for this pilot study

brown hair and appeared to the researcher to be a southern European. After exchanging pleasantries, the young man realized he would soon be saying things in this secluded second floor library of the Multicultural Center that he never thought he would tell anyone.

because it is undergoing rapid racial demographic change. With a student body that had been predominantly white since its founding in 1887, the entering freshmen class had by 1994 become 50 percent of color. I picked the name "Pico" in honor of Pio Pico who was the first governor of California—dating all the way back to its settlement by Spanish explorers. Many are unaware that Pio Pico was part black.

"I am Assistant Director of Student Affairs," Mark Marjorian heard himself saying. **(6)** "But in a few weeks I will be moving from the West coast to take a job in the Midwest."

When the researcher said he was studying race harmony at Pico, Mark stiffened before speaking again. "Well—there was a very successful student retreat last year. We also have a very strong Peer Mentor Program."

He was finding it difficult to choose between his strong feelings of loyalty for Pico—and the opposing need to get some things off his chest.

"Okay, we do need more programming on multiculturalism," he heard himself saying. **(7)** "The problem is, it seems people are either 100 percent for it—or dead set against it. Some see us as flag bearers for positive change, but others see us as 'diversity police.'

6. Access. Access to Pico College was obtained initially through an inside administrator who had been a classmate in my Ph.D. program. Her contacts subsequently opened more doors for me, like this one. How much does fieldwork depend on a lucky tip? In this case, a great deal since this informant was about to leave town and felt he could speak freely with me— well, almost.

7. Unit of Analysis. The unit of analysis in this study is "the process of transition from a monocultural campus to a campus defined by cultural difference." In applying a unit of analysis of this kind (and part way through the process), I found I had to focus on such varied tropes as multiple voices, power, resistance back, and privilege—all within a shifting context of disputed, fragmented, and contested cultural terrain.

"We also need to see the professional staffs on this campus go through the same training our students are going through. (8) But there is resistance to that idea."

As he sat in the dark room, Mark realized he was no longer in control of his own story. It was all coming out now, taking on a life of its own. In the curriculum, people were only making changes at the edges. Many professors agreed that multiculturalism was important—but then failed to actually *do* it. English and Comparative Lit only offered a few special courses and that was it. This forces black students to choose between courses about themselves and courses about Shakespeare—and *then* justify how they decide to their peers.

8. Method and Techniques. I wanted to study the feelings and conflicts of the people who were change agents, resisting change or apathetic about the decision to multiculturalize the campus. The data came from sixteen interviews, eleven observations, and multiple document reviews taken in a pilot study conducted over an eighteen-month period. Triangulation was helpful in view of the limited number of interviews conducted. Wherever possible, I adopted the style of letting the interviewee tell his or her own story, and this led to particularly rich emotions and impressions: on many occasions there was conflicting data, with stories of different informants at odds with each other.

The documents included the Pico College five-year strategic plan, student newspapers, college program brochures, student diversity and leadership training workshop guides, the college catalog, and the president's speeches.

The data was placed into a "data dump" from which I culled out ten recurring themes: conflict, power, resistance to power, resistance back, Western vs. non-Western racial identities, whether multiculturalism includes or excludes Whites, the need for a new social unifier, white alienation or fear, movement toward an alternative regime or sentiment, and community.

"But it shouldn't have to be that way," he said and this time he could hear the strain in his voice. **(9)** "Take the Religion Department. Guy comes in and teaches East Asian Religion. Students love it. Then the new prof leaves. The shot of energy is not institutionalized—so it's lost." Sensing he had the full attention of the researcher now, he added for effect, "And this is happening *all over campus*."

9. The Sampling Strategy was to interview administrators and professors who were most active in the move to multiculturalize the campus. This strategy was later amended when an administrator insisted that I interview several student leaders who gave me surprising information about race relations and especially about white students. The interview sample consisted of an even sampling of women and men— and people of different ages and ethnicities. Observations were random.

Watching the researcher's eyes get big, he knew he would tell the researcher about the backlash. **(10)** How the president of Pico had articulated his vision so well—but that no one had thought out the possibility of a white backlash against multiculturalism.

Ah, this researcher is thirsty for tidbits like this last one— ones that tell him where the tensions really are at Pico. The soon-to-depart junior administrator

10. Resistance Back. The outgoing student affairs administrator believed that tension from Whites who were feeling threatened by multiculturalism was being applied to the president— a thought confirmed by the dean of students, who strongly urged me to interview the president about this. An interview with the president yielded the opposite claim—namely, that the college and its trustees were still fully committed to the mission of

knew he would be telling this researcher about the extent to which Godot had underestimated white resistance to multiculturalism—and this is *from his own high level staff!* And no one had even thought to prepare the *alumni* for what was coming.

Now he would finally tell someone that the first seven appointments Godot made without searches were all white males. **(11)** *All seven.* He would tell this researcher the story about the one senior white professor who stood up one day and announced that he would resign as a faculty member if one more white male was appointed to a top administrative post— and then not long after that, accepted an offer to be next dean of students!

Would words ever be enough to describe all his emotions about Pico? How can you explain to an outsider how hard it is to work here? That it's in your face every day? That it enters into room rates, where the single room dorms are all white because it's the whites who have the money to pay for more expensive rooms.

multiculturalizing the campus. My own impression was that the president was telling me the company line and that inside, he was trying to cope with swirling emotions and tensions about the constantly changing levels of support he was receiving from faculty, trustees, staff, and students. Here at Pico, multiculturalism certainly meant different things to different people—and these meanings were transforming.

11. Culture. I am still using "culture" to refer to "shared meaning" (e.g. Lett, 1987; Geertz, 1973). What's different is that I am going beyond ethnic derivations to include meanings based on race, class, gender, sexuality and age (see Park, 1993). This extends Rosaldo's (1989) critique of static definitions of culture— but I feel it is the only definition that makes sense at Pico where there are so many identities rubbing up against and overlapping so many others.

Thus, the idea of having one fixed ethnic history reside in one geographical locale now seems archaic. To have continued meaning, the term "culture" must now operate as a broader rubric that accounts for identities formed around such disparate categories (themselves far from monolithic) as race, ethnicity, gender, class, sexual orientation,

It hits you in the stomach when you read the first page of the student newspaper—and find that the U.S. Office of Civil Rights has found Pico College guilty of sexual harassment. That two other people in the counseling office are suing for race discrimination. That two more employees are suing for age discrimination. All this in one week's issue of the paper!

immigrant status, age, religion, and physical capability. These meanings change over time, and in most cases an individual will have more than one basis for culture. Under this broader definition, the shared meanings of lesbians of color, for example, might constitute a "culture." Or, culture might derive from gender by itself. Being "a white male" could encompass shared meaning. This is not inconsistent with Rosaldo who emphasized the importance of "process" and "layers" rather than seeing culture as one fixed structure or ordering mechanism. At Pico College, I definitely found process more meaningful than structure because social relations were changing so rapidly. Even such stratifications as "race" and "gender" were constantly being reshaped, recombined, and recontextualized as the campus transitioned from one dominant worldview to multiple ones.

Mark was in his late twenties. As he sat staring straight ahead, he let his shoulders drop. His eyes were focusing on a spot between his body and the far wall—as if imagining an object hanging before his face. In a steady, droning voice, he told the researcher a recent story about the Alumni Office. Citing the alarm a proposed article might have caused within the ranks of

12. Is Multiculturalism A Temporary Way Station? At Pico, patterns of change could be traced to different periods of time corresponding to shifting understandings of multiculturalism. As a result, there was no one campus-wide understanding of the transformations necessary to accommodate that change, and some members of the community were holding on

a conservative white alumni base, **(12)** the director pulled an article from the forthcoming issue of the alumni magazine. Students were up in arms.

The article had been about "Reggae and Rastefarians" and it described the success of a new, charismatic professor of psychology. The professor, who was from the West Indies, taught that every culture should have a voice. Tall and wiry with fine, smooth facial skin, this professor wore dreadlocks down to his shoulders. His bearing was one of deep intelligence. The intensity and meter of his voice had a mesmerizing effect on students—who were flocking to his classes as if drawn to a magnet.

With all the lawsuits—and the reggae story left out—was there any hope?

But then, I want to explain to this researcher that I will dearly miss this place, too. Do I dare tell him that I think the students here are truly great because they question everything? That the president is a truly superb human being?

As he paused, the young man saw what was really going on in this interview. But he realized it did not matter and sighed. Yes, this researcher is a sly one. He tricks me into telling him everything that peeves me. He knows I am a sucker for unloading all my frustration on him. He knows I am leaving. But I am a

to meanings that others had long ago abandoned. Here, the alumni base was believed by some administrators to equate multiculturalism with race intrusion. Recall also the resistance to multiculturalism demonstrated by some professors in their late twenties and early thirties that came as a surprise to professors in their forties who had experienced the liberalism of the sixties and saw in multiculturalism a promising way to reorganize the campus community in the wake of the social upheaval of those times.

Was there an alliance forming between the youngest (white) faculty members and some older professors who had come out of Western tradition? If so, would it change the pace and trajectory of the movement to "multiculturalize" the institution? In contrast to what the president of Pico was claiming, this development implied a new and unanticipated "resistance back" by a potentially growing number of white professors.

While more fieldwork is necessary to confirm these developments, one indication is that there is now a need for a new space *after* multiculturalism that will give people from the "dominant" group—white males—a new and positive role in the new campus culture. This was one setting where a polyphonic novelistic approach worked well—

willing participant in this charade, am I not? And, of course, this is when the researcher asks, "What about the white students?"

So now I will have to tell him how white students often feel they are owed something because they are reaching out to help students of color and then get rejected.

I will tell him that many white students don't realize this is a lifelong process and that you're not in it if you think you are owed something right away.

It has taken me some time to admit it, **(13)** but now I know you have to be in it for yourself in the sense that you have to risk something personally when you learn about other cultures—you have to be willing to change *yourself.*

At the same time, I will have to say that this thing of multiculturalism is not about you personally. If you are raised in the dominant group and then some Latino student comes along and tells you there are two kinds of whites—racists and paternalizing liberals—you know it's not about you personally but about one Latino student who's had certain experiences and is still trying to work through his perceptions.

What have I learned? I have learned the self-doubts white students are feeling are what students of color have to go

by allowing for surprise and contradiction, and by including the voices of white professors and students who had been somewhat alienated by the relatively sudden transition to multiculturalism.

13. Positionality. As a person of color, I have experienced the sharp sting of cultural domination in the academy—often by people I believed were acting in my best interests. One professor told me to take my interest in multiculturalism and study somewhere else. Another angrily told me his division had not hired a single white male professor in five years because of "overemphasis" on diversity. In fact, his division had not hired *anybody* in five years—and his colleagues remained *all white!*

When another professor asked how I could be a third-generation American and in the United States longer than his family had—I could only conclude from his shocked look that as a second generation Irish American he believed he had more of a right to be in the United States than I did.

through every day. I have learned that the feeling that you always have to prove yourself is not the normal experience for white students. And also . . .

At the same time, my position in the field defined the power I held as researcher. I found the two positions often merged—my power as researcher and the emotions that came from prior life experiences. This shaped the way I perceived, recorded, and now represent events: initially, this caused me to be looking for or receptive to certain pieces of data others might not consider important or might miss (like pain or hopelessness). Later it caused me to want to write up only what I felt was important.

Nonetheless, the conflicts are represented as undiluted and multilayered as I found them. Here, I think it was crucial for me to convey the tensions as action, as unresolved experience—that is, in Bakhtin's sense, in the form of *unfinalized* event. I think this urge to convey the unfinalizability of events will compensate in some immeasurable way for the bias contained in my high authority and pain.

The president of Pico College was finally forced to chuckle. **(14)** His second-floor office also afforded an unobstructed view of the Old Student Union building farther down the hill, and large, garish, multicolored posters were hanging from the false balconies of that aging, off-color Spanish-style building. This week, there were more than usual:

14. Historicizing and Recontextualizing. In a sense, Pico College seemed to be acting out a flipped application of power and resistance where people of color now held control (the president, multicultural program administrators and professors, and some students of color)—and Whites were on the defensive. But at the same time, some

Planned Parenthood. May 10th!
Amandla—New Governance—
   New South Africa!
Suburban Alphabet—Art Week
Ancient Celtic Witchcraft. May 23
Zeta Tau Communis
Women's Forum—Discuss
   with/about Black Women,
   May 26
Porn Panel! May 24
AIDS & College Campuses.
   May 24
Asian American Heritage Week.
   May 16–20!

The festive atmosphere of the student marquee always gave him hope. The emotions that emanated from the students every year in the spring were always rejuvenating for him, too. Seeing these banners, the serious man realized that he cherished moments like this and let himself feel emboldened. It's almost like the students are telling me, "You're on the right track, you're on the right track, keep it up!"

Godot now let his emotion turn into a fleeting sense of elation. It had taken five hard years to make this campus into a place where difference could be engaged openly and discussed with good humor.

But was this all an illusion, he asked himself? You keep going back to the board of trustees and each time you leave feeling that you have their support. But don't fool yourself. The leading trustee committees are manned by white males. Sooner or later

senior white professors, trustees, and alumni also retained much power by virtue of their seniority and numbers—in the sense that "power" means control over others and over one's own life. The latter had the wherewithal to stall, hold back, even sabotage efforts to add more gender, race, and class perspectives to the campus.

What I am here calling "resistance back" by white males ironically mirrors the resistance one finds in classical studies of resistance *against* the West written about colonized peoples or by women around the world (e.g., Martin, 1987; Ong, 1987; Chatterjee, 1989; Scott, J. W., 1991; Stoler, 1991; Scott, J. C., 1992; Nordstrom & Martin, 1992; Kondo, 1993; and Tsing, 1994).

What could unite this campus? As a monocultural worldview gives way partially to a multicultural one, will new social unifiers supersede a totalizing Western way of knowing? With no new organizing framework, there was confusion about what should constitute truth or *be valued*. As one informant indicated, the decentering forced students to choose artificially between traditional knowledge (as presented in a course on Shakespeare) and a new and as yet unsettled view of "multiple" perspectives.

On the other hand, at least one informant (the associate

they will get fed up with all this controversy and demand someone's head. And my fine, cultured head is black!

dean of students) observes that if there is going to be a new sense of community at Pico, it will be a "process" of working to learn about one's own differences and seeing the link between that pain and the pain experienced by others. This means that if there is going to be new unity, it might very well be a *process or sentiment*—and not a new structure at all.

Was this a case where multiculturalism was moving so quickly that it left out the European American story—or at least failed to rearticulate that story within the new, shifting context? One result was that some white supporters, alumni, faculty, and administrators had begun to experience a kind of fear or anomie. If so, I do not attribute this to a failure of proponents of multiculturalism at Pico College to plan for it, so much as the newness of multiculturalism as an epistemological thrust—and the inability of that movement to break entirely free of its initial need to distinguish itself from and gain freedom from a rooted, totalizing Western epistemology.

At the same time, the alienation of whites at Pico might be a direct result of their own inability to let go of unexamined positions of privilege, a mindset which could deprive them of future ability to know pain, construct new identities and attain connections to others (community) not based on superiority.

In the basement of the Old Student Union, a tall, well-built student sat alone at a table in the snack bar. **(15)** White picnic-like tables ran down the length of the room. Loud noises were coming from two places at once—from diners who were sitting to his left and from a young woman cashier who stood behind the counter to his right screaming something though a cubbyhole at the cook in back.

Antonio sat up stiffly as he came to a sudden thought. "Class difference matters a lot around here," he blurted out with a force that caught him by surprise. A light complected Latino, Antonio had a large, square head with very short brown-black hair. He was broad-shouldered and had the appearnce of a high school football player. He wondered how he would explain to the others how he had reached this conclusion.

He would tell Minerva and Liz to check it out for themselves: the upper-middle-class students sit in the *old* cafeteria and the lower-class students sit in the *new* cafeteria.

Funny, isn't it? It's the old cafeteria that the upper-class students eat in. The long rows of tables are crammed too closely together—so these students eat

15. Interculturalism. One of the things surfaced by this pilot study is the need for a new cultural mapping that neutralizes the hurtfulness of vertical social or racial hierarchies. One of the most promising is "interculturalism" (e.g., Marranca & Dasgupta, 1991) which promotes exchange *across* cultures. An intercultural approach differs from the "bazaar of ethnic cultures" where one can buy this culture or that culture "straight off the rack," as Mike Davis (1992, p. 80) once described the L.A. Art Festival's early approach to implementing multiculturalism.

In a more intercultural approach, the different identities—ethnic, racial, gendered, etc.—are not arrayed like cans of soup on a supermarket shelf. Instead, they are seen in *interaction* with each other, in all the splendor and disorder one might imagine where there are competing interests, overlappings in identity and multiple plays of power. (Compare Burbeles & Rice, 1991, regarding the hopefulness in dialogue across difference.)

Interculturalism is not unlike the "cross-culturalism" discussed by Lucy Lippard (1990) and Partricia Hill Collins (1986) in visual art and sociology,

like together sardines packed neatly in a can. Then there's the *new* cafeteria—where students from working-class families eat. Loads of space. Go figure. In fact, with all the space, why is it that the ten tables there are bunched tightly together in the middle of the room? It's almost like this is to protect the diners from a large predator.

Will Minerva and Liz listen to me?

Back at the Multicultural Center, a young woman with amber skin and hazel eyes was shaking her head in a heated debate with another woman. "We need to remind ourselves that the Peer Mentor Program *is working.*"

A tall, stocky young black male stopped by and whispered something in Elizabeth's ear, but before she could respond the man stood, laughed, and moved away. Elizabeth's hair was both blond and kinky. She smiled then, and her whole face lit up.

"Wait, Elizabeth," Minerva said. "Don't you think we should be telling people what needs to be done to *improve* the program, too?

"I mean, okay, a few weeks ago we had Value Diversity Week. Then last semester we did Sexuality and Political Thought. But it's not all roses. I mean, is our work *only* for students of color--and women and gays and lesbians?"

respectively. Here, art or discourse is centered within the person and then compared across ethnic or gender groups. Interculturalism also shares a kindred spirit with the "border crossing" metaphor of Anzaldua (1987) which refers to movements of racial or ethnic groups across geographic terrain in the manner exemplified by Mexicans crossing the U.S. border. (See also Rosaldo, 1989; Gomez-Pena, 1990; Giroux, 1992; McLaren, 1993; and Giroux & McLaren, 1994.)

In border crossings, some cultural patterns are lost, others are retained, and still others are merged in a kind of "mestizaje." One could now ask, might "border crossing" aptly describe the experience of the European American student who comes to Pico College from a homogeneous (white) middle-class suburb?

In a similar tracking of movement, Clifford (1992) analyzes how cultural groups come into contact with each other as "traveling cultures."

The most intriguing cultural mapping of all, however, may be "transculturalism" (Ortiz, 1940; Daniel, 1992), which moves away from a dominant-minority or binary view of acts of interrelating and instead focuses on the mutual process of change that occurs when multiple cultures come into contact with each other. G. Reginald Daniel (1992) in particular stresses the need to move beyond the limits of vertical social arrangements—and toward an arrangement that is more "horizontal."

In this instance, I am using interculturalism to encompass not only the way in which distinct identities interact but also the way in which this richness of perspective defines a new wholeness in human experience—what Bakhtin had once called "an eternal harmony of unmerged voices" (1924/1984, p. 30).

The fact that Pico College does not yet reflect that wholeness is not what is important. What is important is that *some* people at one private liberal arts college—its president, dean of students, key faculty, student leaders, and others—feel a strong emotional need to carve out something new, something like harmony, while keeping the development of separate identities alive. I think it is not inaccurate to conclude that this campus is struggling to identify a feeling or sentiment that would exemplify Bakhtin's full sense of polyphony.

"Yeah," Elizabeth said after pausing for a split-second. "Yeah, okay, Whites. **(16)** We know our white classmates are feeling left out of all this, but

16. Bias. In an ironic twist, I now find Western crisis and dissolution fascinating. As a third generation Japanese American, I came into this study with scars

what will our friends say if we tell them about this? Her voice was straining. Will they listen to us?"

Minerva had dark brown skin and long black hair. She thought for a moment before making a face. "Well, it's true. A lot of whites just want the food and the dance—the nice ethnic stuff. So they are a little behind the times. They need to learn there's more to us than that.

"But to tell you the truth, I see my job as MECHA chair to help Latino students first. The whole system is still set up to support whites. So why should we give them *our* help?"

At the Old Student Union, Antonio was almost finished with his sandwich when he came to a second realization. "I am going to have to tell Minerva and Liz about this, too. I have to remind them we have a financial crisis at Pico. We're *losing money*. We're dipping into our endowment at the rate of 5 percent a year for operating expenses. Even two years of this would be really hurt our endowment fund.

"We have to remind other students that our overall student retention rate is only 70 percent—not good for a school with our reputation. Students are leaving this place in droves! It shouldn't be like that for a small private residential college like us. Minerva and Liz will have to

from having grown up in a dominant culture not always friendly to my family's ethnic history (a total stranger once yelled to me it was "my people" who bombed Pearl Harbor—when in fact my father was U.S. born and a junior at UCLA when that war broke out). As a result, I have a tendency to look for or expect racial tension. In this study, I had a recurring tendency to consider the "dismantling" of Western (or white male) domination an important trope. I *looked* for evidence of it.

At the same time, I have another bias that comes from my own ethnic history which demands "undying optimism." I think it is the *combination* of fascination with breakdown and wanting to find hope that led me to represent what I in fact represented in this write-up. In doing this, I may have missed seeing some information or left out others I had seen—for example, the college president's belief that "excellence" would cut across cultural difference and thereby create unity. Very conceivably, I read in a significance for either disintegration or renewal that was partly of my own making.

With a concern for ethics in naturalistic fieldwork (e.g., Clandinin & Connelly, 1994), I conclude that there are several pitfalls in this study I had to watch out for in particular: (1) a tendency to look for dramatic

listen to this. They have to. It affects us all."

At the Multicultural Center, Elizabeth and Minerva were giving each other knowing looks. When they address the student rally, they will have to emphasize the *positive* things, too.

A large polished wooden desk stood at one end of the Pico College president's office. On one side of the desk there was a personal computer. A large framed painting of a tiger hung on the wall directly behind the desk. The walls were of dark oak and the rug dark brown. A soft couch ran along the bay window facing due west. At the south end of the room, nearest the door, there was an oval-shaped hardwood table with four wooden chairs.

Alone in his thoughts, Godot was fully aware of the resistance to multiculturalism at Pico. White students were frustrated. Alumni were unhappy. The forty-member board of trustees maintained a wide range of enthusiasm about multiculturalism. Some will up and decide that we have gone far enough— and seek a return to a Western Civilization emphasis.

Still, he believed that excellence did not have a color tag. Multiculturalism was not anti-white or anticommunity. It was *enabling*.

problems and dive into the first earth-shattering story I encountered, (2) a tendency to romanticize the subject or unit of analysis; (3) a need to become emotionally involved in events; and (4) an inclination to either defer to power or actively resist it.

Here, for example, I was captured by the aura of power to transform held by the president of Pico College. While I tried not to defer too much to that power— or critique it too severely—it was also clear I could do only so much to control my emotions and hunches. One of the advantages to presenting data in a polyphonic novelistic way was to counter those tendencies by including points of view that were not my own—even when I did not like them.

Did we send out a signal to Whites that they don't count? **(17)** Well, they *do* count. And this is what's missing from multiculturalism so far. Now we have to bend back the other way to make whites feel they can belong here, too.

Take the catalog. Last year it had a cover photo showing a black, a Latina, and an Asian student talking with a Chicano professor. Boy, did that get the white alumni all hot and bothered! The thing is, the same people who say we should have included whites in the cover photo would not have been surprised if the picture had contained *only* whites. To calm the waters, we are revising the catalog by not making multiculturalism so blatant.

But what I want to tell everyone is that we are about something larger than all this—that there is more than just all this difference. But how? I need to tell the students—and trustees— that there will be no "community" if we are nothing but a loose collection of differences.

There's a reason I took this job. It had to do with my being black in America. It had to do with my being lucky enough to have opportunities—and wanting to make sure others had the same kinds of chances in life. But have things now changed?

Are we now beyond that original purpose? Don't we need a

17. The End of Social Theory?

In observing the beginning of the end of a one-culture view of history and knowledge at Pico College, I could not help but conclude that all the recent movements—poststructuralism, deconstruction, feminist theory, multiculturalism, queer theory, new history, postmodern art and architecture, subaltern studies, postcolonial studies, and even critical theory—are fueled by the same sentiment, which is the driving question of whether and how to dismantle a mono-racial, male-centered hierarchy of knowledge born of Western colonialism. Implicit in this inquiry is the question of where whites will now fit in.

Pico College could not of course address overnight all the questions raised by all the dismantling thrusts in social theory. The fact that it had decided to move in a *con*structive direction was admirable.

But toward what end? Why do this?

If C. Wright Mills (1959) was right about locating the need for new social theory at that place where social theory cannot explain a problem that is important and personal to the researcher—then we are perhaps at a turning point. Isn't it here— at a place like Pico where dissolution and re-creation seem to co-reside—that new theory must be born? If so, I had a feeling

new   arrangement—where Whites aren't at the center but they aren't excluded either?

My role? I was hired to make this place multicultural—and now I'm trying to make this place better for whites!

Well, it's paying off. I can't complain. Our fund-raising efforts netted $1.6 million in one month alone. We are up in both percent of alumni donors and total dollars raised for the year.

Godot sucked in his breath and let it out slowly. Well, we are not taking a straight path, but we are making progress. Wait, what are all those students doing down there?

social theory would not come back as a way of structuring knowledge—not *that* kind of theory. At Pico, theory would become a way of taking into account both process *and* feeling.

Bakhtin was himself quite taken by the idea of death and renewal. To him, the whole reason for writing about crisis and catastrophe was to discover a new way of social relating which would be life affirming—that is, to find a "place for working out . . . a new mode of interrelationships between individuals, counterposed to the all-powerful socio-hierarchical relationships of noncarnival life" (Bakhtin, 1924/1984, pp. 122–127).

And this brings me to my own passion: When existing social theory cannot explain why race, gender, sexual orientation, power, and class differences continue to confound citizens and their social institutions in a "democratic" society, then perhaps theory has become "unhinged" from its social context. The need for new theory is implicit.

Two rows of lab counters ran down the length of a 20 by 60 foot room at east campus. **(18)** The counters were loaded with scientific equipment. Flasks. Burners. Measuring tools. Copper wires. Several students sat hunched over their work.

18. Significance/Contribution to the Field. This writing is an experimental attempt at applying Bakhtin's concept of polyphony to the reporting of social science research. Despite several methodological problems that I encountered, this

Except for the sound of their tinkering—and the soft music from a radio—the room was still.

An Asian woman, a Latino male, a white woman, and an Asian male were all fingering their equipment in the biochemistry lab. At one end of the two rows a white woman in her thirties sat reading a manual.

Watching all this from the doorway, Professor Stevens recalled how hard it had been when she first started out here. It had been brutal to be a research scientist, do cutting-edge work, teach eager students—and raise a family—all at the same time.

We did do well in the sciences during my tenure here. What was it? In the last ten years, 192 of our students went to medical school. Another 79 went on to do graduate work in the sciences. Still another 127 had gone on to professional schools.

But getting approval for the new course on "Gender and Science" was what hurt the most. I have kept this inside me all these years. It hasn't been easy—but I'm still here. Stevens looked gaunt from all the wear.

What do you do when the senior professors in biology, physics, geology, and physiological psychology are all white men? It's the subtle forms of discrimination that are the real killers—like not getting guidelines or helpful critiques from

early effort suggests that Bakhtin's approach can make two immediate contributions to research:

1. *First, it appears that a polyphonic novelistic writing allows the researcher to represent the multiple voices and emotions of a heterogeneous population in a more nuanced fashion than traditional reporting.* I could show, for example, that some students saw the fiscal crisis at Pico as truly devastating, while the president saw it as another operating problem that required him to project an image of control for an institution that was receiving "record alumni contributions."

Writing in a novelistic form thus allowed me to discover and express the complexity, conflicts and surprises of the people I studied by empowering them with their own voices and authority—something that is not easily developed in the traditional reporting form, which is linear and requires reducing findings to fixed categories.

A polyphonic novelistic style can be superior to traditional forms when writing about issues of race, gender and power differences—since the traditional writer's own position as author never gets discussed and is left, as a result, to influence the write-up without examination.

I also think a polyphonic novelistic writing is particularly effective in times of high cultural

senior professors along the way.

Professor Stevens shook her head slowly. Someone had to be in the vanguard. Someone had to take the "hits" on the forehead.

But why do they resist us, she asked finally. The amazing thing is to watch them. Many of these professors feel terribly threatened by diversity. My own husband is tenure track here—and he can't deal with it!

Then there's Larsen who feels that as a white male there is no longer a place for him—and *he's* one of the ones who's trying! But most of them just shut up. They won't even confront diversity, even if it's in front of their own eyes. Well, except for Tenille, who says, "Why change if it's been so successful?" You see, they only want to teach what's worked for them.

Gathering her notes for the next class, Professor Stevens wondered whether anyone even cared about her travails.

Two floors below the president's office, Drew Lockerby was preparing a speech—on sexual harassment, race, ethnicity, what it means to be a woman and a man, what it means to be gay and bisexual, and what it means to be disabled or Jewish.

With long thin bones and sinewy arms and legs, Drew had a youthful appearance. His face

fragmentation and change—conditions which are only awkwardly or reductionistically navigated by traditional modes of representation. I find it offers flexibility where there are issues of power and resistance, where people have multiple or conflicting loyalties, or where the story is one of joy or other deep human emotion.

At Pico, for example, two students of color empathized with the alienation felt by classmates who were white and not included in the movement to multiculturalize the campus— and in contrast, at least one entrenched professor continued to frustrate attempts by a female professor to teach gender in the sciences. A polyphonic rendition captures this multiplicity of emotions without having to comment on it.

In addition, the polyphonic concept of "unfinalizability" seemed very powerful to me in the sense that I did not ever feel forced to reduce the findings to final resolution or clarity—or steer them into fixed categories. Except for the data dump which I completed as a matter of form more than anything else, I did not feel that I had to conform findings to any preexisting vocabulary. What mattered more was the dialogue *between* characters and, in some cases, between two sides to one person. I think this focus on multiplicity and

was angular and alive. In a few minutes, he had a scheduled meeting with the organizers of "Faces in the Crowd." As associate dean of students, he knew he played a big role in its continued existence. In fact, he could scarcely contain his energy when it came to this project.

Who could guess that Faces in the Crowd would be such a smashing success. We take ten or twelve returning students and get them to look into themselves by confronting their diversity—then let them act out their stories on Orientation Day to entering freshman. Now in the spring, they were putting the finishing touches on their pieces for next August.

Has this year been *too* successful? Was "too much" pain dripping off of these students' stories? Drew did not want next year's entering students to become frightened of Pico before setting foot in their first classes.

A tall white man leaned his head into the open doorway and smiled broadly. He seemed to take pride in interrupting Drew's thoughts. We're ready," said Trent McWilliams, a junior.

Drew remembered how upset Trent had been when other students in "Faces" started fighting and crying earlier in the year. All it took was someone saying "Gesundheit"—and then an atheist yelling at the well-wisher not to make a religious state-

incompleteness allowed me to capture the surprise, contradiction and incompleteness of events at Pico College.

Finally, as a researcher of color I find that writing in a polyphonic style lets me see that there are multiple identities within me. This was not possible in my earlier writing—where I had to either write in the authoritarian manner of the dominant culture or express myself in a very fragmented and unsatisfying way. Here, the characters of a polyphonic writing each touch a different part of me—and this multiplicity creates a feeling of release for the parts that have been repressed. It creates a euphoria. It is a new way of seeing humanity.

2. *The second contribution that Bakhtinian polyphonic novelistic writing makes to social science research is a new capability—an ability to track and report the progress that a racially heterogeneous community makes toward a social arrangement of "unity and difference."* Is one reason why we can't break the deadlock between Western retrenchment (monocultural unity) and early multiculturalism (difference at the expense of unity) the fact that we write and know in the mode of a Cartesian "either/or" dichotomy? (e.g. Daniel, 1992) Polyphonic novelistic writing might offer a way out of this impasse by freeing the writer

ment! Others then complained about the "overemphasis" on homosexuality—and about race being left out.

But Drew knew that for Trent the greatest moment of release and suffering was yet to come. He was "coming out" in front of the entire freshman class next fall. The returning students at Pico did not know that he was gay.

It's all about taking risks and being very vulnerable, Drew concluded. Some of the stories will be negative. But there is always the hope that freshmen will embrace the diversity and pain—and that this will make their own adjustment to college a little easier.

Drew reluctantly reached another conclusion: not everyone would see that antisemitism was related to "classism"— which was related to racism, and sexism, and "ablism."

Well, just knowing you have permission to examine all this, to feel human, to have a safe place to do this—isn't that what we're all about? It's all about—

"Process. It's all about *process!*" Trent was bending his head into the open doorway one more time, this time finishing Drew's sentence for him. And just as suddenly, the smiling Trent had whipped his head away and was gone from view.

We're movin' in the right direction, Drew consoled him-

from always having to reduce findings to one fixed result or synthesis that freezes out the possibility of multiple perspectives.

At Pico College, I had hoped to find harmony but instead encountered multiple levels of conflict. Unity and difference did not yet co-exist at this campus setting. Ironically, the European American identity seemed for the moment the most marginalized from the move to multiculturalize the campus. It was clear to me, however, that there would be no social unity until the European American student was "re-included."

This is not to say that unity and difference will never co-exist—and I tend to think that places like Pico College will be among the first to arrive there. But is the celebration of difference—and resulting dislocation of the centrality of European Americans—the necessary precursor to unity and difference at some later date? Or instead, will the acknowledgment of cultural difference forever preclude new unity—as it had done so far for some European American students who wished to participate?

But just when oppressed groups are beginning to articulate their identities and histories free from the totalizing voice of Western knowledge—who will dare ask them for unity across

self. But we live in a capitalistic society which says there must be somebody on the bottom in order for there to be somebody at the top. There has to be oppression, right? Otherwise, capitalism falls apart.

And the European American? He's struggling with "I am a bad person because we've oppressed so many people of color." So, what can be done for them?

Well, *the first step is to validate their fear.* It's wrong to assume their pain is any less than the pain of students of color—or of women, or lesbians and gays and bisexuals. We know what it feels like to have pain and we need to validate how they feel when they are giving up a little bit of their control.

Step two is to move from that pain to recognizing that other people have pain, too. If we all begin to do that, it means I can take my happy black behind to—

Drew could not finish the thought because this time Trent came in and playfully bit him on the back of the neck. Time to go.

The dark oak walls of the president's office echoed the somber mood of the carpet. At the bay window, one could stare for long hours, envisioning another time and place.

Exiting his office, the middle-aged man with large hands stopped and looked at a white

groups? Even if cultural differences could be nurtured to clarity, can these differences be made to exist over a sustained period of time in dynamic tension with unity?

The question of whether social unity and cultural difference might coexist adumbrates the larger question of what happens to human beings when institutions change radically the rules by which value is accorded, worth is felt, and meaning is constructed.

And here I have to ask: if Whiteness has been excluded from efforts to multiculturalize—here and elsewhere—then why so far have social scientists overlooked this? Are some white social scientists blind to examining their own shifting positionalities? These are questions that demand attention over time. It is a call that beckons.

3. *A comment needs to be made here about "carnival," which refers to Bakhtin's vision of how a utopian social order might come to be.* It would require a separate paper to do justice to this concept, but there is in the data here a hint of the "carnivalesque"—here at Pico College.

Bakhtin (1929/1984) refers to carnival as a "pageant without footlights" where "everyone is an active participant, everyone communes" and where "the laws, prohibitions and restrictions that determine the struc-

haired Mrs. Knorr. Her smile held a strange mix of hope and despair. There's something you need to know. There are lots of students gathering in the foyer. Seems they are protesting our catalog for next year. Saying we have taken the word "multiculturalism" out of it, that this means we are backing away from multiculturalism. Oh, yes, and Dean Wilder is on the phone.

Oh, my, was all he said, and he reversed course, heading back into his office.

ture and order of ordinary, that is, noncarnival, life are suspended." In the carnivalesque moment, everything which buttresses the existing social hierarchy—its "forms of terror, reverence, piety, and etiquette"—is discarded. In place of official order, there is a new way of interrelating characterized by the profane: by "free and familiar contact" with others, by parodies or debasings of the sacred text, by laughter, and by a mocking or decrowning of the person who occupies the top of the social hierarchy (in rural Russia, that would be the mayor of the town).

While Bakhtin's wish for the carnivalesque might seem too utopian or dated for us—arising as it did from an almost nostalgic fixation on rural Russia of the late 1800s—it is impossible, I feel, to ignore the at times crazed mood of "carnival" that struck me with all the upendings of social order I encountered here in my research.

I tried to imagine what it felt like to see fraternity brothers in a pitched battle with students from the Black Students Alliance. I wondered how it felt to be a student on this campus when the campus paper reported in one issue that the college had been found guilty of sexual harassment—*and* that several more lawsuits were on the way based on age discrimination and race discrimination.

What was happening here—in this place where multiculturalism was supposed to be embraced and everyone's culture was going to be valued?

Was there a "profaning" of life at Pico College? Had Pico embarked on a course where a social structure based on a Western, male view of what counts was being tipped over? If so, then perhaps the "mayor" here is not a person at all but rather Westernism. In this tilting, some might feel threatened—like those who blocked efforts to include gender issues in the hard sciences and those who prevented an Asian religion professor from being rehired. Recall how the alumni affairs office had withdrawn an article about reggae and rastefarians from the alumni magazine—in order not to alarm a conservative alumni base?

But the most graphic example of this mood of departing from the existing rules of social hierarchy is the one provided by "Faces in the Crowd," where returning students present entering freshmen with their stories of pain and arrival—the coming out of lesbians and gays, the difficulties with being Jewish, the feelings by some whites that they don't have a culture.

Whether the end of one social hierarchy will lead to a rebirth at Pico College of lived life, community, and human interrelating (Bakhtin, 1984/1929, pp. 166–169) remains to be seen. I have to say that I sometimes wondered if all the introspection here was initiating a healthy process of renewal—or merely a painful and drawn out process of social fragmentation. One hopes (and I believe) it is the former.

4. There is a fourth issue. It is the question of *what is lost by the representation of ethnographic findings in a polyphonic novelistic form?* As in Dostoyevsky's writing, there are limitations to the application of polyphonic novelistic writing to social science research. First, I think the idea that a writer can take his or her voice out of the narrative is illusory: I still found myself putting in what I wanted to put in—and leaving out what I wanted to leave out.

In this chapter, for example, I could repeat almost verbatim the Pico College president's words about his commitment to multiculturalism coming from his own experience as a black man growing up in America—but I had to "read in" my own emotions about the "shiny steel arcs" of the fountain based on my take on his personality. This bias can to some extent be compensated for by giving each informant his or her own voice. But I think it is important to do more than that—to actually admit personal biases as part of the write-up, that is, to make the admission of relevant bias *de rigueur.*

Second, the Bakhtinian emphasis on interaction between characters and on the "uninfinalizability" of events and ideas flies in the face of the categorizing that we as Western researchers are taught to do. I find that the emphasis on incompleteness and multiple perspectives makes it difficult to have the narrative itself engage in a dialogue with prior research— which is written in a different key. I miss that direct exchange.

Third, it was impossible to put linear, compartmentalized analysis into the text of the narrative (and indeed, this is not allowed under Bakhtinian polyphonic novelistic writing). The result was that the analysis got crammed into the sidenotes— and my own voice and authority constantly wandered into the story. The "dialogue" between the narrative and the sidenotes therefore became increasingly strained: the more I sought to make each writing pure (either polyphonic or analytical), the harder it was to relate one to the other. As a result, I think both writings suffered.

Fourth, it was truly a trying task to create a "plot" out of the data I had gathered. As it turned out, the college itself provided a momentary denouement when over 100 students occupied the administration building for three days and demanded a written promise from the institution that it will not back down from its commitment to multiculturalism. The fear among many students of color was that the college was going too far in its recent attempts to reach out to white applicants and wealthy alumni—and that these developments were signaling the end of an era of multiculturalism on this model campus. But in this ironic flip in power relations, it becomes appropriate to ask: Don't people of color have to be willing to change, too? Don't they have a responsibility to reach out to whites? Unfinalizability, indeed.

Even with all the difficulties I encountered in writing this experimental text, there is one point that makes it all worthwhile. Somewhat mischievously, I find the polyphonic novelistic style "subversive" in that it almost renders monological expression small.

A novel examines not reality but existence. And existence is not what has occurred, existence is the realm of human possibilities.

—Milan Kundera, *The Art of the Novel*

References

This experimental text is about multivocality and how to re-present it. In a multivocal text, all voices count and even the system of citing to references would ideally reflect that way of valuing. To encourage a more open exchange of ideas and to give full credit to all who have contributed to this text, the above references therefore include important conversations and timely efforts without which this text could not have been completed.

Anzaldua, G. (1987). *Borderlands/La frontera: The new mestiza.* San Francisco: Spinsters/Aunt Lute.

Astin, A. W. (1995). About writing and musical polyphony. UCLA.

Atkinson, P. (1991b). *The ethnographic imagination: Textual constructions of reality.* London: Routledge.

Bakhtin, M. M. (1965/1984). *Rabelais and his world.* Bloomington: Indiana University Press.

——— . (1981/1930s). *The dialogic imagination.* Austin: University of Texas Press.

——— . (1984/1929). *Problem of Dostoevsky's poetics.* Minneapolis: University of Minnesota Press.

——— . (1990/1919–24). *Art and answerability.* Austin: University of Texas Press.

——— . (1993/1924). *Toward a philosophy of the act.* Austin: University of Texas Press.

Behar, R., & Gordon, D. A. (Eds.). (1995). *Women writing culture.* Berkeley: University of California Press.

Bell, D. (1992). *Faces at the bottom of the well: The permanence of racism.* New York: Basic Books.

Bennett, W. J. (1988). *Our children & our country: Improving America's schools and affirming the common culture.* New York: Simon & Schuster.

Bloom, A. (1987). *The closing of the American mind: How higher education has failed democracy and impoverished the souls of today's students.* New York: Simon & Schuster.

Burbules, N. C., & Rice, S. (1991). Dialogue across differences: Continuing the conversation. *Harvard Educational Review, 61*(4).

Chatterjee, P. (1989). Colonialism, nationalism, and colonized women: The contest in India. *American Ethnologist, 16*(4).

Cheney, L. (1989). *Fifty hours: A core curriculum for college students.* Washington, DC: National Endowment for the Humanities.

Chesler, M. A. (1996, January). *Resistance to the multicultural agenda in higher education.* Unpublished manuscript.

Clandinin, J. D., & Connelly, F. M. (1994). Personal experience methods. In N. K. Denzin & Y. S. Lincoln (Eds.), *Handbook of qualitative research.* Thousand Oaks, CA: Sage.

Clifford, J. (1986). On ethnographic allegory. In J. Clifford & G. E. Marcus (Eds.), *Writing culture: The poetics and politics of ethnography*. Berkeley: University of California Press.

————. (1988). *The predicament of culture: Twentieth century ethnography, literature, and art*. Cambridge, MA: Harvard University Press.

————. (1992). Travelling cultures. In L. Grossberg, C. Nelson, & P. Treishler (Eds.), *Cultural studies*. London: Routledge.

Clifford, J., & Marcus, G. E. (1986). *Writing culture: The poetics and politics of ethnography*. Berkeley: University of California Press.

Collins, P. H. (1986). Learning from the outsider within: The sociological significance of Black feminist thought. *Social Problems, 33,* S14–S32.

Dabney, E. (1995). Transcribing fieldnotes. Loyola Marymount University.

Daniel, G. R. (1992). Beyond black and white: The new multiracial consciousness. In M. Root (Ed.), *Racially mixed people in America*. Newbury Park: Sage.

Davis, M. (1987). *City of quartz: Excavating the future in Los Angeles*. New York: Vintage Books.

Deloria, V. (1969). *Custer died for your sins*. New York: Macmillan.

Dostoyevsky, F. (1951). *Crime and punishment*. New York: Penguin.

————. (1951). *Notes from the underground*. New York: Signet.

D'Souza, D. (1991). *Illiberal education: The politics of race and sex on campus*. New York: Free Press.

Duster, T. (Ed.). (1991). The Diversity Project. Institute for the Study of Social Change, University of California at Berkeley.

Earle, T. (1995). About ethnographic style, research design, and novelistic reporting of fieldwork. UCLA.

Fabian, J. (1983). *Time and the other: How anthropology makes its object*. New York: Columbia University Press.

Fanger, D. (1965). *Dostoevsky and romantic realism: A study of Dostoevsky in relation to Balzac, Dickens, and Gogol*. Chicago: University of Chicago Press.

Fersen, N. (1968–1969). Conversations about *pochva*, Dostoyevsky and writing. Williams College.

Flores, R. (1996, March). *A critical view of student development services*. Unpublished manuscript, Loyola Marymount University.

Foucault, M. (1976). *The history of sexuality*. New York: Vintage books.

————. (1980). *Power/knowledge*. New York: Pantheon Books.

Frankenberg, R. (1993). *The social construction of whiteness: White women, race matters*. Minneapolis: University of Minnesota Press.

Gardiner, M. (1992). *The dialogics of critique: M. M. Bakhtin & the theory of ideology*. New York: Routledge.

Gates, H. L., Jr. (1992). *Loose canons: Notes on the culture wars*. New York: Oxford University Press.

Geertz, C. (1973). *The interpretation of cultures*. New York: Basic Books.

Giroux, H. (1992). *Border crossings: Cultural workers and the politics of education*. New York: Routledge.

Giroux, H., & McLaren, P. (1994). *Between borders: Pedagogy and the politics of cultural studies*. New York: Routledge.

Gomez-Pena, G. (1992). Border Brujo. Performed at Highways.

Guha, R., & Spivak, G. C. (1988). *Selected subaltern studies*. New York: Oxford University Press.

Gwaltney, J. L. (1993). *Drylongso: A self-portrait of black America*. New York: New Press.

Hernandez, G. (1995). Multiple subjectivities and strategic positionality: Zora Neale Hurston's experimental ethnographies. In R. Behar & D. A. Gordon (Eds.), *Women writing culture*. Berkeley: University of California Press.

hooks, b., & West, C. (1991). *Breaking bread: Insurgent black intellectual life*. Boston: South End Press.

Hughes, R. (1993). *Culture of complaint: The fraying of America*. New York: Oxford University Press.

Hunt, L. (Ed.). (1989). *The new cultural history*. Berkeley: University of California Press.

Hurston, Z. N. (1935). *Mules and men*. New York: Harper Perennial.

Hurtado, S. (1992). The campus racial climate: Contexts of conflict. *Journal of Higher Education, 63*(5).

Hwang, D. H. (1994). Facing the mirror. Foreword to K. Aguilar-San Juan, *The state of Asian America: Activism and resistance in the 1990s*. Boston: South End Press.

Jacob-Huey, L. (1995). Conversation about novelistic ethnographies. UCLA Department of Anthropology.

Janesik, V. (1995). Conversation about writing with novelistic detail. American Educational Research Association annual conference.

Kimball, R. (1990). *Tenured radicals: How politics has corrupted our higher education.* New York: Harper & Row.

Kjetsaa, G. (1987). *Fyodor Dostoyevsky: A writer's life.* New York: Viking.

Kondo, D. (1990). *Crafting selves: Power, gender, and discourses of identity in a Japanese workplace.* Chicago: University of Chicago Press.

Kristol, I. (1991, July 31). The tragedy of multiculturalism. *The Wall Street Journal.*

Kundera, M. (1986). *The art of the novel.* New York: Harper & Row.

Lett, J. (1987). *The human enterprise: A critical introduction to anthropological theory.* Boulder, CO: Westview.

Lippard, L. R. (1990). *Mixed blessings: New art in a multicultural America.* New York: Pantheon.

Lodge, D. (1990). *After Bakhtin: Essays on fiction and criticism.* London: Routledge.

Lorde, A. (1983). The master's tolls will never dismantle the master's house. In C. Moraga & G. Anzaldua (Eds.), *This bridge called my back: Writings by radical women of color.* New York: Kitchen Table Women of Color Press.

Marcus, G. E., & Fischer, M. J. (1986). *Anthropology as cultural critique: An experimental moment in the human sciences.* Chicago: University of Chicago Press.

Marranca, B., & Dasgupta, G. (Eds.). (1991). *Interculturalism & performance.* New York: PAJ Publications.

Martin, E. (1987). *The woman in the body: A cultural analysis of reproduction.* Boston: Beacon Press.

Matthieson, P. (1962). *Under the mountain wall: A chronicle of two seasons in Stone Age New Guinea.* New York: Penguin.

McCarthy, C., & Crichlow, W. (Eds.). (1993). *Race, identity and representation in education.* New York: Routledge.

McLaren, P. (1994). White terror and oppositional agency: Towards a critical multiculturalism. *Strategies,* vol. 1, UCLA.

Mills, C. W. (1959). *The sociological imagination.* London: Oxford University Press.

Minh-ha, T. T. (1990). Not you/like you: Post-colonial women and the interlocking questions of identity and difference. In G. Anzaldua (Ed.), *Making face, making soul—Haciendo Caras: Creative and critical perspectives by feminists of color.* San Francisco: Aunt Lute Books.

Mohanty, C. T. (1988, Autumn). Under Western eyes: Feminist scholarship and colonial discourses. *Feminist Review, 30.*

Myrdal, G. (1944). *American dilemma.* New York: Harper & Brothers.

Narayan, K. (1993). How native is a "native" anthropologist? *American Anthropologist, 95,*(3).

Nordstrom, C., & Martin, J. (Eds.). (1992). *The paths to domination, resistance and terror.* Berkeley: University of California.

Oakes, J. (1993–1995). Conversations about qualitative research methods and new forms of writing. UCLA Graduate School of Education.

Ong, A. (1987). *Spirits of resistance and capitalist discipline: Factory workers in Malaysia.* Albany: State University of New York Press.

Ortiz, F. (1940/1947). *Cuban counterpoint.* New York: Alfred A. Knopf.

Park, K. (1993, Spring). "Public ethnographer: In pursuit of intercessory ethnography. *Anthropology UCLA, 20,* 1–26.

———. (1992–1994). Conversations about the need for ethnographies which take into account multiple voices and social fragmentation. UCLA Department of Anthropology.

Ramirez, M., & Castaneda, A. (1974). *Cultural democracy: Biocognitive development and education.* New York: Academic Press.

Rosaldo, R. (1989). *Culture & truth: The remaking of social analysis.* Boston: Beacon Press.

Sacks, K. (1989). Toward a unified theory of class, race and gender. *American Ethnologist, 16*(3).

———. (1994). How did Jews become white folks? In S. Gregory & R. Sanjek (Eds.), *Race.* New Brunswick, NJ: Rutgers University Press.

Sandoval, C. (1990). Feminism and racism: A report on the 1981 National Women's Studies Conference. In G. Anzaldua (Ed.), *Making face, making soul—Haciendo Caras: Creative and critical perspectives by feminists of color.* San Francisco: Aunt Lute Books.

Schama, S. (1991). *Dead certainties (unwarranted speculations).* New York: Knopf.

Schlesinger, A. M. Jr. (1991). *The disuniting of America: Reflections on a multicultural society.* Whittle Direct Books.

Scott, J. C. (1992). Domination, acting, and fantasy. In C. Nordstrom & J. Martin (Eds.), *The paths to domination, resistance, and terror.* Berkeley: University of California Press.

Scott, J. W. (1991). The evidence of experience. *Cultural Inquiry, 17,* 773–797.

Solarzano, D. G. *Notes on social and cultural reproduction and resistance models.* Manuscript.

Sterling, M. (1995). Conversations about the importance of thick description. UCLA Department of Anthropology.

Stoler, A. L. (1991, May). *Sexual affronts and racial frontiers.* Paper presented at TNI Conference, Amsterdam.

Tamanoi, M. (1993–1994). Conversations about power and resistance theory, postcolonial frameworks, and gender studies. UCLA Department of Anthropology.

Tanaka, J. T. (1994–1995). Conversations about computer formatting.

Taussig, M. (1987). *Shamanism, colonialism, and the wild man: A study in terror and healing.* Chicago: University of Chicago Press.

Tierney, W. G. (1992). An anthropological analysis of student participation in college. *Journal of Higher Education, 63*(6).

———. (1993a). *Building communities of difference: Higher education in the twenty-first century.* Westport, CT: Bergin & Garvey.

———. (1993b). The cedar closet. *Qualitative studies in education, 6*(4), 305–314.

Tsing, A. L. (1993). *In the realm of the diamond queen: Marginality in an out-of-the-way place.* Princeton, NJ: Princeton University Press.

Tyler, S. A. (1987). *The unspeakable: Discourse, dialogue and rhetoric in the postmodern world.* Madison: University of Wisconsin Press.

Visweswaran, K. (1994). *Fictions of feminist ethnography.* Minneapolis: University of Minnesota.

Wagner, R. (1975). *The invention of culture.* Chicago: University of Chicago Press.

West, C. (1993). *Race matters.* Boston: Beacon Press.

Williams, P. J. (1991). *The alchemy of race and rights: Diary of a law professor.* Cambridge, MA: Harvard University Press.

Zinsser, W. (1988). *On writing well: An informal guide to writing nonfiction.* New York: Harper & Row.

12

Textual Gymnastics, Ethics, and Angst

Thomas A. Schwandt

Ethnography's encounter with postmodernism has yielded new wisdom but greater anxiety about the authority of the ethnographic enterprise. General acceptance of the wisdom of the postmodern perspective is accompanied by a great deal of uneasiness and ambiguity about developing an intellectually sound and ethically responsible approach that permits the expression of that wisdom. This is so because postmodern wisdom undermines the traditional authority of ethnographic scholarship.

The essays in part II of this book accept and embrace the wisdom of postmodernity. This wisdom lies in the diagnosis of contemporary life:

> What the postmodern mind is aware of is that there are problems in human and social life with no good solutions, twisted trajectories that cannot be straightened up, ambivalences that are more than linguistic blunders yelling to be corrected, doubts which cannot be legislated out of existence, moral agonies which no reason-dictated recipes can soothe, let alone cure. The postmodern mind does not expect any more to find the all-embracing, total and ultimate formula of life without ambiguity, risk, danger, and error, and is deeply suspicious of any voice that promises otherwise. . . . The postmodern mind is reconciled to the idea that the messiness of the human predicament is here to stay. (Bauman, 1993, p. 245)

Tanaka, for example, cites approvingly the Bakhtinian notion of the "unfinalized" or unresolved event or idea and the "complexity, conflicts and surprises" of the social lives of the people he studies. Denzin begins his exploration of ethnography as performance from the assumptions that identity, gender, race, and sexual orientation "are socially constructed on the postmodern cultural terrain" and that the postmodern world stages existential, liminal crises. And McLaren searches for a new identity for the ethnographer who has little choice but to travel through the urban spaces of the postmodern metropolis. In sum, these essays are foregrounded in the postmodern diagnosis of the "messiness of the human predicament." However, they also testify to the struggle to develop an epistemology and an ethics that will supply an intellectual and moral justification for the scholarly response to and authoring of such wisdom.

This struggle to author (to write, to utter, to re-present) postmodern wisdom arises in part because of the widespread endorsement of radical perspectivism as a general methodology of postmodernism. This Nietzschean idea is summarized by Dreyfus and Rabinow (1982): "The more one interprets the more one finds not the fixed meaning of a text, or of the world, but only other interpretations. These interpretations have been created and imposed by other people, not by the nature of things. In this discovery of groundlessness the inherent arbitrariness of interpretation is revealed" (p. 107). Of course, if all interpretations are indeed truly arbitrary (that is, per *The Random House Dictionary of the English Language, The Unabridged Edition,* subject to individual will or judgment without restriction; contingent solely upon one's discretion), there is no need to say more about them. No need to argue about which interpretations are better or worse, who has what kind of authority to make interpretations, and so on.

But the essays of part II are evidence that these authors at least (and I suspect the rest of us as well) do not believe that interpretations are arbitrary. They do not act as if this is so, for they worry about better or worse ways of re-presenting social life. What is implict if not explicit here is the assumption that postmodern ethnographic interpretations matter even if they cannot be absolutely certain but only at best contingent or conditional in many ways, corrigible, rhetorically crafted, politically motivated, and imaginatively offered. Hence, importing radical perspectivism into ethnographic methodology has meant learning to deal with messiness, ambiguity, and uncertainty. It has revealed a horizon of troubling issues about reflexivity, aesthetic and narrative form, agency, authority, and re-presentation. But, it has not meant, in the testimony of these authors, what Calinescu (1987, p. 305) called a radically skeptical "epistemological impossibilism" or "a pervasive sense of a radical, unsurpassable uncertainty, a sort of epistemological nihilism."

Having not abandoned all interest in knowing, having accepted the contingency and fallibility of ethnographic interpretations (not their arbitrariness), having embraced the wisdom of the postmodern picture of human life, we are filled with angst: Wherein lies the warrant to represent the truth of the postmodern picture? What is the source of our wisdom? Perhaps angst is not the right diagnosis here: It is less of a feeling of anxiety and dread and more of a profound worry (*Beunruhigung*; harder to say, but perhaps a more accurate translation.) This anxiety or worry expresses itself in the continuing search for new and better answers to questions definitive of the ethnographic undertaking: What is a good, satisfying, useful, intellectually and morally responsible way to compose a text that re-presents the postmodern condition of social life? What is a good, satisfying, useful, intellectually and morally responsible way of doing fieldwork that takes full account of the "messiness of the human predicament"? What is a good, satisfying, useful, intellectually and morally responsible role for the ethnographer in a social world best characterized by "twisted trajectories," "ambiguities," shifting identities, irreducible "doubts," and "moral agonies" never to be completely straightened up or resolved?

Tentative answers to these questions are to be found in these essays. Lather and Tanaka especially, and McLaren to a lesser degree, engage in textual gymnastics. These are efforts to physically rearrange texts to decenter the omnipotent author; to, as Lather notes, "interrupt the restricted economies of representation that characterize mainstream social science" and to produce a "broadly accessible text that fosters brooding about the issues involved in telling other people's stories." Tanaka experiments with a "polyphonic novelistic style" that helps "render monological expression small." The goal is not simply to call into question but to dismantle ethnography as a kind of factual description of other's lived reality; to undo, as Denzin explains, "the voyeuristic gazing eye of the ethnographer."

Denzin's explication of performance texts is an even more sophisticated gymnastics in which ethnography is quite literally a staged physical performance with an audience. But Denzin is concerned with more than textual form. Ethnography as performance address the issue of an appropriate kind of fieldwork for a postmodern ethnography. His critique of natural performance texts caught in a representational mode and his defense of mystory texts that simultaneously criticize what they produce is a commentary on fieldwork. Denzin seeks a form of doing ethnography that works against realist strategies of 'being in the field' (i.e., participant observation, accumulation of verbatim transcriptions, the straightforward "collection" of the narratives of others) that are typically reproduced in the textual expression of having been in the field.

This concern for a new way of doing fieldwork is intimately related to the search for a new role for the ethnographer as is evident in the essays by McLaren and Lather. McLaren is concerned with how ethnographers-as-intellectuals/scholars can live simultaneously in the academy and the everyday world. As a "means of unmooring ethnography from some of its debilitating modernist discourses and of demoting the epistemological certainty that surrounds them," McLaren advises a new ethnographic identity and agency. He argues for a complex conception of the ethnographer that combines the image of the urban *flâneur* as traveling player with Bourdieu's passion for epistemic reflexivity about the practice of sociological investigation coupled with a postmodern Marxist conscience that allows us to theorize postmodernism as a cultural logic and develop a new form of radical politics. Lather seeks to define the role of ethnographer-as-cultural-critic who occupies some kind of intermediary position between artist and scientist.

Although she does not address the role of the ethnographer per se, McWilliam speaks to the issue of the role of the postmodern feminist scholar/intellectual. In keeping with the interest of postmodern feminist ethnography to reread the ethnographic enterprise, McWilliam calls for renewed attention to the performance of feminist scholarship wherein we critically inspect all forms of poses (written, oral, and body) in relation to knowledge and in relation to others for what they reveal about intellectual and scholarly authority.

The temptation is strong to view the expression of ethnographic angst in this set of essays—this exploration of issues surrounding (and new ways of thinking about) ethnographic texts, ethnographic writing, and the ethnographer's role—only as exemplifying the contemporary intellectual criticism of modes of inquiry (disciplinary activity) in the human sciences. That is, we might naturally be inclined to say that 'what's going on here' in these essays addressing the editors' goal of exploring the "implications of postmodernism for representational practices" in qualitative inquiry is extensive commentary on the epistemology and methodology of ethnography in conditions of postmodernism. And, of course, this kind of reading of the essays is both possible and correct. Lather, for example, wishes to develop a new "methodology of the imaginary;" McLaren argues for a kind of "epistemic reflexivity" purged of "fashionable forms of ethnographic apostasy;" Denzin seeks an ethnography as process and product that exploits the insights of standpoint epistemologies; Tanaka writes about a methodology and textual form that will make it possible to "better represent the multiple voices and emotions of informants." In sum, the postmodern implications for representational practices in qualitative inquiry look to be largely epistemological, methodological, and political concerns. Where once we were concerned with implications for ethnographic practice of the epistemologies and associated methodologies of rationalism, realism and idealism we now worry about implications of the new "-ism," postmodernism.

These essays are composed in the register of epistemological and methodological concerns. Although a full defense of that claim requires a more careful archaeology of the essays and a more thorough explication than I can give it here, consider the following: These essays rehearse to a greater or lesser extent long-standing debates about what it means to know, what can be known, and so forth. We hear echoes of an existential phenomenology that aims to characterize the ordinary experience of human beings living in the world in such a way that avoids the ontologies of both idealism and scientific realism, emphasizes the intrinsically practical and bodily character of knowledge, understanding, and intentionality and rejects empiricist methodology for explaining human action. Simultaneously, we hear at least a veiled defense of empirical claims to having been an eye-witness to an event, to having 'been there,' to having captured some kind of lived postmodern reality.

But I submit that this is not the sense in which it is most profitable to read these essays. Following the advice of Greenhouse (1995), who has begun to explore the significance of postmodern debates for the discipline and profession of anthropology, I invite readers to consider that the intellectual criticism evident in these essays on postmodern ethnography as process and text is a kind of *ethical* debate. Although the essays are foregrounded in methodological and epistemological conundrums of postmodernism that is not only (or even) what they are about. They are about the ethics of the ethnographic undertaking. They are part of an ethical discourse concerned with the implications of postmodernity or postmodern wisdom for the way we ought to be in the world as ethnographers. Postmodern ethnographic experiments are a site where the traditional attention of social scientific inquiry to issues of ontology (with its leading ideas of self, consciousness, identity, being, subject, object) and epistemology (with its concern for justifying knowledge claims) are being challenged by the primacy of ethical behavior, that is, by concerns about the quality of one's relations to others and one's responsibility to each of them (see, e.g., Donoghue, 1996).

By "ethical discourse" I do not mean the traditional consideration of the ethics of professional practice, that is, examination of ethical situations, dilemmas, obligations, duties and so on that arise as the result of ethnographers' activities in interacting with respondents, co-researchers, informants, and the like. This way of framing ethical discourse reflects modernist notions that morality "rather than being a 'natural trait' of human life, is something that needs to be designed and injected into human conduct" (Bauman, 1993, p. 6). This kind of ethical discourse is located squarely within the modernist search for the universality of ethical prescriptions or virtues (that which will compel every human being to recognize a particular prescription, virtue or trait as right or good and obligatory) and the pursuit of foundations for morality (p. 8). The notion of "ethical discourse" that I have in mind here is more like postmodern philosophical anthropology—an examination of the nature of being human, being for and being with the Other and so on under conditions of profound ambiguity and uncertainty in sociopolitical life. This kind of work is specifically undertaken by Zygmunt Bauman, Charles Taylor, and Emmanuel Lävinas, to name a few. It confronts the *Beunruhigung* arising from our struggle to find an ethic that matches our wisdom.

In the present essays we can read this kind of ethical struggle. It is evident , for example, if we read the argument that ethnographic texts only "evoke"—they are no longer cursed by the burden of presentation or representation because they are largely accounts of the ethnographer's subjectivity not descriptions of the native as object (Tyler, 1986)—as a statement about the moral obligations of the ethnographer. It is evident if we deconstruct the postmodern *flâneur*—a tourist who moves *through* the spaces that others live in, who plays at playing in an aesthetic space that is essentially solitary—as a character who Bauman (1993) argues is bad news for morality. It is evident if we read McWilliam's recounting of an episode of her performance in a forum for postgraduate students as telling us something about moral responsibility—about being for the Other before one can be *with* the Other.

Discussions of textual and representational practices in ethnography (or, more broadly, qualitative inquiry) are sites of information about the ethics of ethnographic practice under conditions of postmodernity. It would be wise to undertake more careful readings of these concerns even though the debate about postmodern ethnography unfolds in the register of epistemological and methodological matters. The less we attend to this kind of ethical discourse the more we allow it to remain on the periphery of what is considered relevant discourse in defining the practice of social inquiry.

Note

My thanks to Colleen Larson for her comments on an earlier draft.

References

Bauman, Z. (1993). *Postmodern ethics*. Oxford: Blackwell.

Calinescu, M. (1987). *Five faces of modernity*. Durham, NC: Duke University Press.

Donoghue, D. (1996, March 21). The philosopher of selfless love." *The New York Review of Books*, 37–40.

Dreyfus, H., & Rabinow, P. (1982). *Michel Foucault: Beyond structuralism and hermeneutics*. Chicago: University of Chicago Press.

Greenhouse, C. (1995, September). *Ethics and critics: The case of contemporary ethnography*. Paper prepared for the Poynter Center Seminar on Religion and Morality in the Professions of America, Indiana University, Bloomington.

Tyler, S. A. (1986). Post-modern ethnography: From document of the occult to occult document. In J. Clifford & G. E. Marucs (Eds.), *Writing culture* (pp. 122–140). Berkeley: University of California Press.

CONTRIBUTORS

Norman K. Denzin is Professor of Communications, Sociology and Humanities at the University of Illinois, Urbana. He is the author of numerous books, including *The Cinematic Society, Sociological Methods, The Research Act, Interpretive Interactionism, Images of Postmodern Society,* and *The Alcoholic Self,* which won the Cooley Award from the Society for the Study of Symbolic Interaction in 1988. He is the editor of *Studies in Symbolic Interaction: A Research Journal* and *The Sociological Quarterly.* He is also co-editor of the Sage publication, *Handbook of Qualitative Research* and co-editor of *Qualitative Inquiry.*

Carolyn Ellis, Professor of Communication and Sociology, University of South Florida, lives in Tampa with Arthur Bochner and their four dogs. She is the author of *Final Negotiations: A Story of Love, Loss, and Chronic Illness* (Temple University Press) and co-editor (with Michael Flaherty) of *Investigating Subjectivity: Research on Lived Experience* (Sage). Her current work focuses on narrative, autoethnography, subjectivity, and illness.

Joe Kincheloe is Professor of Education at Penn State University. He teaches courses on curriculum theory and cultural studies.

Patti Lather, Associate Professor of Educational Policy and Leadership, Ohio State University, teaches qualitative and feminist research methodologies. Her publications include *Getting Smart: Feminist Research and Pedagogy With/in the Postmodern,* and *Within/Against: Feminist Research in Education.* Her current project is *Troubling Angels: Women Living with HIV/AIDS,* which combines interview data, researcher reflexive notes and commentary, and an informational primer on the work of living with HIV/AIDS in a multilayered, split-text format designed to reach a broad-based audience.

Yvonna S. Lincoln is Professor, Department of Educational Administration, Texas A&M University. She is the co-author of *Naturalistic Inquiry, Fourth Generation Evaluation,* and *Effective Evaluation,* and the co-editor of the *Handbook of Qualitative Research* and the journal *Qualitative Inquiry.* She is currently working on a book about policy problems generated by the competition among paradigms.

Peter McLaren is Professor of Education at UCLA. He writes extensively on critical literacy, multicultural education, and critical ethnography.

Erica McWilliam is a Senior Lecturer in the School of Cultural and Policy Studies (Faculty of Education) at the Queensland University of Technology in Australia. She has published in new feminist pedagogy and research, and is author of *In Broken Images: Feminist tales for a Different Teacher Education (1994)*, published by Teachers College Press.

William F. Pinar teaches curriculum theory at Louisiana State University, where he serves as the St. Bernard Barish Alumni Endowed Professor. He has also served as the Frank Talbott Professor at the University of Virginia and the A. Lindsay O'Connor Professor of American Institutions at Colgate University. He is the author of *Autobiography, Politics, and Sexuality* (Peter Lang, 1994), and the senior author of *Understanding Curriculum* (Peter Lang, 1995).

Donald E. Polkinghorne is Professor of Counseling Psychology at the University of Southern California. He is author of *Methodology for the Human Sciences* and *Narrative Knowing and the Human Sciences*.

Thomas A. Schwandt is an associate professor in the Inquiry Methodology Program, School of Education, Indiana University. His scholarship and teaching is devoted to issues in philosophy of social science (particularly the union of social science and moral inquiry), intellectual foundations of interpretivist approaches to ethnography, and theory of program evaluation.

Greg Tanaka is a lecturer in Education at the UCLA Graduate School of Education and Information Studies, and has a Ph.D. in education. He is pursuing graduate studies in anthropology, and is the 1996 recipient of the James Clavell Literary Award.

William G. Tierney is Professor and Director of the Center for Higher Education Policy Analysis at the University of Southern California. His most recent book is *Building Communities of Difference: Higher Education in the 21st Century*. He has written extensively on qualitative methodology, higher education, cultural studies, and democracy.

INDEX